Sept 25, 1991

bought at the

Famous "Green

Book Store" in

Dublin, Ireland!

Susan & Lee Shenton

DUBLIN
THE FIRST THOUSAND YEARS

DUBLIN
THE FIRST THOUSAND YEARS

Peter Somerville-Large

Appletree Press

This edition first published and printed by
The Appletree Press Ltd
7 James Street South
Belfast BT2 8DL
1988

British Library Cataloguing in Publication Data
Somerville-Large, Peter
Dublin: the first thousand years.
1. Dublin. Social Life, 847-1978
I. Title
941.8'35

ISBN 0-86281-206-2

9 8 7 6 5 4 3 2 1

There's no beatin' the ould town . . .

Gogarty

Contents

Acknowledgements

I would like to thank Terence de Vere White for reading my manuscript, Mrs Sheelagh Harbison for checking the early chapters and Caroline Tonson Rye of Hamish Hamilton for undertaking the formidable task of copy-editing it. Christopher Sinclair-Stevenson and Giles Gordon have consistently given me encouragement. I am enormously grateful to the staffs of the National Library of Ireland and the Royal Irish Academy for all their help. In particular I wish to thank John Rowe of the National Library who patiently searched for illustrations. The Friends of Medieval Dublin have kindly given me permission to to reproduce Peter Walsh's map, The Bodley Head to quote from James Joyce's *Ulysses*, and Macmillan, London and Basingstoke, to quote from Sean O'Casey's autobiography. I have hesitated whether to dedicate this book to my wife or to my bank manager, but on the whole I think that Gillian Somerville-Large contributed more towards its completion. She likes the dedication made in 1895 by the Rev. C.T. M'Cready, D.D., curate of St Audoen's, at the beginning of his *Dublin Street Names Dated and Explained*:

TO
MY WIFE
(WHOM GOD PRESERVE)

Introduction

Dublin has had a tumultuous history from the moment a little Norse fortress first perched above the Liffey. She has suffered her periods of hardship and tragedy with gallantry and a measure of that gaiety, eloquence and battered elegance that has fascinated outsiders. Recent years, ravaged by economic recession, have not been good ones for the city. Nevertheless, the haggard old lady, who has long disguised her age, is showing her usual valour in declaring that in 1988 she is one thousand years old. To some jeering from her citizens, the millenium has been marked with a fairly subdued round of festivities.

What millenium? Whatever happened one thousand years ago that could be construed as a significant landmark in Dublin's history? What about the old story of Dublin being founded by the Vikings in A.D. 841? Were there not Celtic settlements and monasteries in the area whose foundations, prior to the coming of the Scandanavians, might be said to have marked some sort of beginning? That may well be, but in looking for a reason to celebrate, someone has delved into the *Annals of Ulster*. These tell us that in A.D. 988 King Mael Sechnaill of Leinster inflicted a defeat on the Vikings after a twenty day siege. The Hiberno-Norse citizens had to pay a ransom of one ounce of gold for each Dubliner taken captive.

Cynics may declare: We are celebrating a thousand years of paying taxes. A firmer objection to the choice of A.D. 988 for the founding of Dublin is the question of the accuracy of these Annals, whose dates, it seems, were incorrect by one year up until A.D. 1014 and the Battle of Clontarf. Mael Sechnaill's victory over the Danish Dubs actually occured in A.D. 989. It is Millenium Irish Style.

But the biggest objection of all for choosing this curious date must be the determination of the city fathers to ignore the alien aspects of Dublin. Louis MacNeice's fort of the Dane, garrison of the Saxon, Augustan capital of a Gaelic nation, has a more complex creation than a start as the conquest of the King of

9

Leinster. The same ungenerous spirit is at work that condoned the destruction of Georgian houses as foreign buildings, beat back into the clay the newly discovered Viking town, and now plans a four-lane highway to run by the walls of St Patrick's Cathedral. It refuses to recognize the slow miracle of Dublin's evolution from beleaguered fortress to a capital that is not only Gaelic, but encompasses the traditions of all those who have chosen to live beneath the scimitar of hills that curves around the Liffey.

Enough grousing — let us look for reasons to rejoice. Forget about hospital closures, homelessness, drug abuse, AIDS, emigration. As you can read in these pages, Dublin has faced intractable problems for centuries. There is progress — for example, in spite of medical cutbacks, any doctor will tell you that Dubliners are healthier than they were even twenty years ago. There have been things to be proud of, like the recent success in bringing stylish housing to the inner city, the DART and the reconstruction of the Royal Hospital at Kilmainham. In a city that has the youngest population in Europe, in spite of the corrosive effects of unemployment, there is resilience in a new generation. The young have shown increasing interest in creative arts, have made their mark internationally in pop culture, and in general show more tolerance than their elders. Everyone likes a party; let us roll out the red carpet, make merry and salute a thousand years — and more — of the fair city's history.

1

The Vikings A.D. 837–1170

The Celts were Agrarian people whose wealth was in cattle. Outside the complex structures of monastic settlements, their way of life did not include the concept of towns. For this reason, after much controversy, Dublin is generally accepted to be a Viking creation – a Norse community older than Oslo or Bergen. When in 1170 the Normans captured the little walled stronghold dominated by the wooden structure of Christ Church, they took over a thriving town that had functioned and flourished for over two hundred years.

But what was on the site of Dublin before the Vikings arrived? No kings seem to have lived here, and no important battles were recorded as having taken place near Ath Cliath, the Hurdle Ford, before the Ostmen came. Early chroniclers seem to have been more interested in describing how the crossing of the river was first made when a monster, regurgitated from Newgrange on the Boyne, swept up the Liffey and became wedged between both banks. The *Annals*, those medieval compilations of dates and events from which we can deduce much of the progress of Irish history, make references to ecclesiastics associated with Dublin, but they do not provide evidence to show that it had any importance as a religious centre. However, none of the surviving records are local; any *Annals* of Dublin, if they existed, might have presented another picture.

We know that the area had been occupied by man for a very long time. Primitive Mesolithic shore dwellers who have been given the name of Larnian man, lived a precarious existence around the shores of Dublin Bay over 5,000 years ago. To the south of the Bay an excavated midden on Dalkey Island has revealed that Larnian fishermen burned oak, ash and holly as charcoal, kept dogs as domestic animals and ate ox, sheep and pig in addition to fish and birds. They may also have eaten bear and grey seal. Middens at Sutton on the north of the Bay contained polished stone axes acquired from more sophisticated Neolithic contemporaries. How much Neolithic and Mesolithic communities overlapped in time is speculative. Neolithic farmers, who had developed the stone axes

11

which enabled them to clear patches of forest by ringbarking trees, avoided the shore and the marsh of the river valley and lived on higher ground, mainly to the south of the river Liffey. They have left behind such massive traces as the portal tombs at Brennanstown, Kilternan, Mount Venus and Larch Hill and the gallery graves on Kilmashogue and at Ballyedmonduff, all within ten miles of the river. Later, during the Bronze Age, Dalkey Island again proved attractive to settlers. A decorated pottery beaker has been excavated there which was made by people named after their craft – Beaker Folk. They flourished from 2050 B.C. to 1300 B.C. A decorated pottery bowl found beside a skeleton in Drimnagh, Co. Dublin, was also made by Beaker Folk. Other Bronze Age finds in the Dublin area are two shell necklaces round the necks of male skeletons found in a stone chamber at Knocknaree in Phoenix Park. Near the actual site of Dublin traces of early man have been overlaid by later city dwellers and seem to be limited to a cist tomb found in 1857 in Parliament Street which contained a skeleton, axe heads, funerary urns and a bronze pin dated to 1500 B.C.

Some things do not change within man's experience – the sweep of Dublin Bay and the familiar outline of the Wicklow hills punctuated by the Sugarloaf mountains. But during the years when Christianity was developing in Ireland, the land where modern Dublin is spread was largely flooded by the Liffey and its meandering tributaries and estuaries. The area around modern Townsend Street was under water; so was much of O'Connell Street and the land of Trinity College. There was a beach at Merrion Square and a fringing marsh extended from there to Ringsend. The Liffey, shallow and tidal, was wide – about three hundred yards across. When the tide went out massive mud banks were revealed. It was known as Ruirthech, the turbulent river. The Dodder met it where the American Embassy has been built at Ballsbridge, and the land east of there round Lansdowne Road, was slob. The Poddle, the tributary of the Liffey which is now a miserable underground stream, flowing partly under Dame Street, was then quite a substantial little river. It was tidal, perhaps as far upstream as its confluence with another stream at the junction of modern Dean Street and Kevin Street. (This second stream ran along the Coombe, which means 'valley.') From there the Poddle meandered down towards the Liffey, too wide to be forded, dividing into two to form an island on which a church would be built – St Patrick's, which was known as *in insula*.

North of the Liffey forest clearance had been under way for a long time and some of the richest land in Ireland was partially developed. The plain of Moynalty, which stretched westwards from Howth, had the reputation of being the first meadow land in Ireland, and is supposed to have been cleared of trees as early as 1500 B.C. To the south, only a few areas around church land and scattered farmsteads had been cleared and were suitable for grazing. Elsewhere dense forest containing wild boar and wolves spread southward to the hills linking up with the oak trees that crammed the mountain valley of Glencullen. It was uninviting, and during the following centuries much of the hinterland south of Dublin Bay would remain unoccupied because of the constant threat of pirates and undesirables living safely in the woods.

With the coming of Christianity Dublin Bay was soon scattered with monasteries and hermit cells. St Fintan settled on the south side of Howth Head, St Begnet on Dalkey Island and St Nessan founded his cell on remote Inis Faithleann, now called Ireland's Eye. Some miles up the Liffey the two important monasteries of Finglas and Tallaght stood on either bank, known as 'the eyes of Ireland'. On the south bank of the Liffey near its confluence with the Poddle was a church dedicated to St Martin who had a considerable cult in Gaelic Ireland; St Werburgh's was built later beside the same spot. Along the Poddle stood four churches, St Patrick on its island, St Brigid, St Kevin and St Mac Taill located on its right bank. There is no actual documentary evidence that these were pre-Viking churches, but it is extremely likely. The dedications to St Brigid and St Patrick suggest Celtic foundations rather than Viking, while St Kevin and St Mac Taill were popular Leinster saints. Mac Taill was the nickname of Aongus, Bishop of Kilcullen, whose monastery stood beside the Liffey. His small church was later Latinized as Michael Le Pole; the 'pole' was the monastery mill dam or pool which also gave its name to Dame Street. The church had a free-standing round tower, which, like other round towers, served as a belfry from which hand bells were rung. It survived the longest of pre-Viking churches, and contemporary drawings show what church and tower looked like before their destruction in the late eighteenth century. The existence of a round tower is suggestive of a monastic site, and probably most pre-Viking churches near the Liffey were associated with monastic foundations.

The church of St Patrick's which would be replaced by a cathedral in medieval times, may well have dated back to the sixth century so that it was contemporary with the saint. But it is now impossible to sort out the Patrician traditions which claim that he founded it himself. He is supposed to have been here during the time he was a missionary and to have prophesied that the capital of Ireland would be at the mouth of the Liffey. In 1901 an inscribed seventh-century cross on a carved block of granite was found on the site of the saint's well near the Cathedral. He is said to have conjured this up, from which water still flows, by striking the ground with his staff in order to have water to baptize converts.

Ath Cliath, the Hurdle Ford, was a pre-Viking structure located somewhere near the mouth of the Poddle. It was built on piles of stones spaced at short intervals across the Liffey, which was much shallower and wider at that time. (In 770, according to the *Annals*, a victorious Ulster army was drowned as it tried to wade across it.) On these piles of stones were placed a series of logs or beams overlaid with branches, the whole forming a causeway similar to several which have been excavated in bogs. At the river bank there was probably a fort to guard it. The Hurdle Ford was sited where several important highways met – the Slige Mhor coming in from the west, the Slige Midluarchara continuing on the north bank, the Slige Dala meandering up from the south. Its importance in Gaelic life continued long after the Vikings settled nearby. The *Chronicum Scotorum* states that in the year 999 King Mael Sechnaill made a *tocher* or causeway at Dublin which spanned half the river. He did not bother about the other half, because when a river divided the territories of Irish kings, each was only responsible for his half which was bounded by the Midstream. Around this time or soon afterwards a bridge was built, linking the Viking town with the north bank, probably a causeway with a wooden structure across the swiftest flow of the current. According to chroniclers, some of the most dramatic action of the Battle of Clontarf in 1014 was connected with Dublin's bridge.

There has been much thought given to pre-Viking Dublin. Theories about its appearance vary from the intelligent guess of the author of *Anthoglogica Hibernica* in 1793 who visualized 'cabins in a rath on an elevated spot where the Castle and its buildings now stand' to the elaborate vision of Dr G.A. Little who imagined 'a regal-monastic city'. He believed that monasteries founded round about the Liffey valley developed into full sized towns with 'paved streets, wooden houses and workshops, gardens and farmlands'. The latest ideas about Celtic Dublin put forward by Howard Clarke of University College, Dublin, propose that the area contained two settlements. This would explain why it had two names – Ath Cliath, the Hurdle Ford, and Dubhlinn, the Black Pool.

The original small settlement, Ath Claith, may have been beside the Hurdle Ford at the cross roads of the Slige Midluarchara and the Slige Mhor on the south bank of the Liffey. Within its boundaries on a sharp ridge along the river would have been located the church of St Columcille, which was replaced in the twelfth century by St Audoen's. The so-called lucky stone on the portal of St Audoen's is Celtic. To the east below the steep ridge on which St Columcille stood the Poddle met the Liffey, forming a 'pool' – *Linn Dubh,* the Black Pool. The open space behind Dublin Castle was not built upon during the Middle Ages, probably because it was marshy, and this patch of marsh may have been the site of the Black Pool. To the south in an area known as Dubhlinn there seems to have been a second settlement of the same name founded in the sixth century, a little later than the original Ath Cliath. The curve of Whitefriars' Street and upper and lower St Stephen's Street, a curve to be found on the earliest maps of the city, suggests that they may well have formed the boundaries of an enclosure. Within this enclosure there was in all probability some sort of monastic complex, including a cemetery and a sanctuary. It is significant that the *Annals* never refer to holy men of Ath Cliath, but always of Dubhlinn; in particular there is some mention of Abbots of Dubhlinn. The name Peter Street may record the site of an ancient church existing in pre-Norman times. The area continued to be a location of holy places throughout the Middle Ages, containing a medieval church of St Peter, St Mary's Priory belonging to the Carmelites and the leper hospital of St Stephen. Like Dr Little's more grandiose ideas, the theory of the two settlements must remain speculative. It can only be proved by archaeology.

So the Vikings seem to have imposed themselves among some well-established communities. There is a story that when they arrived they snared some swallows and put lighted wicks under their wings. When the birds returned to their nests under the eaves of the flimsy houses belonging to the settled population, they set fire to them. The Vikings used this dirty trick in other places.

According to the *Annals* they sailed down from Scotland and Orkney and reached Dublin Bay in the summer of 837. They had sixty-five ships. Probably they had previously explored the eastern seaboard and realized the advantages of the site; their prowed ships had come 'sniffing the Liffey' in Seamus Heaney's vivid phrase. They saw one of the few sheltered havens on the east coast of Ireland, a harbour closed off to the south by Dalkey Island and protected to the north by Howth Head which has been compared to a mousing cat with eagerly outstretched head preparing to jump on Ireland's Eye. Dalkey and Howth are both names of Scandinavian origin.

In much the same way as modern landing craft disgorge soldiers, the flat-bottomed, highly manoeuvrable, shallow-draught longships belonging to the Vikings, brought their passengers onto the sandy beach near the mouth of the Liffey. Later the ships were pulled above the tide mark. The traditional Norse method of choosing a landing site may have been used, where the ship's captain threw overboard his 'highseat pillars', the wooden beams framing the place of honour where he was accustomed to sit. He would let the tide carry them ashore, and at the place where they were washed up he and his crew would land and build a shelter or a flimsy house. A temple to the gods might be set up nearby. The first Vikings in Dublin Bay made a number of landings, one of which was marked by a slab of upright stone twelve to fourteen feet high, planted in the same spirit as later colonists raised flags. This standing stone, called the Steyne, survived until the seventeenth century at the spot which is now the corner of Townsend Street and Hawkins Street; it gave its name to a whole district, the Steyne of Dublin. Since in Viking times its location must have been pretty well waterlogged, it was probably erected on a sandbank. In 841, four years after their landing, the invaders built a permanent structure, a *longphort*. Initially this was nothing more than a specified area where ships were drawn up to safety above the tide and guarded from attack by a stockaded earthwork.

These newcomers were Norwegians. The Norwegian area of expansion, designated largely by geographical considerations, extended southwards among islands off the north of Scotland, down along the west coast of Scotland and north England to the Isle of Man. Then to Ireland. From the bases they established on these routes raiders could make forays to the continent of Europe and down to the Mediterranean. Swedes and Danes concentrated more on the Baltic and eastern England for their raiding and colonial adventures, although in due course the Danes would take a prominent part in the Viking presence in Ireland. There would also be strong trading links between Iceland and Ireland when Iceland was colonized.

Was it only the spirit of adventure activated by marvellous seamanship that set in motion the Viking age? Certainly a dominant motive for the Vikings' restless wanderings was greed. Plunder made possibly by swift ships hewn from timber supplied by dense Scandinavian forests promised rich rewards. After plunder came trade. Other reasons have been given for the Scandinavian migrations which ultimately took the Norwegians to America and the Swedes to the shores of the Volga. They include overpopulation aggravated by the widespread practice of polygamy, political dissensions and a social system of primogeniture which resulted in a surplus of disinherited unemployed young men. From evidence of increasing numbers of place names and burial sites throughout Scandinavia, some sort of population explosion took place just before the Viking expansion.

Before they made their landing Norwegians had been raiding the Irish coast for some decades. The earliest raid was at Lambay Island in A.D. 795, and they increased in intensity after A.D. 800. Several museums in Scandinavia display objects which were found in ninth-century graves on the west coast of Norway. They include mountings which originally belonged to caskets, reliquaries or book covers, and large hanging bowls fitted with hooks for chains which would have been suspended as we might hang bowls of geraniums. There are brooches and fragments of bronze ornaments and jewellery with enamel, glass and amber decoration. Many of these objects have parallels in design with material found in Irish crannogs and bogs, and experts conclude that most of them came from Ireland. Dating has matched them to the written material which lists Norse raids on Ireland. None of them are strikingly important, and it is not suggested that the wild rovers set out from Norway with the purpose of collecting metal scraps for bookbinding. But they are assumed to be loot – souvenirs, perhaps snatched up while a monastery burned.

The landings in Dublin Bay and the marking out of the *longphort* meant that there was a change in the simple pattern of raiding. Now, instead of having to brave the open sea for thousands of miles, the plunderers could carry out their expeditions from calmer river waters. Their new base on the east coast of Ireland was ideally located for the processing of slaves and loot. The Irish called the original settlers *Fin Gall* or White Strangers, or *Lochlannach* meaning northerners. Later, when other Scandinavian warriors joined the original settlers they were known collectively as Ostmen, a word derived from the Norse meaning men coming from the east. Their arrival must have seemed a catastrophe to those to whom their longships, battleaxes and two bladed swords represented a brutal superior technology.

From the time of the earliest raids Irish scribes, invariably clerical, inconvenienced by attacks on unprotected coastal property, eloquently condemned the Norse seafarers. They initiated a whole literature of lament. Their protests were climaxed by the main Gaelic text describing the ill effects of the Viking intrusion, a twelfth-century work called *Cogad Gaedel re Gaillaib* or *The War of the Gaedhil with the Gaell*. 'Until the sands of the sea or the grass of the field or the stars of the heaven are counted' wrote the author, 'it will not be easy to recount or enumerate or to relate what the Gaedhil all without distinction suffered from the foe.' He may have exaggerated. He did not attempt to give the whole picture, because he was writing about the career of Brian Boru and wished to enhance the exploits of his hero. The Irish Norse left no literature in self-justification to suggest that they were not altogether the monsters portrayed in medieval texts. True they were addicted to plundering monasteries, but so were the Irish themselves. Beside the 309 recorded occasions when the Vikings robbed ecclesiastical sites can be listed an almost equal number of similar raids by Irishmen. Monasteries were vulnerable to looters because the greatest proportion of economic prosperity in the country centred round them. Raids were not only for treasure, but for weapons, tools and the replacement of ships' provisions from stores which were likely to lie in guarded churches.

The sacking of monasteries seems to have been motivated entirely by greed, and there is no record of even casual vandalism directed towards the high crosses which were being erected at this time. That the Vikings of Dublin practised religious tolerance is indicated by the continued existence of early Christian churches along the Poddle within a few hundred yards of their settlement. (But they may merely have done a deal with the ecclesiastical authorities as they had done elsewhere.) In fact when they were not raiding, the Vikings behaved exemplarily. They came to be on terms of friendship with a good proportion of their new neighbours, and their chieftains married the daughters of Irish leaders. They brought much that was new to Ireland in concepts of trade and standards of craftmanship. They explored the coast and rivers, probably the first time this was done systematically. They introduced towns. They created Dublin.

But benefits from their presence were not immediately apparent when they stepped ashore. From the first they spent their time raiding and fighting. Not only did the people among whom they planted themselves make constant efforts to drive them away, but they had to face a number of attacks from other unfriendly Scandinavians. However, close relations were maintained with Vikings in the homelands up in Norway, the colonies in Scotland, England, the Hebrides and the Isle of Man. These contacts ensured a ready market for slaves and plunder. Along the east coast of Ireland the Norsemen raided monasteries so frequently that over the next two centuries these religious centres lost their importance, and the great Irish monastic tradition became concentrated in the west at monasteries like Clonmacnoise and Clonfert.

In the last quarter of the ninth century the colony became less aggressive, largely because its members were quarrelling among themselves. The Irish were able to seize another opportunity to attack them, and this time they managed to expel them. When the army of the King of Leinster descended on them in A.D. 902 they were forced to sail away hurriedly, leaving a large part of the fleet behind and taking their wounded with them.

Ireland was left alone for a time, remaining free from Viking attacks for a dozen years or so until the arrival of 'a large new fleet of Gentiles' at Waterford which devastated Munster. In Leinster the inviting patch of land on the east coast had too many advantages to be abandoned for good, even if it had to be perpetually contested. In 918 the longships reappeared in Dublin Bay. The men who manned them were Danes; by this time colonial emphasis in this part of the Viking empire was Danish. They landed and seized stretches of coastline to the north and south of the Liffey, and a substantial piece of territory to the west. The Irish resisted, and a year later, on 17 December 919, there occurred one of the decisive battles of Irish history, the wintry Battle of Dublin which resulted in Viking victory and the permanent presence of the Norsemen in eastern Ireland. A Gaelic poet lamented:

> Fierce and hard was the Wednesday
> In which hosts were strewn under the feet of shields;
> It shall be called until judgement day
> The destructive morning of Ath Cliath.

The Vikings returned with a new purpose. No longer were they content to have a mere toehold on the Liffey from where they could dispatch raiding parties. They would build something more elaborate than the riverside construction which Irish scribes called their 'ship fortress'. They intended to settle, and, following the normal pattern of Viking expansion, create a trading empire.

Again the Liffey bank was an obvious place for their operations. The two most important Norse settlements in Ireland, Waterford and Dublin, were founded at the coastal extremities of the natural borders of Leinster and Munster on the one hand and Leinster and Meath on the other. This siting was important, although perhaps initially its political significance was accidental, or at least secondary to its geographical advantages. Since the Liffey divided the kingdoms of Leinster and Bregia, the Norsemen could benefit from the traditional hostility between the Leinstermen and the Uí Néill who overran the Meath plain.

We know exactly where they founded their new town; the traditional location of Viking Dublin has been confirmed by archaeology. Running parallel to the south bank of the Liffey west of the confluence of the Liffey and the Poddle was a long narrow ridge approximately fifty feet high. Even today the sharpness of its incline can be seen by the steepness of the slope between Cork Hill and Dame Street, and the steep gradients of Fishamble Street, Werburgh Street and Nicholas Street. The ridge, probably covered with hazelwood, formed a spur which was ideal for defensive purposes. And just below it where the Poddle and the Liffey met was the 'pool' which gave the town its name. Viking towns elsewhere have shown preference for a 'pool' of some sort, a spread of water at the base of a river that made a natural harbour where ships could be pulled up. *Dyfflin* – the Norse variation of the location, was ideal. At the western end of the ridge were situated the highways and the ford of hurdlework which had long given the area its strategic importance. The stronghold the Vikings built on the site of Dublin Castle not only had the best possible natural harbour, but dominated the comings and goings of Leinster travellers.

We do not know if they had made previous use of this position. Where was the original *longphort*, a construction with the impermanent atmosphere of a frontier fort which had lasted for sixty years in spite of continuous efforts to eliminate it? It must have been intelligently sited, and the 'pool' seems to be the obvious spot for its location. But no material from the recent excavations has been dated before the beginning of the tenth century – the time of the Vikings' return. The *longphort* may have been elsewhere. There is the possibility that it was well upstream, somewhere in relation to Islandbridge. In the middle of the nineteenth century navvies digging out a cutting southwest of Islandbridge in order to lay a railway line exposed graves of men and women buried together beside the river together with weapons, tools and artifacts, brooches, glass and amber beads, lead and bronze weights, axeheads, spear heads and fragments of shields. Forty swords survive from this find, including some Frankish weapons – the equivalent of the Toledo steel blades of another age. Unfortunately most of the rest of the material was dispersed. However, what is there has been dated to the ninth century – contemporary with the *longphort*.

Another cemetery, a military one, was found at Islandbridge in 1934 by workmen digging out the Longmeadows War Memorial Park. One of its occupants lies in the National Museum attended by a dagger and a worn iron sword. At first sight his skeleton might be that of a giant, but we are used to seeing ancient skeletons which are nearly always small. He was a warrior of five feet eleven inches in height, and must have towered over the Celts whose land he invaded. His skull is slightly elongated, a condition technically described as dolichocephalic, which means long-headed. At the time he died such long skulls were characteristic of people whose origins were Scandinavian. He died in the ninth century. Can he be regarded as an early Dubliner? Archaeologists and historians do not like to site the original *longphort* at Islandbridge. The site at the Poddle seems so much more suitable. They tend to explain the presence of two full cemeteries, both dated to the ninth century, so far upstream very simply by proposing that there were several Norse settlements on the Liffey. There may have been another by the Poddle near to the Steyne. Only the one at Dubhlinn prospered. If this is so, it seems strange that there is no mention of other settlements in the *Annals* and that no evidence of its existence has yet been excavated. The puzzle of the *longphort* is another problem that can only be solved by archaeology.

Whatever the truth about the Vikings' previous activities, the ridge above the Black Pool was definitely exploited after they had returned and fought the Battle of Dublin. Giraldus Cambrensis has described how Vikings took precautions wherever they decided to settle in foreign lands. They 'erected a town of their own surrounded with deep ditches and strong walls which secured them against the attacks of natives'. European sites like the artificial harbour at Breda in Sweden and the solid ten-foot ramp found at Fyrkat in northern Jutland have revealed how skilled they were as engineers and architects. At Dublin their stronghold was surrounded by a ditch and earthern bank with a palisade. It was strong enough to withstand a siege of twenty days and nights in A.D. 988 when the Leinster king Mael Sechnaill attacked the Vikings. Later, probably after the Battle of Clontarf, the walls were rebuilt of stone.

Outside the town were some burial mounds at Hoggen Green, a cemetery, and the Thingmote at a spot above the river which today has become the angle formed by Church Lane and Suffolk Street. The Thingmote was a little artificial conical hill forty feet high, specially constructed as a place of assembly and judicature with a seat on top for the king and seats on tiers beneath for his sons and for noblemen according to their rank. Most Norse settlements had similar parliament hills, built with access to water. Political decisions were made here and games and archery contests took place on the flat land beneath. Possibly the Vikings sacrificed their prisoners of war at the Thingmote to appease their gods in the way described by the *Annals of the Four Masters*. 'In the year A.D. 857 Meolgualoi Mac Dungain, King of Cashel, was killed by the Danes, that is, his back was broken with a stone'. Judicial executions took place on another hill to the east, a natural one called the Hang Hoeg or Gallows Hill, a decent distance from the town at what is now Lower Baggot Street. Late in the eighteenth century the Hang Hoeg was quarried away to supply material for street improvements, but it is remembered in the names of Upper and Lower Mount Streets.

Dominated by its earthworks, the little town expanded quickly to become the centre of a small empire, rich in cattle, always a source of wealth for men in Ireland. The tenth century saw the rise and decline of Fingal, the land of the foreigners. On the whole, Viking settlers in Ireland were forced to be town dwellers. Colonists in Shetland and Orkney became farmers and shepherds, who imposed hundreds of Norse place-names on country landmarks. In Ireland Viking place-names are comparatively few and mostly confined to places along the coast. The northern limits of the kingdom of Dublinshire were Swords and Lusk, while to the south it took in the eastern littoral down to Wicklow and Arklow. The suffix 'low' is derived from the Norse *lue* meaning flame or blaze, and there must have been a system of warning beacons on the headlands. Bullock, once Blowick, Dalkey, Lambay and Skerries are names of Norse origin. Westward Dublinshire extended to Leixlip 'as far as the salmon could swim upstream'.

The Danish king, Olaf Cuarán, who reigned from 944 to 980, is generally credited with the foundation of the kingdom. He also crossed over to England on a couple of occasions to rule as king of York. The trading importance of the flourishing Danish colony at York has become apparent during excavations that have taken place there in the past few years. York was quite accessible from Dublin, in spite of its situation on the east coast of England. A traveller could sail from Dublin Bay to the Clyde, and then after an overland journey of only twenty miles, could take another ship on the Forth which would carry him down the east coast. But the development of York proved a distraction for the Dublin Ostmen which became a contributing factor to the curbing of their military expansion in Eastern Ireland.

Like York, Dublin was an important trading colony. In addition to exploiting her geographical situation and the agricultural richness of the territory she had acquired, she developed manufacturing industries like the making of gold and silver ornaments and textile weaving. The contacts with Norway continued and the old trading connection naturally expanded to include other Norse colonies. Iceland was settled around this time, and Dublin is frequently mentioned in Icelandic sagas. One relates how an Icelandic trader, Thorir Kladda, came on a trading expedition to Dublin 'as was usual in those days'. Another tells how in the year A.D. 1000 a boat arrived in Iceland from Dublin whose cargo included a trunk containing 'bedclothes, beautifully embroidered English sheets, a silken quilt and other valuable wares, the like of which were rare in Iceland'. Iceland had persistent links with Ireland; sagas hint there were Irish settlers, probably monks, before the Vikings arrived, while later it had a large Irish slave population.

Among Dublin Vikings slaves were one of their chief commodities of trade. It has been suggested that the town's importance and the fact that it was ruled by a king rather than a mere earl was due to its activities as a clearing centre for slaves. They would be gathered at Dublin from places of capture or purchase – probably the majority were from England – and exported to Scandinavia and other places in Europe and even further afield. Some ended up in Arab Spain or north Africa, while others were captured during raids on remote places such as the Barbary coast. An Irish account describes how a number of negroes were brought back from a raiding expedition, and undoubtedly black faces were to be seen in Dublin in the slave population. Elsewhere in Ireland slavery flourished, encouraged by the Viking example. It persisted during the eleventh and twelfth centuries, when William of Malmesbury and Giraldus Cambrensis remarked on its extent. Giraldus wrote that the Saxons in Britain sold their children both to the Norse and to the Irish.

Although the emphasis was now on trade, the men of Dublin still went raiding. At times the town must have contained similar plunder to that taken at Viking Limerick in A.D. 986 when the Irish victors obtained satins, gold, silver and foreign saddles, possibly looted from Spain. When Dublin was sacked by Brian Boru after the Battle of Glen Mama, in addition to gold and silver ornaments, the victors took 'precious stones and carbuncles, gems and buffalo horns and beautiful goblets'. This was an occasion when the Vikings went into slavery. 'There was not a farm between Howth and the coast of Kerry without a foreigner working on it, and not a handmill without a foreign woman; so that no Irishman put his hand to the flail and no Irish woman ground flour or kneaded a cake or washed her own clothes'.

In addition to refinements of slavery, the Irish learned much about concepts of trading from the Vikings. Gaelic words like *margad* (market) and *mangaire* (dealer) derive from Norse. Irish contacts with Norse Dubliners included not only formal alliances but social mingling, helped along by intermarriage. The number of Scandinavian women shipped to Ireland was limited, and from the first Vikings took Irish women, either forcibly or by proper weddings. Throughout the kingdom of Dublinshire the farming communities came to be of mixed Irish and Viking blood. Vikings had the reputation of being exuberantly polygamous, and the Irish, too, overburdened their households with women, in spite of the official discouragement of the church. This led to a natural blending of Hiberno-Norse stock within a few generations. Vikings began to conform to Gaelic custom. A tenth-century text mentions that they spoke halting or broken Gaelic. They took to adopting local customs such as marking with the sign of the cross and fostering with Irish families. They began to accept Christianity.

They were predisposed to do so. Their own religion with its numerous gods and confused ideas about the afterlife was less attractive than the concepts of Christianity with their emphasis on monotheism. A catalogue of tenth-century Dublin kings shows them to have been nominally Christian. The first King Sitric of Dublin was baptized in 925; his son Godfrey, having been converted by the Saxon King Edmund during a visit to England in 943, returned to Dublin where he founded the Abbey of St Mary del Ostmanby on the north side of the Liffey. This foundation is sometimes given as the official date for the conversion of the Dublin Norse to Christianity. The great Olaf Cuarán, responsible for so much of the town's development, died on a pilgrimage to Iona 'after penance and a good life' and his daughter and grandson were given Christian names.

But there was a long period during which Christianity and the Norse religion were practised side by side; the vigorous Nordic pantheon which included Odin with his guard of wolves, one-armed Ty, Heimdall, the god of the war-horn, and Loki, half devil and half god, was not to be abandoned lightly. In particular, the red-headed warrior Thor, god of war, who made thunder, caused the crops to grow, was invoked at weddings to ensure fertility and worshipped by sailors, fishermen and blacksmiths, had a strong following as patron of the common man. Probably the beliefs of Helgi the Lean cited in the Icelandic *Landnámabók* were typical of Vikings at that time: 'he was very mixed in his faith; he believed in Christ, but invoked Thor in matters of seafaring and dire necessity'. In many parts of Scandinavia the old religion persisted for centuries; the Lapps were only forcibly converted to Christianity at the beginning of the seventeenth century. In Ireland as late as 994 the *Annals* mention the plunder by an Irish attacking force on Dublin of two ceremonial objects, the sword of Carlus and Tomar's ring. Tomar was another name for Thor, and his gold ring, probably similar to a Celtic torque, may have been placed on an altar during sacred ceremonies or else been worn by the Thorsman or priest. The significance of the gold ring as a votive object had parallels in Celtic paganism, where it often appeared on images of gods or was worn by princely heroes, not only as ornamentation, but as a mystical symbol of power. Tomar's ring vanished for good after it had been looted, but the sword reappeared, shorn of its old associations, in the regalia of Irish kings. On a less exalted level, excavations at High Street in Dublin have brought to light a small soapstone mould for casting the sign of 'Thor's hammer', Mjöllni, which the god used for killing numerous giants. This inverted T was used as a Viking sign on coins, in colonies like York, long after Christianity was accepted. The old gods lingered, and the Battle of Clontarf was considered by many writers of annals to be the final struggle between dark pagan forces and those of the true religion, earnestly led by Brian Boru. The lapsed Christianity of his killer, the Viking chieftain Brodar, enforced his personification of evil.

The development of Dublin during the tenth century continued amid a succession of fierce wars and sieges, particularly after the Vikings became involved in the rivalry of the northern dynasty of the Uí Néill and the forces of Brian Boru, who was forming an empire spreading over the south and midlands in pursuit of his ambition to create a High Kingship which would enable the country as a whole to be united under a strong monarchy. Viking interference in this struggle accelerated the colony's decline; the triumph of the kingdom of Dublinshire was very brief, a few decades at most. The Battle of Tara in 980, a heavy defeat for the

Ostmen, was followed by three separate sackings when Dublin was forced each time to pay a heavy ransom. Ransoms largely consisted of cattle; when Mael Sechnaill, the Leinster king besieged and captured the town in 981, he claimed 2,000 head. He also made his famous proclamation that 'as many of the Irish nation as lived in servitude and bondage with the Danes should presently pass over without ransom and live freely in their own countries according to their wonted manner'.

After Mael Sechnaill had inflicted several crushing defeats on the Norsemen he made a fatal decision and accepted them as allies. They formed a disastrous alliance which led to the Battle of Glen Mama in A.D. 999 when the combined forces of Leinster and Viking Dublin were defeated by Brian Boru who subsequently sacked the town with exceptional thoroughness. The fortress was invaded, the wicker houses burned, many of the townspeople went into slavery while their wealth was dispersed. But Dublin stubbornly survived its defeat as it had survived other sackings. Trade resumed immediately as ships continued to call. Just about the time of Glen Mama the town had begun to mint its own coins. (Coins from England and the Continent were already in circulation.) They were small and silver, based on the English penny and stamped with a portrait of King Sitric Silkenbeard on one side, and on the reverse, not the sign of Thor, but a cross, a positive indication that in the fusion of paganism and Christianity, the old religion had lost its official status. These first coins are considered to be the finest the Dublin Vikings produced; later their coinage became debased and was less in use, so that by the time the Normans arrived its issue had ceased altogether. The Ostmen never took to carrying coins about because they did not use purses; instead money was rolled up in rags, or in times of emergency glued to armpit hair with beeswax.

The Battle of Clontarf on Good Friday, 23 April 1014 has often been considered the last of a series of episodes which sapped Viking dominance in eastern Ireland. But the power of the Ostmen had already been checked by previous defeats and sackings. Clontarf was less a contest between Irish and Norse than the conclusion of a revolt of the Leinstermen against Brian Boru in which the Vikings of Dublin took part in their new role as allies of the Leinstermen. Brian's forces won, but they were so weakened that his concept of a United Ireland would never materialize. The Vikings only played a secondary role in the conflict.

Why, then, did the battle, which took place before the bewildered gaze of the townspeople of Dublin achieve such prominence in the works of the chroniclers, annalists and writers of sagas? It was fought on a larger scale than previous conflicts, and attracted international attention. The Viking ruler of Dublin, King Sitric Silkenbeard, had personally visited Sigurd, Earl of Orkney, and Brodar and Ospak on the Isle of Man to gain their support, even offering Sigurd and Ospak his formidable mother, the much-married intriguer Queen Gormflaith, as a careworn prize. Ospak actually joined the other side and fought with Brian Boru.

The battle was exceptionally bloody. The warriors, according to an Irish chronicler, were cut down like corn in a harvest field. Differing accounts of the long day persuade us to see it less as a landmark of Viking–Dublin history and more as a visual spectacle that Hollywood might reproduce. Norse sagas emphasized dreadful portents such as showers of scalding blood, swords and axes fighting of their own accord, and a web of entrails studded with skulls designed by the Valkyries up in the Orkneys. More mundane details included the Viking fleet cut off from giving assistance by the tide, the slaughter of Dubhghall's bridge, the quarrel between King Sitric and his wife in which she received a black eye and possibly broke one of her front teeth, and the disembowelling of Brodar, who may or may not have been legless, as his intestine was tied to a tree and he was led round it. Fighting raged from sunrise to sunset, when the Viking survivors fled into the sea 'like a herd of cows in heat from the sun and from gadflies and from insects'. Meanwhile the saintly Brian, who would not fight because it was Good Friday, sat in his tent trying to influence events with fifty psalms, fifty prayers and fifty paternosters. Brodar approached, and they fought a duel in which Brian (according to Irish sources) cut off Brodar's left leg at the knee and his right leg at the foot. But Brodar split Brian's skull in two.

After the battle life in Dublin seemed to go on much as before. A year later in 1015 the town was sacked by Mael Sechnaill who burned the fortress and the surrounding houses. In 1018 there was another attack and in 1029 Sitric Silkenbeard's son was captured and only released on payment of '1,200 cows and six score British horses' – they actually came from Wales – 'and three score ounces of silver and his fetter ounce'. But gradually the old state of war declined, for Clontarf had initiated a peaceable era. Although they still indulged in occasional foraging expeditions, the Vikings ceased to take part in the dynastic struggles of Irish tribes. Many Norsemen, missing the old aggressive spirit, preferred to emigrate, particularly to Cumberland.

This period of transition was dominated by the long reign of Sitric Silkenbeard, during which Dublin continued to make progress as a trading centre. The Pool of Dublin, the Steyne, and the harbours of Howth and Dalkey all attracted considerable commerce from English, Welsh and continental ports. At the same time distinctions between the Irish and the Vikings were increasingly blurred. All round Europe small colonies of Vikings were being absorbed by the native populations among whom they had planted themselves, losing language, religion and ultimately national identity. Iceland, which had been virtually uninhabited, was the only permanent Viking state to survive outside Scandinavia. In Dublin the Norse language became choked with Irish words and syntaxes, while Viking marital practices continued to encourage the merging of cultures. Kings married Irish wives; by Sitric Silkenbeard's time the ruling dynasty, however much of it cultivated Norse traditions and fostered ancient connections, can hardly have represented a real Viking presence. After Silkenbeard's death there were no more Norse kings because the line had died out. Instead Dublin's Norse rulers acknowledged the supremacy of various Irish kings.

By now the people were wholly Christian. Their first bishop, Donatus, an Irishman, was consecrated in 1028. At the time of Clontarf, Silkenbeard's Christianity appears to have been equivocal, but afterwards he made two pilgrimages to Rome, and like his father, Olaf Cuarán, died a monk on Iona. On his return from his second pilgrimage in 1037 he patronized the foundation of the Church of the Holy Trinity by Bishop Donatus. This Church would later be replaced by Christ Church Cathedral. In 1042 he founded St Mary's Church at Howth. The churches of pre-Norse origin, St Patrick's, St Brigid's, St Columcille's and St Michael Le Pole were revived and became parish churches. Another pre-Viking Church, St Kevin, became the parish church of the most extensive parish in the Dublin diocese. The earliest parish church to be founded by the Vikings was dedicated to St Olaf, a Norwegian king killed in 1030; it stood south of Christ Church near another Viking parish church located at the upper end of Fishamble Street. To the

north of the Liffey, St Michan's, named for a Danish saint, was
founded in 1095 to become the only parish church on the north side
for 600 years. Beside it spread St Mary's Abbey, the town's first
Norse Christian foundation, which would be taken over by the
Cistercians – an unusual move on the part of the order, since
Cistercian monasteries were nearly always located in isolated places
in the countryside.

Christianity in Dublin was a little different from that practised
elsewhere in Ireland. To judge by the dates of the foundations of
Norse churches, it had taken a long time to overcome the old pagan
beliefs. After its comparatively late establishment it ignored the
Primacy of Armagh and sought to cultivate links with England.
The second bishop of Dublin, Giolla-Padraig, was not only
consecrated by Lanfranc, Archbishop of Canterbury, in 1074, but
introduced Benedictines from Winchcomb and Worcester to form a
monastic chapter in the Church of the Holy Trinity. Although he
and his successors were Irishmen, they all began their careers as
monks in the Canterbury Province and persisted in acknowledging
Canterbury's supremacy. Bishop Samuel of Dublin, consecrated by
Anselm, Archbishop of Canterbury, in 1096, typically promised his
English superior that he would 'keep canonical obedience in all
things to you and your successors'. This subservience to
Canterbury was possibly maintained because the Irish church was
considered to be primitive, or it may have been the result of the
Vikings' lingering desire to maintain a separate identity from the
Gaels. In 1152, in spite of protests from Armagh, Dublin was
considered important enough to be elevated to a metropolitan
centre. Gregory, the town's only Norse bishop, became its first
archbishop.

Recent archaeology has given us a completely new understanding
about the day-to-day lives led by the Vikings of Dublin. When
Charles Haliday published his *Scandinavian Kingdom of Dublin* in
1881, his sources derived almost entirely from literature and
tradition. He had little archaeological material to help along his
ideas. One of the earliest of the scattered finds which directly
related to the Norse presence in the town was a trench uncovered
when the Rotunda gardens were laid out in 1762 revealing human
bones and some items now lost. The Islandbridge cemetery was
discovered in the 1850s. Further Viking finds in the Dublin area
included material from Kildare Street, a mass grave out at

Donnybrook containing battle casualties, and the military cemetery at Islandbridge. In the late 1850s workmen laying sewers in the Dublin streets came upon many items of Norse origin, significant because they indicated that any casual excavation within the known area bounded by the old city walls might reveal Viking material. But nothing was done systematically. Elsewhere in Ireland Viking discoveries were meagre and their provenance often went unrecorded.

The area south of the Liffey which comprised Viking and medieval Dublin was covered over with later buildings which remained virtually untouched until the 1960s. A significant section of the tenth-century Viking town and its medieval successor has come to light since 1962. In that year the National Monuments Branch of the Office of Public Works investigated a small piece of ground under the east wing of Dublin Castle. It was the beginning of a long archaeological exercise that has continued amid controversy ever since.

Four major sites have been investigated; two to the south of the old medieval city centre at High Street, one to the south of Christchurch Place, and the large area at Wood Quay between Winetavern Street and Fishamble Street. Previously these sites had been largely covered by late seventeeth- and eighteenth-century houses which had cellars whose foundations were sunk deep into the rubble of earlier buildings. Beneath these foundations was a layer, averaging six feet in thickness, of a dark compact substance resembling turf. This had been known about for a long time, and used to be considered as evidence that Dublin was built on a bog. Now it was identified as the compressed core of Norse and medieval refuse that had accumulated since the tenth century. At its highest level it ceased abruptly at a layer dated to the beginning of the sixteenth century, just beneath the Georgian cellars. Since it had accumulated on boulder clay which is impervious to damp, it became waterlogged, a process that helped to preserve much fragile organic material. This powdery black compost concealed a mass of objects discarded during the city's early existence. Already more than 30,000 have been discovered, mostly humble things. A list of finds from a section of the Wood Quay area includes wooden barrel staves and hoops, turned wooden bowls and plates, wooden spoons, textile fragments, iron locks and keys, fish hooks, shears, needles and needle cases, knives and a gimlet. Some objects remain a mystery like the beautifully carved instrument of wood with four horses' heads which may have been a wool winder. From discarded bones we can tell what animals were kept and eaten. The quantities of bones and shells that have been recovered have been so vast that they have been merely sorted and measured by weight. From refuse we can learn what else they ate. Dr Frank Mitchell, who analysed Viking and medieval garbage and the contents of ancient cesspits, has even isolated a Viking flea.

The narrow elevated ridge rising sharply on an east–west axis above the banks of the Liffey, defining the area that became settled after the Battle of Dublin in A.D. 919, was a tiny elongated patch covering about sixty acres, bounded by the river to the north and running about a mile from east to west and much less from north to south. A portion of the Viking wall that surrounded it, the only substantial remnant of Viking engineering left in Ireland, was discovered at Wood Quay. It stretched from east to west below Christ Church along the old bank of the river. The eastern section was built on a shelf of bedrock that formed the ancient shore line. When the rock ended, the wall bent sharply inwards until it found a solid foundation again and was able to follow its original course. On average five feet thick and up to ten feet high, it was carefully built with a smooth cutting face on the outside and a number of offsets which gave it stability. The mortar on the river's side was weathered away, but on the inner south side it was as fresh as the day it was plastered on. At one place along the shore just within the wall a platform of flagstones was found on which the mortar was mixed, and beside it a heap of sand left by the builders.

On the east side of the little town at the edge of the river a bank of mud has been traced which was thrown up along the old shore line. It was topped with a post and wattle wall, while the sloping front face had many old planks secured to it with wooden stakes. This construction may have been a protection against flood or a sudden sea flowing up the river estuary at neap tides. The skeleton of a dog was found in the ditch outside the bank; either it drowned, or died in the town and someone threw its small body out over the bank. A more mysterious discovery is that of large leather saddlebags decorated with an incised pattern of crosses and containing the claws of a golden eagle.

By 1100 the bridge over the river, known as Dubhghall's Bridge linked Dublin to a new suburb of Oxmantown (originally

Ostmantown) which seems to have had its own separate walls and gates. The clearing of the forest on which it was built took place in the closing years of the eleventh century. It was another indication of the gradual advance of Christianity, since that particular grove of trees had been Tomar's Wood, sacred to Thor. The oaks went over to England to make the roof of Westminster Hall, where spiders are still reputed to be unable to build webs. After 1098 it was said that at Oxmantown 'he that diggeth all the day to any depth shall find the ground full of great roots'. He that diggeth there now, no doubt, shall find more revelations about Viking and medieval life.

Within the walls, dominated by a few squat wooden church spires that rose above the wide grey river, were clustered hundreds of small single-storey houses made of wattle daubed with earth that must have looked like African kraals. Perhaps more than anything else wickerwork conjures up Viking and medieval Dublin. Of course, it was used as a building material throughout Ireland, even for the construction of churches. Some Dublin houses seem to have had specifically Viking characteristics because similarities in the post and wattle design and the oak doorways and door-frames have been found with buildings excavated at the Viking town of Hedeby in north Germany. The vast majority of those found here not only had woven walls, but also woven floors which were often strewn with rushes. Some had double walls with a space between them for insulation. They were small and more or less rectangular, measuring twelve to eighteen feet in length and about fourteen feet in width. The forests south of the town supplied building materials, oak for the doorways, hazel, ash or elm for the woven wattle. Wattle was also used for pathways, partitions, boundary fences and cesspits.

It was not quite a universal material. Several of the earliest houses at Wood Quay were made of planks. One had an underground cellar lined with planks which may have been used for storage, while the part above ground was the usual post and wattle. Along Fishamble Street were a number of wooden houses with long narrow gardens stretching towards the Liffey. At the end of these gardens were the remains of sheds containing accumulations of dung – presumably places where animals were stabled. Although literature indicates that there were at least two houses of stone, no traces of them have been found, nor is there any trace of a great hall like those discovered in Scandinavia. However there may have been some sort of large building on the site of Dublin Castle.

The ground plots in High Street are irregular in length which may indicate that the town grew in a piecemeal fashion. These plots may be examples of *garths*; when Mael Sechnaill made one of his sackings he imposed a tax of one ounce of gold on every *garth* in Dublin. Houses were easy to erect and easy to dispose of. They tended to go on fire not only by accident, but as the result of sackings. Reconstruction was simple. Even if houses did not go on fire their inhabitants preferred not to stay in them too long. After about twenty years of habitation they became greasy and smoke blackened, and half smothered in the refuse that piled up outside. In due course a house would be levelled and another built on top of it. On one site in Christchurch Place the remains of six different houses have been found, one on top of another, like a cardhouse. Carbon dating has proved that very little time elapsed between each new construction. At Wood Quay the northern edge of St John's churchyard has revealed an artificial cliff consisting of twenty-eight feet of houses in layers, beginning with the foundations of Viking houses and working up to the thirteenth century and beyond.

Interiors were unsophisticated – there were no windows or chimneys. The best that can be said of them is that they were cosy. People in Ireland lived in similar structures for thousands of years. Furniture was of the simplest kind. Benches built along the wicker walls served as beds. Among the loot taken from a sack of Dublin in 1100 was listed 'bedding and feathers'. Not many pieces of household furniture have been found – a four-legged stool and some barrel shaped locks and keys for securing chests. Food was cooked in iron or soapstone vessels (stored simply when not in use by being piled on the floor) on a clay or stone-lined hearth in the centre of the floor. The presence of large stones in some houses indicates the possibility that householders may have adapted the Irish method of heating water by throwing hot stones into it. Unleavened bread made from rye, barley or sometimes peas could be baked under hot cinders. Boiling instead of roasting was a preferred method of preparing meat, probably because roasting was more of a fire hazard. Even in Valhalla the boiled flesh of the hog Saehrimni was served to chosen warriors as a delicacy. The excavated bones indicate that both Viking and medieval Dubliners ate large quantities of goat and swine in addition to beef and mutton – more pigs were consumed than any other domestic animal. The remains of horses have been found, and they, too, were probably eaten; the Viking diet included horseflesh, although the Irish had taboos against eating it.

Fish was netted or caught with the barbed fish hooks which have been among the most consistent of mankind's tools; three dozen were found in Winetavern Street. The one sinker that has been recovered could have done for either line or net. Dublin Bay has been a generous source of shellfish since the time of Mesolithic man, and excavations at every level abound with oyster, mussel, cockle and whelk shells. From the cesspits have come the pips and stones of wild strawberries, cherries, rowan berries, pears, damsons, apples, sloes, plums and fruaghans (bilberries), together with the shells of hazel-nuts. Hazel-nuts were important enough as an item of food in Ireland to make the annals. For 1907 the *Annals of Ulster* recorded 'a great nut crop this year'. From written sources we know that cabbages and onions were common items of Norse diet, which could have included the parsnips and leeks favoured by the Irish. Peas and beans also had their place on the Viking menu. Staple cereals for bread and porridge were oats and barley, which were also used for brewing. Mead and beer were drunk together with a certain amount of wine from the Continent. There are references in literature to the tributes of wine received by Brian Boru from Viking imports that had arrived at the Shannon.

Vikings elsewhere ate two meals a day, one in the morning and one late in the evening, and probably Dublin Ostmen did the same. Plates, bowls and drinking vessels were of wood. A little imported eleventh-century pottery has been identified – three sherds of Anglo-Saxon Stamford ware, another wheel-stamped Anglo-Saxon potsherd and some sherds of Slav ware from eastern or northern Europe. But the relative absence of Viking pottery is consistent with excavations outside Ireland; the craft of the potter's wheel did not appeal to Scandinavians of the period. In Norway pottery almost disappeared at this time, and very little of similar date has been found in Denmark or Sweden.

As well as the more familiar cereals, persistent traces in the cesspits of fat hen (*chenopodium album*) and three species of polygonum have suggested to some historians that a proportion of citizens must have lived at starvation level. Their use as cereals dates back to the earliest days of the settlement; traces of fat hen were found beside the skeleton of a girl at the tenth-century level of boulder clay, and it is presumed that they formed part of her stomach contents. A town that supported a slave population and was constantly subject to the terrors of warfare must often have provided an environment where food was scarce. But these particular plants are respectable foodstuffs of great antiquity which have been found on Neolithic sites. Three of them have a curious connection with Scandinavia, since they formed part of the last ritual meal of Tollund man before he was sacrificed. The leaves of fat hen were regularly eaten all over Europe until spinach was developed; the seeds contain fat and albumen, and the coarse porridge they made was a valuable dietary supplement. It is a common species that prefers disturbed soil, and appropriately its grey mealy plants have grown in abundance above the excavations.

Clothes were home produced, wool spun on spindles weighted with whorls; the bone count gives ample evidence of the sheep that provided the fleeces. Linen was stretched with smoothers after it had been spun, yarn was wound on wooden reels and sewed with needles made of bone, bronze or iron which were carefully kept in needle cases. Two of these cases have specifically Scandinavian decorations. Small pieces of tenth- and eleventh-century cloth have turned up, mostly material in twill and coarse plain weave. A few show more varied taste in colour and decoration, such as a border decorated with gold thread and another with traces of red dye. Some fine netting has been tentatively identified as material for hairnets. Bronze and bone strap-tags were used as fastenings, as well as D-shaped buckles. The style of clothes probably resembled those shown in the ninth-century Oseburg tapestry found in a burial ship at Oseburg in south Norway which depicts men in coats or tunics reaching to the thigh over trousers resembling plus-fours. Women of status had long sleeveless dresses and a sleeveless cape worn in cold weather, which, with a very little manipulation could reveal white shoulders, a feminine attribute much admired among Vikings. Young girls dressed less formally, sometimes even wearing short dresses with boots.

Jewellery is more durable than cloth. Dublin Norse jewellery includes pewter and bronze gilt brooches whose humped shape has given them the name of tortoise, amber and green glass beads, a cornelian, two gold armlets, gold and silver rings, a small inlaid dress pin topped by a stylized man's head and lignite bracelets. A tortoise brooch decorated in the tenth-century style known as Borre-Jelling with an interlaced animal pattern is a direct link with Scandinavia. So are animal and bird-headed bronze and bone pins, and a small open-work bronze brooch similar to others found in Sweden and at Hedeby.

The Ostmen never adopted Irish dress, but literature has recorded some regional differences in fashion. When the Norwegian king, Magnus Barefoot, visited Dublin in 1102 he was prominent in his 'red surcoat over his mailshirt and clothes worn in Westland [Ireland] and had short skirts and overcloaks. . .so that. men called him Barelegs or Barefoot'. Evidently he preferred a Gaelic kilt and ample cloak to the trousers and tunic favoured by Norsemen. King Magnus married an Irishwoman.

> 'Why should I return home
> Since my heart is in Dublin;
> There is an Irish girl whom I love
> Better than myself.'

His son, Sigurd, is supposed to have paid a visit to Norway in about 1127. He spoke only a little Norse, and like his father generally wore Irish clothes. For a running race he appeared in a hybrid outfit; a shirt, trousers which were bound with ribbons under his soles, short cloak, an Irish hat, while he carried a spear shaft.

Among warriors chain-armour was probably only worn by chieftains; other ranks had leather armour and carried, in addition to their weapons, two kinds of shield, one circular and one long enough to protect a man when he knelt. Helmets were pointed casques. Later, Viking armour became more elaborate. Giraldus noted the amount that Ostmen wore during their attack on the Normans outside Dublin in 1171. They fought 'in Danish fashion completely clad in iron; some in long coats of mail, others with iron plates cunningly fastened to their tunics and all bearing round shields painted red and rimmed with iron. Men with iron hearts as well as iron arms.' No armour has been found in the Dublin excavations and surprisingly few weapons. There is little evidence of 'hideous barbarous quivers and polished shining bows and strong broad green sharp rough dark spears' such as were used at the Battle of Clontarf. The arrow fragments, arrowheads, axeheads, javelin heads and spear butts discovered at the pre-

Norman layer of excavation do not amount to more than a few
dozen weapons spread over a couple of centuries. Could swords
and Viking axes have been buried with their owners? The graves at
Islandbridge containing weapons are dated to the ninth century and
after the coming of Christianity the practice of burying a man's
sword with his body ceased. However since Christianity was slow in
establishing itself, it is possible that weapons were buried with
corpses until a comparatively late date; no cemetery contemporary
with the excavated Viking town has yet been found. At Clontarf
neither King Sitric nor the people of Dublin actually fought on the
battlefield. Although scarcity of weapons undoubtedly reflects
the increasing tendency of townspeople towards peaceful pursuits, the
town was in a constant state of war alert, and many male citizens
must have possessed arms. Excavated material derives mainly from
rubbish heaps which were not places where prominent things like
weapons would end up. A brooch or a lignite bracelet could quite
easily be lost in a basket of filth, but weapons were not so easy to
lose. One sword pommel of Viking type dated from about the
eleventh century has been found, in addition to a fine iron sword
inscribed SINIMIAINIAIS and dated to the twelfth century.

In the narrow pathways outside the lines of wicker houses there
was rudimentary town planning. At Wood Quay well-built wooden
pathways were made from runners with cross timbers of scrap
planks and split logs placed on them like railway sleepers. Near
Christ Church a broad paved street had walls of post and wattle
along each side. A wooden conduit in Winetavern Street suggests a
possible eleventh-century water supply. Cesspits of two sorts have
been found, one a mere wicker basket, the other a more elaborate
pit which may have been regularly emptied. The Havamal, the
celebrated Norwegian poem packed with aphorisms and advice,
specifically recommends men to get up in the night to relieve
nature.

Little in the way of recreation was possible within the town walls,
but a short distance outside the gates three greens provided space
for athletic or military pastimes. Indoor activities involved dice,
and carved gaming pieces made out of wood and antler for chess
and a game like draughts. Children played with bone whistles,
spinning tops and wooden models of ships. One bone Viking skate
has been identified. Another with a pointed toe which contains a
hole for a leather lace has been dated as post-Norman, but it is

tempting to assume that some of the earlier Dubliners indulged in what was a way of life in Scandinavia. An early Norse king boasted to his brother: 'I was so skilful on skates that I know no one who could beat me – and you could no more skate than an ox.' Many bone skates have been found in Viking York, indicating a colder climate there. But in Ireland many winters, like those of 914, 1000 and 1095 were recorded in the *Annals* as being exceptionally severe, and generally the climate was harsher than it is now. Skates were made for use – perhaps on the frozen slobland around Ballsbridge.

The town was a centre for craftsmen. Bronzesmiths, tanners, weavers, blacksmiths (who by Viking tradition were often jewellers) leather workers, carpenters and cobblers have left tools, equipment and debris such as shavings and heaps of sand connected with metal working. The sites of their workshops dating back to the tenth century, grouped round High Street and Winetavern Street, have produced chisels, punches, awls, tongs, knives, shears, a saw and a gimlet with its turned wooden handle still in place. Knives were sharpened on grindstones shaped like rolling pins rather than on the wheels used at a later date. Viking craftsmen seem to have specialized particularly in comb-making and bronze working.

Combs have been found in scores. One reason for their great number may be that Dubliners used them for barter; Jocelin's *Life of St Patrick* mentions that the inhabitants of Dublin paid tribute to the Archbishop of Armagh in shoes, gloves, knives and combs. But unruly Viking hair had to be kept in order, and the Vikings may have had a more positive attitude towards combing than the Irish – a study of the Gaelic word *cior* indicates that combs were first used specifically for scratching lice. By the early medieval period they were treasured possessions, sometimes protected in comb bags, or comb caskets which are mentioned in Irish literature, or carried about from cords attached to belts, as well-worn holes found pierced in Dublin examples have proved.

It has been debated whether or not the Vikings were clean people. The Havamal describes how a guest should be greeted by his host with 'water, a towel and a hearty welcome'. It also recommends how 'freshly washed and well filled with food, every man should set off to the Thing, even if he is not too well dressed'. Saturday was named as the day for washing. However, the Swedes who lived in the Volga region were considered by an Arab observer to be perfectly filthy. The Danes in England, on the other hand, are said to have combed their hair, had a bath on Saturday and changed their linen frequently 'in order the more easily to overcome the chastity of women and to procure the daughters of noblemen as their mistresses'. Brodar, the slayer of Brian Boru, 'left uncut his long black locks which he tucked into his belt' and less extreme hair styles also needed a lot of combing. Dubliners, who had close affiliations with the wholesome Danes of York, appear to have taken care of their toilet; in the Winetavern Street area over two hundred combs have been found, although comb-makers did not work there. They were simply discarded by their owners.

The comb-makers practised their craft around High Street in what was more or less a medieval industrial estate where workshops and houses of artisans were concentrated. Combs were sometimes of bone, but more usually of antlers of red deer. The bones from the refuse pits indicate that venison was a rare item of diet. Deer hunting is a rural pastime, requiring packs of larger dogs than the numerous little bow-legged terriers which have left their skeletons in Dublin's compost. Chasing the stag was not a pursuit for people whose interests were predominantly urban or naval. The deer may also have flourished some distance away.

Most of the stocks of waste antlers found in High Street show signs of having been discarded naturally by stags during the shedding season. People living near the herds must have gathered them up in the late spring and brought them down for sale to the comb-makers in the town. Debris around the workshops has demonstrated every stage of manufacture. The antlers, or the odd bone, were sawn into thin plates to make blanks in which the teeth were cut. Single-sided combs were later packed with pairs of sawn antler strips to make fillets. Single-sided combs are the commonest, a small Viking technical advance. Some have sheaths and many contain decoration – hatching, chevrons and dot and circle patterns.

Bronze working was a major craft from the tenth century onward. This has been proved by the dating of furnace slag and eight clay crucibles in which bronze was melted. Seven hundred decorated bronze pins for fastening clothing – many more than could be accounted for by careless losses – have been found in the High Street area. Chippings of amber indicate waste from setting pieces of jewellery in bronze fitments. Then there are the trial pieces. There are animal bones or occasionally pieces of wood and stone on which craftsmen carved designs which served as patterns for casting thin bronze panels used to cover objects such as croziers and reliquaries. The bones used were jawbones, thighbones and ribs of oxen. The designs on them vary from rough doodles and preliminary sketches to intricate geometric weavings compared by Seamus Heaney to 'an eel swallowed in a basket of eels.' One piece showing intertwined animals is very similar to a panel on the shrine of the Cathach of Columcille which was made between 1062 and 1098 by a craftsman with the splendid Hiberno-Norse name of Sitric Mac Aeda. His father was a bronze worker associated with the monastery of Kells in County Meath. Another piece shows a Hiberno-Norse version of the Ringerike style which flourished in eleventh-century Scandinavia, a style which greatly influenced the ecclesiastical art of Ireland. It was copied on metal objects such as the book shrine known as the Misrach and the crozier of the Abbots of Clonmacnoise, in addition to being used generally in the decoration of manuscripts and the patterns on stone sculpture.

The trial pieces show that the standard of bronze making in Dublin was very high. Could so small a community produce craftsmen capable of such beautiful work over a long period? Such bronze work might well have been an extension of the skills practised during Ireland's finest period of artistic expression. But one theory accounting for this fine workmanship proposes that a group of bronze workers from a Scandinavian settlement in London came over to Dublin in a body after the Norman conquest of England, bringing the Ringerike style with them.

Shipbuilding and the maintenance of merchant vessels and men of war were integral to Viking expansion and power. In their raiding days they had undisputed mastery of the sea. They were skilful navigators and outstanding ship's architects, building fleets of fast comfortable vessels for their armies and empire makers. Their longships have been described as the pinnacle of their material culture. In Dublin there were no burial mounds containing the remains of a great ship like those found at Oseburg or Gokstad. The vessels associated with Viking Dublin were far more modest. As Viking aggression declined longships became outnumbered by the small merchant vessels whose design ultimately derived from Roman shipwrights. Two of them have been sketched on boards which were found in Winetavern Street, and are similar to the four small model ships from the same area which were carved out of a single piece of wood and were probably intended to be toys. These sketches and models all date from the· eleventh century and illustrate small-keeled vessels identical to the stocky Scandinavian *knarr* with high raking bows and sterns. They are single masted, the mast set in the middle of the hull to carry a sail that usually lacked a boom, although one ship has a spar which seems to be adapted as a boom. Such vessels could sail seventy-five miles a day; voyages from Norway to Dublin would take about ten-and-a-half days.

Viking shipbuilding techniques were copied extensively throughout Europe. The numerous ships, both English and Norman illustrated in the Bayeux tapestry, which is believed to have been embroidered in the 1080s, are very similar to the drawings and models found in Dublin, although the Dublin boats lack decorated sterns and prows. The Bayeux craft vary considerably in size; one longboat is shown carrying ten horses. The masts were movable so that they could be unstepped on landing. Several panels of the tapestry illustrate stages in shipbuilding, from the felling of trees and cutting and planing of planks, to vessels being launched with a pulley attached to a post. Similar activities must have taken place along the banks of the Liffey. But the wash of the river has destroyed much of the evidence relating to the work of shipwrights. Ship's timber has been preserved in two ways – it has been found well above the river bank, indicating that it had been carried up to the town, probably for firewood, or else it forms part of the stack of discarded ship's timber that was used in twelfth-century engineering when the Normans built their great revetment on the south bank of the Liffey to lessen its width. Numerous large boat nails have been identified as well as stakes, ribs and a stave-built wooden pail with a lid and a spout for use on board ship, since the lid prevented water being spilt by any movement of waves. A specially worked cone-shaped block of wood is an attachment for a steering oar of characteristic Viking design. It allowed the steersman to guide a ship with minimum effort and, if necessary, raise it clear of the water. Oar rudders are shown on Bayeux ships.

The Irish learned much about shipbuilding from the Vikings, especially after the sack of Dublin in 902 when the Ostmen left behind many of their ships as they.fled. The armed navy that Viking Dublin possessed at the beginning of the eleventh century was used by Brian Boru in 1005 when he sent a combined Hiberno-Norse fleet to harass Scotland and England. There is a literary reference to boat-building in Dublin in the story of the escape of Auda, the widow of an early Viking king of Dublin. After the death of her husband 'she...caused a ship to be secretly built of wood, and when the ship was completed, placed all her wealth on board, and with all those of her kindred who remained alive she sailed away to the Orkneys...'

The excavations indicate that the town of Dublin was a tenth-century foundation, confirming the written sources. The new discoveries must change many preconceived ideas about the Norse townspeople. Anyone imbued with medieval propaganda is bound to feel a twinge of surprise at the prosaic nature of the thousands of objects found lying on the boulder clay. Can these fragments of domestic and industrial refuse really derive from the 'brutal, ferocious, furious, untamed implacable hordes' referred to by the author of *The War of the Gaedhil with the Gael?* Are the people who left behind these tools, artifacts, bones and shells to be associated with the figures of terror described so graphically by Irish scribes? The answer appears to be yes with one important qualification. The excavations also confirm the literary evidence that the Vikings turned from being pirates to traders as they realized that more peaceable occupations were ultimately more profitable. This change of purpose also took place at other Viking towns in Ireland – Waterford, Limerick and Cork. The military activity did not immediately cease, as the dreary list of wars, battles, sackings and sieges noted by the *Annals* indicates; but parallel with it went the bustle of trade.

2

The Coming of the Normans 1170–1300

Outside St Audoen's the smell of malt comes from Guinness' brewery and a cold wind from the river gushes up the steps. Here was the heart of medieval Dublin. Traces of the city wall can be seen in the recently reconstructed arch and wall overlooking Cook Street. Its uncertain route can be followed by Wood Quay, past Bridge Street, up Cornmarket and at the Castle where some chunks of broken masonry survive. Portions are embedded in the Iveagh Buildings. Bull Alley, Golden Lane, Cornmarket and Ship Street, once Sheep Street, give hints of how the old town was laid out. From the main thoroughfare of High Street, Winetavern and Fishamble Streets descend to the river.

Apart from material recovered by excavation, the city's medieval remnants are few. They include the Archbishop's palace of St Sepulchre, now a police barracks, where all that remains of the old structure is a vault and a small sixteenth-century window. St Mary's Abbey has left behind its half-buried chapter house. St Werburgh's shelters a double tomb whose battered thirteenth-century effigies portray a Purcell Knight and his lady who originally lay in the monastery of All Hallows. A later monument, dated 1482, under the tower of St Audoen's, commemorates Sir Rowland FitzEustace, Baron Portlester, and his wife.

The painful nineteenth-century reconstructions of Dublin's two cathedrals, St Patrick's and Christ Church, were so comprehensive that it is difficult to recall that the most impressive medieval monument in Dublin is the great 150 feet limestone tower of St Patrick's raised by Archbishop Minot in 1362. St Patrick's contains some brasses and two ecclesiastical effigies, one of Archbishop Faulk de Saunford or perhaps his brother, the other of Cornish-born Archbishop Tregury, crowned with an ornate mitre, his arm raised in blessing. Christ Church has suffered even more than St Patrick's by restoration. The Victorians encased much of the building fabric in new stonework and unforgivably removed the fourteenth-century choir. But they left the soot-blackened Romanesque doorway in the south transept, topped by its double row of chevrons, one of which supports a small elongated head which may represent Henry II or Dermot Macmurrough. On the stone capitals in the nave medieval decoration includes crowned heads, a leering monster and two portrait busts framed by dragon's wings. The crypt is pre-Norman, while some of the chapels contain shrines dedicated to notable figures associated with the Norman conquest. A small heart-shaped metal box holds the heart of St Laurence O'Toole which survived the destruction of the Reformation. There is an effigy of his successor, Archbishop Comyn. Best known of Christ Church's medieval survivals is the striking black polished limestone knight who is supposed to be Strongbow. His arms, however, are those of FitzOsmund. Strongbow was probably here in the first place, but after his effigy was damaged by a fall of the roof, FitzOsmund may have been put there in his stead. The smaller figure, thought to be Strongbow's son, is more likely to be a container for his intestines.

For the medieval townsfolk the towers of their two cathedrals – an excessive number for so small a community – were symbols of man's hope and salvation. For those who lived elsewhere on the island they were permanent reminders that the men who built them and worshipped in them were of alien stock. St Patrick's, begun in 1192, was modelled on Salisbury Cathedral, while Christ Church, enlarged from Bishop Donatus' foundation of 1037, copied Glastonbury and Wells. Although the external walls and towers of St Patrick's are made of Irish limestone and the spire and battlements of the tower are of granite from the cliffs behind Dalkey, interior refinements are from England. White wrought stone was hauled over from quarries outside Bristol, while the black marble in the columns which decorate the triforum was transported from the Isle of Purbeck in Dorset. Many of the craftsmen responsible for medieval Christ Church were in the entourage of King John during his visit in 1210. Nicholas of Coventry, known as Cementarius, Osbert the quarrier, Urricus the engineer and Alberia the ditcher were Englishmen. So was the unknown craftsman, 'the Master of Christ Church', who built the nave and was responsible for much of the carving. There is similar work in St Andrew's, Droitwich, believed to have been done by him, and he seems to have come to Ireland in about 1213.

The banishment of Dermot MacMurrough, ruler of Leinster, led to his seeking Norman intervention in a local squabble. Ireland's great traitor had many associations with Dublin. He was born in

the town about 1100; he had a house there, surrounded by a
garden, which like the residence of the Ostman governor, was of
stone and stood out conspicuously among the wattle and daub. His
piety, which manifested itself in founding monasteries at Ferns and
Baltinglass, was responsible for two of Dublin's most famous
monastic foundations – the Priory of All Hallows, whose High
Altar was located just where the Campanile of Trinity College
stands, and the nearby Augustinian Nunnery of St Mary de Hogges
on Hoggen Green. The nuns of St Mary de Hogges, according to a
manuscript in the British Museum, 'were not of the younger sort,
but of elderly persons and. . .those who desired to live single lives
after the death or separation of their husbands'. Among them was
Dermot's wife, also Archbishop O'Toole's sister, who entered after
she had separated from Dermot, bringing inside with her all his
wealth. A more murky piece of family history concerned the
murder of Dermot's father in the hall of his court of justice, and his
burial, together with a dog. This demonstration of ill-feeling by the
townspeople towards the MacMurroughs helped to initiate the
events that culminated in the invitation to the Normans.

By the twelfth century any Irish king who claimed to be the Ard
Rí or (High King) made a point of asserting his supremacy over
Dublin which had long been the most important town in Ireland,
rivalled only by Waterford. It was an ecclesiastical centre with its
own archbishop and the base of the king of Leinster. But its true
importance still lay in its position as a prosperous trading port. It
possessed a fleet of over 200 ships which, following Viking
tradition, sailed to distant towns on the continent. However, the
bulk of trade was with English ports, particularly Chester and
Bristol. In Dermot's time Dublin was directly governed by Earl
Ragnall Mac Torcaill, a member of the Ostman family which had
ruled since the death of Sitric Silkenbeard. The prefix 'Mac' is a
clue to the extent of Hiberno-Norse integration. In 1162 Dermot
had been acknowledged as overlord of Dublin, but in 1166 he was
supplanted when Hasculf Mac Torcaill, who had succeeded his
brother Ragnall, accepted Rory O'Connor, king of Connacht and
aspiring High King as his superior. When Dermot sought help
abroad in his attempt to regain the high kingship his contact with
Bristol traders, begun during his residence in Dublin, led him
straight to that port. It was a Bristol merchant, Robert Fitz-
Harding, who may even have had family connections with the Mac-

Murroughs, who provided him with an introduction to Henry II.

The small group of Normans which landed at Bannow Bay early in May, 1169, consisted of experienced knights backed by Welsh archers armed with modern crossbows who reinforced Dermot's army. On August 23rd these first arrivals were joined by Strongbow with 200 knights and 1,000 soldiers. The combined forces captured Waterford and Strongbow married Dermot's daughter. The following summer he and his father-in-law marched on Dublin, a prime target for any invader.

Earl Hasculf called upon his new overlord to save the town. Rory O'Connor, the recently installed High King, had a far larger army than the 5,000 men who made up the forces of the enemy, while the defence of Dublin appeared to be simplified by the natural barrier imposed by the Wicklow mountains. O'Connor posted his main army at the moor of Clondalkin, east of the range, and placed forces at the traditional passes that led up from the south, the Scalp above Enniskerry and Windgates on the coast south of Bray. But elsewhere the forested hills were not impenetrable for mobile troops moving quickly during a summer campaign. Dermot and Strongbow came across the mountains by way of Glendalough, Glencree and down by Rathfarnham to the outskirts of Dublin.

Taken by surprise, the defenders sent out their Archbishop Laurence O'Toole to mediate. In due course the Archbishop would co-operate with the Normans, following the approved ecclesiastical rule of acknowledging the strongest temporal power. But now he confronted Strongbow and his brother-in-law and listened to Dermot's demands for hostages and for the town to recognize him as High King once again. While these points were being discussed, two Norman knights, Raymond le Gros and Milo de Cogan, led a small party of knights in an unauthorized attack; they breached the walls of Dublin and slaughtered the townspeople. These were the people who had killed Dermot's father, an independent Hiberno-Norse blend, who for all their long years of integration remained an isolated group, separate in spirit from other Gaels. Out at Clondalkin Rory O'Connor made no move to help them, as he was boycotting the peace negotiations. A strong medieval opinion believed that the Dubliners deserved their fate 'for having violated their word to the men of Erin'. Some thought that Dermot, wishing to take revenge for his father's murder, encouraged the slaughter. Portents indicated divine justice; there was a thunderstorm and lightning set fire to wicker buildings as the Normans slipped over the walls. The crucifix in Christ Church refused to be moved when the escaping Ostmen tried to seize it. Earl Hasculf and some of his followers briskly abandoned the town to its fate, ran to the ships which had been moored in the Liffey for just such a contingency and sailed away. The date was 21 September 1170.

Dermot retired to his capital at Ferns while the Normans settled in the town for the winter. Their position was far from secure, and made less so in the spring of 1171 when Dermot died and Strongbow, who had marched to Wexford to be with him on his deathbed, declared himself High King instead. Meanwhile Earl Hasculf returned with a large fleet containing men recruited from Norway, the Hebrides and the Isle of Man to launch an attack on Dublin by sea. The Normans had one great advantage over the seafarers: horses. The Ostmen were turned, and as they fled back to their ships Hasculf was taken prisoner. The Normans would have spared his life for ransom, but he refused to bargain. So they took off his old balding head in the hall of his stone house.

After that the Irish sent a huge pan-Gaelic army to attack Dublin. Since they lacked skill in siege warfare, they hoped to force the Normans into surrender by starvation. Strongbow hurried back from Wexford to help his men in their plight. Not only were they cut off from other Norman strongholds at Wexford and Waterford, but Strongbow could expect no help from England. He had been on the wrong side during the recent English war; in addition Henry II was alarmed at the possible creation of a rival Norman kingdom in Ireland. One of the defenders of Dublin, Maurice Fitzgerald, uttered the first recorded lament of the colonist in Ireland. 'We are considered as Irish by the English and each island hates us as much as the other.' The attitude of the Normans in England contrasted with the solidarity of the Viking colonies, still prepared to help remote kinsmen with whom they had retained links for over 200 years. The Normans shut up in Dublin could only help themselves. They proved aggressively resourceful. Three mobile units, commanded by Strongbow, Milo de Cogan and Raymond le Gros, each consisting of thirty to forty mounted knights, sixty bowmen and a hundred foot soldiers, set out to attack O'Connor's main army which was camped at Castleknock. The Irish were routed, and after that the Norman presence in Dublin went unchallenged.

Unlike the Vikings, the Normans and those who subsequently moulded Dublin left a good deal of information about themselves. The *Calendar of Ancient Records,* which has been edited by Dublin's own historian, John Thomas Gilbert, contains nineteen volumes of the muniments in the possession of the Corporation. They comprise royal charters and grants, the Assembly Rolls, the White Book, the Chain Book and other documents concerned with the city. The White Book, composed of 111 sheets of vellum, has transcripts of documents relating to city affairs which were copied between the thirteenth and seventeenth centuries. The Chain Book which was chained to the Guildhall for reference by the citizens, contains memoranda of the city's laws and usages, and miscellaneous material such as directions for pageants. The Assembly Rolls in Latin and English consist of enactments of the City Council. There are a hundred and two charters and grants dating from 1171 to 1727.*

'Henry II, King of England, Duke of Normandy and Aquitaine and Earl of Anjou notifies that he has granted and confirmed to his men of Bristowa his city of Duvelina to be inhabited and held by them from him and his heirs, with all liberties and free customs which they have at Bristowa and throughout his entire land.' The royal city of Bristol, much of whose prosperity had been based on its trade with Viking Dublin, had been granted special privileges which would henceforth be shared by Dubliners. Later the 'Liberties of Bristol' were enjoyed by four other cities in Ireland – Waterford, Cork, Limerick and Galway.

Henry made this first grant to Dublin during his state visit to Ireland. His distrust of Strongbow had not been alleviated by his subject's reappearance in Gloucester offering him the spoils of conquest. More was needed to ensure a conquest that would involve the English crown. In the Middle Ages it was not enough to obtain territory by proxy; the physical presence of the sovereign was necessary to assert his strength and receive oaths of loyalty.

---

* Noel Carroll, the publicity officer for the Dublin Corporation showed me some of these charters, together with city regalia. Because there is no museum in the City Hall, the things are not on display. Mr Carroll vanished, and in a few moments returned carrying the huge Dublin City Mace, the City Sword, the ancient city seal and various charters and seals, many small enough to put comfortably in the pocket. He casually placed this remarkable collection on his desk for me to examine. There can be few other capital cities whose treasures are produced with such delightful informality.

The subsequent disinclination of English monarchs to visit Ireland did not help the fluctuating fortunes of the Anglo-Normans. Henry also wished to avoid some papal legates due to arrive in England and ask embarrassing questions about the recent murder of Thomas à Becket. He had an idea of regaining lost prestige by bringing the eccentric Celtic church back under the influence of Rome. He came to Ireland armed with *Laudabiliter* and a quantity of wax to be used for seals on charters and documents. His fleet of 400 ships contained an impressive retinue and the largest foreign force which had ever landed in Ireland. A succession of Irish chieftains viewed its strength and acknowledged his rule. He was an able and energetic monarch whose ideas had contributed to the development of the English judicial and fiscal system. He ruled great areas of France. He could only spare six months in Ireland, four of which he spent in Dublin.

Instead of shutting himself behind the walls of the town he had the imagination to build a palace beside the Thingmote which was constructed of 'peeled osiers, according to the custom of that country'. Powerful Normans had castles of stone; Henry's wattle palace was an exercise in psychology. At Christmas he gave a lavish reception. Giraldus Cambrensis wrote how 'very many of the princes of the land repaired to Dublin...and were much astonished by the sumptuousness of his entertainments...and having places assigned to them at the table in the hall by the king's command, they learned to eat cranes, a food they loathed'. In England Henry's banquets had the reputation of being so unappetizing – with four-day-old fish, meat from diseased animals, bread made hastily from yeast out of the ale tub and sour wine – that people dreaded attending.

The king left Dublin on 2 February 1172 and departed from Ireland two months later in an atmosphere of reasonable good will. Strongbow was confirmed in the Kingdom of Leinster, John de Courcy in Ulster, while Hugh de Lacy was granted Meath. The unsatisfactory half-conquest was initiated. For Dublin, where Hugh de Lacy had been appointed as Justiciar, the visit and the new charter were crucial to its development. Within a rapid space of time the little Viking seaport was reshaped and given gloss and organization characteristic of Norman efficiency. It became the seat of centralized government. Prosperity brought civic consciousness and high living standards to be enjoyed by people who were newcomers. The town, or city as it had now become, filled up with strangers.

The Ostmen had seen their Earl beheaded, their strong men emigrate and had been reduced in numbers by slaughter. We do not know the population of Dublin when the Normans arrived, but Bristol contained about 5,600 people and Dublin was smaller. Soon after Henry's visit the majority of Dublin Ostmen crossed the river and went to live in the suburb of Oxmantown. There was already a community there served by St Michan's parish and attended by the new Cistercian Abbey of St Mary's. Whether they went voluntarily or were forced to go because their presence in the city was regarded as a threat, is not known. Waterford, Cork and Limerick also acquired their Ostman suburbs. The Ostmen do not seem to have been discriminated against in the same way as the Irish were. Norman and Ostman shared a common ancestry and the Ostmen as traders, craftsmen and sailors could contribute valuable skills and experience to the life of the city. No enactment was made against them and they had the same rights and privileges as incoming settlers. Nevertheless they declined and vanished as a separate race. An early roll of freemen issued just after the new charter shows that out of 148 names only ten belonged to Ostmen. In subsequent years Viking names sometimes cropped up in the city records. A sept known as the Harolds had a castle near the foot of Kilmashogue and land at Harold's Cross. In 1350 there is mention of the election of a 'Captain of the Harolds and a Captain of the Archbolds' in County Dublin. The names of the ruling Ostman family of Mac Torcaill occurred occasionally as owners of small pieces of property. A Hamo MacTorkil figured in a law case, and the Justiciary Rolls of 1313 told of the attempted escape of a member of the family named Walter MacTorkil who had been imprisoned in Dublin Castle. Today the occasional surname like Searson, derived from Sigurson, indicates Norse ancestry.

Henry's charter opened the way for a massive flow of immigrants. Although it specified that newcomers should be men from Bristol, the early settlers came from all over south-west England and from south Wales. They were mainly tradesmen and artisans, people with urban backgrounds. A roll believed to date from the late twelfth century, giving names of citizens and their occupations – goldsmith, tailor, shoemaker, carpenter, miller, vintner and so forth – lists only fourteen names out of 1,600 as having originated from Bristol. (Just one name on the list is noted as *Hiberniensis*.) But there were undoubtedly men from Bristol in the body of citizens which sallied out of the city walls on Easter Monday 1209 for a hurling match on a pitch located on the flat land at Cullenswood beside modern Sandford Road. Local Irish septs interrupted the camaraderie of ex-patriots by an ambush in which an appalling 500 were killed which must have amounted to a quarter of the male population. New Bristol settlers were quickly encouraged to come over and replace those who had perished. The slaughter would be commemorated for 600 years. Richard Stanyhurst wrote how in Tudor times when hostile Irish still posed a threat, the mayor and citizens recalled Black Monday by an anniversary feast on the sylvan site, eaten under guard so that 'the mountain enemie dareth not attempt to snatch so much as a pastrye crust from thence'.

By 1209 the Norman conquest had long been an indisputable fact of Irish life. By the treaty of Windsor in 1175 Rory O'Connor recognized Henry as king, and two years later Henry's son, Prince John, was made Lord of Ireland at the age of ten. In 1185 the prince made the first of two visits to Ireland – the second was after the Cullenswood massacre when he came as king. This first visit was considered by Giraldus Cambrensis to be a public relations disaster – the prince brought over a shipload of sportsmen and dogs for his amusement and insulted the Gaelic lords who came to do him homage by pulling their beards. But it had significance. It brought over the founders of the Butler and Geraldine dynasties who were to have great importance in Irish affairs. John's presence in Dublin resulted in a new, more extensive charter which set out for the first time the legal rights of citizens and formed the basis for municipal legislation. It also defined the city's boundaries. There were provisions protecting Dublin merchants from foreign competition. Foreign merchants were forbidden to buy corn, hides or wool except from citizens, while no foreigner could sell drink in the city, but only on his own ship.

A building programme began which would continue throughout the thirteenth century. The two cathedrals rose amidst a squabble initiated by Archbishop Comyn who wished to establish his own jurisdiction outside the authority of the Justiciar and the control of the Prior of Christ Church. Christ Church, rebuilt by Strongbow, possessed a regular chapter under the rule of reformed Arroasian canons who followed the rule of St Augustine with modifications borrowed from the Cistercians. These rules, approved by St

Malachy, were adapted to some extent to the special demands of the Irish church. St Patrick's had a secular chapter wholly constituted on the English model. Archbishop Comyn raised the rank of St Patrick's to a collegiate church and built the palace of St Sepulchre where he installed 'a college of clerics of approved life and learning'. His successor, Henry of London, raised the collegiate church to the dignity of a cathedral in 1213. Two cathedrals in the same dioٲese caused continual friction which was only eased in 1300 when the older Christ Church was accepted as the mother church with the right to consecrate archbishops and to be the treasure house for church insignia. This was little more than a sop to local pride, because St Patrick's continued to be the more important cathedral during the entire medieval period up until the Reformation.

Apart from Christ Church the most impressive ecclesiastical building within the city walls was St Audoen's. St Werburgh, west of the castle, rebuilt on the site of a Norse church which had been dedicated to St Martin, and St Nicholas, were new spires within the walled area, joining St Audoen's west of Christ Church, St John and St Olaf north of Christ Church, and St Mary del Dam inside the eastern gate, the history of whose foundation is unknown. City parishes were tiny; St Olaf's, for example, only covered 40,000 square yards. In the suburbs St Andrew's, St George's and St Peter's all east of the city and St James, and St Catherine's to the west added their number to the old pre-Norman churches in the valley of the Poddle as churches outside the walls. All the time the cathedrals were being transformed. The city was crowded with masons and workers heaving masses of stone which arrived at the Liffey in boatloads from quarries scattered around Ireland, Wales and England. It had to be unloaded and laboriously carried up the steep hill and outward to sites where yet more buildings were being erected to the greater glory of God.

Secular buildings also required boatloads of stone. The records show that there were six by now, some of which may have had tiles, although the excavated green-glaze tiles dated to the thirteenth century may also have come from churches. The city was dominated by the largest secular building of all, Dublin Castle, which probably replaced a defensive motte and bailey construction pushed up by the Normans when they first took the city. In 1204 King John ordered 'a castle. . . for the use of justice in the city and if need be for the city's defence with good dykes and strong walls'.

It was a rectangular enclosure with a circular tower at each corner and a gateway with a portcullis at the centre of the North Gate. Apart from the royal administrative offices, it contained the exchequer, treasury, a chapel, mill, kitchen and buttery with a stock of a hundred dishes, one cauldron, two platters, five cups and five pitchers. From the first it was used as a prison, since there is an early reference to a great chain to guard prisoners. Between 1243 and 1245 a new hall, modelled on one in Canterbury, was constructed under the patronage of Henry III, who, although he never visited Ireland, took great interest in its progress. It was probably the most lavishly equipped building of its time in Ireland, with its marble columns, a dais surmounted by a fresco showing the king and queen surrounded by barons, a rose window and piped water – the first site in Dublin to enjoy this luxury.

The Poddle river was dammed around this time to facilitate the defences of city and Castle. It ceased to be tidal, the Black Pool dried up, and the Poddle now was channelled to run beside the Castle walls. This meant that Dublin was surrounded by water except on the west side where there were large ditches to keep off enemies. The city walls had been reconstructed to Norman specifications. Grants for building stone towers along them began to be given to selected citizens like John Garget who was granted a tower 'upon Gurmund's gate' or William Picot a 'clerk of the city' who built Buttevant near Isolde's Tower. The walls were also being extended northward, considerably increasing the area of the enclosed city, as the silted Liffey was pushed back and land was reclaimed.

The Liffey was changing. There was a process whereby the river narrowed and some sort of natural silting was taking place, possibly associated with the construction of Dubhghall's Bridge. The water below the Viking city wall was too shallow to provide berths for the Normans' big ships. Therefore the river had to be pushed back. The original Viking wall which stood beside the old river bank was kept to become a second line of military defence. All the streets north of Cook Street running at right angles to the river developed after the process of land reclamation; Winetavern Street was the most important. Numerous gates in the old wall along Cook Street opened up the older parts of the town to the newly reclaimed area. Directly below Christ Church, where the river was first made to retreat around 1200, a post and wattle fence has been traced, which was later replaced by a massive wooden revetment made largely from ship's timber. Behind it was packed river mud, gravel and garbage. Large wooden drains, later replaced by stone, helped to carry away liquid effluent into the river. On the old shore level just below the Viking wall a number of human skeletons have been found which were roughly thrust into the silt of the shore. One was an adult holding a child in its arms; there were also some severed heads and limbs. Probably they were casualties from a raid which occurred in Viking times when their bodies were thrust over the existing city wall into the mud of the river.

The thirteenth century was the great age of urban growth, although very likely Dublin would have expanded, even without the impetus provided by the Normans. St Audoen's had to be enlarged to cater for the increase in population. What this may have been we can only guess; perhaps at the height of Anglo-Norman development there were about 8,000 people in the town. The permanent head of administration was the Justiciar, who held supreme powers, only subject to the king, although he ruled together with a municipal government. The city acquired bailiffs, a sheriff's court, trial by jury, a system of weighing and measuring and a mint. Early coins showed King John wearing a diadem with five pearls. A pottery piggy-bank has been found with a thirteenth-century coin inside it. There was now a mayor. Previous first citizens had been styled Provost, but in 1229 Henry III arranged for the annual election of 'a loyal and discreet Mayor' who in due course had power to try 'felonies, trespass, misprisions, contempts and concealments within the city'.

The community was small and intimate enough for townspeople to be recorded by their Christian names and occupations, like Robert the Moneychanger, William the Clerk and William described as 'with the coif' a form of cap associated with lawyers. Beneath the Justiciar ranked the municipal and ruling classes, then the commonalty from merchants down to lowly villeins and betaghs. At the top of the salary scale the Justiciar received £500 a year while a porter earned 13s. 9d. a year. To give some indication of thirteenth-century values, a chicken cost a penny.

Medieval towns usually developed distinct quarters and Dublin was no exception. Cooks, prone to accident by fire, were situated just outside the old Viking wall in Cook Street. Leather workers concentrated at High Street and Skinners' Row; fishmongers congregated in Fishamble Street. Wine merchants and also sellers of ale were to be found in Winetavern Street, although at its upper end was a colony of wood-turners and coopers producing barrel staves and wooden bowls and platters. In 1235 Castle Street was referred to as Lormeria, a reference to the lorimers who worked there making spurs and other small iron objects. People still lived and worked in houses of daub and wattle or wood similar to those in use before the Normans arrived.

On the whole the diet was good. The dung and refuse of medieval Dublin has been analysed, not only from the contents of cesspits, but from the remains of agricultural produce that was sold outside the west gate of the city on a site which is still known as the Cornmarket. There were fields beside the city walls; a proportion of manure was carried out to them in dung carts. The Normans managed to harvest the corn crop before the siege by Rory O'Connor's army. Animals could be grazed on common ground on Hoggen Green and the green area of St Stephen's.

In addition to cereals the Cornmarket sold hay and straw, together with bracken for bedding animals. Straw was not only used for animals but for floor covering in houses during summer; trampled straw has been found in many excavated houses. In winter rushes were used instead. Bundles of moss served in privies as we use lavatory paper. Winter wheat was ground into white flour. Spring wheat was considered inferior because it became infested with the ground black seeds of corncockle (*agrostemma githago*), a weed now almost extinct because of modern farming methods, which gave the flour a speckled appearance, an unpleasant taste, and although no one realized it, rendered it toxic when eaten regularly. Another common cereal was buckwheat (*fagopyrum esculentum*), a food crop which does well on poor acid soils and comes quickly to seed. It is still eaten in eastern Europe and in America where it was imported because it suited the skimpy soil of New England.

Material from the cesspits has shown that in addition to the range of food eaten by the Vikings, medieval citizens enjoyed imported foods such as figs, raisins, and walnuts. Shellfish continued to be a favourite item of diet, while the animal bones in the medieval layers of excavation indicate that by far the greatest source of meat was still pig. Beef was usually salted down in winter. But cattle was raised mainly for milk and hides and sheep for wool, so that the ratio of beef and mutton bones to pork is relatively small. Other items of meat were obtained casually. They included hare and wild birds such as greylag or white fronted geese, snipe and wild duck caught in the sloblands by the river. Sea eagles and ravens have been identified; they could not have made good eating. Bones from early medieval levels do not include rabbit. Rabbits were introduced to Ireland by Anglo-Normans who probably kept them in cages and ate them as French peasants do today. Escapes would have quickly built up the wild population. By the fourteenth century rabbit had become a mundane item of diet; the Prior of Holy Trinity is recorded as eating rabbit for breakfast, while a shopping list in the Chain Book itemized: 'for two good rabbits three pence'.

Dublin was largely self-sufficient and imports contained luxuries like jewellery, spice, dried fruit and a good deal of wine. Quantities of wool were imported from England since local wool was too coarse for any fine weaving. Exports included hides to Italy in great numbers, reflecting the wealth of Irish cattle, small fast horses, much in demand in England since Henry II took some home with him, hawks and other birds associated with falconry, and any surplus in corn, beans, peas and dried fish that had not been confiscated by the King's Purveyors. Frequent enactments by the Justiciar enabled the English monarch to claim a proportion of Irish food and commodities.

Trade was somewhat inhibited by the Liffey's tendency to silt up, a problem which would remain for centuries. Already in the thirteenth century after the reclamation of land along its banks, its main channel was fouled with sandbanks and old wrecks. There were slips at Merchants' Quay and Wood Quay and a crane or weigh-house existed, but increasingly merchant ships were unwilling to tackle the hazards of the river. By now they were heavier and built with deeper keels than their Viking prototypes. They needed extra draught and preferred to anchor in the pools of Clontarf or at Howth or in Dalkey Sound off the important port of Dalkey. The merchants of Dublin suffered and would continue to do so. In 1358 they petitioned Edward III, complaining that 'for want of deep water in the harbour...the large ships from abroad...have to anchor at the port of Dalkey...the merchants of the city have usually purchased wines, iron and salt and other merchandize from such large ships in the port of Dalkey and removed them in barges and boats to Dublin' where they had to pay customs at three pence in the pound. Nearly a century later facilities for landing cargoes had not improved. Citizens complained in 1437 how 'merchants...to the great and manifest injury of Dublin proceed to Howth, Baldoyle, Malahide, Portrane, Rush and Skerries'.

The powerful Guild of Merchants, known as the Guild of the Holy Trinity, excluded Irishmen from learning any of the fifty or more trades it controlled. Irishmen could not hold civil or clerical office. *'Et non Hibernicae nationis'* was one of the principal qualifications of a freeman of the city. It is probable that although there was little initial inclination among the Gaels for living in towns, their influence on civic life in centres like Dublin and Limerick has been underestimated. They trickled in over the years, so that the population, especially its poorer strata, became mixed, much as it had been in Viking times. They sought to live in the city to avoid the consequences of war and famine or to escape the manor servitude imposed by the feudal system. A Dublin bye-law of 1315 stated that 'villeins and betaghs who by permission of the mayor and commonalty remain in the city for a year and a day are thereby freed from their lords'. Irish names appeared more frequently in civil and judicial documents. Men of Gaelic stock accepted foreign custom willingly like Robert de Bree, who presumably originated from around Bray in County Wicklow, but became in 1290 a citizen of Dublin with 'a grant of special grace...that during his whole life he may use English laws'. Many other Irishmen obtained municipal jobs or received ecclesiastical benefice provided they were known to be of good character and 'continually and unswervingly remained in loyalty and obedience to us'.

'Conquest draws to it three things' Richard Stanyhurst wrote in the sixteenth century, 'laws, apparel and language – and if any of these three lack, the conquest limpeth.' Conscious that their existence was the result of conquest, medieval Dubliners took more care than the Vikings to prevent their language being swamped in Gaelic syntax. The aristocracy spoke French, the official Norman language, while the majority of the rest spoke the language of their origins, a southern dialect of Middle English. The Kildare poems written by 'Michael Kildare' early in the fourteenth century were in this form of Dublinese. Some of them were satirical, holding up to ridicule those who did not give enough to the 'wretched poor', tailors who made wrong hoods and bakers with their 'loaves small'. A verse from a hymn written around 1300 conveys the language's sub-Chaucerian flavour:

Dis world is lue is gon awai
So dew on grasse in sumer dai
De pour ches ssal be pi nest
Pat sittist bold a bench...

Early Dublin medieval dress was simple in style. Both men and women wore the same basic garments, an inner tunic, or smock in the case of a woman, and a surcoat or mantle topped with a hooded cloak. In Christ Church two effigies of women in thirteenth-century clothes show one wearing a long plain tunic and surcoat set off by a pillbox hat, the other dressed in a more voluminous gown and mantle with a wimple. Armour was of an international type, its styling as variable as car bodies are now. From the meagre evidence of effigies it seems that later on in the fifteenth century Irish armour assumed various provincial characteristics consistent with its remoteness from centres of European heraldic fashion. Names of fifteenth-century armourers, Richard West, Nicholas de Hodderode of Scarlet Lane and William Corner of St Werburgh's parish, have been preserved in civic records.

The most sumptuous wearing apparel was donned by the clergy. In 1293 the belongings of the former Archbishop of Tuam who became Justiciar included 'a chasuble of red samite, a great cross of pearls, two precious embroidered capes, a clasp for a cape with an image of the deity, and precious stones, a gilt crest for the head of the cape with divers shields and precious stones and an amice with pearls of varied work'.

Such richness was indicative of the enormous power of the church. Interiors of churches and cathedrals also emphasized the importance of display. There were benches against the wall and a solitary 'shriving pew' or confessional, but no other seats, nothing to take away from the glory of arching pillars. The grey stone walls were usually whitewashed or painted with yellow ochre. Under the sprinkling of straw or rushes floors were richly tiled; many fine tiles with elaborate designs have survived from Christ Church and St Mary's Abbey. Often the lighting was as bright as it would be today. A saint's feast would be the occasion for the lavish use of candles. Henry III once authorized the use of 800 lighted tapers for the feast of St Thomas and St Edward in the Abbey of St Thomas – a kingly gift of expensive wax. Frescos illustrating biblical subjects for the benefit of the illiterate – the majority of people – included paintings of the story of the Passion on the rood screen of Christ

Church and a fresco in St Audoen's showing the Trinity. Carved statues, jewelled insignia and lavishly embroidered vestments were on daily display to citizens living crushed together in ramshackle little houses.

Together with the Merchants' Guild – whose Guildhall gave importance to Fishamble Street – the ten religious houses encircling the city controlled the main sources of wealth. Among them St Mary's Abbey, the richest house in the Pale, owned over 5,000 acres in north Dublin, 134 houses in the city, most of them rented out, and the huge estate of Monkstown in south Dublin which stretched from Blackrock to Dun Laoghaire. It possessed a private quay at Bullock harbour and its own little harbour at the mouth of the Bradoge river known as the Pill – a word of Scottish origin – where the Cistercians carried out their own exclusive trading operations. The fish landed at the Pill was sold to the inhabitants of the north side of the Liffey. There was a Fisher's Lane north of Pill Lane which is marked on Rocque's map of 1756.

Another very wealthy Abbey, belonging to the Augustinians, played an important part in the city's life for centuries as the Abbey of St Thomas Court. Because it was a royal foundation – Henry II had taken special interest in its dedication to the martyr of Canterbury – it had valuable grants which varied from the exercise of justice, including the power to execute criminals, to mundane privileges like brewing its own ale and baking bread. Like the Archbishop, the Abbot of St Thomas, who sat as a peer in Parliament, was totally independent of the authority of the Mayor and Bailiffs.

The Knights Hospitallers of St John of Jerusalem, founded in Dublin by Strongbow, also had huge possessions. The impressive main house of these veterans of war, situated at Kilmainham, must have looked like an independent small town. A castle, two dormitories for the brethren, lodgings, and a great hall were surrounded by a strong wall with towers and outer enclosures. In addition to its endowment of lands, orchards, shrubberies and a valuable two mile stretch of river bank, Kilmainham received 500 acres of what is now Phoenix Park from Hugh Tyrell of Castleknock. It owned granaries, had milling interests and possessed a charter which gave it, like St Thomas Court, considerable independence of the laws that governed the rest of the community. After the suppression of their rival the Knights

Templars, with whom they had carried on a century long feud, the Hospitallers acquired the Knights Templars' extensive property at Clontarf. They not only dispensed hospitality as their name implied, but provided a nucleus of men of military experience loyal to the government and ready, in the words of Edward I, 'for the repulse of the king's enemies...warring upon his liege people'. Their Abbey was strategically sited, guarding the western approaches to the city.

The Templars and the Hospitallers provided the city with the medieval equivalent of hotels, not only dispensing almost regal hospitality at their headquarters, but offering more modest accommodation at special guest-houses in Dublin for their members. The Templars kept in Winetavern Street 'a stone house near the church of the Holy Trinity with decent entertainment and stable, white cloth, white salt, white candles and cooking utensils'. Other religious houses accommodated the poor, while strangers to the city could stay at the hostelry run by St Mary's Abbey. St Thomas', which was frequently used as a residence by the Justiciar, received royalty; included among its rooms was 'John's Chamber' where the king had stayed in 1210.

Travellers could also stay at the small hospice belonging to the Priory of Holy Trinity. We know quite a lot about life in this priory which was attached to Christ Church. Some of its records survived until the Record Office fire in 1922, and before they were destroyed a number of them were published. They consisted mostly of detailed notes about housekeeping and expense lists for a wide variety of purchases such as needles and threads for sewing bags, Wicklow boards and grease for the Priory carts. There is a good deal of miscellaneous information such as records of debts: 'To Edward the fisherman for an old debt of Robert de Sain Neot, late kitchener, 19d.' The parchments cover the period just preceding the Black Death, but the intimate glimpse they give into the life of a wealthy institution has details which would have changed little in a century.

The Priory of Holy Trinity, like St Mary's and St Thomas's, was extremely well endowed. North of the city it possessed the manor of Glasnevin and Gorman; the name of the Priory Grange is preserved in Grangegorman. To the south it owned a great manor called Clonken, covering the parishes of Stillorgan, Killiney, Kill and Tully. Kill o' the Grange was a church on a Priory farm. By this time the forests on the flat land below the hills had been cleared and turned into farms and manors run on feudal lines. Until they were covered by suburbia, they left traces in sitings of villages and arrangement of field systems characteristic of imported Norman manorial patterns of land tenure which were quite different from Gaelic ways of handling land. Much of the farmland around the city was in the possession of ecclesiastic communities.

In the city the only surviving traces of the Priory buildings are the ruins of the chapter house and garden beside Christ Church. Nearby the Prior had his chambers where the present Synod Hall is now; they were of stone with close fitting doors, glass windows and the luxury of a chimney. The furniture included coffer chests, benches, flock and feather bedsteads and chairs. 'Hire of a certain man making straw stools for the Prior's chamber as well as at Glasnevin – 16d.'

The Priory's duties as a hostelry meant that its accounts stress the expenses of the kitchen which contained twelve dishes, twelve plates and twelve sauce vessels in addition to such items as two large pewter dishes made by Walter the Goldsmith at the cost of 9d. Plates were for feast days; more generally trenchers, thick slices of stale bread, were used to carry food instead. The use of pottery, neglected by the Vikings, had now become general, although the Priory accounts make little mention of it apart from a record of four shillings for clay sold at Clonken to one Dowenild O'Helyn for making earthenware. Potters were concentrated in Crockers' Street outside Newgate. At the Wood Quay excavations more than half the pottery sherds found on the site seem to be of local manufacture, although much imported pottery came from the same provenance as many Dubliners – Bristol. The armorial green-glaze 'knight jug', one of the most spectacular items that has been recovered, which is decorated with stylized apes and knights, came from Ham Green near Bristol. Gloucester and west of England ware are well represented; Chester and the east of England less so. Other medieval pottery found in Dublin has been traced to several regions in France and a handful of majolica sherds to Italy.

The Prior and his guests were hearty eaters. Generally he was served with three meals a day. A breakfast for the Prior, Master John Hackett, Master Thomas de Kylmor, Thomas Pypard and others included a roast goose and cooked pigeon eaten with sixpence worth of wine obtained from a merchant called Stephen de

Gascogne, who almost certainly sold wine in or around Winetavern Street within a stone's throw of the Priory. Wine drinking was a Norman habit. Prince John's charter had specified that the king was to receive tribute in the form of two tuns 'from each ship which happens to come thither with wine – one before the mast and one behind'. Houses near Winetavern Street have been found with well built timber-lined cellars which were probably for wine storage. In one of them a complete jug, and in a nearby cesspit sherds from other jugs, came from the wine-growing areas of south-west France, particularly from the Saintonge region near Bordeaux. The best wines are known to have been shipped from La Rochelle; Back Lane was once known as Rochelle Street. Inferior vintages known as *vini corrupti* came from Spain and England and had to be flavoured with additives like ginger and cinnamon. Spiced wine was drunk with every feast.

The midday meal was served about noon and supper was early. Diners would wash their hands at table from vessels with acqua manile spouts in the shape of animals or grotesque heads, several of which have been excavated. Courses were accompanied by paindemain, a fine white pancake, while meat was cut into small pieces or minced because there were no forks. The Prior and his associates ate larks (often made into lark pie with a tasty crust known as the coffin, supplied by the cooks in Cook Street), oysters from the beds at Clontarf, geese, chickens, capons, rabbits, pears and imported figs and dates. Herbs and spices flavoured many dishes. Beans and peas were merely fit for feeding labourers or animals, while the only vegetable mentioned as appearing at the Prior's table is the onion. Fish was essential for fast days and Lent. Expenses for one Ash Wednesday consisted of: 'Herrings 6d. Whitefish 12d. Salmon 18d. Baking the salmon 3d. Almonds and rice 4d. Ginger and mustard ½d.' Strong spices were used to flavour many dishes, and there is controversy as to whether this was to hide the taint of not-quite fresh food or whether the medieval palate enjoyed strong flavours. Almonds were a staple of contemporary recipes like blandissorye, almonds simmered in a fish stock to which rice flour was sometimes added, very likely the dish for which the almonds and rice on this menu were used. The elaborate sweet dishes called *subtletys* – which concluded banquets – also required almonds; these were moulded, brightly coloured cakes of sugar and almond paste fashioned into religious, or hunting scenes, heraldic devices of models of fully armed ships. Henry II brought 569 pounds of almonds with him on his Irish visit. Honey was used as a sweetener, or occasionally as a medicine. When the Prior, Simon de Ludgate, was dying in 1346, he was treated with rosewater and sugar. The last entry in the Priory's surviving records was written in 1347 just before the Black Death decimated its members.

There were a number of matters over which church and laity disagreed, mostly relating to property. One of the most frequent subjects for contention was the fishing along the river, since the Hospitallers, the monks of St Mary's Abbey and members of the other foundations downstream had been granted fishing rights which conflicted with the inclinations of ordinary people. (Salmon fishing was one of the city's most important commercial preoccupations throughout the Middle Ages.) But on the whole the citizens accepted that religious wealth was justified. The church was the chief civilizing influence of the time. Religious communities possessed libraries, organized schools, distributed charity and ran hospitals like the leper hospital of St Stephen's south of the Castle and the Hospital of St John the Baptist outside Newgate which admitted both men and women. There seems to have been an easy familiarity in Dublin towards religion which was not always found elsewhere. Heresy was almost non-existent. Only one dubious case of a heretic being burned at the stake has been recorded, when in 1327 an O'Toole of Leinster is said to have been burnt on Hoggen Green because 'he denied obstinately the incarnation of our Saviour...as for the holy scriptures he said it was but a fable; the Virgin Mary, he affirmed, was a woman of dissolute habit...'

The most popular places of worship were churches associated with the Friars – Augustinians, Dominicans, Carmelites and Franciscans – who were in touch with religious thinking on the Continent and supplied fiery revivalist preachers. With many churches to choose from, other congregations were attracted by advertisement, often in the form of relics. Although Dublin could not compete with centres like Canterbury, it possessed a number of local exhibits. There might be a shortage of saintly corpses, but St Thomas's had managed to obtain the head, and later, after a dispute that had to be settled by the Pope, the body of Dublin's first Justiciar, Hugh de Lacy, who had been beheaded with a battle axe. Christ Church contained Strongbow, St Laurence O'Toole's heart and the miraculous *Bachall Iosa*, the Staff of Jesus shod with iron, and covered with gold and jewels by Christ himself, who gave it to a hermit on a Mediterranean island with instructions about its delivery to St Patrick. The Normans, who had lifted it from Armagh during the early years of the invasion, continued the Irish custom of swearing oaths and treaties by placing the hand upon it. In wartime it was carried as a talisman.

Another miracle-working relic in Christ Church which attracted gifts from rich donors, was the cross of the Holy Trinity, the one that had refused to budge when the Ostmen tried to remove it during the sack of Dublin. Archbishop O'Toole used to talk to it; a penny offered to it leapt back twice and was only accepted after the giver made suitable penance. In 1174 Strongbow had granted lands at Kinsaley to supply it with a perpetual light. In 1270 someone bequeathed it a silk girdle and two rings, while the King's Mandate of 1244 had instructed that 'four wax tapers, each 1lb in weight shall continually burn before the cross in the Holy Trinity'. This Mandate also made 'provision to cause the anchorite in the church of St Mary del Dame to have three half pence a day...with ten shillings a year for his clothes'. The anchorite may well have been on show to worshippers and pilgrims.

Pilgrims, whether voluntary or undergoing compulsory penitential pilgrimages imposed by confessors or courts of law, travelled to other centres in Ireland or went abroad. The shrine of Our Lady of Trim was well known, while centres like Croagh Patrick or St Patrick's Purgatory attracted penitents from all over Europe. Irish pilgrims went abroad to places in England such as Canterbury – an ampulla with a half-length figure of Thomas à Becket has been found in the revetment garbage – to Rome or to Santiago de Compostella in Spain. Around 1220 Archbishop Henry de Loundres founded a special hospice on the Steyne which was supported by lands at Shankill belonging to the diocese of Glendalough. It was known as Lazar's Hill because St Iago, or St James was patron of lepers. Here pilgrims gathered from all over Ireland, having made their way along the western highway to Dublin through St James Gate. This was not a gate in the city wall, but a landmark and barrier about half a mile to the west. The hostel put them up before they embarked for Spain. Wearing a costume that included a fringed cloak and a cross (the broadrimmed hat came later), carrying a pouch and a staff with a metal tip, the traveller would step into a small crowded boat.

When he returned he might say prayers of thanksgiving for having survived a long dangerous journey at the shrine of St James outside the gate, which later became the Church of St James. He was now entitled to wear a badge. These badges were more than mere souvenirs; they were charms which could work miracles. They could be used to prove that the wearer was entitled as a pilgrim to exemption from certain tolls and taxes, or as proof in a court of law that the wearer's property was immune from distraint or debt. Most major sanctuaries sold lead badges, but two found in Dublin and dated to the thirteenth century are of pewter. One, showing St Peter and St Paul, may have been brought back from Rome. The other, inscribed IN HONORE SANTI VVLSTANI, 'in honour of St Wulfstan' is in the form of a miniature flask. The cult of St Wulfstan, who was bishop of Worcester from 1062 until his death in 1095, enjoyed great popularity in Dublin. After his canonization in 1203 he became famous as a miracle worker and devil exorcizer. Pilgrims who visited his tomb at Worcester took away these flasks which would have been filled with healing water.

Religious houses controlled much of the city's milling and produced the wheat, barley and oats which were converted into the citizen's ale. The dignified good cheer of religious hospices would have been on a different level from the hospitality imparted by the city taverns. Drinking was one of the few ways that people could compensate for the lack of social activity. Few games could be played within the city – there was a prohibition against games in cemeteries, which suggests that the lack of open spaces was keenly felt. People did not read or go to the theatre. Some infrequent amusements were organized, like dancing and rhyming or cockfighting. Citizens could go out on excursions to the hamlet at Hoggen Green, where, possibly because of the presence of the nunnery and the Augustinian priory, there seems to have been a permanent holiday atmosphere. Hoggen Green had archery butts, a bowling alley and a public gallows which provided regular festive entertainment.

But there was ample time for imbibing ale, beer brewed from hops, wine and whiskey which was distilled by the Irish. In Winetavern Street a hoard of over 2,000 pewter tokens has been discovered which must have been in the possession of a tavern keeper for the use of his customers. The coinage did not provide small enough change to pay for single drinks, so that a penny or a halfpenny would be exchanged for a number of tokens, each of which would represent a measure of alcohol. The largest collection ever discovered, they were stuck together in a clump in a cesspit in the form of a dozen rouleaux similar to the rolls of coins handed out by banks today. The subjects engraved on them which vary from an ecclesiastic with a crozier, an Agnus Dei, a pilgrim drinking from a bowl to a deer wounded by an arrow, have been traced to Scotland where a mould for casting similar tokens is in the National Museum of Antiquities. A thirsty thief may have thrown them away rather than be caught red-handed. However, it seems more likely that when such tokens were superseded by the introduction of the brass farthing in 1295, this consignment became instantly obsolete and was declared illegal; for this reason all the tokens were thrown away together, before they could be put into circulation.

Women were allowed equal rights in regard to drinking. They also had a monopoly as brewers although they were forbidden to sell wine or meat. Ordinances set out rules for brewing and penalties for infringements – 'No .woman brewer shall brew with straw under penalty of twenty shillings'; 'the fine on any woman brewer for inferior ale is fifteen pence for the first offence, two and six pence for the second, and for the third suspension from her occupation for a year and a day'.

The *Calendar of Documents* gives numerous examples of local crimes through the centuries, some commonplace, some bizarre, like the murder of a friar in 1379 by eight of his fellow friars, including John Hollywood, Vicar, who concealed and later buried the body. A less serious ecclesiastical criminal occasion followed a row in 1220 between the Archbishop and the citizens, when two of the Archbishop's men violently assaulted a townsman and the wife of another in the market place. Brawls were frequent of the sort that is recorded as having taken place in 1310 when a Raymond Fraysal was charged with the death of a John Cachfrens in a tavern. A Mayor of Dublin, Geoffrey de Morgan, was accused of using the seal of the city for his own purposes. De Morgan was violating a position of trust; it is not recorded if any citizen incurred the huge penalty of forty shillings fine on his behalf 'for reviling or insulting the Mayor in any manner or place outside the Guildhall and Tholsel'. In 1311 one Phillip le Clerk was charged 'that by night he lay hid in the church of the Holy Trinity and broke a trunk therein which money arising from oblations of divers people for the aid of the Holy Land was deposited'. The *Calendar* lists innumerable burglaries; a man is charged with entering the house of Andrew Tyrel and stealing six capons and hens worth 2d.; another robber in 1308 stole two cups, 12d., the skin of a fish called 'sele' and a pair of spurs worth 8d.

The dark streets were dangerous, and the appointment in 1305 of three city watchmen could not have been very reassuring. One had charge from Gormond's Gate to the 'great Bridge', another from Newgate to St Patrick's Gate and a third from the Tholsel to the gate of St Mary del Dam. 'Each watchman shall have three others with him on every night, and for them he shall provide daily repast under penalty of 6d.'

Jail accommodation was very limited, so that a term of imprisonment was a relatively infrequent form of punishment. It was easier to whip or hang a casual criminal. Vagrants were dealt with ferociously. Some 'infirm poor' were licensed to beg in certain areas, but if found outside these boundaries they were 'stripped from the middle up' and whipped. Beggars were a general nuisance, the more so after the Black Death since plague came to be associated with 'exhalations' breathed by mendicants. In addition, homeless wanderers, who were usually Irish, might have been sent into the city as spies from the clans in the hills.

Justice was meted out equally by the King's law and canon law. There was not much distinction, since it was believed that in any case divine justice ruled the universe. The city and its outskirts were dotted with places of execution like Hoggen Green, the Viking Hang Hoeg, the gallows maintained by the Archbishop at Harold's Cross, and the new Tholsel which doubled as a prison and had a gibbet outside on which criminals like 'David O'Tothill, a stout marauder, an enemy of the king, a burner of churches and a destroyer of the people' were dispatched. Religious houses like the Abbey of St Thomas kept their own domestic gallows. In 1300 the Archbishop of Tuam, who was Justiciar, argued that he was at liberty to 'execute English robbers for a day and a night in prison, he claims also to have gallows, trebuchet, pillory and tumbril and this likewise from old'. Gibbets could be improvised; the Chain Book states that a miller convicted of stealing corn to the amount of 4d. 'shall be hanged from the beam of his own mill.'

3

Siege, Fire and Pestilence 1300–1347

Dublin had a local problem; it lived in fear of another disaster like the slaughter of Cullenswood on Black Monday, 1209. While land to the north of the Liffey was protected by the secured territories of Meath and Kildare, the forest-covered hills to the south, concealing unfriendly Wicklow septs, were only a few miles from the city walls. The Normans never made much attempt to settle in hill areas. But as they consolidated their rule in other parts of Ireland, colonial towns allied themselves for defence and other common interests. In 1252 Dublin and Drogheda made a compact, and in 1285 this was extended to include Waterford and Cork. Envoys met regularly at Kilkenny, where disputes were settled by a common council. However, towns were isolated by the difficulties of travel, and defence pacts were soon seen to be unrealistic. Ultimately each community had to be self-reliant, with defence an obligation of every citizen. In the closing years of the thirteenth century which saw not only continuing wars against the Irish, but the beginning of the Geraldine-Butler feuds and the break-up of Anglo-Norman settlements, independent strength became essential. In vain did Edward I write to the Archbishops and Bishops of Ireland imploring 'that unity and mutual love may prevail amongst barons, knights and others in Ireland'. Sir John Wogan's first parliament, held in Dublin in 1297, had been a show of unity, but by 1317 quarrels between Dublin and other settlements had reached such a pitch that Edward II had to order parliament to meet elsewhere because he feared 'that damage might be done in the majority of Ireland and their men enter the city on account of the disputes between them and the men of the city'.

At that time trouble came to Dublin not from the Irish nor from the quarrelling Anglo-Normans, but from Scotland. In 1317 the town faced one of the greatest threats in its history with the arrival of the army of Robert and Edward Bruce. Scotland's hero was descended from Strongbow and Dermot MacMurrough, and his brother Robert's wife was a descendant of Rory O'Connor. These genealogical considerations influenced the enterprise of May 1315

69

when Edward Bruce landed near Carrickfergus with 'six thousand Scots fighting men' who proceeded to fight their way southwards. Early in 1317 the army, commanded by both Bruces, reached Castleknock, and from the tower of St Audoen's the terrified citizens of Dublin saw the fires of the camp. They were totally unprepared for the emergency. The preceding years had been relatively quiet, a period when the menace of the Wicklow septs had temporarily receded. As always happened in times of peace, the wall had been allowed to fall into disrepair. Some portions had been adapted as sides of houses which were built against them illegally. Towers were in decay; one had collapsed altogether when its tenant tried to enlarge his living quarters.

Superhuman efforts had to be made. The walls along the quays were extended, fortifying the land reclaimed by the Normans, by demolishing St Saviour's Abbey and the tower of St Mary's Abbey across the river and using the stones. Gaps were filled in and St Audoen's arch and Winetavern Gate reinforced. Any houses against the walls that interfered with defence were taken down. Roger le Corviser of Bristol, a settler in the city, was ordered to remove a mill; the authorities 'deeming this mill injurious and perilous to the Castle and too close to the King's mills, caused it to be taken down'. The bridge across the Liffey was destroyed to prevent the Scots using it to approach the city from the north side. For decades the river would have to be crossed by ferry; the bridge with its row of shops and shrine dedicated to the Virgin was not restored until 1380, largely because of the efforts of the Dominicans at St Saviour's on the north side who had a school across the river at Usher's Island.

A public safety order prescribed that any woman crying out within the walls in the time of war should be fined 3s. 4d. and lose all the clothes she was wearing. Another order decreed that 'at least one man should come to muster from every house at the tolling of the public bell by day or night, while the land is troubled by the Scottish enemies'. The Mayor, Robert le Nottingham, set fire to the suburbs of the town, the most drastic measure that could be taken. The fire was much larger than had been intended, and spread so quickly that soon four-fifths of the suburbs were destroyed, in addition to part of Christ Church. However, the Scots army, lacking a proper siege train, did not take advantage of the devastation. It retired to Leixlip and Dublin was saved. But the outskirts were smouldering ruins and the economy was destroyed, although Edward II graciously pardoned the Mayor and citizens for the burning and gave them relief from taxes. The 'mean people of Dublin', blaming their betters, petitioned unsuccessfully for compensation.

The havoc wrought by the Bruce invasion initiated the decline of the colony and the authority of the Dublin-based government. Norman Ireland had reached its zenith during the reign of Edward I from 1273 to 1307. As the fourteenth century advanced the empire began to dwindle; the new Middle Nation, a blend of Anglo-Norman and 'the wild Irish, our enemies' would gain in strength while Dublin would be increasingly threatened, particularly towards the vulnerable south. There would be times when outposts like Tallaght had to be abandoned and the settlers there would come crowding in for safety behind the protection of the walls. Citizens were reduced to expedients such as paying 'blackrent' to Donall MacMurrough Kavanagh to prevent him marching on them. The Prior of Kilmainham contributed, others gave valuable horses, one man gave his bed which was worth thirty shillings.

But habitual medieval perils such as fire, famine and plague could be more devastating than any invasion. Mayor le Nottingham's uncontrolled blaze in the face of Bruce's army was an example of the constant danger of fire. In normal times Dublin burnt regularly; wicker houses easily crackled into flame, and there was a lack of water to put out conflagrations. A burnt house excavated in Fishamble Street contained a charred sack of grain and a scorched knife handle. In 1190 a part of the town was destroyed by fire; in 1282 High Street was burned. In 1304 a blaze on the north side destroyed St Mary's Abbey, together with the chancery rolls stored inside it. In 1362 a fire broke out in St Patrick's destroying the north-west corner with towers and bell. The blaze, ascribed to the carelessness of 'John the Sexton' resulted in the construction of Archbishop Minot's tower by 'sixty idle straggling fellows'.

Laws tried to lessen fire risks by prohibiting hazards of wood, straw ricks or kilns within the city walls and requiring a container of water to be placed outside the door of each house. Blame for a fire was put squarely on the householder in whose hovel it started. In 1305 an ordinance of the Common Council decreed that if a fire took place in a house, the owner was liable to a fine of twenty shillings. Anyone causing the destruction of a street was drastically punished; 'he shall be arrested, cast into the middle of the fire, or pay one hundred shillings'.

Famine was endemic, the result of war, weather and a European agricultural recession that brought declining prosperity throughout the first half of the fourteenth century. Henry la Warr, writing in his commonplace book, the *Black Book of Christ Church*, described with horror a famine in 1296 when the starving ate the bodies of men hanged on gibbets. The Scottish invasion coincided with a famine that affected many countries, a result of bad harvests and a murrain among cattle. It was followed by a number of epidemics, probably of typhus. Cattle disease persisted during the years before the Black Death. During a famine in 1331 the people of Dublin were saved from starvation by the stranding of a school of whales at the mouth of the Dodder at Ringsend. Called 'turlhydes' by medieval chroniclers, they measured thirty to forty feet, and were large enough to prevent a man standing beside a carcass from seeing another on the far side. The poor were allowed to cut them up and carry them away. (Stephen Dedalus, walking on Sandymount Strand, pictured 'a horde of jerkined dwarfs, my people, with flayers, knives, running scaling, hacking in green blubbery whalemeat.')

Only five years afterwards the economy had recovered sufficiently for customs to be charged on a wide variety of goods brought into the city, including fish, ashes, honey, tallow, figs, raisins, dates, salmon, herrings, wood, wine-skins and even coal. In 1338 the Liffey froze over so that from 2 December – 1 February the people enjoyed themselves on the ice, dancing, running, playing football and making fires on which to broil herrings. Probably many perished in the cold, but the scene makes a pleasant vignette, a respite before the deadliest peril of all – the Black Death.

Dublin was no more susceptible to disease than other medieval centres, and the records even show that in matters of general municipal care the city was rather more progressive than similarly sized English towns. There was rudimentary street lighting; an ordinance of the Common Council for 1305 stipulated that 'two warehouses whose lights are displayed are to contribute to the watch an amount equivalent to that paid by one hall'. By 1329 a number of streets had been paved, long before many English towns attempted the task; Bristol only got its first public paving in 1488.

Admittedly the work of extending Dublin pavements, carried out over the next two centuries and paid for by tolls and grants of murrage, was never very thorough and records are full of complaints about its inadequacy.

The water supply was more efficient. It had been engineered back in 1224 when citizens began to receive their water from the juncture of the Dodder and the Poddle. It came along a three-mile conduit known as 'the Tongue' to a reservoir or cistern west of St Thomas's Abbey where the overflow was stored. In 1308 another cistern of marble was built by Mayor John de Decier near the east door of St Audoen's. The water flowed down Thomas and High Streets as an open stream. An early grant allowed the Dominicans to lay a pipe across the river to receive water from this supply at their monastery at All Hallows. The pipe had to have an opening which might be stopped by the insertion of a man's little finger. The Dominicans were lucky; other grants specified pipes 'no thicker than a goose quill'. Other sources of water were wells, including two associated with St Patrick, the one with legendary origins beside the cathedral, the other in St Patrick's Well Lane – later Nassau Street – which had special properties and attracted the sick to visit it on the saint's day to obtain holy water.

But in spite of having a relatively adequate water supply, Dublin, like all medieval towns, was filthy. Cesspits were quite unable to deal with old food, let alone excrement. The smell of latrines and privies filled the narrow lanes. Properly built latrines were few and confined to some of the religious houses and the houses of the wealthy citizens. Such constructions were supposed to drain outwards so that their contents dribbled down the city walls or flowed into the Liffey. In 1341, for example, a couple called de Granalset are recorded as having been granted permission to rebuild their house with a lavatory opening into the river. There seems to have been some sort of public latrine at Isolde's Tower. Otherwise every householder was supposed to be responsible for keeping clean the portion of the street before his door. A later ordinance of 1456 gave constables the right to fine anyone a penny who failed to remove a nuisance from outside his house. Other laws tried to clean up rivers which were garbage-filled sewers. Even the watercourse running through Thomas Street could not have been very pure, since upstream it turned the wheels of Mullinahack whose Irish name, *Muileann a Chacca*, translates as Shitty Mill. A completely different place called Schytclapp Mill appears in a rent roll in St Patrick's Cathedral around 1350.

The Assembly Rolls were full of references to 'dung'. Car-men were charged 'the pain of 11d' if they unloaded dung behind the Fleshambles, and an order by the Assembly directed where it could be placed: 'That no person or persons cast dung at no site nor in any place in the city, but only without Hankmany land in the hollow pits there, or else in the hole beyond the Hogg's Butt and on the other side of Francis church on the pain of 12d.' A good deal of dung resulted from the abundance of animals. Edicts against wandering animals were extremely common, though of course a lot were confined. Horses were stabled; a horse's skull from the twelfth-century level of excavation is in the Museum of the National Stud. Dairies were kept within the city, a practice that would continue until the twentieth century. There were poultry runs, and the remains of a medieval hen showed her still sitting on an egg. Cats and dogs, whose skeletons have been found, would have kept down vermin and assisted in clearing the mountainous filth. However, most scavenging was done by pigs. In autumn they might have been driven outside the walls and fattened on acorns from the forests before being slaughtered to make salt pork for the winter. But there were always herds allowed to wander around loose rather than be confined in sties. Between 1200 and 1500 there were at least fifteen ordinances relating to the control of stray pigs which could be killed on sight. The much quoted letter of Garret More, Earl of Kildare, to the City Assembly in 1489 complained that 'dung heaps, swine, pig sties and other nuisances in the streets, lanes and suburbs of Dublin infect the air and produce mortality, fevers and pestilence throughout the city'.

Excavations have brought to light the shattered skulls of butchered oxen poleaxed in the Fleshambles. The tanners carried on their smelly work for the benefit of leather workers. A mass of scrap leather found in High Street and dated to the twelfth and thirteenth century consists of clippings and worn soles of boots and shoes. The leather came from local sources. No medieval Dublin tannery has been investigated, but a Viking tannery unearthed in York gives some indication of the nature of this occupation. Fresh skins were stripped of fat and animal fur which accumulated on the site; chicken dung was used in the curing, while maggots and blow flies fed on the decaying flesh.

The few hospitals, in the charge of religious orders, were located outside the city, out of reach of infection. The earliest, dedicated to St John and located outside Newgate, was known as Palmer's Hospital after its founders, Ailred le Palmer and his wife, Norse inhabitants of the town at the time of the Norman conquest. In 1225 Archbishop Marianus O'Brien wrote that this place 'is so charged with a multitude of sick persons that it is barely able to maintain them'. It was used not only by the sick and incurable 'bedridden in the bonds of God', but also by the destitute and orphaned. Like many buildings outside the walls, it was largely demolished during the Bruce threat, but by the time of the Black Death it was functioning again as one of the few places where people could get some sort of nursing care. The hospital of St Stephen, located within what is presumed to be the original pre-Viking settlement of Dubhlinn near the common land of St Stephen's Green, cared for lepers. That Dublin, like other medieval cities, had its wretched community of lepers is indicated by the leper window in St Audoen's outside which these outcasts could gather to hear the drone of the Mass.

The earliest epidemic in Dublin recorded in the *Annals* was in 949 when the Vikings attacked Kells and other religious centres; for once, divine punishment was forthcoming. 'God did soon revenge on them, for there broke out a great disease, leprosies and the running of blood upon the Gentiles of Dublin.' Between 1200 and 1500 there were eleven different epidemics, the earliest probably of typhus, the later ones of plague.

Remains of black rats have been identified. The black rat, *rattus rattus*, the specific agent for spreading plague, had spread to Europe from the Middle East, brought by ships bringing returning crusaders. It thrived in the medieval clay and wattle houses which Philip Ziegler, who has written the most lucid history of the Black Death, considers 'might have been built to specifications approved by a rodent council as eminently suitable for a rat's enjoyment of a healthy and carefree life'.

The fleas of the black rat, carrying the deadly plague bacilli, hopped onto humans whom they bit and infected. Bubonic plague was the form of the disease that invited the epithet 'black' because its most prominent symptom was the black buboes that developed under the arms and on the thighs of the victim. In seventy per cent of cases death followed in two to seven days – usually in three or four. There were other forms of the disease that were even more lethal. The highly infectious pneumonic plague, which could be caught from nose droplets, was said to occur in late winter. 'Men suffer in their lungs and breathing and whoever have been corrupted or even slightly attacked cannot by any means escape nor live beyond two days.' Recovery from pneumonic plague was virtually unknown. A rarer, even more devastating, form was septicaemic plague, in which the bloodstream became infected with plague bacilli within an hour or two, killing the victim long before buboes had time to form. A man might go to bed in good health and never wake in the morning. Bed is perhaps an ideal term. Among the poor beds were rare enough and often shared by whole families. Overcrowding was a feature of medieval life. Within the wicker interior of houses, rustling with rats, up to a dozen people might have to find accommodation. Through the night a flea could jump from limb to limb, spreading devastation with its bite; a sneeze from grandfather lying near the fire could infect most members of a family, exhausted by the rigours of winter.

The Black Death first appeared in Europe in 1347. How it came to Ireland can only be guessed. Probably it arrived from Bristol, reaching Howth and Drogheda almost simultaneously, and spreading from these towns to the interior of the country. It could equally well have come from some French port in Gascony or Brittany. The exact date when it reached Ireland is also obscure. John Clyn, a Franciscan friar from Kilkenny, who left a moving and graphic account of the devastation caused by the disease, wrote that it arrived in August 1348. He wrote that both Dublin and Drogheda were almost destroyed within a few weeks, and stated that in Dublin more than 14,000 people died between August and Christmas. This number was undoubtedly wrong, but most chroniclers of the Black Death wildly exaggerated the mortality figures –. they simply did not have any idea. A more serious discrepancy in Clyn's account is his dates. In August 1349 Richard Fitzralph, Archbishop of Armagh, told the Pope during his visit to Avignon that the plague had not yet done any conspicuous harm to the Irish and the Scots. He had travelled out to the south of France from Ireland, and it seems incredible that he and Clyn had been living in the same country. There are other facts which cast doubt on the Franciscan. The Archbishop of Dublin did not die of the plague until 14 July 1349, and the Bishop of Meath in the same month.

The *Annals of Connacht* record 'a great plague in Moylurg' for 1349. Philip Ziegler comes to the unsatisfactory conclusion that John Clyn must have got his dates wrong. Certainly he was under heavy strain. Of his order of Friars Minor twenty-five died in their house at Drogheda and twenty-three in Dublin. Monastic communities were particularly susceptible to infection; the Church was so reduced in ranks that after 1348 not a single new monastery was founded in Dublin.

'This pestilence was so contagious' wrote Clyn, 'that those who touched the dead person or persons sick of the plague were straightway infected themselves and died, so that the confessor and the penitent were carried to the same grave. And from fear and horror men were seldom brave enough to perform the works of piety and mercy, such as visiting the sick and burying the dead. For many died from boils and abscesses and pustules on their shins or under their armpits; others died frantic with the pain in the head and others spitting blood.' Some people thought it was the end of the world. Clyn's last footnote reads: 'I leave parchment for continuing this work if happily any man survive and any of the race of Adam escape the pestilence and carry on the work which I have begun.' He added '*magna Karistia*' which means 'great dearth'. Someone with different handwriting put a postscript: 'Here it seems that the author died.'

Bubonic plague had arrived from some unknown source of infection in the eastern hemisphere. Now it became a part of life; pockets of infection smouldered in nearly every town of size. The last serious outbreak in Ireland of this particular pandemic took place after the Great Rebellion in 1649; the last in Europe was the 'great visitation' which afflicted London in 1665. After that cities largely ceased to confine themselves within walls and sanitation improved. The brown Norwegian rat ousted the black rat as civilization's chief nuisance, mainly because clay, straw and wood became obsolete as building materials when living standards rose. But before then plague had been liable to flare up and kill at regular intervals. In Dublin the first terrible outbreak was followed by two more in 1362 and 1370 'in which many nobles, citizens and innumerable children died'. Outside the city there may have been other visitations or the disease may have merely travelled slowly. An English chronicler known as Geoffrey the Baker stated that the Anglo-Normans were almost wiped out, but the Irish themselves were unaffected until 1357. It seems probable that the Irish in their scattered rural communities were much less susceptible to infection, and it is even possible that the 1357 outbreak mentioned by Geoffrey the Baker was not the plague at all.

After the first major outbreak Dublin, like other Anglo-Norman towns, petitioned for relief of taxes. The citizens requested a special allowance of a thousand quarters of corn. Hardship caused by the Black Death continued; in 1354 the tenants of royal farms near the capital were complaining of the 'plague lately existing in the said country' and 'the excessive price of provisions' exacted by certain crown officials. Such farms, like others all over Europe, had labour problems as a result of the great mortality, but in addition they were threatened by 'the destruction and wasting of lands, houses and possessions by our Irish enemies'. The 'other many misfortunes' mentioned in the petition had been precipitated by increasing internal differences aggravated by the relentless warfare with the Irish foe. The power of the Dublin-based government, already eroded by internecine quarrels, was further weakened by mortality among civil servants and administrators attached to the Castle. In fact the Black Death had a particularly destructive effect on the small Anglo-Norman empire where numbers had always been of prime importance in the matter of survival.

4

The Late Middle Ages 1361–1536

In spite of frequent demonstrations of loyalty, early medieval English rulers were indifferent to the troubles of their Irish colonies and tended to stay at home. Occasionally a person of rank would journey across the water on behalf of the king. In 1308 Piers Gaveston, Edward II's favourite, appointed King's Representative, sailed over to Dublin from Bristol for a short stay, during which he entertained lavishly and kept up a splendid court in the Castle. A more significant visit was that of Lionel of Clarence, second son of Edward III, who landed in Dublin to take up the position of Justiciar in July 1361. He had ordered the Castle to be renovated for his arrival, the gardens laid out with arbours and space left for a jousting ground with a wooden tower. But the important features of the Castle remained defensive. Its massive bulk formed the cornerstone of the city walls which were pierced with gates and towers. Defence was stressed all round the landward side of the city by the ditch outside the walls, nineteen feet deep and forty feet wide. In an emergency it could be flooded, but usually it was kept as a dry moat which tended to get clogged with garbage and entrails of cattle. Oxmantown across the river was also walled. There was still no bridge linking the two, since the old bridge destroyed during the Bruce invasion had not been rebuilt. Ferries served instead, or fords, since the Liffey was still relatively shallow. Two fords are mentioned in later fifteenth-century documents. One was associated with the Augustinians at St Saviour's; in the 1450s they were forbidden to use it since it had become too dangerous. Another was blocked off to prevent 'Irish enemies' from infiltrating the city.

Citizens had little temptation to go far beyond their defended homes. Even round the arc of Dublin Bay, fringed with mills, orchards and market gardens, travel was not safe. A fifteenth-century chancery roll referring to the 'Bothyr de Bree' or the Bray road to the south, states that this was the route the O'Byrnes and the O'Tooles usually took on their raids to the city. The only safe direction in which to travel was north for a little way towards

Meath and the lands which supplied Dublin with most of its grain and cattle.

Outside the walled section of the city with its elaborate system of defences there was a considerable amount of suburban development, including the numerous monasteries and their spreading possessions. Although they covered far too wide an area to be defended in the same way as the walled city, the main approach roads beyond them had guarded gateways which were some gesture towards defence. St Kevin's Gate, New Street Gate, St Francis' Gate, the Coombe Gate and Crockers' Bar to the south and west and Whitefriars Gate and the Blind Gate at Hoggen Green to the east indicate how much of Dublin was outside the walls.

Inside, the city's main street was the thoroughfare which, running from east to west along the ridge that formed Dublin's backbone, was made up of Castle Street, Skinners' Row and High Street. At its east end was the Castle. To the west at the junction of Skinners' Row and Castle Street with Fishamble Street stood the pillory in a little building with curved eaves, which, according to an old drawing, was almost oriental in style. The next intersection was where High Street met Skinners' Row outside Christ Church with St Nicholas Street and Christ Church Lane running from south to north down to the river. In the middle of this cross roads stood the High Cross before which public proclamations, papal bulls and sentences of excommunication were read; penitents stood there shivering in their white garments. Wills were proved by being read three times at the Cross within a year and a day of the testator's death. Shops seem to have been concentrated in this area; seven are mentioned in an edict of 1326 as being located opposite Holy Trinity Church. At the corner of Skinners' Row and Nicholas Street was the Tholsel, the small medieval town hall in which were located the mayor's offices, a lockup and a speedy sort of gallows. It was fairly new; in 1336 a grant was made to the Mayor, Bailiffs and Commonalty to levy customs on goods imported into the town to pay for the Tholsel and paving the streets. They included local produce from the countryside such as corn, honey, onions, cheese and butter, imported items like figs and raisins, animal skins, important for clothes, including sheep, lamb, goat, kid, rabbit, hare, wolf, cat and deer, wood, tiles and lead for building, and spade irons and ploughshares.

Winetavern Street, running steeply down to the river, was

convenient to Merchants' Quay, and at their junction was located the city crane where cargoes from foreign ships were discharged. Wood Quay, one of the earliest quays in Dublin, was probably named after the timber-retaining wall constructed in the twelfth century. A line of twelfth-century warehouses has been excavated at Wood Quay, along a cobbled street-way right down on the water's edge. Neighbouring streets had markets. Corn was sold in the Cornmarket, meat at the Fleshambles in High Street and fish in narrow Fishamble Street which was so steep that it had to have an artificial bend to get up the hill. After the Black Death regulations for slaughtering animals and disposing of fish became more stringent as filth and decaying animals' flesh was associated with plague. Slaughtering now took place outside the walls. At the lower end of Fishamble Street was a boat slip where local boats unloaded their fish. In 1459 an ordinance decreed that 'every fisher that hath a board in the Fishambles and casteth guts under their boards and wash not their boards after they hath done their market shall pay a groat...'

There was only one common schoolhouse in the city; Thomas Brasyll is mentioned in the Franchise Rolls as Master of Grammar in 1477. However, religious foundations and chantry chapels provided some education. An unsuccessful attempt was made in 1321 to found the University of St Patrick with two faculties, theology and law. Friar John Clyn considered the place 'a university as far as its name meant, would that it were in fact!' This failure, along with others, to create a higher place of learning has been cited as an indication of the poverty and isolation of Ireland. Elsewhere in the country Bardic schools might survive, but they remained totally outside the mainstream of European thought.

A network of narrow lanes no more than eight to ten feet wide ran between clusters of houses and along the walls which formed boundaries of a surprising number of orchards and gardens. There were, of course, no street numbers. Stone residences were still a rarity, and so were chimneys, which were regarded by some hardened householders as degenerate affectations. Windows were either unglazed or filled with thin plates of horn, mica, bladder or oiled canvas. The odd pane of expensive glass, small, green and stamped with a bottle end, might be found in a rich man's home.

Limited interior light came from rush candles or tallow dips. Tallow, derived from mutton fat, was relatively expensive, but wax was only for the wealthy, although wax candles were much in demand for lighting churches. The rush and tallow lights were made at home. Wax candles must have been made by candlemakers, although there is no mention of them until 1558, by which time they were also using tallow. An ordinance forbade butchers to sell tallow to anyone except private citizens; only when they had been supplied could the surplus be sold to the candlemakers of the city.

Flint and steel lit the hearth. Fuel was not so much for heating, although it fulfilled that function, but for cooking. Most of it was still wood supplied from the forests, but turf was also burned; in the Holy Trinity Accounts for 1334 the Steward of Clonken recorded the sum of 3s. 1d. as having been received for turf sold that year. Coal came to Ireland probably early in the fourteenth century and is occasionally mentioned as an article of trade or part of a cargo. The Assembly Rolls for 1454 contain an ordinance that salt, iron, pitch, resin and coals coming with the franchises in ships should be purchasable only by buyers for the city. This reference could be to charcoal, although the word used in the plural usually referred to coal as we know it. Its early use was a luxury. The first proper recorded shipment of coal to Dublin was from Bristol in 1504.

Rather than sit by the smoking hearth in the smelly half-light of a tallow dip, people went to bed early. They wore no nightgowns until the sixteenth century when women first put on 'night rails', although men continued to sleep naked except for nightcaps of wool or velvet. Beds had no bedsteads; mattresses, mainly of flock, or feathers for the wealthy, were covered with a limited amount of bed linen, seldom enough, and usually shared with one or two other people. It was seldom washed in the homemade soap of lye and ashes which was all the household had available. Soap was not a commercial commodity until the sixteenth century, when the Customs Accounts for Bridgwater in Somerset mention the export of soap to Ireland. This would have been for washing clothes. There were some laundresses in Dublin since the Holy Trinity Accounts have a reference to one. They may have washed by the side of the city watercourse in Thomas Street – no other suitable water supply has been suggested. When in 1458 the Hospital of St John obtained a grant for some of the water flowing through Thomas Street, the Mayor and Commonalty reserved the easements as to washing and wringing.

Furniture consisted of items such as wooden coffer chests, backless benches and the occasional settee. Tableware was of tin or expensive pewter; in the Franchise Rolls of 1468 to 1485 containing the names of 660 freemen, only two pewterers appear. Pewter ware was confined to knives, usually the property of the diner, and spoons. Forks, an Italian innovation, did not make their appearance until the sixteenth century. The rich had sophisticated effects. A John Kyng and his wife, who lived in the parish of St Nicholas Without the Walls in 1475, possessed according to a will, ten round basins, two round bowls, brass pots and a pitcher, a frying pan, a chafing dish with a brass pestle and mortar, six candlesticks of latten (pinchbeck), sheets, napkins, towels, blankets, three leather bottles, a girdle ornamented with silver and some elaborate jewellery. Among the goods left by Dame Margaret Nugent in 1474 was a silver cup called a nut – probably a wooden bowl decorated with bands of silver, silver spoons, coral beads and that prized medieval ornament, a coconut mounted on a stand.

Through the streets men and women paraded in their parrot-coloured clothes, strictly Anglo-Saxon in style. However, the Irish mantle, which Edmund Spenser was to describe as 'a fit home for an outlaw, a meet bed for a rebel and an apt cloak for a thief' was such a useful garment that colonists in Ireland wore it illegally, prized it highly and often sent one as a present to English friends. (The Vikings, apart from eccentrics like Magnus Barefoot, had never taken to the mantle.) Men were either bearded or more or less clean-shaven, since those who chose to dispense with beards were required by law to shave at least once a fortnight, rather than let a barbarous moustache grow on the upper lip in the Irish manner. They wore tight doublets with waistcoats known as colehardies, which were later replaced by jackets or jerkins; or they favoured the 'houpeland', a gown belted at the waist. They assumed extravagances like the long pointed shoes known as crackowes or poulaires from their place of origin in Poland. A picture dated around 1384 depicting medieval occupations and displaying a fine assortment of clothes includes a supposed Mayor of Dublin who wears a long red robe and a blue pleated cape with two large buttons on the right shoulder; his shoes are long and pointed and his large brimmed hat is either conical or shaped like a lemon squeezer. Women's clothes were equally flamboyant. The effigy of Margaret Jenico in St Audoen's, dated 1482 illustrates the dress of a high born lady. Her long gown is pulled up, revealing the rim of her petticoat; she has a horned-head-dress and a girdle with a pendant cross.

The rich included merchants belonging to the guilds, clerics like the Prior of Holy Trinity, whose robes, according to the accounts, were trimmed with fur – 'skin with fur for Prior's mantle: 3s.'; 'one skin for the Prior's hood: 2d.' – and officials like water-bailiffs, mace bearers, the Stable Court Sword Bearer, Master of the Works or Keeper of the Keys of the Treasurer. Friars wearing the uniform of their particular order were an essential part of the scene; in a threatened city so were knights and men of arms. Among lesser citizens the most numerous were minor guild members, apprentices and journeymen whose duties included measuring and weighing commodities as well as transporting them. Porters staggered up and down the steep lanes under their heavy loads – one lane, Keysers, was known as Kisse Arse from the number of people who slipped in it. The cries of sellers in the markets mingled with the ringing of church bells, the jingling of harness and creaking of carts bringing in produce from outside. Down on the river fishermen landed their catch. Everywhere there were furtive beggars with their rags and dangerous breath.

Such was the summer scene that greeted Clarence as he arrived with the task of restoring order to the progressively weakening area of Leinster and the outlying stretches of territory which were under the control of the March lords and the 'degenerate English'. His best known achievement was shepherding the Statutes of Kilkenny through the Parliament of Kilkenny in February 1366. The thirty-five enactments sought to preserve English influence in Ireland by a series of anti-Irish measures, some direct attempts at apartheid like the forbidding of marriages between colonists and Irish, others ostensibly eccentric, like the prohibition of riding in the Irish fashion without stirrups. The Statutes were less a great divide in history than an affirmation of previous attitudes conveyed typically in an earlier Dublin statute of 1297 which had instructed that Englishmen 'should relinquish the Irish dress at least in the head or hair'. Dublin had long played host to a national parliament composed of a single body with no Irish representative. But although the Irish, unless specifically Anglicized, had no role to play in civic affairs, there was continual intercourse between the communities in matters involving mutual benefit. Trade and commerce were largely unrestricted and whenever the Statutes were impractical they were ignored. One of their least successful passages forbade merchants to visit fairs or to supply Irish enemies with victuals.

By now most of the Normans who had settled elsewhere in Ireland had abandoned Norman French for Gaelic. But in Dublin the survival of the local version of English demonstrated the city's isolation which partly arose because it was the centre of administration. Irish chieftains who had contact with the central government persisted in claiming that they could not understand English, so that in 1465 a special clerk had to be appointed to write letters in Latin to the Gaelic lords. The language of law and of the statute books continued to be Latin or French until 1495 when at last officialdom considered that laws and charters were becoming too difficult to read and adopted English instead. Meanwhile Gaelic seeped into the Pale in spite of efforts to keep it out. Innkeepers were forbidden 'to seyll their ale to them but such as beeth of gode conversacioun and English borne'. In vain; by the sixteenth century children of English descent were being coerced to learn their own language at their parent's expense. In 1600 Fynes Moryson could still report that 'the very citizens (except those of Dublin where the Lord Deputy resides) though they could speak. English as well as we, yet commonly speak Irish among themselves'.

Clarence transferred the Exchequer to Carlow, a shift towards a more strategic centre for the area under English control. But for all other purposes Dublin remained the capital city where the Justiciar, the Archbishop and most government officials had their headquarters. His six year term of office heralded a period during which Dublin became closely associated with the fortunes of English royalty. The next royal personage to visit Dublin was Richard II, who in 1394 was the first English king to land in Ireland since John a century and a half before. Richard brought over a large army to expel Art MacMurrough Kavanagh and other chieftains from the English-held territory in Leinster. His military aims achieved, he moved up to Dublin, where flying the flag of Edward the Confessor, he received the submission of four Irish kings – O'Connor of Connacht, O'Brien of Thomond, O'Neill of Ulster and MacMurrough himself. His intention was to obtain their oaths of fealty and then give them legal status under the English crown.

Henry Castide, an English squire who could speak Irish, was given the task of instructing the kings on social niceties. 'I must say' he remarked in tones of later Empire builders dealing with Rajahs, 'these kings...were of coarse manners and understanding'. He tried to make them wear English clothes 'As they sat at table they made grimaces, and I resolved...to make them drop that custom...they would also make their minstrels and principal servants sit beside them, eat from their plates and drink from their cups.' The kings were discreet when asked about Castide's humiliating attentions. 'He has prudently and wisely taught us the manners and usages of his country...' Castide noted that 'they were much stared at by the Lords and those present...for they were strange figures and differently countenanced to the English and other nations.' Citizens must have been equally unaccustomed to 'the novelty to see four Irish kings' and stared just as much as they watched them riding from the Castle through the crowded streets to Christ Church to receive their English knighthoods.

Richard's aims of uniting Ireland under the English crown were thwarted, and the Irish chiefs were to remain outside English law until the Tudors revived his policy with the scheme of surrender and regrant. In 1413 Richard's usurper, Henry IV, sent over his second son, Thomas of Lancaster, a boy of fourteen, as King's Lieutenant in Ireland. The city, by now accustomed to royal visits, worked out a traditional welcome for him; he was met at some distance from the walls by sheriffs and escorted by a troop of horse and trumpeters to Hoggen Green where the Mayor waited to receive him. He remained in Ireland for twelve years, a period when Dublin became increasingly vulnerable to the effects of the Gaelic resurgence. In 1402 Mayor Drake and his men killed 500 O'Byrnes at Bray, an exploit which earned the Mayor and his successors the privilege of having a gilt sword carried before them. But the territory surrounding Dublin shrank dramatically as the Pale came into being and then shrank again. At one point loyalist possessions south of the city only reached as far as Dalkey. But while it wrestled with local troubles that threatened its very existence, Dublin was distracted by the rivalries of English monarchs. The arrival in Howth in 1449 of Richard Duke of York concentrated its political allegiance during the Wars of the Roses. The city became fiercely Yorkist and remained so for forty years.

In 1463 the Yorkist king, Edward IV, began a policy of allowing Irishmen to rule from the Castle. He appointed as King's Representative in Ireland Thomas, Earl of Desmond, head of a Hibernicized Norman family whose Gaelic connections gave promise of confident government. He did indeed prove a strong and competent ruler in the English interest; while he relaxed the Statutes of Kilkenny, he ordered the Irish living in Dublin colony to take English surnames, to 'go as English' and to be sworn lieges within a year. But he had only been Lord Deputy – his title, since the Duke of Clarence over in England was nominally Lord of Ireland – for five years when he was arrested in Drogheda in 1468 and beheaded for treason, an execution widely regarded as judicial murder. He was succeeded by Thomas Fitzgerald, Earl of Kildare, a member of a powerful house which was virtually to rule Ireland for over half a century.

Thomas's son, Garret More, the Great Earl, succeeded his father as Deputy in 1478 to become the most powerful of all governors of Ireland during the Middle Ages. He ruled in Dublin under three English kings. As a fervent Yorkist he encouraged the citizens to stage an episode, which although it contained elements of farce, provided one of the most magnificent set pieces in the city's history – the reception of Lambert Simnel, the last dubious hope of the Yorkist cause. Garret More accepted the fair-haired ten-year-old boy as Edward, Earl of Warwick, rightful heir to the throne of England, and the citizens rapturously reinforced the idea. On Whit Sunday 1487, Lambert Simnel was crowned as Edward VI in Christ Church with a gold circlet taken from the statue of the Virgin Mary in the church of St Mary del Dam. After the crown was placed on the child's head by the Archbishop of Dublin, Walter Fizsimons, he was lifted on to the shoulders of Great D'Arcy of Platten, the tallest man in Ireland, and preceded by clergy and mayor, was brought into the Castle. The triumph was brief. A month after his coronation he went to England where he was taken prisoner and set to turn the spits in King Henry VII's kitchen. Sir Richard Edgecombe was dispatched to Dublin to receive the sheepish allegiance of the Great Earl and other nobles in King John's room at Thomas Court where the Earl was residing. The Mayor, Jenico Marks, apologized on behalf of the citizens. 'We were daunted to see not only your chief governor whom your Highness made ruler over us, to bend or bow to that idol whom they made us obey; but also our father of Dublin and most of the clergy.'

While Dublin was the stage for Yorkist intrigues and for Ormonde-Geraldine feuds, the citizens demonstrated their loyalties passionately. As the fortunes of the Ormondes and the Geraldines wavered, their divided support for the two great families resulted in periodic violence. A later English official wrote to Thomas Cromwell that the Irish of the Pale 'count more to see a Geraldine reign in triumph than to see God come among them'. In 1434 the Mayor and citizens were forced to make public penance and walk barefoot through the streets for sacrilegiously breaking open the doors of St Mary's Abbey and taking the Earl of Ormonde prisoner. In 1493 there was a bad riot on Oxmantown Green; the fighting spread across the river as mobs of Geraldine and Butler supporters roamed about burning each other's property. The worst riot of all was in 1512 when a row broke out in the churchyard of St Patrick's and some Butlers were chased inside, pursued by a group of archers. When a shower of arrows damaged statues and the rood loft, the Earl of Ormonde was forced to take refuge in the chapter house, where he barricaded himself behind a door in which can still be seen the hole that was chopped through which the rival leaders eventually shook hands. This episode was also considered sacrilege, and once again the Mayor and Corporation, who had Geraldine leanings, were considered responsible. They were ordered to walk round the city in subsequent Corpus Christi processions, naked, except for their shirts, carrying lighted candles.

Along with this intense political activity went the events which medieval chroniclers loved to list, storms, plagues and fires. An Archbishop of Dublin, carried off by pirates, was rescued by his faithful parishioners who chased the ship up the coast to Ardglass, County Down. Mayor Jenico Marks was murdered. The Liffey dried up for the space of two minutes. A storm swept over the city destroying the east window of Christ Church together with many holy relics, although the *Bachall Iosa*, St Patrick's crozier, was miraculously saved.

Holy days and other holidays divided up the year. Musters, where the citizens paraded in front of the Mayor took place four times a year. There was the ceremony attending the official known as the Mayor of the Bullring who was annually elected to be captain of all bachelors in the city. They paraded before him on May Day on Oxmantown Green; at other times he had the privilege of attending the wedding of any bachelor, who in his turn was obliged to kiss the iron ring in the Bull Market where the bulls used in baiting were tied. Every St John's Eve the Mayor and Commons visited Palmers, the Hospital of St John's where a bonfire was lit. A more important annual ceremony involved the Mayor leading a procession round the franchises or fringes of the city. A description of Riding the Fringes in 1488 tells how the Mayor and his companions 'proceeded well horsed, armed and in good array, taking their way out of Dame's Gate, turning on the left hand of the strand and from thence straight forward to the longstone of the Steyne...' Their long ride brought them to St Mary's Abbey, where the Abbot, worrying over the extent of its boundaries, informed them that they had taken the wrong route. 'But the Mayor and his brethren said "Nay! for by our book we did return back from the Tilkan, we should have ridden by our Lady Church of Osmany..." ' and so they departed, every man repairing to his own lodging.' The ride, whose purpose was to mark out the city limits, included a pause when a spear was cast ceremoniously into the sea.

Riding the fringes came to involve the guilds; in due course twenty-nine of them were represented, each preceded by a large platform with a tableau showing its craft. The function of the guilds, members of which were obliged to be 'of English name and blood, of honest conversation and also free citizens', was social, economic and religious. A guild was made up of a Master, two wardens, an annually elected council and members, who ranged from master journeymen to apprentices. Unlike Gaels, women could join. An apprentice spent seven years training at his craft, after which he had to undergo a test, executing his 'masterpiece' to show that he had not been wasting his time. All members were expected to defend the city, providing themselves with their own weapons. An enactment of 1454 stated that 'no prentice of merchande shude be admitted into the fraunches of the saide cittie till he have a jake-bow, shefe, sallet [helmet] and swerde of his owne, and all prentices of other craftes to have a boew, arrouys, and a swerde'. The military Guild of St George went further. Created in 1447, commanded by the King's Representative and the most important military personages in the four shires, it was virtually a private army, maintaining 120 mounted archers, 40 horses, 40 pages and 500 crack troops.

By the end of the fifteenth century the original Merchants' Guild had branched out into numerous craft guilds, each of which was under the patronage of the Virgin or a saint and had its special church, chantry and hall. The feast day of its patron was celebrated with ceremonies which all members had to attend and culminated with a banquet. The tailors, for instance, who were under the patronage of St John, had their banquet on St John's Day at midsummer. In addition, all guilds celebrated religious holidays like Lammas Day, Holy Rood Day and Shrove Tuesday, while the most important Christian festivals honoured in the city, Christmas, Corpus Christi and St George's Day, were marked with pageants, *tableaux vivants* and morality plays.

The church's initial tolerance for actors may be indicated by the carving on one of the capitals in Christ Church which shows a trio of strolling players, one with a violin, another with cymbals, the third protruding his leg through a split gown in what appears to be a dance step. As elsewhere, drama began in the church, when the clergy staged simple representations of the biblical story at appropriate points during the Mass. Dumb shows were later followed by dramatizations where the dialogue was sung in Latin. Two specimens of liturgical plays performed in Dublin have been preserved, *Abraham's Sacrifice* and *The Lay of the Sacrament* which are copies of English manuscripts. There are a few records of church dramatics. A liturgical play of the fourteenth century which was given at Easter in the church of St John the Evangelist, consisted of six characters, three of whom were Marys with veils, surplices, silk copes and boxes of ointment. During the early sixteenth century, St Patrick's gave miracle plays at Whitsuntide. An entry in the cathedral accounts of 1509 lists a payment of 4s. 7d. to players who included the Great and Small Angel and the Dragon.

Dublin had no cycle of plays like Coventry or York. Only one morality play has survived, dated to the early fourteenth century, written in a form of Middle English and most probably composed in England, which has been given the name *The Pride of Life*. It was found on the back of an Account Roll of the Priory of Holy Trinity where it was probably scribbled down by a scribe who approved of its theme involving the salvation of the soul, which is rescued by the intervention of the Virgin.

Wat schold i do at churg wat
shir bishop wostoner
nay churc his no wyl cot
hit wol abid yer.

Such church plays and the approval of the clergy encouraged citizens to stage secular productions, always with a religious theme. There had been a theatrical tradition involving the guilds before the decree of 1498 by the Mayor and Commons of Dublin who declared that guilds were to perform on the feasts of Corpus Christi and St George. Crafts which failed to put up a production would be fined, but this proviso was unnecessary, since the stage-struck apprentices and journeymen willingly undertook expenses. The plays, probably in dumb show, were staged on platforms which were wheeled from one public place to another, so that citizens could witness all of them in rotation. On Corpus Christi day, 1498, twenty-eight different occupations presented stories from the Old and New Testaments, playing incidents vaguely relevant to their own crafts. The goldsmiths presented the Three Kings, fishermen played the Apostles, and others associated with the sea 'maryners, vyntners and saumon takers' gave Noah and the Ark. Presumably the 'vyntners' had something to do with Noah's drunkenness. In other plays butchers took the parts of executioners and tormentors. Performances included the Sacrifice of Isaac by the weavers and a presentation of the Flight into Egypt by the skinners, house carpenters, tanners and embroiderers who had to provide 'the body of the camell and Oure Lady and Hir Childe well aperelid with Joseph to lede the camell and...the portors to berr the camell' – just as two people make up a pantomime horse today. 'Steynors and peyntors' had to 'peynte the hede of the camell'.

Records of other theatrical presentations in Dublin include an indoor pageant presented by the Guild of St George on St George's Day when St George's Chapel in Christ Church was 'well hanged and apparelled to every purpose with cushions, rushes and other necessaries'. The theme offered no surprises. St George appeared on horseback, while the Dragon was led by 'a maid well apparelled with trumpeters and a large retinue'. Outdoor plays were sometimes performed on crude stages, like those on Hoggen Green on Christmas Day 1528 which were witnessed by the Mayor, Arland Ussher, and Francis Herbert and John Squire who were city

bailiffs. Before these chilled dignitaries the Guild of Tailors acted
Adam and Eve while the Priors of St John of Jerusalem and All
Hallows presented two plays about the Passion and the martyrdom
of the Apostles.

Meanwhile during the years preceding Silken Thomas's rebellion
Dublin had been reduced to an uneasy political state. In 1492
Garret More's support for another claimant to the English throne,
Perkin Warbeck, earned him a spell in the Tower of London. The
notorious Sir Edward Poynings was sent to reduce the Lordship of
Ireland to 'whole and perfect submission'. Part of Poynings'
energies were directed towards a pressing need; he authorized the
defence of the Pale by ordering its boundaries to be dug by local
inhabitants with 'a double ditch of six feet high above the ground
on the part with nereth into Irishmen'. Of course fortifications of
Pale territory had existed long before Poynings arrived. The Pale
had come into existence as four obedient shires of Meath, Dublin,
Kildare and Louth small and ultimately defendable piece of land.
The first mention of the word was in 1446, when the idea of
enclosing such an area was adapted from the Pale of Calais. Before
then the only defences on the outlying borders of the shrunken
shires had been castles built by individuals assisted by grants of
£10. Guarding the Pale was never a properly organized
programme, and there were times when it hardly seemed to exist. A
letter sent to Henry VI in 1453 from the Parliament in Dublin
complained how 'in the nether parts of Meath, Dublin, Kildare and
Louth there is scarcely left out of subjection of enemies and rebels
thirty miles in length and twenty in breadth as a man may safely
ride or go to answer the king's writ'. Dublin's vulnerability
continually oppressed the citizens, who complained in 1464 how
'the walls are decayed and weak, the liege subjects and inhabitants
are unable to sustain the cost of repair in consequence of the
continuous burden on them in daily defending the lands and the
people'.

The threat from the hills continued throughout the last part of
the fifteenth century and the early years of the sixteenth. Garret
More died in 1513 to be succeeded by Garret Oge, who lacked his
father's massive authority. The powers of the King's Deputy had
been greatly reduced since Poynings had curbed the importance of
Dublin as the capital of the Anglo-Irish estate. The Parliament,
which had been virtually independent, was now forbidden to meet

in the city except with the direct royal approval. Most of the responsibility for civic and military administration was transferred to the direct control of the crown. This decline in authority, combined with prolonged civic weakness, increased the deficiencies in the city's defences. Dublin had always relied on peaceful conditions in the Pale and elsewhere for its food supply. But the Wicklow clans had become bolder, raiding the city and its environs on a regular basis and carrying off prisoners, and what was almost worse, cattle. Sometimes the depredations of the enemy actually resulted in famine, while generally a shortage of beef became commonplace. A year before Silken Thomas's rebellion John Derrick, a prebendary of St Patrick's, wrote to Thomas Cromwell: 'all the butchers in Dublin hath no such beef to sell as would make one mess of browes; so as they use white meat' – food made from milk 'except it be in my Lord of Dublin's house or such as have of their own provision'.

There was general civic discontent which culminated in Garret Oge's summons to London to answer various charges of maladministration. Before leaving Dublin he entrusted his position to his eldest son, Lord Thomas Fitzgerald, a young man of twenty known as Silken Thomas because he and his followers wore silken fringes on their helmets. A rumour that his father, whom he knew to be imprisoned in the Tower of London, had been executed, drove him into immediate open revolt. On St Barnabas Day, 11 June 1534, he rode into Dublin with seven companions, crossed the river to St Mary's Abbey and burst in on the Council which was awaiting his arrival. In the chapter house, which today is all that survives of the Abbey, he renounced his allegiance to the English crown. It seems surprising that this famous scene should take place in a religious establishment, but Dublin as yet had no adequate public buildings, which could accommodate a large assembly of people. The Castle was for national administration and sometimes even Parliament was obliged to meet outside it. In 1422, for example, it had assembled in the Carmelite monastery. The law courts usually had their sessions in the Dominican Priory, while other bodies found accommodation in other substantially built religious houses. A few years later, during the turmoil of the Reformation, when the parish of St Olaf was united with that of St John in 1538, St Olaf's church, together with its priest's chamber, were let out for secular use.

The course of the rebellion was confused by factors such as plague within the city and the O'Tooles outside, who controlled much of the territory to the south. The Geraldine faction in the city took to rebellion easily enough. But there were also loyalists, many of them officials and civil servants, who proceeded to make arrangements with Silken Thomas about a siege. His own forces were allowed within the city walls on the understanding that they would not injure any of the townspeople, while the supporters of the crown, who included the Constable of the Castle and Archbishop Alen, were permitted to withdraw into the Castle loaded with provisions and gunpowder. This was a fatal move on the part of the rebels, because their lack of gunpowder would bring about their downfall. The Archbishop, who detested the Fitzgeralds, became an early casualty of the siege when he attempted to escape to England in a ship which foundered on a sand spit near Clontarf. He was taken prisoner, and Silken Thomas handed him over to his followers who 'brained and hacked him in gobbets', an impious act which earned them all excommunication.

Silken Thomas drifted down to Kilkenny to engage some Butlers, while five of his captains and 100 men planted small guns called falcons at the Castle gates. The Constable, John White, had received what were called King's Letters promising support from outside, and he used these to persuade the wavering citizens to join him. The city gates were closed and the rebel forces beaten off. When Thomas returned in September he ordered the city water pipes to be cut while his forces at Thomas Street prepared to assault the Newgate as a preliminary to storming the Castle from Ship Street. Since about 1485 this massive two-towered gateway on the western section of the city wall had acted as the city prison. The Chain Book gives an inventory of its grisly contents. There were gyves, small bolts for the dungeons, legbolts with shackles, bolts with collars for men's necks, a pair of manacles weighing one stone and two bolts with small-sized shackles for children. The city jailor was Richard Stanton, a renowned shot, who aimed at the rebels 'as they would skip from house to house', wrote Richard Stanyhurst, 'causing some of them with his peece to carry their errands in their buttocks. One rebel who was about to fire at him...took him so trulie for his marke, as to strike him with his bullet in the forehead, and withall turned up his heeles...Stanton...issued out of the wicker gate, stripped the varlet mother naked and brought in his peece and his attire. The rebels then tried to fire the gate...four hundred men rushed out of Newgate through flame and fire of the rebels and dispersed them.' The only loyalist casualty was said to be one apprentice.

After the unsuccessful storming of Newgate a relief force sailed over to Dublin under the command of the newly appointed Lord Deputy, the fierce Sir William Skeffington. He went down to Maynooth to attack the Geraldine castle there and to hang the defenders after they had surrendered. 'The pardon of Maynooth', the first example of English ruthlessness during the Tudor wars in Ireland, followed standard European treatment of the defenders of besieged castles, but it shocked the Irish. A new era of violence was initiated. Silken Thomas was captured and taken to London where his father had died in the Tower during the course of the rebellion. In 1537 the young man and five of his uncles were hanged, drawn and quartered at Tyburn.

5

The Reformation and After 1536–1603

In 1536 Henry VIII acceded as King of Ireland, using as a pretext the oaths of submission made by Irish kings to Richard II a century and a half before. Between this date and the death of Queen Elizabeth sixty-seven years later the Reformation made its impact on Dublin, while elsewhere a sequence of savage wars culminated with the defeat of Gaelic Ireland. The conflict strengthened Dublin which became the main base of English operations against the Irish. The city entered a robust period during which the confines of medieval custom were abandoned and vigorous political and religious changes were absorbed. The centre of a strong alien government reinforced by a military presence, known as 'the Irish London', 'Young London' or 'the royal city of Ireland', Dublin was now the seat of a series of Lord Deputies who were powerful ambitious Englishmen, and the headquarters of a horde of officials, lawyers and adventurers who came over to benefit from the spoils of conquest and Reformation. The presence of these strangers helped to end the old cultural isolation from the rest of Europe. At the same time the city enjoyed a period of commercial prosperity, strengthening trade links with Chester and Liverpool and reaffirming old associations with Bristol. Waterford was supplanted at the point of entry to Ireland for the old southern route from Bristol and New Milford. Foreign trade thrived, particularly in wine, inducing a new wave of foreign merchants to move in and set up their signs. They included the first religious refugees 'of the reformed church from the Low Country' who arrived in 1576.

The Reformation was swept in immediately after Silken Thomas's rebellion by George Browne, ex-Provincial of the Augustinian Friars, who was appointed Archbishop of Dublin in 1537, succeeding the murdered Archbishop Alen. Browne efficiently organized the destruction of the holy artistry of the cathedrals and churches. 'The Romish reliques and images of both cathedrals in Dublin took off the common people from the true worship' he wrote to Thomas Cromwell. Outside the doors of

96

Christ Church a great bonfire blazed to consume statues and other things; when the *Bachall Iosa* was tossed on the flames no miracle saved it. Churches lost their plate, and the gold circlet that had crowned Lambert Simnel was melted down. The statue of the Virgin that stood in an alcove above Dame's Gate was knocked from its niche. Not much escaped; of the combustible religious effects the heart of St Laurence O'Toole has survived and so has the graceful oak figure of Our Lady of Dublin. Of all the religious orders in the city that were suppressed, only the Calced Carmelites eventually returned to their original location, and it is appropriate that their church in Whitefriars' Street should contain the only statue to have escaped destruction. According to tradition it was used for a time as a hog trough. Comparisons with other pre-Reformation statues have dated it to just a few years before the Dissolution; further tradition propounds that it came from St Mary's Abbey. Certainly it turned up in penal times in the Mary's Lane Chapel on the site of the old Abbey. In 1816 when a new church was being built, the statue was considered too shabby for veneration and thrown out; eight years later the Carmelite priest, Father John Spratt, saw it in a junk shop and rescued it.

Inside the denuded cathedrals the Lord's Prayer, the Creed and the Ten Commandments were displayed in gilded frames, written out in English in ornamental lettering. To replace 'picture and Popish fancies', Dr Heath, Archbishop of York, presented the cathedrals with two large bibles.

The break up of the monasteries began. In England a history of corruption in religious houses made their suppression acceptable to many. This was less the case in Dublin where corrupt practices were considered to be at a minimum. Nevertheless confiscation proceeded smoothly. Only one house, the Priory of the Holy Trinity, was allowed to continue for religious purposes, a circumstance that led to the preservation of its accounts. The others were sold, acquired by influential supporters of the government, or demolished for building material and speculation. In July 1539, the Priory of Friars Preachers was handed over to be turned into lodgings for lawyers and in due course to become the site for the Four Courts. In the same month the great Abbey of St Thomas Court was surrendered by Abbot Henry Duff and granted to William Brabazon, under-treasurer to the king. The rich prize, for which the ancestor of the Earls of Meath had to pay a rent of

18s. 6d. a year, included 'the site of the monastery with a malt mill, a wood mill and two double mills...ten acres of meadow, two pastures and ten of underwood...' He also acquired the Abbey's ancient Liberty which would become the Liberty of the Earl of Meath. The site of the monastery for friars of the Order of Augustine Hermits would later fall into the hands of William Crow, whose name is perpetuated in Crow Street off Dame Street. Here William Petty would work in the Down Survey, and one of the city's most prominent eighteenth-century theatres would be built. King Henry gave the Priory of All Hallows to the citizens for their support during the rebellion; it provided a site for a university. The crown kept the Priory of the Knights Hospitallers at Kilmainham, where the buildings were converted at a cost of £100 into a residence for the Lord Deputy. Abbot Laundy appealed in vain for St Mary's Abbey, pointing out that it had not only provided free hospitality to rich and poor, but had given supplies to loyal citizens during the rebellion. But even a letter from Lord Deputy Grey and his Council could not prevent St Mary's suffering the same fate as the other houses. Their contents were confiscated for the benefit of the king. Inventories show that very little escaped the scrutiny of the King's Commissioners – lead, bells, plate, jewels, ornaments, corn, stock and stores were all listed as material that would replenish the royal treasury. So was the property owned by religious houses outside their walls which brought them in rent. The list of possessions of the dissolved nunnery of St Mary de Hogges included rented houses in Cook Street, Winetavern Street, Wood Quay, Fishamble Street and Oxmantown.

The citizens may have regretted the destruction of their relics and the social trauma induced by the departure of the monasteries that provided civic benefits available nowhere else. But initially they welcomed the new religion. The accession of Henry as King of Ireland and head of the church was greeted with celebrations. There was an amnesty for criminals – excluding traitors, murderers and ravishers – casks of wine were broached in the streets, bonfires were lit and salutes fired. Large numbers of people went into the cathedrals to gather round Archbishop Heath's bibles 'on purpose to read therin for the small bibles were not so common then as now'. By 1551 Lord Deputy St Leger's promulgation or pronouncement of the Book of Common Prayer in English was accepted with minimum opposition. There was little enthusiasm for the change of emphasis in 1553 when the ardently Catholic Queen Mary came to the throne of England, although many people, including the Earl of Desmond, Primate Dowdall, Archbishop of Armagh and Archbishop Browne himself thought it prudent to return to the old religion. In 1554 Hugh Curwen was appointed Archbishop of Dublin and Lord Chancellor with the brief of bringing back Catholicism. St Patrick's was restored to its former position and Mass was celebrated there. The Priory of St John at Kilmainham also resumed its Catholic trappings. Few further changes were made before Mary died, Elizabeth succeeded and the Reformation again gathered momentum. Curwen became a Protestant.

The prevailing religious character of the city had changed. Instead of clergy there were now soldiers, a good many of them from England. They were a nuisance, and would sometimes be a danger, when, hating the Irish wars, they threatened mutiny. The city had no barracks, so that many were billeted on reluctant citizens who also had to contribute to the upkeep of successive armies. In addition to the usual rounds of taxes, a process of confiscation was introduced in to the Pale known as the Cess where provisions were seized and paid for at a price much lower than their market value in order to feed the garrisons and the Lord Deputy's household. Administration of the Cess led to hoarding, which became a serious problem. But in spite of it people in Dublin found that they were prospering. In England the Elizabethan age had brought in higher living standards, and the impetus for improved conditions came largely from the newcomers pouring into Dublin. By 1577 Sir Henry Sidney could write to the Queen that the houses of Dubliners were 'so far exceeding their ancestors' that they have thought rather to be another and new people than descendants of the old'.

Medieval wickerwork was rapidly superseded by more comfortable dwellings built of local timber and plaster and roofed with slates and wood. The houses of prosperous burghers were very similar to the black and white Tudor buildings which survive in their thousands all over England. In Dublin the oak-beamed cagework houses that made up much of the late sixteenth-century city have completely disappeared. Not only did wars, rebellions and other uncertainties make their tenancy haphazard, but they decayed rapidly in a climate that is damper than England's. By the late eighteenth century the few that survived were considered 'pest houses'. There are records of what some of them were like, such as the stately house in Cook Street with Roman lettering over the door and the imposing residence beside it, demolished in 1745, which bore a Latin inscription carved on an oak beam which translated: 'Thou that madest the heavens and earth bless this house which John Lutrel and Joan caused to be built in the year 1580 and in the twenty-second year of the reign of Queen Elizabeth.' John Lutrel was Sheriff of Dublin in 1567 and 1568. Nothing remains of the original buildings of Trinity College begun in 1591. The only sixteenth-century building still intact was located some way outside the city: Rathfarnham Castle, built by the Lord Chancellor, Archbishop Loftus, about 1585. The last cagework house which stood at the corner of Castle Street and Werburgh Street was demolished in 1813.

We know the outward appearance of Elizabethan Dublin from a detailed report written for the Lord Deputy, Sir John Perrot, in 1588. The city was still enclosed in its medieval jacket, the walls, accompanied by their great ditch encircling an area comparable in size to Chester or York. Although the surrounding country was still actively dangerous, a certain amount of suburban building had been put up within the shadow of the walls which contained a total of thirty-two towers and gates. There were six main gates: St Nicholas' Gate, Newgate with its two towers, Gormond's Gate, Bridge Gate, Pole Gate and Dame's Gate with the Poddle running beside it, whose site is still indicated by a narrowing of Dame Street opposite the Olympia Theatre. Each gate was now protected with a small cannon provided after the rebellion. The walls were incomplete along the Liffey for a distance of about 280 yards; however, not only were the quays well above the water, which would have made it difficult for any enemy to invade the city by ship except at high tide, but they were fortified by three free-standing towers – Prickett's Tower on Merchants' Quay, Fyan's Castle at the foot of Fishamble Street and Case's Tower further east. The base of Fyan's Castle was discovered a few years ago in the course of sewer construction.

An enemy invading by river would have further difficulties; he would be confined to the northern area of the city by a wall following the route of the original pre-Norman city wall which had been retained as an inner defence; it ran from a point north of

Newgate westward towards Dame's Gate.

Irregular or postern gates were constantly being bored by citizens whose premises adjoined the outer wall. In any emergency these had to be filled in or barred with iron gratings, while the ditch outside the walls had to be cleared of ramps of earth and heaps of garbage and offal from the slaughtering premises. Each tower and gate had an individual history, the towers usually taking their names from citizens who had built or rented them over the centuries. Of the gates only Gormond's Gate followed this custom, since William Gormund gave it his name around 1233. Many towers were substantial little buildings. Case's Tower had been granted to Robert FitzSymon in 1471. He 'built it up with stones and buttressed it about and put a roof of timber thereupon and halled it with slates.' It was still owned by his family in 1585, but a few years later was referred to as Case's Tower. The towers were dominated by the bulk of Isolde's Tower, a round tower forty feet high situated at the east end of the city wall at the confluence of the Liffey and the Poddle.

Five towers belonged to 'the woeful Castle of Dublin' which stood on the south-east corner of the city, its south and east walls bounded by the Poddle. It was enclosed by a curtain wall and a ditch so that an enemy would find it impregnable, even if the city were taken. This internal defence system had defeated Silken Thomas. Inside its functions were as complex as those of the Pentagon. Parliament often met in its great hall. It contained the courts, mint, exchequer, state paper office, a barracks and dungeons for captured rebels and priests. The two drum-shaped entrance towers had special rooms for important prisoners which were guarded, not only by exceptionally high walls and the moat, but by a corps made up of a Constable, gentlemen porters, warders, archers and pikemen. Even so a number of prisoners managed spectacular escapes, including the most famous escaper of all, young Hugh O'Donnell who managed to slip down a rope on two separate occasions and make his way to the inhospitable Wicklow hills.

Hostages were confined in the Castle, like Silken Thomas's female relations or the Earl of Desmond's young son, held during the Munster rebellion 'without any learning', lamented his mother, 'or bringing up or any to attend to him'. On at least one occasion a gladiatorial contest took place in the Castle's courtyard as two Irish chieftains brought their differences to be settled under the patronage of the new government. The fight was an echo of medieval trial by combat as Teigh MacKilpatrick O'Connor and Connor MacCormack O'Connor fought stripped to their shirts before an audience of court officials. MacCormack received two wounds in his leg and one in his eye, and had his head chopped off and presented to the watching Lords Justice on the end of Teigh's sword.

It was to the Castle that chieftains came to make submission, like the Earl of Tyrone whose humiliation took place in April 1603 'upon his knees in the Castle of Dublin in the presence of the Lord Deputy and Council, solemnly swearing upon a book'.

During the fifteenth century heads of administration had preferred to live at Thomas Court where the tradition of hospitality associated with the old Abbey was extended so that its palatial accommodation and siting outside the city limits was chosen for the King's Representative. After the Reformation, when Thomas Court was no longer available, Kilmainham was used as an official residence for a few decades until it was damaged in a storm during the administration of Sir Henry Sidney. He moved into the Castle whose living accommodation had been neglected for years so that it had become 'ruinous, foul, filthy and greatly decayed'. The last redecoration scheme seems to have been provided for the Duke of Clarence in 1361. Now it resumed its old function with suitable comfort and splendour for the Lord Deputy and his entourage; the Council Chamber was repaired, the courts of justice embellished and space made for records. However, by the time Strafford became Lord Deputy in 1633 the residential section had once again been allowed to fall into disrepair. The Castle was never a satisfactory residence, probably because too much that was unpleasant went on there.

An engraving illustrating the attack on the Castle by Silken Thomas in Stanyhurst's *History of Ireland*, published in 1577, gives a good idea of the walls of Dublin. Another, by John Derricke, also shows a portion of the walls as the Lord Deputy, Sir Henry Sidney, leaves the Castle with a troop of corseted soldiers. Some heads are displayed on poles.

> These trunckles heddes do playnly showe
> Each rebelles fatall end

And what a haynous crime it is
The Queen for to offend.

The sequel depicts Sidney's triumphant return, when he is received in state by kneeling dignitaries. Behind the raised portcullis of the gate can be made out a row of houses which are captioned 'Dublin'. Sidney, regarded as the ablest colonial administrator of his time, was one of a series of governors sent over to Ireland who typified the bold changes that were being imposed on the city. The experiment of allowing the government in Dublin to be in the charge of Irishmen like the Fitzgeralds was considered a proven failure. While the country was undergoing conquest and complex reorganization, men of distinction were put in charge at Dublin Castle, strong Tudor personalities, ruthless and accomplished. They included Sidney, Sir Anthony St Leger, who served as Deputy on three occasions, the hot-tempered Sir John Perrot, rumoured to be a bastard of Henry VIII, and Lord Mountjoy who destroyed the Gaelic armies by fighting them in winter. The position carried great power. The Lord Deputy – who sometimes received a higher title of Lord Lieutenant – could grant pardons, except to traitors to the monarch, was responsible for the armed forces and could impose forcible recruitment on the Old English of the Pale. But it was never popular. Sir John Perrot called Ireland 'a slimy country'. Sidney considered his fourteen year period as Lord Deputy as 'that thankless charge' and on his retirement in 1578 described himself as 'fifty-four years of age, toothless and rambling, being five thousand pounds in debt'. Lord Fitzwilliam complained that he was 'a banished man wearing himself out amongst unkind people, a people most accursed who lusteth after every sin'. Apart from the anxieties of trying to bring order to Ireland, there were the adjustments necessary in exchanging Elizabethan luxuries for provincial austerities. Sir Peter Carew was warned that while most provisions could be bought in Dublin, such as fish, flesh or fowl, he would be well advised to bring over a cook, physician and surgeon. The voyage over was time consuming and dangerous. Sidney was wind-bound for two months in Wales and Cheshire before crossing. The Earl of Essex, arriving on 15 April 1599, found that a boatload of noblemen sent out to greet him had sunk in mid-channel.

The Lord Deputy headed a flow of merchants, accountants,

lawyers, civil servants, soldiers and adventurers. There had been times during the Middle Ages when the city had been more crowded, as people had come in as refugees from the surrounding countryside. But not since Henry II's original charter had there been such swift changes in the composition of the population. Many newcomers were migratory and only spent a brief time in Dublin before seeking their fortunes elsewhere in Ireland. For those destined to suffer the hazards of travel and battle and to encounter the 'wild shamrock manners' detested by John Derricke, the grey silhouette of the city rising above the Liffey offered a last opportunity of experiencing Anglo-Saxon civility before setting out into a barbarous country. But many found Dublin expensive and squalid. 'My brains are tried by captains who expected to find a city of London in Dublin' wrote Lord Burgh to Sir William Cecil. 'Almost everything is wanting, and the general misery, lamentable to hear as I am sure in your ears, but woeful to behold in Christian eyes.'

The best known critics of Dublin at this period are Fynes Moryson, Lord Mountjoy's secretary, who complained interminably about Ireland in general, and the ex-soldier, Barnabe Rich. Rich's comments often seem trivial as when he objects to one custom that citizens had adopted from their Gaelic neighbours, the wake, 'which you shall hear by their howlying and hollowing' or observes patronizingly that 'the ladies of Ireland were not acquainted with curling sticks, they knew not what a coach meant'. His complaints about high prices were more justifiable. 'This city of Dublin is principally beholden by the English for the residence of the Deputy and his officers. This maketh the citizens to raise their prices in all things; their houses, chambers and lodgings are dearer rented in Dublin than they are in London.' According to Moryson only a few residential inns existed to provide the occasional luxury of a feather bed – usually lousy. Many travellers made alternative arrangements like Andrew Trollope, who on his visit in 1581 'lodged in a lawyer's house, a man of my profession, where I found my entertainment better than my welcome as all Englishmen shall do'.

Together with the newcomers came a cultural awareness which was a by-product of the Renaissance, even if its impact was muted. Books were now readily available, a good many to do with religion. After 1551 when the first Book of Common Prayer was printed in

Dublin, a King's Printer was appointed, who, together with other printers, produced numerous tracts, including one in Irish, extolling the Protestant faith. By now Dublin had its own regular band of musicians who paraded through the streets three times a week wearing light blue livery. In 1569, after he had been greeted with the customary state banquet, Sidney witnessed the first modern drama that departed from the old medieval miracle play to be presented in the city. Subsequent Lord Deputies were entertained with the new drama. After the Armada victory in 1588 a group of strolling players called the Queen's Players came over from England with a repertory. Amateur performances of plays also took place, like the one recorded in September, 1601 when the Gentlemen of the Castle, encouraged by Lord Mountjoy, performed a tragedy called *Gorbode* to celebrate the Queen's birthday.

There was now the germ of a literary society. Men of letters included two Barnabes – Barnabe Rich and Barnabe Googe, the author of a book on husbandry – Geoffrey Fenton, who translated Guicciardini, and Ludowick Bryskett, son of a Genoese merchant and a protégé of Sidney. Bryskett, described by John Aubrey as 'a little man, wore short hair, little bands and little cuffs', held a remunerative position as Clerk of the Council and Controller of the Customs of Wines, but like many other civil servants, considered his main solace as 'literary work'. His *Discourse of Civil Life*, actually a translation of Giraldi Cinto's *Dialogues,* describes how one conversation 'grew out of a visitation of certain gentlemen coming to my little cottage near Dublin'. His circle of acquaintances included Dr Long, Primate of Armagh and the genial Thomas Smith. Dr Smith was the first apothecary to be appointed to the city. In 1556 he was granted a 'concordatum' of twenty shillings and one day's pay from every soldier in the garrison to encourage him to stay and supply 'fresshe and new drugs and other apothecarye wares in plentiful manner to the needful and be of good helpe to such of English byrthe in this realm resident.' Bryskett's most eminent friend was Edmund Spenser, who lived in Dublin for seven years, first as secretary to Lord Grey, then as Clerk to the Court of Chancery, before going off to Munster. It is thought that he worked on the second part of the *Faerie Queene* during the time he was in the city.

A local historian and poet, Richard Stanyhurst, wrote more

sympathetic material about Ireland than that produced by Moryson and Rich. He was a Dubliner, a member of one of the old families like the Usshers which had given service to the city for centuries. In 1571 he contributed to Raphael Holinshed's *Chronicles of Ireland* a section called *Description of Ireland* which includes his well known impression of Dublin's situation: 'if you would traverse hills they are not far off. If champion ground, it lieth in all parts. If you be delighted with fresh water, the famous river Liffey runneth fast by...' He also listed the churches and streets, the markets and fair days on Wednesdays and Fridays, and pointed out such details as the well-stocked shambles for corn and meat and the organization of alms for the needy. He emphasized a virtue which nearly every traveller noted: Dublin was already famous for hospitality. Mayors – of whom he had two in his family – gave a lead to ordinary citizens by the numerous lavish state functions they organized, where banquets glittered with the city plate. In 1599 it included a basin and ewer 'parcel gilded', a nest of bowls, one salt double gilded and 'a fair standing gilt bowl' which had been donated by Sir John Perrot and was engraved with his crest, a parrot, and his motto *Relinquo in Pace*. Edmund Campion, Stanyhurst's tutor, who visited Dublin in 1571, considered that 'this Mayoralty, both for state and charge of the office and for bountiful hospitality exceeds any city in England except London'. Private entertainment was also lavish, if Josiah Bodley's visit to Sir Richard Moryson was typical. On one occasion he was feasted with brawn, stuffed geese, venison pies, pastries and tarts eaten with claret, sherry, a Spanish wine known as the King of Spain's daughter and native Irish whiskey. 'Returning home, card tables and dice are set before us and amongst other things that Indian tobacco of which I shall never be able to make sufficient mention.'

New civic appointments included drummers, trumpeters, a sword bearer and one Fergus Dowdall 'for keeping the Tholsel clock'. The guilds became Protestant and expanded. Fynes Moryson noted that by the end of the century the first coaches were brought over from England by some lords and knights 'but they are not generally used'. Merchants included numerous foreigners whose activities were restricted in case they became too successful. Among local tradesmen was the type described by Moryson as 'a merchant...with only a barrel of salt or a bar or two of iron in his shop'; others were 'very wealthy and men of good ability, they have their shops replenished with all sorts of wares'. The import of cheap ready-made goods helped them. There was a thriving trade in linen, woollens and silks, and in some cases Dublin merchants were considered to have better wares than those in London. Although edicts against overcharging were numerous, the presence of a large official class which included 'servants, friends and followers...maketh the citizens to raise their prices in all things'. It was considered that imported luxuries like spices, wines and fine wearing apparel 'would never be vended among the Irish themselves'. Fashions were more strictly English than ever. Some Dublin tailors went on special trips to London to bring back the latest 'hats and swords, broadcloths, kerseys, velvets and silks'.

Senior aldermen paraded in scarlet robes, the more junior in violet, traditional colours of rank; 'turkey-gowns' of orange-red were worn by other civic officers. The guilds strictly regulated clothes worn by their members. A bye-law of the Guild of Merchants in 1573 gives details of the sort of costumes required: 'a coate of clothe decently made without gardinge cutting or sylke to be wrought theron...a doublet...a shurt of this cowntry clothe...the ruff thereof to be one yard long...a payr of hose...the breche of the same hose shall not be bolsterede out with ether wool, heyre or eny other thinge.' Apprentices, who were stylish dressers, tended to disregard such restrictions, although those who wore long hair or did not conform to these and similar minute regulations were liable to be ceremoniously whipped in the hall of their guild in front of other guild members by porters in disguise.

The changes did not remove all the trappings of medieval life. If the religious orders were suppressed, church bells continued to ring. The bells of St Audoen's rang at six every morning to call people to work; there was another peal at 11 a.m. for the midday meal and a third at eight in the evening to warn people of the curfew. The great Boebell of Christ Church was rung at four in the morning and nine at night. A bell was tolled if a disaster happened or 'in tyme of greate tempest and storms, so well-disposed citizens may be remembered to pray for their neighbours who are in danger upon the seas'.

Penitents were still dressed in white sheets and hats, a wand was thrust into their hand and they were exposed to the populace either before the High Cross or in the precincts of Christ Church. They included Catholics who were convicted of allowing priests to celebrate baptisms or marriages, or adulterers like George Bateman of Kilmainham or 'a said Eyeland alias Hinchliffe'. In 1571 this Eyeland was ordered to show himself 'with a white shete from his shoulders downe to the ground rounde about him and a paper above his head' on which was written: 'For Adulterie – leaving his wyfe in England alyve and marryeng with another here.'

In the mud of broken pavements cattle and unringed swine 'a danger to little children lying beneath the stalls' continued to roam filthy streets. After 200 years the work of paving was far from complete, and an edict of 1573 compelled the inhabitants of Thomas Street to pave their street 'unto the two separate streams coming from the cistern'. The cleansing cart and specially appointed city scavengers who had sworn to 'cause the streets with your ward to be kept clean from time to time' could not prevent the accumulation of dirt, the ditches of Newgate 'grown...full stoppid', the muck in ill-named Rosemary Lane including entrails of cattle, the garbage thrown over the low wall near Gormond's Gate into Colman's Brook. Stinks came from bad herrings brought into the city by foreign fishermen which were 'not fit for humans to eat'. Wood Quay, another place to dump garbage and 'oulde barks' as well, had an innovation – 'a common jakes made upon such place of the Wood Quay'. Street lighting was still basic, limited to a lantern or candle shone from every fifth house 'on every dark night from Hallowtide to Christmas'.

Contemporary writers were censorious about the taverns of Dublin. Barnabe Rich complained about 'nurseries of drunkenness' where 'their drink is double the rate of London'. 'There is no merchandize so vendible' he wrote, 'it is the very marrow of the commonwealth of Dublin...the whole profit of the town stands upon ale-houses and the selling of ale.' Taverns were open not only during the week 'night and day, and in every minute of the hour' but on Sundays during divine service. 'Every filthy ale-house is thronged full of company...young idle housewives that are verie loathsome filthie and abominable, both in life and manners, and these they call tavern keepers.' Since early times women had traditionally been brewers. This encouraged the situation whereby the sixteenth-century drinker could not only enjoy fresh Dublin oysters or a salmon at his local ale-house, but also a harlot. The city council, encouraged by indignant English settlers, issued many edicts to deal with the problems of 'fornication'. Apprentices were considered particularly susceptible to prostitutes, with unfortunate consequences. 'It is complained that an excessive number of evilly disposed women are at this present keeping of taverns in this city, whereby prentices are enticed to whoredom and consumation of their master's goods in embezzling.' In 1561 no unauthorized 'woman or maid' was allowed to sell wine, ale or beer 'but such as should keep a sign on their doors with the intention to extirpate whordom'. Any householder keeping an unmarried servant woman in his house 'that doth use any mysgovernance as fornication' could be fined. In spite of edicts harlots continued to flourish 'whose ungodliness of life can do no less than procure the indignation of God against the honourable city'.

Stanyhurst, who knew that beggars were also a problem in English cities, noted of Dublin 'the extraordinarie number of beggars that dailie swarm there'. More than ever came in as a consequence of the wars, undeterred by the prospect of being 'beaten with whippes through the market town or other places til his body be bloody by reason of such whipping' or perhaps being tied to a horse's tail and dragged through the streets. In 1579 Barnabe Tathe was made Beagle and Master of the Beggars with the brief of killing swine and ridding the city of vagabonds and beggars. Both Tathe and succeeding Masters of Beggars found the task impossible; it seems to have induced a nervous breakdown in Tathe, who, after appealing to the City Assembly to relieve him of his post, was retired to the House of St John.

Beggars and plague continued to be associated in the public mind. There were two major plague epidemics during this period. During the first in 1575, 3,000 people died between June and October, while thousands of others fled, some seeking refuge on Dalkey Island. The second in 1604 virtually emptied the city, and anyone who could rushed into the countryside. Grass grew in the streets and church doorways. Prayers and litanies were said on Wednesdays and Fridays, while those left in the city were commanded to burn faggots at their doors on Wednesdays and 'such other nights as the Maior shall think fit'. But the Mayor had departed with the Sheriff and his court, while the Lord Deputy was safe in Drogheda. A short time before this plague a pesthouse had been built on Hoggen Green. Named the Bridewell after St Brigid's well nearby, it provided a prison for any unfortunate vagrant who was rounded up. A year after it was built it was moved farther out to a section of city property at All Hallows where four stong men were appointed to prevent infected persons running abroad. In spite of the penalty of eighty days' imprisonment for those who failed to disclose an outbreak of disease, sick people were apt to 'keep the same secrete' rather than risk a sojourn in the horrible building at All Hallows. As a consequence neighbours who visited them were often 'trapped in the same disease'.

Buildings continued to catch fire easily in spite of a primitive fire service that provided 'lathers and buckettes'. They were also liable to fall down, since the maintenance of churches and civic buildings was neglected. The churches may well have suffered because of the upheavals caused by the Reformation, but the neglect that made Newgate Prison ruinous and left the old Tholsel 'ruinated and decayed' must be put down to the uncertainty of the times. Leinster was not yet subdued, and the old pattern of raids and counter raids from the southern hills continued. Neglect may also have been responsible for bringing down the south wall of Christ Church in 1546, damaging Strongbow's tomb. But Christ Church had a structural weakness which was not remedied until the nineteenth century; its walls were too thin and there was too much window space to support the roof.

The most terrible damage to buildings was the result of an accident on 11 March 1596 when more than twenty houses were thrown to the ground and many others damaged by gunpowder. Forty-four barrels had been brought by boat up river to the buildings known as the Crane which served as the city's custom-house, where imported merchandize was weighed. It stood at the northern end of Winetavern Street beside the river. The barrels exploded with such force that the bell in Christ Church Tower was cracked and 'no less than six score bodies were identified, besides sundrie headless bodies and heads without bodies, that were found and not known'. In an examination of witnesses various small children and unemployed persons who rolled the barrels were blamed; so was the clerk of the storehouse, an Englishman named John Allen who was believed to be a recusant or Catholic, which was quite enough to have him put in prison. The tower of St Audoen's took much of the force of the blast, which caused two large cracks in the inner walls just above the apex of the louvers which can still be seen.

Almost every Lord Deputy during this period had to organize a local hoisting against the Wicklow clans. Some were successful, like Lord Fitzwalter's routing of the Kavanaghs in Powerscourt in 1556, when he hanged seventy-four of them. But Dublin had no reason to forget old fears. In 1565 Walter Fitzgerald led a force of O'Byrnes to the village of Crumlin, and citizens watching from the walls saw it burn. Although Fitzgerald was captured and hanged soon afterwards, a state of emergency continued for some years. In 1580 Lord Grey de Wilton, Spenser's employer, was ambushed disastrously in the wilds of Glenmalure. A year later an attempt to overthrow the government and capture the Castle resulted in the execution of forty-five people, including Nicholas Nugent, a member of the Pale aristocracy and Baron of the Exchequer. In particular the Tyrone rebellion at the end of the century demonstrated the city's continued vulnerability. A report in the *Calendar of State Papers* of October 1597, described how 'the rebels rage all over the Pale so that almost no part of it is free from their killings, burnings, preying and despoiling'. It had become usual for the city to have plenty of soldiers to defend it; in 1586 there had been 1,200 armed men with weapons that included various great pieces and twelve hundredweight of powder. But now many soldiers were fighting rebellion elsewhere in Ireland. Dublin was inadequately defended, with arms that included ancient culverins from the Tower of London which were 'likely to lie and consume with rust'. The postern gates and walls had to be repaired with earth four yards thick. Citizens were formed into watches; there were muster points at the Cornmarket, High Cross, Pillory and Gormond's Gate. Every evening after drums were beaten and St Audoen's bell tolled, the gates were locked. Any Irishman or suspicious person was immediately brought before the Mayor. In the event Tyrone was defeated, and the danger receded for another forty years.

6

Dissent, Rebellion and the Commonwealth
1603–1662

In the summer of 1603, a few months after the death of Queen
Elizabeth, the ceremony of 'Riding the Franchises' or Fringes,
combining civic duty with festival, took place as usual. Authority
had to be asserted over those who considered that they lived far
enough out in the suburbs to be beyond the control of the
municipality. Sometimes this led to outright violence; in 1626 there
was a tussle 'wherein some affronts and assaults were offered'. But
in 1603, according to the *Calendar of Ancient Records,* the ride went
peaceably. The Mayor, sheriffs, recorder and sword bearer
escorted by 300 horse, followed the long established route through
Dame's Gate, along to Ringsend 'where the trumpets sounding, the
company came together'. Then by Donnybrook, Clonskeagh and
back to the heart of the city. At several places citizens refreshed the
riders with drink, and when they reached the river 'Puddell' planks
were placed across it for their convenience. The horsemen rode by
the Abbot's Meadow near St Thomas Court, past more meadows
and a great old hawthorn. A clatter of hoofs down Murdering Lane
on their way to Kilmainham, and then they all went back to Christ
Church where in another meadow near the small Camock river
tents had been erected. The company 'lighted and dyned'. Fully
replete, it took a trip by boat up the Liffey to Kilmainham bridge
where horses awaited. Further riding brought it along the north
bank, past the gardens of Oxmantown Green to Glasnevin and out
to Clontarf, then a return to the stone wall which was all that
remained of St Mary's Abbey. Finally 'they rode in good order
over the bridge and about the city the longest waye til they came to
the Maior's door, where everyone, blyssing the Kinge's Majestie,
took leave of the Maior and parted to their houses.'

The king they blessed was James I. The historian Richard
Bagwell has considered that 'the change from Elizabeth to James I
marks the transition from a heroic age to one very much the reverse
– public affairs were administered by a smaller race of men'.
James's accession coincided with O'Neill's defeat and submission.
The flight of the Earls would follow and the settlement of Ulster by

Protestants. In Dublin many of the city's problems on that day when the Mayor made his rounds concerned religion.

In 1603 a large part of the populace was Catholic. Only seventy years before their grandfathers had accepted Archbishop Browne's vigorous campaign of change. But the Reformation had not made a permanent impact. There is no easy explanation why this should be so. Undoubtedly people in Dublin were influenced by the propinquity of those who did not wish to be converted or civilized by 'the greatest murderers and proudest people in all Europe'. Dublin also had a reputation for tolerance. Bloody Mary's reign had brought no terrors; when Elizabeth acceded there were no persecutions. In 1570 Archbishop Loftus could request Sir William Cecil that the newly appointed Chancellor should be 'neither a dissembling Papist nor a cold or cruel Protestant'. Dublin became a haven for Englishmen fleeing their own religious troubles. A recurring grievance of Fynes Moryson and Barnabe Rich was the nest of Catholic refugees whom Rich called 'Pope's cocktails', including in their number 'English runnigates' or murderers, debtors and recusants who had fled over to Ireland on account of their misdeeds.

The programme of Reformation included the establishment at the end of the century of Trinity College on the confiscated land which had belonged to the Priory of All Hallows. Earlier Sir John Perrot had the idea of turning St Patrick's Cathedral into a university, but this had been thwarted by Archbishop Loftus. (In his rage Sir John threatened to send the City Council out of Dublin on cabbage stalks and to pull the Archbishop into small pieces like grass between his fingers.) In 1591 the alternative site was decided upon, and a new charter proclaimed the founding of the college 'in a certain place called All Hallows'. The Green in front changed its name from Hoggen Green to College Green. The College began very modestly with a chapel, buttery, kitchen, hall and main square court paved with thin red Dutch bricks. There were four fellows and three lectures a day, followed by a disputation in the afternoon when each tutor spoke in Latin on some subject connected with divinity. In the words of Archbishop Loftus, Trinity was 'a counterblast to Popery', founded with the purpose of converting the Irish to the Protestant religion. This was a formidable undertaking.

Increasing Gaelic influence in the Pale was immediately apparent in language. By now the old Middle English dialect had become extinct, except for pockets in north Dublin and Wexford. The modern English that replaced it was not always pure. Stanyhurst wrote how 'the meaner sort spoke neither good English nor good Irish, but rather a mingle mangle of gallimaufrie of both languages'. He repeated the old medieval complaint that Irish names spread insidiously in the city, 'for noone with his good will will be called Henry, Edward, Richard, George, Francis...but rather, Morrough, Moriertagh, Tirlogh...for language they do so despise ours as they think themselves worse when they hear it.'

The Anglo-Irish families who had been part of Irish life for centuries were now known by the Irish as *Sean-Ghaill* or Old English as opposed to the *Nua-Ghaill* or New English, the title given to newcomers. Referring to themselves as 'Inglish gentillmen', the Old English felt at a social disadvantage when they went to England and found themselves lumped together with the Irish they despised. Lord Howth, asked by Elizabeth herself whether he could speak the English tongue, lamented that 'such was the report of the country made to the Queen'. Stanyhurst found that the English 'judge them [Dubliners] to learn their English in three or four days as though they had bought at Chester a groat's worth...and so packed up the rest to be carried after them to London'. Members of prominent families in Dublin and the Pale were expected to speak with a brogue which was already being lampooned on the London stage. Shakespeare had rudiments of stage Irish in Macmorris's speech, while Ben Jonson used it elaborately in his *Irish Masque* in 1613.

At home the Reformation had the effect of antagonizing the Old English. The merchants of Dublin and Drogheda and the landed gentry of the Pale initially wished their children to serve in legal and executive positions in the reorganized administration at Dublin Castle. Some had even gone to England to undergo legal training. However, after 1570 many found themselves unable to stomach the Oath of Supremacy. This meant that almost all legal appointments from the 1570s onward went to new arrivals from England. By then enthusiasm for the new religion had waned. An English official noted how 'in the tenth year of her Majesty's reign they came very orderly to church, but first their women grew weary of it and that being unpunished, their men left'. In 1573 the Jesuit, Dr Wolfe, wrote that Dubliners were 'almost all Catholics, especially the natives, though they were forced to go to the communion and preaching of heretics'. Protestant clergymen had increasing difficulty filling their churches. Barnabe Rich tells of various officials who after hearing Mass and bringing the Mayor to Christ Church, 'convey themselves to a tavern till the service is done'. Archbishop Loftus complained that Dublin lawyers even absented themselves from a public thanksgiving following the defeat of the Armada; this was largely because citizens resented restrictions on their trade with Spain. Instead of sending their children to the new university, many Pale families preferred to ship them abroad to be educated in seminaries at Louvain or Salamanca which had been set up after the Council of Trent. By 1601 the Jesuit, Father de la Field, who returned to the Pale after an absence of twenty-five years, noted with satisfaction that in the renovated churches, in spite of pews and elegant furniture 'they could not get a single Catholic to go to their profane temples'.

Persecution of priests had occurred in Elizabethan times; the most famous victim was Archbishop O'Hurley of Cashel, who, after being kept in chains in 'a dark, dismal and fetid prison' in the Castle was hanged outside the city in July 1584. But such severity failed to stop the impact of the Counter-Reformation, spearheaded by the Jesuits who 'swarmed as locusts through the land'. In 1586 the Dublin Parliament refused to pass specific legislation against priests. Sir John Dowdell wrote to Lord Burghley in 1585 that 'every port town and upland town and also gentlemen's houses are...furnished with superstitious seducing priests'. Many were old Dubliners, like the persuasive Henry Fitzsimons, who became a Catholic at Oxford. When early in the seventeenth century he took the dangerous step of returning to his native city, 'ever since his arrival he hath gathered great multitudes of his Majesty's subjects, perverted their religion and drawn from the church' wrote the outraged Lord Chancellor and the Bishop of Meath to the Archbishop of Canterbury. His missionary activities included the foundation of a sodality for young girls 'who had consecrated themselves to perpetual virginity' and the celebration of Mass in a nobleman's house to the accompaniament of harps, lutes and every kind of musical instrument except the organ. In due course he was imprisoned in Dublin Castle where he made converts who included fellow prisoners and the main gaoler. While he was in captivity he held his famous religious 'disputations' with his distant relative, the

youthful James Ussher, champion of the reformed church, who
had been one of the first students at Trinity which he entered at the
age of thirteen. The contest was a draw, but the publicity did
Fitzsimons no harm, and the authorities deported him to Spain. On
his departure the main gaoler wept. Nearly forty years later he
returned during the Great Rebellion and nearly got himself hanged.
Ussher became Archbishop of Armagh, and in 1613 the Articles of
what has become the Church of Ireland were drawn up under his
direction.

Those who hoped that the old religion might be tolerated when
James came to the throne were disappointed. The gunpowder plot
of 1605 brought a wave of persecution to Dublin, where old
Englishmen like Lord Gormanston and Sir Patrick Barnewall were
imprisoned. Earlier in the same year a proclamation had ordered all
priests to leave Ireland. Many went into hiding; Gilbert mentions a
contemporary document which lists 'places of most publicke note
whereunto the priests did resort to Masse in Dublin' as 'certain
back rooms in the houses of Nicholas Queitrot, Carye and the
widow O'Hagan in the High Street'. Local authorities failed to
persecute them. 'The multitude were ever made comfortable by
edicts and proclamations' declared the Attorney-General, Sir John
Davies. 'If this one Corporation were reformed, the rest would
follow.' In 1613 the newly elected Mayor refused to take the Oath
of Supremacy or go to church. The appointment of a pliable young
man in his place was described as a 'salmon leap' since he was
chosen over many seniors who had refused to compromise their
religious convictions. In the same year when Parliament was called
in Dublin for only the fourth time since 1543, Catholics walked out
after they failed to get their champion, Sir John Everard, elected as
Speaker. Many people continued to suffer fines and forfeitures
rather than accept the reformed church, while priests continued to
be furtively encouraged. In 1623 three city aldermen were named as
giving shelter to 'Jesuits, Fryers and Papish priests' who had 'come
from beyond the seas' to meet in conference and appoint titular
bishoprics and other benefices.

The accession of Charles I in 1625 brought an initial degree of
tolerance. Catholics were allowed to rent warehouses, outhouses
and stables as chapels. Religious communities like the Discalced
Carmelites, who opened a chapel in Cook Street, were seen on the
streets openly wearing the habit of their order. On one occasion

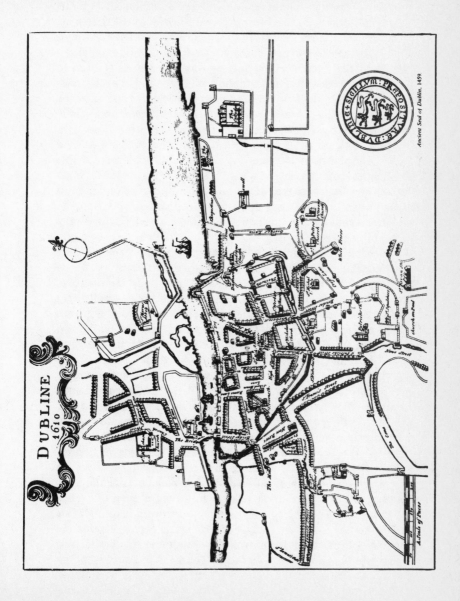

they even held a public procession of the Blessed Sacrament. King
Charles, always in need of funds, proposed a series of agreements
called the Graces, which would provide various concessions in
exchange for sums of money. But the Graces were never honoured,
and soon there were new attempts to curb Catholic activities.
Fifteen of the illicit religious houses which had been allowed to
function were closed. The Catholic University and chapel 'richly
adorned with pictures' which had been confidently established by
the Jesuits in Black Lane and Bride Street, were sequestered in 1630
and the buildings handed over to Trinity. (Trinity had its own
troubles, with attempts by priests to convert students and send
them to Spain.) A feature of the period was the forcible
interruption of Masses. On St Stephen's Day, 1629, when
Archbishop Bulkeley, the Mayor and a file of musketeers tried to
break up Mass in a church run by the Franciscans, a crowd rescued
the friars and the Archbishop was forced to take refuge in a
neighbouring house.

The city, preoccupied with religious turmoil, made few
developments in the first years of the seventeenth century. When
John Speed produced the first published map of Dublin in 1610,
not a great deal had changed since the plans of the city walls were
made for Sir John Perrot in the 1570s. The map shows the walls
intact, and round about are familiar medieval landmarks, the two
cathedrals, the Castle, the Tholsel, mills and a score of churches.
Three ships and what looks like a rowing boat sail on the Liffey
where Merchants' Quay and Wood Quay are marked and upstream
the bridge cuts the river. Buttevant's Tower has been renamed
Newman's Tower after being granted to Jacob Newman in 1602.
On the north side there are communities at Oxmantown and
around St Michan's. Although St Mary's Abbey has long been
suppressed, it is marked as the site for another cluster of houses,
and, unlike other little housing estates north of the river, is
properly walled. South of the river developments outside the walls
converge towards St Patrick's Street in a long avenue of houses
stretching to the outer St James Gate, and eastward in a single line
of new houses along the rough road of Dame Street towards the
bold square of Trinity. In front of Trinity is the brand new
Bridewell for locking up vagrants. To the northwest is a site
marked The Hospital. This was the 'certain plott of the commons
of this cittie' appropriated by Sir George Carew for his Carey's

Hospital which had been intended as a place of retirement for old and maimed soldiers who had fought with him in Munster. It was never actually put to this use, since Sir George lived in it himself. Later it passed to Sir Arthur Chichester and became known as Chichester House. In 1685 it was purchased by the crown for use as Parliament House. In 1728 the new Parliament building, later the Bank of Ireland, took its place. The Bridewell and Carey's Hospital were the first incursions on the common land of Hoggen Green which led to its eventual disappearance.

Dublin did not break out of its chrysalis for another quarter of a century. The only significant new development was the Custom House, erected, together with a crane and wharf in 1621 on the river below Dame Street. True expansion did not begin until the arrival of Thomas Wentworth as Lord Deputy in 1633. Before then the city had become distinctly tattered. Churches dedicated to the reformed faith took up a good deal of space, and the success of the Counter-Reformation had ensured that many had fallen into disrepair. 'I know not whether the churches are more ruinous or the people more irreverent' wrote a contemporary English cleric. 'In Dublin...one church is used as the Deputy's stable, another as a nobleman's house and the choir of the third as a tennis court where the vicar officiates as keeper. The vaults under Christ Church where the Lord Deputy repairs every Sunday are let for tippling houses for beer, wine and tobacco, and these are frequented by Papists.' Protestant clergy, Sir John Bingley considered in 1629, were 'a set of very profane and drunken fellows'. In 1637 the steeple of St Audoen's was 'ready to fall and endanger the whole church; the roof receiving rain in several places...the church wanting all necessaries to become the house of God'. In the Castle the new Lord Deputy had to take down one of the towers 'and the others are so crazy that we are still in fear part of it might drop on our heads'. As he wrote in a long complaining letter to Mr Secretary Coke, Wentworth could smell 'wood reek' coming from the bakery.

In this general picture of decay the property of Richard Boyle, the Earl of Cork, was a crisp exception. The Earl had been one of the most successful of Elizabethan adventurers since his arrival in Ireland on Midsummer Eve, 1588, virtually penniless. In twelve years he had made his fortune and had built a massive town house in Dublin on the site of the old church of St Mary del Dam. He repaired one of the tipsy towers of the Castle at his own expense. A staunch supporter of the Protestant interest, 'no man in either kingdom' wrote Sir Christopher Wandesford, 'hath so violently and so frequently laid profane hands, hands of power upon the church and her possessions...as this bold Earl of Cork'. Lord Cork and Wentworth feuded bitterly. Two days after Wentworth's installation at the Castle Lord Cork's remarks that 'perfect peace and plenty might continue' were badly received, since he had been one of the two Lord Justices in charge of the country before Wentworth was appointed. The feud was highlighted by the farcical dispute about the Earl of Cork's family tomb. In the year of Wentworth's arrival this vulgar monument had been erected over the high altar of St Patrick's in tiers of red, black and gold; it contained 'the bones of my wife's grandmother and of her father and the coffin where my first wife's dead body was enclosed'. Wentworth was determined to remove it from its aggressive site. Although Lord Cork pleaded that it had cost him £1,000 and was the most beautiful monument in Ireland, it was dismantled stone by stone. Today it can be seen where it was re-erected in obscurity on the east side of the cathedral; but the self-made nobleman is elsewhere. When he died, three years after witnessing the execution of his rival, he chose to be buried in his equally florid tomb in Youghal.

For the seven years of his term of office, Wentworth, soon Earl of Strafford, devoted his great energies to making Ireland stable for the crown and creating a beautiful and fashionable capital. Reforms were quickly introduced. The abuses in the churches ceased, while the taverns under Christ Church were closed down. Regulations were brought in to prevent the unbecoming behaviour that had been hidden by pews, and people were forbidden to walk or talk in the aisles during divine service or to urinate against church walls. The Lord Deputy encouraged the linen trade and suppressed piracy along the east coast. Signs of his influence were visible everywhere. A visitor, James Howell, wrote how 'traffic encreaseth here wonderfully and all kinds of bravery and buildings'. Discipline was brought to the army. In order to provide a suitable setting for lavish entertainment, the Castle was redecorated with new rooms and gardens with fifteen uniformed attendants to look after it. There were new gardens along the Poddle, and in 1635 provision was made for open spaces on College Green, St Stephen's Green and Oxmantown Green to be 'kept for the use of citizens to walke and take the open air, by reason this cittie is at this present growing very populous'. Strafford was ahead of his time in contemplating compulsory regulations for ensuring good style in the new buildings with which he planned to 'beautify the city exceedingly'.

Merchant's Quay and Wood Quay, divested of their commercial role by the building of the Custom House downstream, became fashionable addresses for wealthy newcomers like Sir William Parsons and Sir Philip Percival, lessee of the Custom House. Among the 'very stately and complete buildings' observed by Sir William Brereton who visited Dublin during his tour of the British Isles in 1635, was the house in Dame Street erected by Sir Christopher Wandesford 'in a very wholesome air, with a good orchard and garden leading down to the waterside'. Wandesford built the Rolls Office at his own expense 'a stately brick building of three storeys and in it a large room for the safe repository of the rolls'. It had modern conveniences like a handsome chamber for his secretary and clerks of office, a table of fees for everyone's inspection and boxes and presses of new oak with partitions to take material for every year of the king's reign. Another handsome house near to Wandesford's on College Green belonged to Archbishop Ussher 'to...reside for the most part, in regard to the affection he bore the city, being born and bred in it'. Brereton, who hired a horse at 1s. 6d. a day to make his tour, was impressed by the bustling streets filled with 'divers merchandize' which he compared favourably with London. He considered Dublin 'beyond all conception the fairest richest best built city I have met with on this journey (except York and Newcastle). It is far beyond Edinburgh.' Some things he didn't like, the Castle 'much less and meaner than ours' and the 'Commons House', 'but a mean and ordinary place'.

The Earl of Strafford dominated every civic and military function. He was to be seen everywhere, parading before his troops 'clad in black armour with a black horse and black plume and feathers'; receiving the white staff of office from the outgoing Mayor attended by Aldermen in scarlet; opening Parliament on a white Barbary horse, surrounded by a great entourage. One of his most important contributions to Dublin's cultural life was the encouragement he gave to the founding of a theatre. Before his time plays were not a public amenity, but had usually been performed as the last course of a formal meal during the opening of a legal

term or a Mayor's banquet. Dublin's first professional theatre, the
New Theatre, was opened in Werburgh Street in deliberate
proximity to the Castle in 1637 under the direction of a Scotsman
named John Ogilby whom Wentworth appointed 'Master of the
Revells'. John Aubrey described the small rectangular building as a
'pretty little theatre'. For the next four years until the outbreak of
rebellion in 1641, audiences could see works of playwrights like Ben
Jonson, Middleton, Beaumont and Fletcher and James Shirley, an
Englishman who had been induced to settle in Dublin. Among the
plays he wrote for the local stage was *St Patrick for Ireland*, which
is regarded as the first drama in English to show any enthusiasm for
Irish traditions. However, according to one of his prologues, he did
not care for Dublin audiences:

> When he did live in England he heard say
> That here were men lov'd wit and a good play.
> This he believed, and though they are not found
> Above, who knows what may be underground?

A more lively enthusiasm for theatre had been discernible at the
university, but this had been curbed by Provost Robert Ussher –
'no friend to the levitie of theatrical gaities and representations' –
who banned all undergraduate productions in 1629. If they could
not perform plays, the students brought a new raucous element to
the city. By now there were over 200, many from important
families, like Lucius Carey, son of a former Lord Deputy. Before
1641 a proportion were Catholic; they included Thomas, son of
Maurice Fitzgerald and Fergal O'Gara, patron of the Four
Masters. There were now sixteen fellows, none of whom had been
'branded with infamy, convicted of heresy or any dissolute
manners and life'. Students, who entered when they were around
sixteen years old, wore costumes of dark and sombre hue which
they tended to embellish illegally with swords, daggers and
poniards, while they adorned themselves with 'long hair and ruffles
and other new fangles in attire'. In spite of regulations about rising
at six and listening to Latin prayers during Commons, their
schedule allowed them time for climbing the college walls, rioting
in the streets, playing dice, insulting women, wounding citizens,
breaking windows and holding revels in the College. In Provost
Bedell's register for 28 August 1629, student misdemeanours
included: 'Sir Springham to render account for the omitting of his

declamation, said to keep a hawke, not to come to prayers...Rawley for drunkeness...having added to his fault the knocking of Strarack his head against ye seat in ye chappell...' A student named Weld was fined for drinking and lodging in the house of Mrs Jones, an ale-house keeper, 'a suspected place for disorder and vice', while Mrs Jones herself had to stand at the Market Cross with a paper on her head which read: 'For harbouring a Collegian contrary to the act of the State.'

No regulation nor the isolation of the university from the town could prevent students and fellows making the long walk through the mud and dust of Dame Street to visit the city's taverns. After 1635 these were subject to licensing laws. Popular inns included the Red Lion in Werburgh Street near the New Theatre, the Angel Inn on the site of the present Four Courts Hotel and the Brazen Head at Bridge Street which survives today as the oldest inn in the country.

By 1637 city revenue exceeded expenditure by £60,000 as a result of the new confidence in trade engendered by Strafford's reforms. But life was plagued by old abuses. Complaints in the Assemby Rolls or edicts of the City Council continued to involve dirt, whorehouses, hucksters, beggars and fire hazards. In 1638, in addition to the buckets, ladders and hooks stored in churches, the Council sent to England for 'an instrument called a water spout...very necessary for quenching any great fire suddenly'. In 1634 an 'abundance of beggars' was particularly condemned because 'they do most presumptously build cottages upon the commons and highway'. John O'Shea was given the task of expelling them with the help of 'ten armed and well qualified men'. City scavengers continued to be inadequate, the worst offender being one Katherine Strongue, who in 1634 not only failed to do her job properly but extorted money from the poor. She threw dirt into Mr George Beddley's garden, fouled up the river, only used two of the seven carts provided for her work and failed to remove the dung thrown out into the streets by a brewer named Henry Creame 'which procureth a continual stinck'. The Mayor petitioned the Lord Deputy to remove her, but she refused to be budged. In the winter of 1634 citizens made an effigy of her and pelted it with snowballs.

Apart from a few charitable bequests – a new clock given by the retiring Mayor to the inhabitants of Thomas and Francis Streets, a sum of £200 a year left by Ann St Lawrence for the maintenance of 'six poor women such as go to church' – there was nothing in the way of provisions from public funds for the poor, who were totally neglected by civic authorities. Prisoners were in a particularly bad way, since they were expected to be maintained by their families or by casual charity. A petition from prisoners in Newgate described how 'they have not anything allowed unto them but what is exte...ded out of the charity of good people as they pass the gates...they will inevitably perish unless they are relieved with more care...' In 1634 the House of Commons was shamed into giving a donation fr.. n every member for the poor prisoners in the gaols of Dublin, but this was not a usual practice. The notion that criminals should be maintained at public expense would not be considered seriously for many years.

The seventeenth century brought in a craze for gambling and dice. There was enthusiasm for outdoor pastimes for 'stodball, quoits, tennis, cudgels or other unlawful games' which an ordinance in 1612 forbade to be played on Sundays and holidays. A racquet court which was in existence before 1625, located at St John's Lane at the upper end of Fishamble Street, survived until 1972, when three of its walls were demolished; the fourth made a boundary for the old graveyard of St John's Church, where the old facing of its flagstones can still be seen. Bear and bull baiting were such regular features of entertainment that in 1620 the Mayor was asked 'to restrain the common passage of bears and bulls through the city'. A grand confusion of traffic brought problems from the numbers of car-men, the wheels of whose vehicles broke up pavements. Regulations specifying that every car-man should have a licence embellished with the city arms in the forepart of his car did not prevent him or his fellow drivers from galloping about so that 'they hurt many children and put some in danger of death'.

The Liffey continued to silt up. The bar across the mouth of the river between the sandbanks known as the North and South Bull which were located respectively a little to the east of Sutton and due north of Dun Laoghaire, discouraged merchant vessels which preferred to land cargoes at Dalkey, just as they had during the Middle Ages. At Wood Quay and Merchants' Quay, according to a report in the Public Record Office in London written in 1590, the depth of the water varied between three and six and a half feet. Wrecks and local ships like apple ships and fishing vessels crowding the slip at the bottom of Fishamble Street blocked up much of the available landing space. No one removed the debris along the quays – wooden planks, slates, millstones and garbage. The pressure eased, as the confusion down by the docks was moved downstream. But on market days there was chaos throughout the city. In 1633 the authorities tried to sort things out by allocating each trade its separate area. Those who sold oatmeal and flour were given the steps of the High Cross to display their wares, but were forbidden to bring any stools and vessels to encumber the streets. Also standing by the High Cross with free passage carefully marked out between them, were merchants selling butter, cheese and bacon. (The High Cross was considered an essential city landmark, and when it was accidentally broken at the beginning of the century, it was repaired as a matter of course.) Breadsellers with their 'clifes' or giant baskets, were banished to the walls of St Michael's Church. Timber merchants and those who sold earthenware were allocated St Thomas Street and St Michael's Lane. Those selling herbs and rushes, which were still strewn on the floors of houses, were not allowed into the city on Sundays.

We do not know how well this system worked. A year after the departure of the Earl of Strafford the new order that he had ushered in collapsed as rebellion brought castastrophe. Dublin, a prime target for rebel forces, was never taken, although it narrowly escaped destruction. The religious preoccupations earlier in the century had not changed the city's basic isolation. The response of the Old English to the impetus of the Counter-Reformation had done little to bring them into closer sympathy with their Gaelic neighbours. After the rebellion a witness declared during his examination 'that he had heard many bitter words cast out against the city of Dublin, that they would burn and ruin it, destroy all records and monuments of the English government, make laws against speaking English, and that all names given by the English to places should be abolished and the ancient names restored'.

In October 1641 Dublin was in the charge of two Lords Justices in the absence of the Lord Deputy, the Earl of Leicester, who succeeded the executed Strafford but never bothered to come to Ireland. Plans for the city's capture involved separate attacks by picked men from Leinster and Ulster, timed to take place on a day when a public fair would cloak their activities. But the plot was betrayed by a drunken informer, Owen O'Connolly, who after drinking with his fellow conspirators in a tavern in Werburgh

Street, weaved his way by night to Chichester House, tenanted at the time by one of the Lords Justices, Sir John Borlase. Next morning there was a proclamation against 'the most disloyal and detestable conspiracy intended by some evil-minded Papists'. One of the ringleaders, Rory Q'More, escaped by rowing up-river to Islandbridge, from there making his way to the house of his daughter, married to a Sarsfield at Lucan. Two others were captured and hanged, Hugh MacMahon, found in his lodgings, and Lord Maguire, hiding in a cockloft in Cook Street. For the next 200 years a special service was held on October 22 in adjacent St Audoen's which commemorated the anniversary of Lord Maguire's arrest. As in services in other city churches, a sermon was preached 'describing in lurid manner the Papist orgies of blood in 1641'. At midnight the bells would ring out in thanksgiving.

The uprising spread quickly to other parts of Ireland. Dublin not only had to carry the financial burden of war against the rebels, but became the chief sanctuary of uprooted Protestant settlers who came pouring in from all over the Pale and from as far away as Ulster. Propaganda made the most of their sufferings. For many years pamphlets would be published with the purpose of inflaming Protestant opinion by high-lighting grizzly details: 'Sir Patrick Dunstan's wife was ravished and the unfortunate gentleman slowly cut to pieces...they cut off his ears and nose, teared off both his cheeks, after cut off his arms and legs, cut out his tongue and after ran a red-hot iron through him...' In 1646 the partisan Sir John Temple, son of a Provost of Trinity, published his bigoted *History of the Rebellion* which is regarded as having contributed to subsequent English attitudes. But Temple's eye witness account of life in Dublin in 1642 is vivid and undoubtedly accurate. He noted the miserable condition of the refugees: 'Many persons of high quality covered over with old rags – mothers with their children, ministers and others that had escaped with their lives, sorely wounded – all frozen up with cold, ready to give up the ghost in the street'. He described how 'many empty houses in the city were taken up for them, barns, stables and outhouses filled with them; yet many lay in the streets and others under stalls and there miserably perished'. A certain number was quartered on citizens, while others received help from the Marchioness of Ormonde, herself a refugee from Waterford. An attestation in the Ormonde papers tells how at Skinners' Row or St Mary's she 'did constantly relieve to the uttermost the many distressed English children' and took over the perpetual charge of 'twelve poor distressed English children'.

The authorities devoted their energies to protective measures and the persecution of Papists. The Records were brought to Cork House. Assessments were ordered to provide fire, lanterns, candlelight and other necessaries for the courts of guard in the city and suburbs. Loyal citizens were commanded to bring in their plate to be minted for the services of the government – an expedient that raised £2,000. There was little that could be done about 'the crazy old walls,' which as usual had been neglected during the long period of peace. Part of them fell down during the time of greatest panic when people from the suburbs added to the flow of refugees. Many decided that rather than stay in an undefended city they would escape by boat 'in such a dismal stormy season as in the memory of man had ever been observed'. Catholics were disarmed, expelled and occasionally put to the torture at the Castle in order to try and implicate King Charles in the uprising. Priests were sought out and imprisoned and books were kept with the names of 'masters of families as servants that are Papists'. The zealous Parliamentarian, Sir Charles Coote, commander of the Dublin garrison, was 'so violent in his fury that as a rule he was quite beside himself with rage'. Incidents like the burning of Clontarf and the throwing overboard of fifty-six men, women and children who had fled in boats off Bullock, encouraged the Catholic lords of the Pale to join the rebellion and besiege the city. The ensuing famine nearly brought defeat, but relief came from England in time.

For the next six years in varying confrontations between Parliamentarians, Royalists, Government, Confederate and Irish forces, Dublin was seldom free from threats of starvation and massacre. Contemporary accounts give glimpses of the stages of various sieges – the traditional destruction of houses built beside the walls, the moment in 1643 when Ormonde was told of 'nothing being left but a very little biscuit', the scene where the energetic Marchioness and other ladies carried up baskets of earth to repair the walls (during which operation a Viking burial mound on College Green was torn down), the weary reluctance of citizens to care for additional troops, since, according to their petition, 'they were impoverished through work at the trenches, decay of trade, many were pauperized by the pulling down of houses and by the number of soldiers and refugees quartered on them and their

families'. But soldiers were a necessary evil. There came a time
when sightseers looking from the spire of St Audoen's as their
forebears had done during the Bruce invasion, could make out 200
fires started by the army of Owen Roe O'Neill blazing from
Castleknock to Howth.

Many Dubliners were Royalists, but after Ormonde surrendered
to the Parliamentarians in July 1647, they accepted Parliamentary
rule under protest. When King Charles was executed in January
1649, the course of war took a different turn as Ormonde joined
the confederacy. The pressure on Dublin was only relieved by the
outcome of the Battle of Rathmines between Parliamentary troops
and the allied Royalist and Confederate Irish forces under
Ormonde. In the summer of 1649 Ormonde suddenly found that he
had to capture Dublin before Cromwell, waiting in Wales for a fair
wind, brought over reinforcements. He advanced to Finglas,
crossed the Liffey and camped at Rathmines. Rathfarnham Castle
was taken and the city's water supply cut off at Templeogue,
depriving the corn mills of power and yet again bringing the
besieged a step nearer starvation. The disposition of Ormonde's
forces deprived Parliamentary cavalry horses of pasture in fields at
St Stephen's Green and the meadows between Trinity and the
mouth of the Dodder. The Confederates hoped to take the
Parliamentary outpost of Baggotrath Castle which stood where
Waterloo Road now meets Baggot Street. But the Parliamentary
leader, Colonel Michael Jones, helped by a traitor, surprised and
routed them. Ormonde's luggage was captured, together with his
artillery and provisions. The captured confederate camp at
Rathmines was like a fair 'with cloth, silk and all manners of
clothes to be sold; and at Dublin the officers did not know their
own soldiers they were becoming so gallant, they had a good store
of wines which they drank in their hats, knocking out the heads of
the vessels'.

Cromwell heard the news at Milford Sound. 'This is an
astonishing mercy, so great and seasonable that indeed we are like
them that dreamed.' The crossing to Ireland with a fleet of thirty-
five ships was stormy and he was very seasick. On 15 August,
having made his way to Dublin from Ringsend, he was 'most
heroically entertained with a resounding echo of the great guns
around the city'. He addressed a big crowd, standing graciously
with a hat in his hand and saying that 'as God had brought him

thither in safety, so he doubted not but by His divine providence to restore them all to their just liberty and property'. He soon tired of all the rejoicing, and on 23 August issued a second pronouncement. The people of Dublin, rescued from the usages of a bloody enemy, were forbidden to indulge in 'profaning, swearing, drinking, cursing, which were said to be daily practice of the place'. On 31 August he set out to sack Drogheda.

Although Dublin was the only major town in Ireland to have escaped capture throughout the period of war, it suffered great damage. Among the buildings gone to ruin was Ogilby's theatre, converted into stables, 'spoyled and a cowhouse made of the stage'. From the *Calendar of Rolls* we learn of the neglect that made 'the streets in default of scavengers most foully kept, the toll of the market neglected – which used to be worth £150 a year'. There were countless 'hucksters', unofficial street traders desperately trying to make a living, brewers' carts were breaking up the paving, and the walls were broken down. In 1649 the House of Commons was without a carpet, and it was suggested that a fine of £3 imposed on a defaulter named John Betson, or some other fine, might be used to get a new one.

In 1644 a French visitor, the Sieur de la Boulaye le Gouz, had estimated Dublin to be the size of the French town of Angers with a population of between twenty and thirty thousand. At that time, during Ormonde's viceroyalty, it would have been swollen with refugees. In 1650, as if to bring the population more in line with the rest of the country, where a third of the people are said to have perished in ten years, Dublin was stricken with plague. During previous outbreaks people had fled into the countryside, but now the ravaged land could not support them. By the end of the first year something like 16,000 people, weakened by years of malnutrition, are said to have died in 'the great mortality'. William Petty thought that at the peak of the epidemic, the final one to strike Dublin and the worst since the Black Death, 1,300 died in a week. The ghost town was, according to the Common Council, 'exceedingly depopulated, at least one half of the number of houses pulled down and destroyed'. A few years later the census of 1659, the first in Ireland, showed that even after a period of recovery the number of citizens was comparatively small. The total population of Dublin was given as 8,780 of whom 5,459 were styled as English and 2,221 as Irish. The ravages of war were felt throughout the fifties; a tax had to be raised to pay for the relief of the destitute. Provost Winter of Trinity distributed quantities of white bread – a foretaste of famine soup – to those who listened to his sermons. During the rebellion well-fed wolves had flourished, so that in 1652 a public wolf hunt was organized as close to the city as the Barony of Castleknock.

In spite of hardships regeneration was vigorous. Ireland had two commonwealth governors, General Charles Fleetwood and Henry Cromwell, son of Oliver Cromwell, who kept great state at the Phoenix, a lodge on the crown lands at Kilmainham, indulging in his passion for falcons and hunting dogs. The newly created Common Council encouraged men of the trading and mercantile class to come over from England and settle with the status of freemen. Once again the lists of freemen had new English names – Robert Taylor, Gabriel Jones, Edward Whitehead. In 1649 the ceremony of Riding the Fringes was revived after a ten year gap. The suppression of provincial government in Munster and Connaught bolstered Dublin, and the period when it was ruled by a Commonwealth Government laid the foundation for Restoration prosperity.

With peace there was time for the continuation of the educational and cultural progress which had lapsed during the wars. The 'Lord Protector's School' which the government hoped to found never materialized, but the Free School was supported by the Corporation, and William Hill's famous school, founded in 1656, also promoted the Protestant faith. The University, which had been left 'destitute of fellows and students' after the plague which killed Provost Martin, revived under the Puritan Provost, Dr Winter. The emphasis was 'to build up one another in the knowledge and fear of the Lord and diligently to attend public prayer'. Five new professors were appointed in Divinity, Civil Law, Physics, Mathematics and Oratory and Rhetoric. An important new faculty was the 'Fraternity' of Physicians established by Dr John Stearne, great nephew of Archbishop Ussher. One of the original associates was William Petty, who had come to Ireland in 1653 as a doctor in the Parliamentary army. Among Petty's many preoccupations was membership of the Hartlib Circle, a group of savants who made important scientific enquiries into subjects ranging from mathematics to astronomy. Members included the Boate brothers Arnold and Gerard, whose enthusiasms and scientific interests influenced many of their associates, including Robert Boyle.

Petty's medical practice in the city was valued at £1,600 a year. At the same time he was carrying out his famous Downe Survey of forfeited lands which he completed in just thirteen months. Later he was involved in the redistribution of these lands, working in the house in Crow Street known as the Crow's Nest. He disliked his work, not for ethical reasons, but because it turned him into a frustrated civil servant with the 'daily direction of nearly forty clerks and calculators... and giving answers as well to impertinent questions...'

Oliver Cromwell had received an enthusiastic reception because he had been cheered into a Protestant city. Ormonde's departure in 1647 had initiated a pogrom in which Catholics were expelled. In 1651 Colonel John Hewson observed that Dublin had formerly swarmed with Papists, but now 'I know none there but one who is a surgeon and a peaceable man'. The policy of expulsion continued under the Commonwealth. An edict of 1650 declared that 'all Papists are to be turned out of this city; and for the Jesuits, priests, friars, monks and nuns, £20 will be given to anyone that can bring certain intelligence where any of them are'. A few priests took on disguise, but Catholics who stayed risked death, like Edward Hetherington who was tried by court martial in St Patrick's Cathedral in 1655 and hanged with placards on his breast and back which read: 'for not transplanting'. However, nothing could keep people from outside coming into the city, and edicts forbidding them to approach within two miles of any walled town or garrison soon proved impracticable. For a time they were registered – name, age, and appearance were noted – and issued with licences that allowed them to stay in the city up to twenty days. But such policies proved ineffective. In October 1656 there were instructions that 'all Popish shoemakers to be searched for by the Mayor and Sheriffs of Dublin and not to be allowed to inhabit Dublin and its suburbs'. Six months later Protestant coopers complained that Irish coopers were still present in the city. By then ancient complaints were being repeated in the Assembly Rolls which noted that 'there is Irish commonlie and usuallie spoken and the Irish Habbit worne not onlye in the streetes and by such as live in the countrie and come to this cittie... which is highly provoking of God which may justly cause the plague and other judgements to seize upon this cittie'.

Quakers were also persecuted from the time their meetings were first held in 1655 in the house of a tailor named George Lathan. Many were imprisoned like John Perrot who in 1656 wrote from his prison in Dublin to Henry Cromwell complaining of 'my share of suffering and persecution I have & doe under goe as well by beating, threatenings and Cruell mockings & scoffings as by imprisonment & tryalls and hallings before Rulers and Magistrates but all being for the Lord's sake'. His pleas did him little good; later he suffered another spell of imprisonment in the 'Common Gaole of the fower Courtes, Dublin'. It was Henry Cromwell who first advocated sending undesirables as slaves to Jamaica. In 1659 instructions were given to beadles and constables 'to imprison all beggars, idle women and maidens sellinge apples and oranges, and all regraters, all idle boys. . .others trafficked in eggs, hens and various commodities'. They were enclosed in a large cage in the Cornmarket for examination and punishment – in many cases deportation to the West Indian plantations.

7
The Restoration to the end
of the Seventeenth Century
1662–1700

The Duke of Ormonde, who inspired the flowering of Restoration Dublin, returned in July 1662. King Charles II's new viceroy, the best known and most generally loved Irishman of his day, now fifty-two years old, landed at Howth and spent the first night of his return at Howth Castle. On 27 July 1662, the fifteenth anniversary of the day he had surrendered Dublin to Colonel Jones, he was met by a cheering crowd which included old Dubliners from the Pale, Catholics hoping for a better way of life and cruel old Parliamentarians like Lord Broghill and Sir Charles Coote. 'The joy of the city was continued by the plenty of wine that was given in the streets, the ringing of bells, bonfires and several fireworks...'

His arrival initiated the transformation of the city. The development begun by Strafford had been a false dawn. The Commonwealth had contributed to Dublin's revival, but Ormonde's viceroyalty was decisive for its sudden very rapid growth. This can clearly be seen in a map published by Thomas Phillips in 1685, the year of Ormonde's dismissal, which shows the vast changes that had taken place since Speed's map of 1610. Dublin had spilt over its walls, and was now being embellished with numerous new public and private buildings 'raised for beauty as well as for use'. They included the 'Blew Coat Boys' Hospital' on Oxmantown Green, a long building with a clock tower and elaborate gateway. The Royal Hospital for the accommodation of old soldiers was erected between 1680 and 1694. The Tholsel, long neglected, was rebuilt. St Audoen's underwent one of its reconstructions, while Trinity acquired a new front hall and chapel. St Patrick's gained a new roof, completed in 1671, containing forty tons of oak donated by the Earl of Strafford's son from his lands in Wicklow. Both cathedrals received new bells, six for Christ Church, first rung on Saturday 30 July 1670 and eight for St Patrick's, first rung on Friday 23 September 1670.

We can follow the outline of Restoration Dublin in a legacy of street names: Anglesea Street, Jervis Street, Capel Street, Coghill Court, Fownes Street, Ormond Quay, Temple Lane, Temple Bar

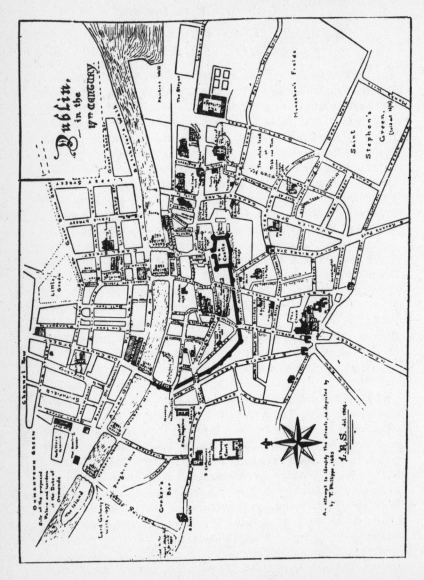

* Dublin in 1685. Reconstructed by Leonard Strangways from T. Phillip's map.

and numerous others. Along them scores of brick houses containing large windows and spacious rooms, their foundations laid on the debris of the medieval city, were replacing old timber and plaster edifices. There were new buildings in the Coombe, in the warren of back streets leading down to the river, and along Dame Street between Trinity College and the Parliament at Chichester House. New houses in Essex Street had overhanging summer houses built on the river bank so that residents could enjoy the sight of boats going up and down. After 1684 proper quays appeared along the river; the work proceeded unevenly since different sections of the bank were in the charge of different contractors. The first land speculators appeared. A new chunk of building land materialized in 1663 when Mr Hawkins built a sea wall along the river from modern Townsend Street to Burgh Quay. It was not always effective; during a storm of 1670 the tide flowed right over it and up to Trinity. Building sites became available when the land around Stephen's Green and Oxmantown Green on the southern and northern outskirts was apportioned to speculators by lot by the City Assembly, always short of money. Seventeen acres of Stephen's Green was 'set to the advantage of the city' to become a park, while round their edges on the west and east sides were eighteen and fifteen lots respectively. On the north and south sides thirty-three and twenty-four sites were measured out. William Petty took one on the north side. His son's title, Earl of Shelburne (in Wexford) spelt a little differently, would be borne by the hotel which would rise on the foundations of his old residence. The Assembly Rolls for August 1664, stipulated 'the fines for each lease to be applied in walling in and paving the Green for the ornament and pleasure of the city'.

Oxmantown Green was similarly divided up with room reserved for Ormond Market, the Blew Coat School and a highway. It had long been in use as a site for civic festivals and a mustering ground for regiments quartered in the city, and before the Puritans were in charge had boasted a maypole. Now it became a fashionable suburb on the north side of the river as Capel Street and Mary Street were created, attracting consequential citizens like Hercules Langrishe, Lord Dungannon and Lord Massereene to take up residence a river's span away from the crowds on the south side. By 1697 the north side needed two new parishes. St Paul's and St Mary's were formed from the western and eastern parts of St

Michan's which had been the only Dublin parish north of the river
for 600 years. Capel Street was linked to the rest of the city by
Essex Street Bridge, the most important of the five bridges that
now spanned the Liffey, and the work of Sir Humphrey Jervis,
Dublin's first acknowledged 'improver'. Jervis was also responsible
for much of the development of the Quays and for Ormond market
to which the butchers were pressed to take their trade. Further west
Smithfield Market, whose usefulness has only just come to an end,
was founded in 1665 for the sale of hay, straw, sheep, cattle and
pigs.

Ormonde, who had directly encouraged the development of the
north side, also played his part in the salvation of the vast open
space to the north-west, an area far larger than the total acreage
covered by the city. Its Irish name of Fionn Uisce (Bright Waters)
had long been anglicized to Phoenix. This land once belonging to
the Knights Hospitallers had been in the possession of the crown
since the Dissolution, and was designated a royal deer park in the
gift of Charles II. After he was dissuaded from presenting the green
acres to his mistress, Barbara Villiers, the park, greatly enlarged
through the energies of Ormonde, reverted to the city.

The changes resulted in the gradual destruction of old
landmarks. Throughout Dublin's history, whenever there were
periods of peace, the city wall had been considered a nuisance, and
breaches in it had always been a serious problem of defence. Now
people living in its vicinity burrowed away at its stones to enlarge
their properties, although it was never systematically done away
with. Portions of it survive today. Towers came down, like Isolde's
Tower which was replaced by Essex Gate. The Blind Gate beside
the Castle, described as 'wholly useless, no ornament to the city'
was demolished. The massive size of the Thingmote had ensured its
long survival. However, by 1681 the unenclosed land on College
Green on which it stood had passed out of public ownership into
the possession of the City Recorder, Sir William Davis, who
painstakingly levelled it in order to enlarge his property by St
Andrew's Church. The mass of earth was carted over to Nassau
Street, then known as St Patrick's Well Lane, a thoroughfare that
had been subject to flooding. Now it was safely raised by eight or
ten feet, a plateau still to be seen if the height of Nassau Street is
compared to College Park. Another Viking remnant that got
shifted was the Steyne which stood for at least seven years after the

erection of Hawkins' wall. How and why it was knocked over is not recorded; it was last seen lying against the College railings before it disappeared.

The background to development and change was expanded trade. Around 1660 the most important exports had been live sheep and cattle sent to England. When the Cattle Acts of 1663-1667, brought about by English breeders, smartly put an end to that trade, the wool and linen trades gained momentum. Among linen merchants Jervis Yeats, ancestor of the poet, W.B. Yeats, presumed an immigrant from Yorkshire, ran a wholesale linen business which was exempted from certain duties by the Irish Parliament. In addition to trade with England, continental markets provided outlets for Irish goods which were mostly old standbys like tallow, butter, beef, mutton, friezes, staves and fish. For a time shipping was interrupted by the French and Dutch wars of 1665 and 1672, particularly the last, when Dutch privateers hovered outside Dublin Bay to prey on ships entering and leaving port. But these wars were interludes in an era that was marked by a previously unmatched period of sustained prosperity.

The Mayor had increased importance after the title was dignified by the prefix Lord in 1665. (The new title was actually created in 1641, but not adopted for twenty-four years.) King Charles further recognized the importance of Dublin by presenting the Lord Mayor, who received a substantial salary of £500 a year for a job which was virtually that of a city manager, with a gold chain of office and a company of foot guards. Among the most grandiose new houses was the 'elegant building' at the entrance to Fishamble and Castle Streets erected by the first Lord Mayor, Sir Daniel Bellingham. According to the Hearth Money returns it had ten hearths.

The population was growing until it would soon nearly double as dispossessed landowners, their tenants, younger sons, artisans and merchants from the provinces moved in. An Act To Encourage Protestant Strangers to Settle in Ireland was passed in 1662. Included in a new flow of immigrants were Dublin's first Jews who came as refugees from Tenerife where the Inquisition was persecuting them. They were known as 'foreign Protestants' like the Dutch who would come in the train of King William, and the Huguenots, who had begun to arrive in Strafford's time, but poured in after the revocation of the Edict of Nantes in 1685. Most

Huguenots settled in the Coombe, where they helped to establish the weaving and linen industries, forming their own guilds. They have been credited with designing the terraced houses known as Dutch Billies which were once a distinctive feature of the Coombe with their roof ridges running at right angles to the streets and gabled fronts concealed by curved quadrants. Among the first Huguenots admitted to the city franchise were an apothecary, a baker, a chandler, four curriers, three periwig makers, a sail maker, a surgeon, six weavers, and three wool combers.

The Frenchmen were horrified at the number of Catholics they found living in Dublin. 'They are more than half the population' a certain Monsieur de Fontaine observed indignantly, 'and there are quantities of friars and Jesuits'. He was threatened with burning by a Catholic doctor. 'He says that he knows I have come to hunt them out, bring in Huguenots instead, and that I was a pernicious Huguenot of Rochelle...'

Encouraged by Ormonde's toleration, many Catholics sought to better themselves in the city. However, the returns of the Hearth Money roll for 1664 indicate that most of them lived in humble circumstances. (The Hearth Money tax was introduced in 1662.) The majority of householders with two or more hearths had non-Gaelic names. At that time, before the new building schemes the better-off were concentrated in St Audoen's Parish and St John's Parish. Some householders had a good many hearths – Lord Dungannon in Church Street ten, his neighbour, Lord Massereene fifteen, the Earl of Carlingford in Winetavern Street fourteen, Lord Ranelagh in Dame Street sixteen, and Lord Primate of Ireland and the Earl of Anglesey, both on College Green ten and twelve hearths respectively. Of sixty-nine Kellys listed in the 1664 roll, sixty-eight had only one hearth; of sixty-three Byrnes sixty had one hearth; of forty-nine Doyles forty-eight had one hearth; and of thirty Connors all had one hearth.

Religious differences had not ceased to provide foundation for dissent. The Act of Settlement passed by Ormonde's first Parliament pleased no one. The public Remonstrance, drawn up by the Franciscan, Peter Walsh, with which Ormonde hoped to gain the loyalty of Catholics in return for the state's authority, was never accepted. Most Catholic landowners had been unable to repossess the property they had lost in the Rebellion. Soon the Popish Plot not only resulted in the death of Archbishop Talbot in

Dublin Castle and the execution of Oliver Plunket at Tyburn but reintroduced persecutions and restrictions. Those who contracted mixed marriages lost their civil rights. Guilds officially remained closed to Catholics, although Dublin was less rigid than cities like Limerick when it came to allowing Catholics to become freemen. This may have been because of Ormonde's influence, or merely because the additional fees were useful to an Assembly perpetually seeking for extra sources of money.

In addition to propensity for religious strife, Ormonde's Dublin continued to retain medieval inconveniences. There might be gracious new houses and squares planted with lines of trees, but the streets were as filthy as ever, and incapable of absorbing the clanking Restoration traffic. The difficulties posed by 'loose, idle and disordered persons who frequent the city and suburbs selling apples, nutmeg, sneezing salt, tobacco and other commodities' were old problems. A petition complained of the number of hucksters sitting under baulks and stalls 'so that coaches and carts could not well pass or turn'. Some beggars were issued with licences, an idea that Swift would endorse enthusiastically. The rest were thrown out or imprisoned. A suggestion by the enlightened Master of the House of Correction, Thomas Parkes, that 'they should be provided with more advantageous work like carding, spinning, knitting, rasping of logwood and beating of hemp' was ignored. Nor was the attitude towards the problem of street cleaning more progressive. While the task of removing garbage was leased out to private contractors, the streets would continue to be 'exceedingly foule and dirty for want of constant sweeping and cleansing'.

People were still familiar with that old fashioned decoration, a rebel's head stuck on a pole. In the *Calendar of State Papers* for the year 1667 there is a record of the assortment of heads sent up to Dublin and what became of them. A hanging committee decided where they were to go. Dudley Costello's originated in the west of Ireland: 'His Grace had ordered it to be put upon St James Gate which is upon that part of the town towards Connacht.' Violence took on forms which would become increasingly popular. Duelling would reach a frenzied pitch half a century or so later. Abduction, a singular Irish pastime, had already come into vogue with the snatching of a young girl named Mary Ware in February 1685 by one James Shirley who was disguised in a black periwig. Rioting was regular. A pretext like the execution of Colonel Blood's fellow conspirators in 1663 could provoke one. Volatile apprentices, performing the functions of dissent appropriated by university students today, ran amok frequently. Even during the traditional annual march to Cullenswood they could not be relied upon to desist from 'disturbances, disorders, debauches and other profanations...committed to dishonour of God or scandal of the Government.' (After the Williamite wars local patriotism took other forms and the Cullenswood march finally ceased.) The apprentices' most famous riot took place in 1671 when they attacked the unfinished wooden bridge that was planned to link Usher's Quay to Oxmantown. Thirty of them were arrested; a few days later when they were being escorted away, thee men were killed by soldiers in an attempt to rescue them. The bridge became known as Bloody Bridge.

To go out and obtain a house in the suburbs was an adventure to be undertaken by the rich and enterprising. Most citizens still preferred the cosy squalor of the old city with places like Skinners' Row which was almost dark, since the roofs of its jewellers' shops almost touched over its seventeen foot width. Signs of progress included several streets now properly paved with 'hard Wicklow granite'. The stenches of fish and meat had been transferred across the river. In 1687 an organized system of public lighting was introduced 'for the prevention of many mischiefs and inconveniences in the streets in the dark nights'. Each street was required to hang lanterns and candles from five o'clock to ten o'clock at night, 'the cost to be borne by citizens'. The social historian, Liam Cullen, has considered that this innovation, as much as the cutting down of the forests which was going on at the same time, marked the death of the medieval world. Another important development was 'a timber house in High Street with a large backside of garden plot reaching to Back Lane, now called the Post House'. (Later it was moved to Fishamble Street.) This post office, according to an early user, 'accommodates all persons with the convenience of keeping good correspondency...most commonly twice a week with any, even the remotest part of Ireland, at a charge of eight pence or twelve pence, which could not formerly be brought to pass under ten or twenty shillings, and that sometimes with so slow a dispatch as gave occasion many times of no small prejudice to the party concerned.' One of the reasons communication was so slow was the state of the roads which reduced travel to a crawl. A journey on the main route between Dublin and Limerick, a distance of 160 miles, took at least four days.

The Assembly Rolls are full of complaints about the deficient water supply with references to the citizens and merchants who used it – brewers, innkeepers, water carriers and house keepers. Again lack of money impeded efficiency. On one occasion a part of the city was without water for a whole year because of the wearing out of lead in an ancient conduit. In 1668 the Assembly borrowed £300 to pay for imported water pipes made of elm – they were too wide in diameter to take lead. Later after a water rate was introduced with specially appointed collectors and a surveyor to supervise the system, the distribution improved.

There was still no proper fire service, although the need was recognized. In 1670 'the Lord Lieutenant, having charged the present Lord Mayor to take care that the city be provided with engines etc. to quench fire in time of danger, the Lord Mayor is empowered to treat with such persons as shall propose to make such engines.' But the Lord Mayor and his successors were lax, for in 1705 a Commons petition noted that 'the city is very much enlarged and in great danger from fire for want of engines etc, and fit persons to make use of the same'. In addition to old houses of timber and plaster, there were many thatched dwellings and cabins; a proclamation of 1670 forbade any more to be built, even in the suburbs, because of the danger of fire. An 'engine' consisted of a pair of plunger pumps dragged on a sled or on small, usually solid wheels. Below the pumps was a cistern that had to be filled by buckets. Water was directed through a swivelling goosenecked branch pipe in a series of pulsations as each pump plunger made its delivery stroke. Not until 1711 was there a co-ordinated fire service; the Assembly Rolls have an entry: 'Ordered...on the petition of John Oates, water engine maker, that he...be allowed six pounds per annum...to keep the water engine belonging to the city and that...he cause six men...at his own expense...to play on the said engine, and on any extraordinary accident of fire to have twelve men or more in readiness.'

No organized fire fighting could have done much about the fire which nearly blew Dublin Castle to bits, together with part of the city. Ormonde's son, Lord Arran, prevented the flames from reaching the powder magazine, so that the only loss was Ormonde's furniture which must have included items from an inventory of goods made in the Castle in 1678: 'a four poster bedstead, turkey carpets, chamber pot and basin...one large silver looking glass, taffeta curtains, a new table covered with Spanish leather...' Silver and Spanish leather and the mounted guards outside the Castle marking Ormonde's comings and goings with long tattoos of drums did not make the great fortress a congenial residence. Ormonde's biographer, Thomas Carte, called it 'a miserable place and scarce afforded any accommodation'. This was in spite of its self-contained community working in the kitchen, wash-houses, mill and a 'room for the sick'. The brigade of servants lived in dismal circumstances. 'Eight boy scullions had only four beds between them and two scavengers in the dark kitchens had no beds at all.' Although duty forced Ormonde to have a base at the Castle, he understandably preferred to live elsewhere, first in Henry Cromwell's hunting lodge, then in a house at Chapelizod where the gardens sloping down to the river were, according to his successor Lord Clarendon, particularly fertile, growing excellent asparagus.

The journey of Lord Clarendon and his wife to Ireland emphasized the isolation of Dublin from London and the difficulties undergone by travellers. The great route through Wales was in such a state that the fourteen miles between St Asaph and Conway took five hours. Between Conway and Beaumaris he had to walk, while his lady was carried on a litter. Sometimes a carriage had to be taken to pieces at Conway and carried to the Menai Straits on porters' shoulders round the dangerous cliffs of Penmaenmawr. At the coast there were often further delays. Robert Leigh, stranded at Holyhead in November 1669, wrote piteously how 'I am still at this comfortless place...the wind is unfavourable...and the weather very stormy and foul...several ships are here...two packet boats, a ship laden with powder for Ireland and the Lord Lt's yack [sic]...no passage has been made for three weeks.'

Even after the crossing was completed the old difficulty of getting up the river to the city often caused further delays. Sir Bernard de Gomme's chart of 1673, the earliest chart of Dublin Bay, clearly shows the shallowness of the water and the exposed nature of the anchorage outside the 'barr' or sandbank lying across the mouth of the river. Although it was 'not drey at lewe water' –

ᴊeing covered to a depth of about six feet – ships could only go over safely at high tide, after which they hurried to specific anchorages at 'Iron Poole' 'Clantarfe Poole' and 'Salmon Poole' just below Ringsend. Anywhere else dried out. Waiting for the tide, they risked shipwreck tossing about in exposed Dublin Bay. It needed another high tide to get from Ringsend or from one of the designated anchorages to the Custom House. Just as they had been in the Middle Ages, ships were reluctant to make the last stage of the journey. A petition of the Lord Mayor and Corporation to the Irish House of Commons in 1698 complained that 'the river is choked up by gravel and sand...and ash thrown in and by taking ballast from the banks below Ringsend, whereby the usual anchoring places...are now becoming so shallow that no number of ships can with safety bide there...much merchandize being unloaded at Ringsend and then carried to Dublin.'

The majority of passengers disembarked at Ringsend. From there they were taken in a rickety vehicle known as a Ringsend Car across the sands towards Townsend Street, first referred to as such during the 1670s. Travellers included Thomas Dineley, author of the famous illustrated *Itinerary* of Ireland, and the Frenchman, Jonvin de Rochfort, who in 1666 rather surprisingly estimated Dublin as 'one of the greatest and best peopled towns in Europe'. Neither of these visitors gave more than a passing glance at the city. A more comprehensive impression of Dublin at this period is given by the bookseller, John Dunton, who came over from England in April 1698 to promote his wares. His letters, which have been edited by Edward MacLysaght, were written a few years after the Williamite victory, and give a vivid idea of the metropolis that was the result of Ormonde's nurturing.

In 1667 a Frenchman, René Mezandière, managed to obtain a virtual monopoly of public transport, after stressing in his petition the lack of coaches and sedan chairs for hire 'to supply and accommodate ladies and other persons of quality either for journeys into the country or to the seaside from Dublin'. However, vehicles to and from Ringsend remained independent, and it was estimated that their drivers collectively earned at least £500 a year. Dunton took a Ringsend Car. 'I saw a large strand, yet twas not be walked over because of a pretty rapid stream which must be crossed'. When he reached Lazy Hill, the name given to the south side of Townsend Street, recalling the medieval Hospice that stood on its site – he paid his driver three halfpence for the journey.

A petition of 1684 against the removal of the courts of justice to the north side of the river mentioned that the majority of houses on the south side 'were set to such as either set lodgings to preachers, solicitors or suitors or kept taverns or ale houses for supply of them'. The petitioners feared that 'if the courts be removed the heart of the city be left destitute'. However, innumerable inns continued to flourish south of the river, some of them providing accommodation for visitors, while more select lodgings were also available like the alternatives mentioned by Arthur Podmore to his friend, Henry Gascoigne in 1677. 'Choice of lodgings are to be had, but few that will also provide diet. The most convenient place I have yet met is in Bride Street at one Mr Gibbs, a gentleman, and a very neat house with a garden that stands well for air, besides the convenience of having no children...Mr Wormington has a fair brick house with good rooms in St Nicholas Street...the back has a way to the city wall and the view and air of several houses adjoining.' Twenty years later Dunton, after a short stay with a lawyer in Winetavern Street, moved across the river to Arbour Hill where his landlords were an elderly couple 'like Adam and Eve in Paradise'.

He was an assiduous tourist who made it his business to see everything the city had to offer. He visited Trinity, the Parliament at Chichester House, and inspected the Liberties crowded with Huguenots, 'brawny weavers and tradesmen'. He went to the Royal Hospital which when it was opened in 1685 on a piece of land once belonging to the Knights Hospitallers, had been described by William Molyneux as 'a most stately and beautiful piece of building perhaps as Christendom affords'. The tower was not built until after Dunton's visit; a bell would be installed in it known as the Old Cow of Kilmainham whose deep note would carry on a fair wind as far as Howth.

At the Blew Coat School Dunton saw the boys in their distinctive blue coats lined with yellow calling attention to an exercise in private charity. Public charity was still minimal and more or less confined to a few Protestant widows or people like 'Thomas Jones, being an ancient inhabitant of this cittie...ninety-six years old...blind and in deplorable condition shall be allowed five pounds yearly'. In 1688 the Assembly considered the erection of a workhouse for Dublin's poor, but the project was interrupted by war and postponed until 1703. In 1669 the Guild of the Holy Trinity had subscribed to the erection on Oxmantown Green of a hospital 'for the poor and aged as well as men and women and the fatherless and motherless children that have not friends nor estates to live upon'. Ultimately, the charity of the Guild was limited to 'the education and support of the children of Freemen, none of whom shall be admitted who were under three feet nine inches in height, or were lame, deformed or afflicted with any infectious diseases'.

In spite of the many new buildings Dublin was still countrified. There were large gardens behind many houses, and fields elsewhere like the 'great meadows' by the side of the river that Jonvin noted at Oxmantown. Dunton mentions the biggest haystacks he ever saw standing beside the Poddle. The Castle had gardens, terraced walks, lines of flowerpots and rows of flourishing lime trees. He climbed the tower of the Tholsel, from where he gained a view out across the rooftops to the open sea. This building, rebuilt and completed about 1682, contained the municipal courts, halls for city assemblies, guild room and public exchange which boasted a clock; in 1687 a widow named Ruth Wittan had the job of winding the city clocks, including this one, for a salary of £4 a year.

Dunton gives the impression of a lively society, well provided with amusements and opportunities for pleasure. There was the racquet court at St John's Lane, which would have been enclosed like a modern badminton court, and bowling alleys in College Green and near Wood Quay. Another splendid bowling alley at Oxmantown had its own banqueting chamber, while its garden walks were planted with sycamores and elms along a stretch of river. Inns included the Swan, the Feathers, the London Tavern, the Bull's Head, the Fleece, the Bear and Ragged Staff and the White Hart where Colonel Blood had dined the night before he tried to seize the Castle. A quarter of Dublin houses were said to be occupied by sellers of liquor. From exile in Rome the Reverend Francis O'Malley directed a Gaelic address to his countrymen in which he called Dublin 'the city of the wine flasks'. Gilbert gives a figure of 1,180 ale-houses and 91 public brew houses for this period. For the second time in the century the convenient vaults of Christ Church were turned into 'tippling houses and tobacco shops'.

The theatre was an attraction not to be missed. It represented part of the new vigour introduced into cultural and intellectual life.

The first Irish portrait painter, Garrett Morphy, had begun to paint bewigged Jacobites and their doe-eyed ladies. Ormonde was the natural successor to Strafford in his patronage of the arts and such institutions as the fashionable 'Society of Friends' founded by a formidable Welsh poetess and snob, Mrs Katherine Phillips. Members of the Society, mainly courtiers and friends of the Duke, addressed each other by neo-Classical names; Lady Dungannon was 'the excellent Lucasia', Ormonde's daughter 'the bright Policrite' and Mrs Phillips herself 'the matchless Orinda'. The same John Ogilby who had founded the New Theatre in Werburgh Street before the rebellion, opened a theatre in Smock Alley (today it is Lower Exchange Street) only three months after the departure of a Puritan government and Ormonde's return. The first recorded performance was of John Fletcher's *Wit without Money*. Smock Alley was frequently patronized by Ormonde who celebrated the marriage of William of Orange to Princess Mary by attending the theatre in state and inviting all the company to supper at the Castle afterwards.

The interior of Smock Alley originally contained rows of cloth-covered benches and three galleries, but in 1680 during a gala performance of Ben Jonson's *Bartholomew Fair* the galleries fell down, killing three people. When Dunton went there it consisted of a stage, pit, boxes, two new galleries, lattices and music loft, all well lit with lamps and candles. Although he did not think much of the theatre's location 'in a dirty lane and a place for making lewd bargains', he was impressed by the acting which he considered equal to anything to be seen in London. Three years after his visit part of the interior collapsed again and several members of an audience watching a performance of Shadwell's *Libertine* were killed. Seventeenth-century playgoers were a rugged lot and not permanently discouraged; Smock Alley soon reopened.

By the end of the century there was a well-established group of publishers and booksellers. The first Dublin newspaper, a weekly called *An Account of the Chief Occurrences of Ireland. Together with some Particulars from England*, had been produced in pre-Restoration times by William Bladen, official printer to Cromwell and Mayor of Dublin. It was succeeded by the *Mercurius Hibernicus or the Irish Intelligencer* which ran for a while in 1663 before folding. 'There is so little news to "stiff" the gazettes in Dublin that their publication has ceased' complained Sir Ellis

Leighton in 1671. In 1685 when political events made the news more lively, the *Dublin News-Letter* edited by Robert Thornton at the sign of the Leather Bottle in Skinners' Row came into being. It consisted of a single page written in the form of letters, one on the front, one on the back, each beginning with the vocative 'Sir:'. The government-produced *Dublin Gazette*, modelled on the *London Gazette* – the idea came from Venice where an official periodical was paid for with a coin called a *gazetta* – was first issued by James II around May 1689. Not a single copy from that period has survived, since documents relating to James were destroyed by his successors. Throughout William's reign the only official government publication in Britain and Ireland was the *London Gazette*. However, the *Dublin Gazette* made its reappearance in 1705, and has continued to disseminate official news twice a week ever since, although now it is called *Iris Oigigiuil*.

The first proper newspaper as we know them was *Pue's Occurrences* founded by Richard Pue in 1703 and published twice a week for seventy years. Pue was proprietor of Dick's Coffee-House, which had been converted from Carberie House, the old stately residence of the Earls of Kildare. The 1st Earl of Cork's Cork House had undergone a similar transformation to Lucas' Coffee-House. Such places were the locations for book auctions, a novelty in Ireland and very popular as social occasions tinged with excitement. Dunton used Dick's for a while to sell his books, but became dissatisfied and moved his business to Pratt's Coffee-House in High Street where, amid the chatter and chink of cups, he wrote his *Conversations in Ireland*. The booksellers he encountered he usually scorned, and it was his opinion that 'learning runs low in Ireland'. They included William Norman at the Rose and Crown in Dame Street, Nat Gunn 'a constant bidder at my auctions', and Eliphal Dobson from the Stationer's Arms in Castle Street 'whose wooden leg startled me with the creaking of it'.

Versatility among those associated with print was general. Early booksellers and stationers had numerous other lines, selling such diverse wares as funeral tickets – grim little invitations to funerals, adorned with skeletons, urns, Father Times, mourning coaches and weeping cherubs – maps, mezzotints, sheet music, musical instruments and 'superfine Black Lead pencils'. However in general shops were less specialized than they were to become later. For example an inventory of the possessions of a Quaker shopkeeper, Isachar Wilcocks, who died in 1694, gives an indication of the wide range of goods sold by a grocer. In addition to foodstuffs such as loaf sugar, spices, sugar candy, raisins, currants, ginger, oil, honey, treacle, vinegar and thirty-three barrels and a half of herrings, Mr Wilcocks had on offer thirty-six pounds of knitting needles, 'Snaffle Bitts', brimstone, three hundredweight of steel shot, gunpowder, billhooks, beeswax, paper, sealing wax, pins, tobacco and horn books.

Many booksellers were publishers, like Joseph Ray, the producer of *News-Letter* and the irascible John Whalley, whose religious opinions earned him a spell in the pillory during James II's stay in Dublin. In addition to producing a series of periodicals which ranted against Papists, Whalley published his highly successful Almanacks which were widely imitated and continued to be popular throughout the eighteenth century. Old Moore's still gives an idea of what they were like; according to a description in Hoey's *Dublin Journal* in 1730 they contained material on 'the Weather, Times, Seasons and Customs...remarkable days throughout the year...Royal Birthdays...Holy Days...Lucky and Unlucky Days...'

Among John Whalley's many sidelines was one as a lucrative compounder of quack medicines. However, a more serious interest in medicine and the sciences was developing. The first public dissection of a human corpse in Ireland was made by a Mr Patterson in 1684. Three years earlier Dr Allen Mullen managed to obtain portions of an unfortunate elephant for dissection. 'The booth wherein the elephant was kept took fire about three o'clock in the morning...multitudes were gathered...and when the fire was extinguished everyone endeavoured to procure some part of the elephant, few having seen him living.' Doctors of the day included William Petty and John Stearne, who after receiving one of the first medical degrees recorded at Trinity in 1662, went on to become Professor of Medicine and first President of the College of Physicians founded by Ormonde in 1667. The Scotsman, Sir Patrick Dun, who would have a hospital named after him a century after his death, was physician to the Williamite army. He had a pleasant bedside manner. 'On Monday last I sent from Dublin...two dozen bottles of the best claret...and two bottles of Chester ale', he wrote to General Ginkel in Connacht. '...I sent a lesser box of which there are a dozen and half potted chickens in an eartheren pot and in another pot fowre green geese. This is the physic I advise you to take.'

The Dublin Philosophical Society, a formalized Hartlib Circle, and predecessor of the Royal Dublin Society, was founded in 1683 by William Molyneux. William Petty became its first president. Members first met in a coffee-house, and then at the Crow's Nest where Petty had worked on the Down Survey. The building was now furnished with a laboratory, museum and botanic garden. At the first meeting in the new premises, Molyneux showed an experiment of viewing pictures in miniature with a telescope, Dr Huntingdon, the Provost of Trinity, read an account of the porphyry pillars of Egypt, and Dr Mullen, the elephant dissector, talked of experiments involving dogs, blood and rennet. Later papers read by Dr Mullen included *On poisons, Dissection of a monstrous Double Cat* and *Dissection of a Chicken with Two Bills*. The Philosophical Society continued meeting regularly until after 1686 when the troubles ensuing upon the succession of James II discouraged philosophical speculation. It did not disband permanently, but after it was reconvened in Trinity in 1693, it never achieved its former lustre.

On 6 February 1685 Charles II died and was succeeded by his Catholic brother, James. The momentous period of change was heralded by the recall of Ormonde. 'It was impossible to express the consternation which that event put all Ireland in' wrote a contemporary, 'and which appeared in every face when the Duke of Ormonde...left Dublin to go to England.' Apart from a gap of eight years, he had ruled in Dublin since 1662. His son, Lord Arran, succeeded him, but died suddenly, to be followed by the King's Protestant brother-in-law, the Earl of Clarendon. During Clarendon's indolent year in office there were few outward indications of approaching catastrophe. At the Smock Alley theatre the curtain call was advanced to four o'clock to accommodate gentlemen dining at taverns and coffee-houses. A newly popular pastime was attendance at the races in the country at the Curragh which was considered to be larger and finer than Newmarket Heath. Clarendon found Dublin 'a tattling town'. He loathed the Castle 'this pityful bit of a castle', and spent much of his time in Ireland trying to convince the Lord Treasurer in London that it was not worth the upkeep as a residence for the King's Representative. 'The reparations are very great...and it is the

worst and most inconvenient lodging in the world.' His brief
viceroyalty passed without incident, but there was apprehension.
Many Protestants had left Ireland with Ormonde, and now more
went with Clarendon. They feared his successor, Richard Talbot,
recently created Earl of Tyrconnell and brother of the Archbishop
who had died in the Castle, victim of the Popish plot. Under
Clarendon, Tyrconnell had been Lieutenant-General of the army in
Ireland, where he had replaced Protestant officers by Catholics.

For the first time since the Reformation the Catholics of Dublin
were on the ascendant. Although Tyrconnell protested that 'there
be no difference made between his Protestant and Roman Catholic
subjects in the city' he determined to favour the Old English of the
Pale and to change the Restoration Settlement. Protestant militia
were disbanded and Catholic judges and lawyers were admitted to
the City Council which ordered that the only oath necessary for
admission to the franchise was that of allegiance. Protestant
clergymen were not allowed to preach on controversial topics. The
Catholic Lord Mayor imprisoned two of the vergers of Christ
Church because 'they did not make the bells ring merrily enough
for the birth of the Prince of Wales'. When friars appeared in the
streets to be laughed at by boys, the Lord Mayor gave them armed
protection. During a further panic-stricken exodus from the city,
the Fellows of Trinity College tried to sell their plate on the English
market, but it was seized in Dublin harbour and put into the King's
stores.

Then William of Orange arrived in England and revolution
broke out. When Tyrconnell raised an army Dublin became filled
with undisciplined recruits from the country whose bad English was
scoffed at by citizens upon whom they were billeted.

In March 1689 King James landed at Kinsale, the first English
monarch to come to Ireland since Richard II. His entry into Dublin
on Palm Sunday, 24 March was an impressive public occasion. The
streets were freshly gravelled, hangings and flowers decorated every
window, musicians played and soldiers lined the procession. At the
city boundary James was met by the new Lord Mayor, Sir Michael
Creagh (whose Protestant faith was an indication of the King's
tolerance), and other dignitaries who presented him with the
freedom of the city while pipes played '*The King Enjoys his own
Again*'. Celebrations continued well into the night, 'the Papists
shouting, the soldiers' muskets discharging, the bells ringing, and

bonfires in all parts of the town'. James was seen to be in tears.

Soon things began to go sour. The Patriot Parliament, called from March to June 1689, proved a disappointment to the Catholic Irish, since although it repealed the Act of Settlement, the yardstick of confiscation was considered not to be religion, but loyalty to the King. Although James's advocacy of religious tolerance was centuries ahead of his time, Protestants became increasingly uneasy as they saw Mass celebrated in Christ Church, and Trinity transferred into a barracks and a prison for Protestants. Tyrconnell took over the Blew Coat School and 'turned out all the poor Blew boys... and sent their beds to the great hospital at Kilmainham for the use of wounded soldiers'. Later it was the turn of the pensioners, who were evicted from the Hospital with forty shillings each to make way for a garrison.

Then there was brass money for which James was long remembered. This was not altogether fair since brass money – which numismatists call gun money – was designed as a temporary expedient, and in any case the financial system had been chaotic for a long time. There were no banks until around 1675 when Hoare's Bank was started in Cork and similar institutions gradually developed in Dublin. Meanwhile banking was in the hands of brokers who were usually goldsmiths. They concentrated in the parish of St Werburgh, where they received deposits and issued their own notes which might be used locally. Between 1650 and 1679 traders throughout Ireland similarly issued their own tokens which were exchangeable for goods. Designs on Dublin tokens included a winged beast issued by Roger Bold of Skinners' Row, Arthur Harvey of High Street's three rabbits, the three cocks and three doves associated with Henry Aston, while Jacob Hudson's tokens bore the inscription 'Come'. After 1679, when heavy-weight copper halfpence were minted officially in England, the distribution of trade tokens ceased.

Since there was no mint, the official coinage was irregular. Foreign coins, both gold and silver, counterfeit and genuine, were in circulation. Pistoles, rix dollars, ducatoons, French Louis, Mexican pieces of eight and so forth were all viable pieces of money, their value determined by weight, a practice that made business slow. If money had to be transferred from one part of the country to another, it either had to be transported under guard or issued by bills of exchange and letters of credit guaranteed by rich men.

James's mints in Cork and at Capel Street in Dublin were the first in Ireland. The debased coinage they produced further muddled the money system. They melted down old cannons, broken bells and pots and pans, turning them into coins. Tin and pewter were used when brass bells became scarce. Shopkeepers who refused money from the Capel Street mint were threatened with hanging. After brass money, the coinage continued to be in disarray and Wood's halfpence did nothing to help. Throughout the eighteenth century there was a constant shortage of change. Publicans refused to serve strangers unless they could pay in small coins. The handling of large sums of money went on being a problem. When, during the 1750s, Mrs Bayly wanted to invest £200 in debentures at Dublin Castle, she had to take a sedan. 'Walked home, but the money was so heavy I could not walk going.'

A witness to James's stay in Dublin was William King, Dean of St Patrick's, who remained in the city and became effective ruler of the diocese. (Later he was Archbishop of Dublin.) He deplored the number of churches taken over and the fact that priests and friars 'multiplied in Dublin to three or four hundred at the least . . . there were not more lusty plump fellows in the town than they'. His journal noted how in February 1689 Protestants were deprived of arms when Tyrconnell commanded citizens to bring their 'swords, bayonets, firearms and others to the door of their respective churches, an occasion for looting by the soldiery detailed to ensure it was done'. At the approach of Schomberg's army Dr King was imprisoned in the wardrobe tower of Dublin Castle, where he and a number of other influential fellow citizens could look down on the courtyard and the rooftops of the city. They listened to rumours.

'August 23rd, 1689: There happened a scuffle in town between some Frenchmen and Irish soldiers, two of ye Irish were killed as reported. September 15th: Word was sent to me . . . the bells were forbidden to be rung and services prohibited in all churches by ye government. September 16th: The scholars were turned out of ye College . . . October 22nd: Mass was said in the College Chapel and the College Library delivered to Dr Moore and some Fryers and priests.' (Only the vigilance of this Catholic Provost, Dr Michael Moore, prevented the library's destruction during the occupation of the college.) 'I heard yre were no less than 12,000 men in Dublin armed. November 17th: The King went to Christ Church to Mass. November 18th: Some soldiers brought in about 38 prisoners into ye Castle yard said to be taken of ye enemy; but others said only 14 of them had bin soldiers, ye rest were poor country people. We observed several little boys about 12 or 14, one of ym was brought in a car being sick and dying, ye rest were tyed with hay or straw ropes to one another...'

Another diarist, the young English Jacobite, John Stevens, was in Dublin during the harsh winter of 1689-90. There was no coal, since the import of coal from England had been suspended, turf was too expensive for most people and the soldiers cut down the available trees. Food grew scarce. Stevens was billeted in Trinity, where he spent his endless spare time bewailing lost opportunities and the frolics of the court at the Castle where the king was trying to reconcile the differences between his English and Irish supporters. Stevens was disgusted by the drunkenness and loose living that he saw in Dublin, 'a seminary of vice, a living emblem of Sodom'. His namesake, Richard Steevens, the benefactor of Steevens' Hospital, also commented on the licentiousness of the period. 'Drunkenness was so easily procured that no liquors were strong enough, nor no days long enough to satiate some overhardened drunkards...the women were so suitable to the times that they rather enticed men to lewdness than carried the last face of modesty.' John Stevens' colonel Henry Fitzjames, a natural son of the king, spent his time 'in following the court, in walking the town...in drinking and such idle and foolish divertisements of youth'. The winter passed; on May 19th Stevens' regiment was reviewed by the King on Oxmantown Green. A little over two months later it was routed at the Boyne and made its way back to Dublin. 'I wonder that I outlived the miseries of this dismal day.'

During the battle the population of Dublin was confined to the city. Gates were closed and Protestants ordered to remain indoors which gave rise to ugly rumours that Tyrconnell intended to take many away as hostages. By five o'clock on the long summer's day they could watch the first stragglers from James's defeated army arriving outside the walls. Soon the streets were filled with exhausted soldiers. James came and went, fleeing through Bray to Waterford and France. On the morning of July 2nd Tyrconnell reached the city to find a state of confusion. Changes were swift; the garrison was withdrawn and Robert Fitzgerald, a son of the 16th Earl of Kildare, took over the Castle. He tried to protect the

Catholic minority whose shops and houses were beginning to be looted.

On July 4th a troop of dragoons from William's army came to take charge of the stores. In their joy people pulled the soldiers out of their saddles and hugged the horses. After camping at Finglas King William rode into Dublin on Sunday, July 6th, to hear a sermon preached by Dr King. A Protestant wrote how 'there was very great joy when we crept out of the houses and found ourselves as it were in a new world'. Another account tells how 'they ran about shouting and embracing one another and blessing God for his wonderful deliverance...the streets were filled with crowds and shouting and the poor Roman Catholics now lying in the same terrors as we had done some days before...'

8

Swift's Dublin 1700-1742

After the battle of the Boyne there was yet another spurt of immigration and more newcomers joined the earlier groups of Old English, Elizabethan, Cromwellian, Restoration and Huguenots. But the population, which rose during the first fifty years of the century to 130,000, was increasingly Catholic in its proportions. Not all Catholics were poor; in spite of formidable obstacles, the century saw the rise of a Catholic middle class as the laws that excluded them from government services and from the army encouraged many into business and trade. Not all Protestants were rich; many of the beggars to whom Swift gave money and who lived in the Liberty surrounding his cathedral were Huguenots ruined by the Trade Acts. But inevitably Catholics suffered a long period of oppression after the Treaty of Limerick in 1691 ensured the reversal of all their hopes. With the abolishment of the Patriot Parliament and the prohibition of Catholics entering Parliament at all went the last vestiges of toleration. The Penal Laws, said to be modelled on laws enacted against Huguenots in France, removed Catholics from every public office. During the period when they were most stringently applied, even the job of charwoman in the Tholsel was carefully given to a Protestant.

At the end of the war the celebrations of King William's triumphs must have seemed interminable. Impressive demonstrations of enthusiasm for the new order were climaxed with the opening of the new Parliament held in Chichester House in 1692 when a great procession wound its way through the city streets preceded by soldiers playing trumpets and kettledrums. Later the speaker congratulated the new Assembly on being 'the choicest collection of Protestant fruit that ever grew within the walls of the Commons House'. On 1 July 1701, as the usual guns were fired and food and drink distributed, a handsome brass equestrian statue of the Orange monarch by Grinling Gibbons was unveiled on College Green. Its main function was to be a pivot for Loyalists to parade around once a year with drums beating and colours flying, carrying green boughs and wearing orange cockades in their hats. Those who felt antipathy towards it included Trinity students who resented William having his back to their seat of learning. Among the first to insult it were two students, who in 1710 were obliged to stand beside it for half an hour wearing placards that stated: 'I stand here for defacing the statue of our glorious deliverer, the late King William.' In spite of protective railings and a little guardhouse, when it was not being decorated with orange lilies and flaming coat and sash, the statue was insulted, daubed, defaced and hacked at for the next two centuries until it was blown to pieces in 1929.

Drinking clubs were founded whose members drank the Orange toast, remembered battles and reviled brass money, wooden shoes, the Pope and the Bishop of Cork. In 1716 the Protestant Bishop Peter Browne had the temerity to attack this swiftly hallowed custom in his *Discourse on Drinking Healths* where he stated that not only was the practice of 'heathenish extraction', but imbibing 'in grateful and glorious rememberance is a sinful profanation of the Holy Eucharist'.

The disruption of the wars meant that the economy throughout Ireland suffered a setback, and in the capital the development initiated by the Restoration was muted and did not fully resume until around 1730. However Dublin continued to change and the destruction of the medieval city went on. Old streets were considered too narrow and projecting cagework houses were old fashioned and uncomfortable. The city walls with their towers continued to fall, and gates had become anachronisms, impeding traffic, as Thomas Pooley and Marmaduke Coghill stressed in their appeal in 1699 for the removal of Dame's Gate which had guarded Dublin's eastern approaches for so long. They pointed out that more people now lived outside the walls than within and that 'the gates of the city are of little use or security to it'. Gormond's Gate was demolished the same year.

New amenities included the great linen hall in Capel Street, opened in 1702; the linen trade increased in importance as the century advanced. New quays were completed by 1711 and a new water supply, stored in the 'city bason' began to flow in 1722. Surviving buildings dated to the first quarter of the century included Marmaduke Coghill's mansion at Drumcondra and the Presbyterian Church in Eustace Street. Half a dozen houses are scattered round the Liberties and Arbour Hill. We are fortunate in the preservation of Tailors' Hall in Back Lane, which was built for use by the guilds; when they did not need it it was let out for social functions, just as it is now since its recent restoration. The Mansion House, built in 1710, predating its equivalent in London by twenty years, remains the official Mayoral residence. Its builder, Joshua Dawson, sold it to the Corporation for £3,500, including in the price twenty-four brass locks, six chimney pieces, four pairs of scarlet calamanco curtains and chimney glass in the Dantzick oak parlour.

The two most successful architects of the period were Edward Lovett Pearce and Colonel Thomas Burgh, the Surveyor-General, both members of prominent Anglo-Irish families. In the late twenties they were joined by a German, Richard Castle or Cassels. Pearce's masterpiece was the Parliament House on College Green, begun in 1729 and later added to by James Gandon. Burgh was responsible for the Custom House on Burgh Quay, the revamped St Werburgh's, the library at Trinity, the design of Steeven's Hospital and the Royal Barracks. The central block of the Barracks – now Collins' Barracks – was put up in 1701 on the site of the property on Oxmantown Green that had been the Duke of Ormonde's 'reward' from the grateful city fathers. The concept of housing soldiers all together instead of billeting them on citizens or shutting them up in defensive castles was new. The system assisted parades, training and discipline; now offenders could be flogged in private.

None of the new buildings is more eloquent an architectural expression of the age than the little L-shaped Marsh's Library beside St Patrick's with its high pitched roof. Archbishop Narcissus Marsh was an immensely learned Provost of Trinity whose skills in languages led him to introduce the teaching of Irish into the university. In 1698 he became Archbishop of Dublin. Having observed that his official residence, the Palace of St Sepulchre, had no chapel or library attached to it, and considered which was the greater need, he commissioned the elderly William Robinson, designer of the Royal Hospital, who had preceded Burgh as Surveyor-General, to design his library. It was begun in 1701. At one time readers, although limited to 'all graduates and gentlemen', were locked into the cubicles with rods and chains.

The most important associations of the library are not with the cleric who built it and endowed it, whose portrait hangs over the door, but with his enemy. Jonathan Swift wrote of Marsh 'no man will be glad or sorry at his death except his successor'. Swift's death mask is here, together with a writing cabinet, the plain wooden table on which he is believed to have written the *Drapier's Letters* and *Gulliver's Travels*, and books he read. Clarendon's *History of the Grand Rebellion* has his angry pencilled notes about the Scots...'mad, treacherous, damnable and infernall'. Directly across the street from the library are the red brick walls of the Deanery, all that survives of the building destroyed by fire in 1781. The new Deanery contains Francis Bindon's portrait in old age of its most distinguished incumbent. In the early eighteenth century the building was surrounded by a generous garden of a quarter of an acre which was added to in 1721 when Swift obtained a lease of the ground once known as the Cabbage Garden, a place which provided pasture for Cromwell's horses. (These animals seem to have been everywhere, even stabled in St Patrick's.) The Cabbage Garden, which is the land on which the Meath Hospital now stands, was christened Naboth's Vineyard by Swift, who was an enthusiastic gardener. He planted it with peaches, nectarines, pears and paradise apples as well as roses and shrubs reached by meandering gravel walks.

He was born in Dublin in 1667. His parents were English immigrants who were staying in a tall Jacobean house on Hoey's Court near St Werburgh's belonging to his uncle Godwin. After school in Kilkenny Grammar School he went to Trinity at fifteen and stayed for nearly seven years until the outbreak of trouble in 1689, when, like a lot of others he sought refuge in England. In 1714 he returned to 'wretched Dublin in miserable Ireland' at the age of forty-six. 'I was at first horribly melancholy but it began to wear off and change to dullness.' In 1720 he told Vanessa: 'I am getting an ill head in this cursed town for want of exercise ...everybody grows stale and disagreeable, conversation is nothing but South Sea and the ruin of the kingdom and the scarcity of money...'

However, although society might be intolerably dull, life in his own Liberty had its invigorating aspect. As Dean of St Patrick's he held an odd piece of inherited power. Before the Reformation, this particular Liberty, like that of the Archbishop of Dublin, had its own gaol and court and the right of according sanctuary to fugitives. Swift enjoyed vestiges of these privileges, maintaining his own seneschal or law officer. The area he ruled consisted of five and a half acres of narrow streets adjoining the Coombe and Spitalfields, which swarmed with impoverished people. Here his charity and his passionate identification with the poor were attractive features of his complex personality. He is said to have given away a third of his income, including all the profits of his writing, except those of Gulliver. He cut down on his drinking wine, to the extent that, according to Samuel Johnson, he even refused to offer it to guests, an unpardonable meanness in the eighteenth century. (However, he still drank half a pint with his mutton pie when he dined alone.) He walked instead of taking coaches or sedan chairs in order that he might empty his pockets, which he filled with coins of all values for distribution. The Huguenot banker, Peter la Touche, likewise filled his pockets with coins for charity before he set out walking from his bank in Castle Street.

Not everyone received Swift's bounty. Mrs Pilkington tells how he refused an old woman who held out a very dirty hand to him. He told her gravely 'that tho' she was a beggar, water was not so scarce but she might have washed her hands'. In *A Proposal for giving Badges to the Beggars in all Parishes of Dublin* he stated: 'Whoever enquires as I have frequently done from those who have asked me an alms what was their former course in life will find them to have been servants in good families, broken tradesmen, labourers...and what they called decayed house-keepers.' But beggars also included those 'of the female sex, followed by three, four or six children' who inspired *A Modest Proposal*.

One of his chief cares was the poor in the vicinity of the Cathedral. As a centre for the wool and silk industries, the area suffered economic blight after restrictions on imports were imposed by the English Parliament in 1699. Hundreds of Huguenot weavers became destitute. 'Their cries can scarcely be out of your ears...it is impossible to have a just idea of their calamity unless you have been an eye witness to it.' He tried ways of encouraging people to buy Irish like writing *A Proposal for the Universal Use of Irish Manufacture* and suggesting to the Archbishop that the clergy should wear Dublin-made black gowns. His epilogue for a charity theatrical performance included the lines (which eighteenth century pronunciation would have rhymed perfectly):

> We'll dress in manufactures made at home
> Equip our kings and generals in the Coombe.

His practical charities included an almhouse for widows and a charity school for the poor inhabitants of the Cathedral precincts. Dr Delany noticed how the poor 'were lodged and never begged out of their district; and they always appeared with a very distinguished decency and cleanliness'. Swift's housekeeper, Mrs Brent, told how he kept £500 of his income for a loan free of interest to the industrious poor, forced to sell or pawn their looms. Small sums lent to tradesmen were repaid at a shilling a week.

He saw himself squatting like a toad in his Deanery. 'I live in the corner of a vast unfurnished house...my family consists of a steward, a groom, a helper in the stables, a footman and an old maid, who are all at board wages.' Although he was a martinet and practised savage household economies, he was also sensitive to their well being. He regarded them as friends. A cook-maid with a plain face 'roughened with age and furrowed by small-pox' he called 'sweet heart'. When his manservant, Alexander MaGee, known as Saunders, was ill, he wrote to Knightly Chetwood: 'I have the best servant in the world dying in the house, which quite disconcerts me.' He put up a monument to Saunders in St Patrick's. To some extent his feeling reflected contemporary attitudes. An advertisement for a missing servant issued in 1719 seems excessively paternalistic: 'He went off in a coat and waistcoat of dark brown serge and a red collar with fustian breeches... He is about sixteen years old, marked with small-pox, with light brown hair and tender eyes. If he submissively returns to his duty in a reasonable time, he will be forgiven.'

Mrs Pilkington wrote of a disastrous 'saturnalia', a feast during which Swift planned for his servants to take the place of their master. It ended with one of them throwing meat in his face and mimicking him. Probably Swift, like others, employed too many, though not, as Samuel Madden considered 'as we do our plate on our sideboard, more for show than use'. Rosemary Ffolliott has noted an estimate in the *Calendar of Records* of the city's population of 1695 which gives over 28,000 adults of whom no less than 6,881 were male or female servants. The majority were male, who were entitled to wear their masters' livery. In *Directions to Servants* Swift advised the footman: 'Chuse a service...where your livery colours are least tawdry and distinguishing; green and yellow immediately betray your office, as so do all kinds of lace except silver, which will hardly fall to your share, unless with a duke or some prodigal just come to his fortune.' Servants were allowed to eat up the remains of the huge meals of the period, while the cook, as the *Directions* make clear, had the right to candle ends. When dining in high society it was customary for guests to tip servants lavishly 'much more than the dinner is worth' grumbled Lord Charlemont in an essay, 'and what would be deemed dear reckoning in a tavern'. In the Wicklow papers the accounts of Ralph Howard, later Lord Wicklow, confirm this custom, which declined as the century wore on. '1748 – Jan 5th – to Servants where I dined – 16s 3d. At Lord Primates and other places where I din'd – £1.0.0.' The accounts of Mrs Bayly, a housewife living in Peter Street, include payments made while dining at the Lord Chancellor's: 'Mr Norman the butler 2s 2d and another footman of my lord's, 1s 1d.'

In time Swift could write:

> The difference is not much between
> St James's Park and Stephen's Green
> And Dawson Street will serve as well
> To lead you thither as Pall Mall.

His Dublin friends included Dr Delany, George Faulkner the printer, and Viscount Molesworth to whom he dedicated a Drapier letter. He admired Thomas Sheridan, and regularly visited his school at 27 Capel Street – once the mint that made brass money – where he took classes. Stella and Vanessa were the most prominent of his many women friends who included Laetitia Pilkington, the tiny, immoral wife of a penniless clergyman who later divorced her. Swift commented savagely on the pair of them – 'he has proved the falsest rogue and she the most profligate whore in either kingdom'. But before things went sour he and Mrs Pilkington had a delightful friendship which lasted seven years. In her memoirs written in 1748 her engaging portrait of the crusty old Dean describes how after the death of her infant son he sent her a letter and a present.

' "Madam, I send you a piece of plum cake, which I did intend would be served at your christening. If you have any objection to the plums or do not like to eat them, you may return them to Your sincere friend and servant J. Swift." I now examined the contents of the parcel, a piece of gingerbread in which were stuck four guineas, each one wrapped in white paper and outside of which was written "plum".'

Her memoirs include a description of Swift watching servants through a pier glass in the dining-room. Once he spotted the butler helping himself to ale, for which he was fined two shillings. The pier glass helped with the composition of *Direction to Servants*.

Perhaps Swift's most charming friend was Mrs Pendarves, a Cornish widow who first arrived in Dublin in the good ship *Pretty Polly* with her friend, Mrs Donellan, in September, 1731. In due course she would marry Dr Patrick Delany, fellow of Trinity and Dean of Down, her beloved 'D.D'. Her letters and pleasant gossipy autobiography are crammed with details about Dublin society.

Her first impressions of Dublin were equivocal. 'I must say the environs...are delightful. The town is bad enough, narrow streets and dirty-looking houses, but some good ones are scattered about; and as for Stephen's Green, I think it may be preferred to any square in London.' Mrs Donellan's sister, married to the rich Bishop of Killala, lived in a new house in the Green designed by Richard Cassels; it partly survives as Iveagh House. Mrs Pendarves wrote in her journal: 'The apartments are handsome and furnished with gold-coloured damask, virtus, busts and pictures.' She also noted 'They keep a very handsome table, six plates of meat at dinner and six plates at supper.' When she drove out to a review at Phoenix Park, the Bishop's coach, pulled by six Flanders mares, surpassed the Lord Lieutenant's in magnificence. Later she would be critical of Mrs Clayton's ostentation.

The first ball she attended was at Dublin Castle on September 26; guests included 'Miss Kelly who is a perfect beauty, sweet Letty Bushe, Miss Ussher, Miss Wesley, Miss Ormsby, but the top beauty is Lady Rosse, a sweet agreeable creature.' During the winter season there were further entertainments, not all amusing: 'The rest of the men are not worth naming, poor dull wretches...I wanted my good friend, Mr Ussher; in his stead I had Captain Folliot, a man six feet four inches high, black, awkward, romping and roaring.' At Thomas Conolly's new house at Castletown she was one of 'four dull women without so much as a cavalier to attend us'. But more often she had fun. At Mrs Palliser's party she abandoned whist and commerce to join the younger set of people and dance until three. She went to another ball at the Castle, where the ballroom had been transformed by the newly knighted Edward Pearce and 'finely adorned with paintings and obelisks'. A painting survives of this ball showing the Lord Lieutenant and his wife, the Duke and Duchess of Dorset, touching hands in a quadrille watched by the crushed ranks of society. 'We were all placed in rows, one above the other so much raised that the last row almost touched the ceiling! The gentlemen say we looked very handsome and compared us to Cupid's Paradise in the puppet show.' In the supper room the guests found 'a holly tree illuminated by a hundred wax tapers and round it...all sorts of meats, fruits and sweetmeats – when the doors were first opened, the hurley is not to be described, squealing, shrieking, all sorts of noises, some ladies lost their lappets, others were trod upon. Poor Lady Santry almost lost her breath in the struggle...'

There were less energetic, more intellectual amusements. In January 1733 she was entertained by her future husband, who regularly held dinners on Thursdays. Swift was there, 'a very odd companion (if that expression is not familiar for so great a genius).' After her return to England she kept up a correspondence with the Dean. 'The cold weather, I suppose, has gathered together Dr Delany's set...I recall no entertainment with so much pleasure as what I received from that company...' When she came back to Ireland fourteen years later, Swift was too ill to visit.

Mrs Pendarves' first arrival coincided with a frenetic new stage in Dublin's development. Half the tonnage of ships coming to Ireland berthed at Dublin, and in spite of trade restrictions, various industries prospered. Linen was doing well; there were minor enterprises like sugar refining, furniture making, glass works and brewing which was the foundation for several fortunes. Dublin poplin, like stout, was said to benefit from Liffey water. Mrs Pendarves' only observation about industry noted that 'they make mighty good gloves here'. An offshoot of commerce was insurance, which had developed early in the century. In 1700 Dubliners had been mystified by the strange reappearance of a ship named the *Ouzel* after its capture years before by Algerine pirates. This had led to the formation of the Ouzel Society in 1705 which henceforth dealt with ship insurance and commercial arbitration.

Around 1730 a number of self-made entrepreneurs were responsible for planning the new fashionable areas of the city. 'The great Luke Gardiner' (Mrs Pendarves' words) laid out the houses in Henrietta Street. On the south side of the river there was another push of development where Aungier Street and Cuffe Street were laid out by Lord Longford in the reign of Queen Anne. After the development of Dawson Street in 1725 Stephen's Green gradually became fully enclosed with houses that had to be at least two storeys high, and made of brick, stone and timber, not of the old cagework.

Like other observers Swift considered that the development of Dublin was taking place too quickly. 'They have found out' he wrote of builders 'all the commodious and inviting places for erecting houses, while fifteen hundred of the old ones, which is a seventh of the city, are said to be uninhabited and falling into ruins.' Swift's opinions were echoed by newpapers. In 1734 an editorial in the *Dublin Weekly Journal* wrote 'that we grow too populous...is very evident from the vast number of shops everywhere seen, more than there were forty years ago'. Twenty years later there were editorial complaints of 'more squares, more streets, more lanes, more courts and alleys being continually added to this overgrown metropolis'. Faulkner's *Dublin Journal* complained in 1757 of 'rows of empty buildings, and our builders still proceed in their folly'. But Dublin would continue to be a speculator's paradise for another forty years, as the glowing perspectives of russet coloured bricks, interspersed with handsome important buildings of stone gave the city its characteristic imprint, which, though battered, has survived.

Those who benefited by this handsome manifestation of capitalism belonged to an age of the self-made man who happened to be Protestant. Most members of the upper strata of society had only been established in their mansions for a few decades. Many prominent aristocrats had very humble origins or were separated by a mere generation or so from an impecunious newcomer who had chosen Ireland, just as men had in Queen Elizabeth's time, as the means to advancement and wealth. The élite consisted of politicals, lawyers, divines, Huguenot merchants and bankers as well as landowners. The Leesons, who were brewers, scraped their way into the peerage and became earls. Lord Molesworth was the son of a Fishamble Street merchant: Members of the newly structured society were proud and confident. 'Last Sunday the Earl of Antrim and his newly married Countess went to St Ann's church in the morning, accompanied by a great number of quality, who all made splendid appearance. After divine service they went to the Strand in their coach and six attended by the same grand company. The populace crowded in shoals to see the shining pair, in so much that his Lordship, 'tis said, ordered the coachman to drive softly to better give room to the populace to satisfy their curiosity...'

For those among whom Mrs Pendarves moved Dublin offered exhaustive entertainment, especially during the winter season when Parliament was sitting, attracting its round of balls and masquerades. There were routs, plays, concerts and gaming of all kinds. After a heavy night the gambler could take the air in Sackville Street Mall or join the throng at Stephen's Green, both localities beautified by double rows of elms. The Green was particularly fashionable, especially the north side, known as Beaux Walk, the Dublin equivalent of Pall Mall. The south side was called Leeson Walk, the east Monk's Walk and the less modish west French Walk on account of the many Huguenots lodged in houses there. In the central area popular and civic amusements took place like concerts or firework displays or the Mayor inspecting the Freemen of Dublin or the Chief Magistrate reviewing the Corps of Guilds on May Day.

On Sunday it was a popular pastime to drive in one's carriage to Phoenix Park. For the more adventurous there were jaunts farther afield, Dunleary* was in the wilderness, and had only one ale-house, but nearer to town Blackrock was famous for its claret drinking. Simple pleasures were available like going and eating cockles at Ringsend 'at a very good tavern, the Sign of the Highlander', and playing billiards at Mrs Sherlock's for 2d a game. Sandymount and Raheny were also celebrated for their cockles, while oysters were the speciality of Malahide and Clontarf. Other country amusements were to visit the spa at Templeogue or the annual meeting of the Florists' Club which gave premiums to flower gardeners at the Rose Tavern in Drumcondra.

In the city the number of taverns and brandy shops and heavy drinkers was notable. Samuel Madden considered Ireland a country 'that flowed with wine as much as the Land of Canaan did with milk...for this affair of drinking is grown so fashionable a vice that there is neither managing any business, gaining any point of interest, carrying any election or procuring any place of preferment without it'. Society drank far too much, mostly claret. 'Drunkenness is the touchstone by which they try every man' Lord Orrery observed in 1736, 'and he that cannot or will not has a mark

---

* Before 1821 this little seaside town south of Dublin was known as Dunleary. In 1821 its name was changed to Kingstown to honour George IV who departed from there after his visit to Ireland. After 1921 it became Dun Laoghaire.

set upon him.' An indication of the heavy drinking that went on is found in an essay by Lord Charlemont. 'After dinner the doors shall be locked, the keys laid on the table, and the guests drenched with wine until they can hold no more; which out of pure hospitality and friendship is poured down their throats and they are left to wallow in filth and beastliness.' This custom did not decline until the second half of the century.

Among the poor whiskey was the most popular drink, especially after 1740 when the excise duty was lowered and it became very cheap. Fortunes and peerages were acquired through ale. Many taverns were foul dens, devoted to the requirements of the very poor. But scores of others had the sort of atmosphere that was recorded and remembered with nostalgia by writers of memoirs. Taverns, eating-houses and coffee-houses were social centres used for a variety of purposes such as meetings, discussions of politics, concerts, games of billiards or clubs for anniversary dinners. Like shops they had painted signs over their doors. Some were named after the famous; – there was one called after Swift, and another after Lord Carteret, the most popular Viceroy of the day. There was a Shakespeare's Head, an Addison's Head, an Isaac Newton's Head, a Whalley's Head and a Burnt Elephant. Each attracted its own clientele and a circle of admirers. Dr William King wrote about the steaks at the Old Sot's Hole, which from early in the century were reputed to be the best in the city:

> Here the Goddess supplies a succession of steaks
> To mechanics and lordlings, old saints and young rakes.

Innkeepers, coffee-house keepers and their wives were celebrated in verse, like Mrs Cartwright, whose husband ran the Custom House Coffee-House.

> Her goods are all both choice and sweet,
> Her vessels neat and clean as meet,
> Her coffee's fresh and fresh her tea...

A retired soldier, Thomas Ryan, landlord of the Cross Keys, provided cheap and plentiful food.

> Each Sunday night we got from that old trooper
> Good barn-fowl with salad for our supper,
> Or some fine ribs of roasted tender beef
> Which to our stomachs was a great relief...

After a church service guild members often met in session at the Rose in Castle Street, which was not to be confused with the Rose and Bottle in Dawson Street or the Rose at Drumcondra. An anonymous poem describes how these honest tradesmen behaved.

> Wine they swallow down like fishes,
> Now it flies about in glasses,
> Now they toast their dirty lasses...
> Now they throw away their poses
> Now they break each others noses...
> Hats and wigs fly all about...
> Now they part with heavy curses,
> Broken heads and empty purses.

Mrs Pilkington said the Rose was also a favourite rendezvous of lawyers. Swift asked his readers to

> Suppose me dead and then suppose
> A club assembled at The Rose
> Where from discourse of this and that
> I grow the subject of their chat...

During the first half of the eighteenth century the two most fashionable meeting places, both situated on Cork Hill, were the Eagle Tavern and Lucas' Coffee-House. The Eagle was the venue for clubs like the Aughrim Club, the Sportsman's Club, and the Hanover Club. In 1739 a dinner for members of the Hanover Club consisted of more than 200 dishes. The Hell-Fire Club, founded in 1735 and disbanded after its chief motivator, Lord Rosse, who was 'fond of all the vices which the beau monde call pleasures' died in 1741, also held meetings at the Eagle, although it also adjourned to the country to Speaker Conolly's exposed shooting lodge on Montpelier Hill. Lucas' Coffee-House could not have been a very restful location to sit and sip coffee, since it was a well-known rendezvous for duels. Mrs Pilkington tells how 'Lucas' Coffee-House is the place to which Irish gentlemen usually resort to decide, in an honourable way, their quarrels. While the combatants retire into the yard to acquire glory, the rest of the company flock to the windows to see that no unfair advantages are taken, and to make bets of them which fall first...'

The traditions of ceremony were part of the old fabric of city life. The procession of the Speaker, dressed in his robes of office and accompanied by the Sergeant at Arms bearing the Mace from his house in Molesworth Street to the House of Commons was a daily sight in winter. The guilds still held their dinners and celebrations on saints' days. Their main function had become dressing up, and numerous regulations were enforced about their spectacular uniforms. An assembly of guild members in 1713 had the Cutlers, Painters, Stainers and Stationers attending their standard at six o'clock at Mr Warden's Wine house on Lazy Hill, 'their hats edged with gold, bearing cockades of red, blue and yellow and wearing yellow gloves stitched with red silk and bound with red ribbon'. They were to accompany the Lord Mayor riding the Fringes, a ceremony that had ceased to be a cause of friction and had become a fancy dress display.

Other relics of the past persisted. Traffic increased all the time, while paving was still inadequate; in 1735 one Winifred Hacket complained that the paving was so bad round Ormond Quay that one of her horses slipped and fell into the river and drowned. Regulations for street cleaning were as ineffective as ever, and the city scavengers complained that the cost of emptying cars made them lose money on the job. Their task was made no easier during 1726 when the Liffey, during one of its frequent floods, overflowed into the city stables, drowning thirty-seven of their horses. Since the scavengers could not do their job properly, filth still abounded. It was not altogether surprising that Swift's obsessions became scatological.

Violence lurked in unsafe areas of the city like Bagnio Slip near Temple Street 'a haunt of the lowest characters' and George and Sir John Rogerson's Quays beside the river. The area beside the quays, practically a town within a town, had its own doctors and ship builders. Before the building of Gandon's Custom House in the 1780s, the quays were the usual point of arrival and departure for cross channel passengers who were shipped over in ferries to and from Ringsend as an alternative to taking a Ringsend Car. Notable arrivals included Swift returning triumphantly in 1723, when he was greeted by a boat decorated with garlands bearing the inscription 'Welcome the Drapier', after which he was escorted in triumph to his Cathedral. Handel landed here in 1741, Peg Woffington and David Garrick in 1742 and John Wesley on numerous occasions. The ferry that brought Peg back from the Ringsend Packet was called the *Lovely Jane* and was owned by the proprietor of the famous Fountain Inn, which, together with the Black Lion Ale-House, had the reputation for supplying guests with good smuggled wines and brandies.

On the quays sailors fought, whores walked, press-gangers lurked and convicts in chains were assembled to be transported. The most famous victim of the press-gang was young James Annesley, kidnapped and shipped out to Virginia as a slave in 1724 at the instigation of his wicked uncle, Lord Altham, who feared that he might be the rightful heir to his title. Annesley's escape and return to Dublin fifteen years later to claim his inheritance was one of the *causes célèbres* of the century. The press-gangs had the effect of making the area more or less free of beggars, and since the only men immune from them were gentlemen, people in the area were always well-dressed. Enterprising footpads sported silver buckles and silk stockings. In February 1767 the *Freeman's Journal* reported how 'a Mr Edward Tobin...was attacked near the Dockyard...by a person genteely dressed, who presented a pistol saying "I am a gentleman" and demanding a guinea which Mr Tobin gave him. He had on a scarlet waist-coat laced with gold, a ruffled shirt, his hair tied behind him and a gold-laced hat.'

Until the American War of Independence city convicts, many of them children in their teens, were transported to tobacco plantations in Virginia. After the American war transportation was resumed, but now it was to Australia; prison ships anchored off Ringsend where they waited to receive convicts ferried out to them, some of whom had been offered an alternative to Botany Bay that was almost as unattractive – joining the army. If a criminal was not transported he had a good chance of being hanged; among the scores regularly executed, since Ireland was subject to the same savage capital penalties as England, were pirates and mutineers who challenged the vital smooth running of merchant and naval transport. Pirates were hanged in chains on outlying rocks round Dublin Bay and left as a warning to other malefactors. Petty criminals were usually sentenced by the Lord Mayor's Court to be whipped at a cart's tail from the Tholsel to the Parliament House, to be placed in the stocks, or 'scourged at the whipping post'. The rest of the criminal population, together with debtors, were lodged in the city's prisons. The Newgate, situated in the old Cornmarket, was superseded by the 'new' Newgate re-erected between 1773 and 1780 in the Little Green to the north of the river hard by Green Street Court House which is still in use. The Sheriff's Marshalsea, known as the Black Dog, was located in Newhall Street, also near the Cornmarket, from where prisoners would constantly shriek at passers-by for charity. The Four Courts Marshalsea off Thomas Street was built in 1775. Both Marshalseas received debtors and criminals alike. Criminals of Dublin County were lodged at Kilmainham. Conditions in all these places were known to be appalling. A report of a committee of the Irish House of Commons in 1729 described how every prisoner had to pay towards the 'penny pot' – 2s. 2d. at the Black Dog and 1s. 4d. at Newgate with another 4d. added for 'not being thrown into the Felon's Room' whose stinking confines were crowded with prisoners sick and dying of gaol fever. At the Black Dog those who could not pay enough were violently beaten and stripped naked, while the really destitute were imprisoned in a small foul room known as the Nunnery, because women arrested by the watch were confined there together with howling and cursing male criminals.

Poverty in Dublin was rather worse than in infamous London. Visitors began recording impressions of crowds of beggars surrounding newcomers 'roaring with hunger' and the primitive thatched cabins that were a feature of the suburbs. Overcrowding was already common; Arthur Dobbs reported in 1729 that '70 persons have been known to live in a house, there sometimes being a family in each room and in the cellars'. Since the supplies of wood from the surrounding forests had long been exhausted, cold was a particular problem for the poor. Often the price of coal was exorbitant. Although turf was available – the turf-sellers went about with their cry of 'buy the dry turf – here's the dry bog-a-wood' – coal was now the largest single import that came to Dublin. In 1718 the Rev. James Wood, describing the view from Phoenix Park, mentioned:

> While thus retir'd I can the city look
> A group of buildings in a cloud of smoak.

Coal was carried over usually during the summer months by coal fleets which came from Bristol and from small coal-producing towns on the river Clyde and along the west coast of England and Wales. Places like Ellenfoot, Workington, Whitehaven, Milford, Ayr and Girvan had their own fleets, some of which had been specially built for the Dublin trade and had no other market but Ireland. When they arrived in Dublin they often had to sell their coal at a loss, especially in summer when big-time 'coal-mongers' bought up supplies and hoarded them against winter shortages. In hard winters the shivering poor were forced to steal coal out of the gabbards on the quays.

At other times merchants hoarded butter, cheese and bacon until their prices rose. There were several famines. During the winter of 1728 Primate Boulter relieved starving people by providing public meals in the dining hall of the new workhouse, while many others were fed by the authorities of Trinity. The terrible famine of 1738, considered the worst natural disaster of the century, was the result of a prolonged period of intense frost. While the more comfortably situated members of society disported themselves on the frozen Liffey, the less fortunate were given relief work or received charity. This famine is recalled by two follies outside the city which were erected to give employment to the poor: the Killiney obelisk, raised by John Mapas, looking over Dublin Bay, and the convoluted Hall's Barn at Rathfarnham which imitated the Wonderful Barn at Leixlip. But thousands died from starvation and the subsequent typhus which decimated the country.

The desperately poor could now seek charity from the Dublin Workhouse which was founded in 1703, as an alternative attempt to deal with the 'sturdy beggar' who, for much of the century, could still be locked in the cage in the Cornmarket. The Workhouse, supported on funds derived from licences issued to cars, carts, brewers, drays and sedan chairs, meted out carefully calculated harsh treatment to its inmates. They slept in vaults or cells on double rows of beds and ate quantities of gruel, bread, milk, porridge and 'burgoo' which was 'oatmeal stirred up in cold water, seasoned with salt and enlivened with pepper'. They were expected to work or be flogged or transported overseas; large numbers of them died.

Even more horrible was the Foundling Hospital, an adjunct to the workhouse created in 1729. During its 130 year existence about half the children reared in it died before the age of twelve. In the ten years ending March 1760, out of 7,781 admissions 3,796 died and 52 were simply unaccounted for. The Hospital, with its famous wheel on which abandoned babies were placed, and bell summoning the watchman to collect them, began with good intentions: 'to prevent the exposure, death and murder of illegitimate children'. A report to the Irish House of Commons in 1758 described how verminous sore-covered children were reared in

the Protestant faith in buildings open to wind and rain. The milk
was watered, the stirabout full of insects and sand, the beef crawled
with maggots, while the treasurer, a man named Purcell, kept order
with a cat-o'-nine-tails and threats of confinement in Bedlam to
staff and children alike.

Records of deaths, printed in news sheets as 'quarterly bills of
mortality' give a wide variety of causes, including 'great fogs'
which killed 100 people in 1753, age, asthma, pain in the belly, pain
in the head, childbirth, chin cough, grief, small-pox, stitches and
fever, perhaps the most lethal killing agent – over the years several
hundred thousand died of unspecified fevers. Ailments could be
treated by quack remedies like Viper's Drops, horse-dung posset,
turnip water, Dr Anderson's Angelic Pills and Bishop Berkeley's
famous Tar Water.

Dublin began the century almost devoid of hospitals, but soon
had plenty. Many survive. Jervis Street dates back to 1721 when six
doctors, whom Maurice Craig judges from their names to be
Catholics, started the Dublin Charitable Infirmary in Cook Street
which was later transferred to King's Inns Quay and finally to
Jervis Street. Mrs Mary Mercer opened Mercer's Hospital in 1734
on the site of the old leper hospital of St Stephen. In 1710 Dr
Richard Steevens, President of the College of Physicians, left
money in trust to his sister Grizel with instructions that after her
death the money was to be used to found a hospital. Dr Steevens'
Hospital was built during her lifetime in 1733 on a site in open
fields to the west beyond Usher's Island, away from infection.
According to 'several gentlemen who have been abroad' Steevens'
was 'commodious' and 'kept the cleanest of any hospital of its kind
in Europe'. For breakfast patients got '3 oz of bread, a pint of
grewel or small beer'. For dinner there was '8 oz of bread, 8 oz of
mutton boyled without bones, a quart of beer or mutton broth and
a quart of small beer'. Nearby St Patrick's Hospital, founded with
money left by Swift 'for the reception of aged lunaticks and other
diseased persons' was equally careful about diet. An early notice
mentions 'that every article of food used in this hospital is excellent
of its kind'. Those who could afford to pay were given roast beef,
milk and butter, but others had to resign themselves to breakfasts
of bread, stirabout and a pint of beer.

Apart from Swift, Dublin's best known medical benefactor was
Dr Bartholomew Mosse, born in Maryborough in 1712, the son of

a clergyman. The conditions of nursing mothers in Dublin passionately concerned him. 'Their lodgings are generally in old garrets' he wrote, 'open to every wind, or in damp cellars subject to floods from excessive rains'. In 1742, after studying surgery and midwifery on the Continent, he opened the first maternity hospital in the British Isles in Fownes Court. There were twenty-four beds and on 15 March 1745, the first patient, Mrs Judith Rochford, was admitted. By the end of 1746, 509 babies had been delivered and the premises were plainly inadequate. Mosse raised money by means of concerts and lotteries with which he leased five acres of waste ground containing some thatched cottages and a large pool of stagnant water located at the northern end of Sackville Street. Within a year he had laid out a public walled garden, planned on similar lines to Vauxhall Gardens in London with flowers and shrubs, a coffee room and pavilions and an artificial waterfall lit by artificial moonlight. The shilling entrance fee provided an income for the new hospital whose tower had a golden cradle on top. The enchanting chapel was decorated by an obscure French stuccodore named Barthelemy Cramillion, who illustrated in vigorous and voluptuous fashion some vaguely appropriate texts such as 'Kings shall be thy fathers and queens thy nursing mothers'. More prosaic but more necessary was the order in 1757 to prepare fifty-four wooden bedsteads, each with straw or hair mattresses, broadcloth sheets, linen curtains and a bolster. Nurses were issued with blue gowns of a glossy woollen material called calamanco, red petticoats, shifts, handkerchiefs, caps and aprons. Patients had to be clean and free of vermin. The first of many generations of Dublin women who had their children here were Mary Rea and Elizabeth Knight, safely delivered of a son and daughter respectively. (But in the first thirty years of the hospital's existence about one baby in six born alive would die almost immediately.)

Mrs Delany has a description of a *gratis breakfast* organized by Mosse in 1751 in one of the hospital's newly built rooms in order to attract subscribers. The meal was to be accompanied by a concert. 'We went...at about half an hour after eleven, the concert to begin at 12...We squeezed into the room, which they say is 60 feet long and got up to the breakfast-table which had been well pillaged; but the fragments of cakes, bread and butter, silver coffee-pots and tea-kettles...and all sorts of spring flowers strewed on the table shewed it had been set out plentifully and elegantly. When they had satisfied their hunger...such a torrent of rude mob...*crowded in* that I and my company *crowded out*... We got away with all speed without hearing a note of the music.'

The hospital received a Royal Charter in 1756 and a year later, when it was officially opened, the Lord Lieutenant and his wife were entertained to a similar programme of breakfast and music. Mosse died in 1759, worn out, we are told, by hard work. Five years later a round building, the Rotunda, which gave the hospital its familiar name appropriate to the shape of its patients, was added to the complex and henceforth concerts and other entertainments were performed there. (For a long time the place continued to be known as Mosse's Gardens.) The Rotunda got additional financial support from a tax on sedan chairs and another on the lighting in Rutland Square. Owners of houses had to make an annual payment for the number of lamps on their hall doors. Each private lamp was rated at £1.14s per annum. No house had less than two private lamps, and Lord Charlemont's mansion had four. Householders had also to pay 1s. 9d. per foot for the lights on the garden rails that illuminated Mosse's fairyland in their midst.

9

Eighteenth Century – The Middle Years

Until 1741 Dublin's main musical venue had been the Bull's Head Tavern in Fishamble Street. Here the Charitable Musical Society gave its concerts in aid of debtors and other unfortunates, Lord Mornington performing on the violin and harpsichord, Lord Lucan playing the flute and the Earl of Bellamont the violoncello. Funds from the Society helped Lord Mornington to found the Hospital for Incurables with the aim of keeping depressing sights off the streets. In October 1741, a printer and publisher named William Neal opened a magnificent Music-Hall designed by Cassels and decorated in white and gold which was situated just across the road from the old tavern. Here on 8 April 1742, the first rehearsal of *Messiah* took place, to be followed five days later by the most important musical event in the city's history. Handel had already been in Dublin for five months, having been invited over by the Lord Lieutenant the Duke of Devonshire, to give a series of six concerts. The oratorio was an extra and had been kept secret; not until March did the newspapers announce its imminent performance. Because of the expected crush làdies were advised not to attend wearing their hoops, while gentlemen were requested to leave their swords behind. Admission was half a guinea and the book of words cost 'an English sixpence', worth a halfpenny more than an Irish sixpence. On 15 April 'the most Grand, Polite and Crowded Audience' in the words of Faulkner's *Dublin Journal,* witnessed a triumph. Handel thought so too. The *Journal* found that 'the sublime, the grand and the tender, adapted to the most elevated, majestick and moving words, conspired to transport and charm the ravished heart and ear'. The proceeds, which came to £400, were divided between the Society for Relieving Prisoners, the Charitable Infirmary and Mercer's Hospital.

Before he left Dublin, Handel had his poignant meeting with Swift. In St Patrick's where a new organ had been installed in 1695, Swift had endeavoured to keep the choir to a high standard, scouring the British Isles for promising singers. His disciplinary notes from the Vicar's Choral, written in 1734 are well known. Mr

Fox, the vicar, appeared at services 'dirty, filthy and very indecent, sometimes intoxicated'. Mr Church was 'very indecent in his behaviour, openly laughing in the time of divine service; he and Mr Fox disputing constantly the performance of the anthem...' Swift disapproved of the secular use of his choir, and such performances as a concert on St Cecilia's Day in 1731 in his cathedral aroused his anger. His last coherent letter, dated 28 January 1741, was to admonish his choir for singing at the Bull's Head. But by the time the choir, together with that of Christ Church, was swelling the chorus of *Messiah*, he was sinking into the darkness of his final years. When Handel arrived at the Deanery he was just able to understand who his visitor was. 'O! A German and a genius. A prodigy! Admit him.' He lived on until 19 October 1745; the crowds filed past the coffin of the greatest Dubliner of all for two days.

In the year Swift died 'the Irish Lord Lieutenant' arrived. Philip Dormer Stanhope, 4th Earl of Chesterfield, immediately set about making himself a friend of the Irish people 'who were worse used than negroes by their Lords and Masters'. Lord Chesterfield was witty, a scoffer at religion, known for his liberal views, his poor treatment of Samuel Johnson and for describing Miss Ambrose, daughter of a wealthy Catholic brewer, as 'the only dangerous Papist I know'. (He also wrote a bawdy poem about her.) The '45 set Scotland ablaze, but his presence did much to prevent a Jacobite rising in Ireland.

He was directly responsible for some of the easing of restrictions against Catholics. After the death of Queen Anne there had been some relaxation of the more outrageous penal laws. Catholic clergy were gradually allowed to return. The 1731 Report on the State of Popery in Ireland mentioned that there were forty-five Catholic schools inside the walls of Dublin and twenty-three without. They were illegal, but were tolerated for a number of reasons. The large population which supported them was hostile to informers. Although the Irish Parliament had passed the Popery Acts, it had no power to enforce them; such enforcement was in the hands of the executive of Dublin Castle which proved ineffectual. Catholic schools were small and information about them derived from the report is meagre: 'St John's Lane Parish, two reputed school masters...Parish of St Michael the Archangel, three Popish schools, two of which teach book-keeping, the other writing and

arithmetic'. Three convents ran schools for affluent girls – the
Benedictines in Channel Row, the Poor Clares in North King Street
and the Dominicans in Channel Row where daughters of noblemen
like the Earls of Tyrconnell and Fingal, Lord Trimleston and Lord
Dunsany attended. Here lived Mrs Delany's friend, Miss Crilly, '*a
nun professed*...an old acquaintance of D.D.'s, is extremely
sprightly, civil and entertaining...' Mrs Delany visited the convent
in 1751, noting 'the chapel is pretty, the altar mightily decorated
with candlesticks, gilding, little statues but terribly bad pictures'.
Miss Crilly did not make herself conspicuous in a habit, but wore 'a
black stuff nightgown and plain linen'. In 1712 when the Poor
Clares had been raided and brought before Judge Caulfield
charged with keeping a nunnery, they wore secular dress; the judge
decided they lived, not in a nunnery, but a boarding house.

In 1750 the Jesuit, Father Austin, returned to Dublin from
France. He had once been a pupil of Swift's charity school, but
Swift, although he supported the aims of Protestant
indoctrination, is believed to have encouraged the boy to become a
priest by advising his parents: 'Send him to the Jesuits who will
make a man of him.' After working for a decade with the secular
clergy in the church in Rosemary Lane off Cook Street, which had
a long and furtive existence during the worst of penal times, Father
Austin founded a school in Saul's Court off Fishamble Street in
1760. Even at that date Catholic schools were nominally forbidden
by law. However, Saul's Court became famous among affluent
Catholic families, particularly those who wished their boys to
become priests.

Before 1745 churches were makeshift affairs, usually converted
from stables, lofts and warehouses. The oldest, the Franciscan
chapel of St Francis in Francis Street, had been rebuilt soon after
the Restoration, but because of the persecution resulting from the
popish plot, was not opened until the reign of James II in 1688.
This 'plain, oblong building', according to a contemporary
description, was the cathedral church of nine successive
archbishops. The Augustinian Father Byrne made a chapel from an
old stable in John's Lane off Thomas Street. A rough chapel in the
yard of Mr Jennet the brewer, now part of Guinness's, served the
old parish of St James.

As long as they were unobtrusive, such places of worship were
tolerated and ignored. But an accident in 1745, while Mass was

being said to a packed congregation in a house in Cook Street, revealed their inadequacy. The floor gave way under the weight of the crowd, and several people, including the priest, were killed. Public opinion was shocked, and Chesterfield gave permission for proper chapels to be opened. A number of modest churches were subsequently built in the Liberties and in the back streets round the Liffey. By 1770 the city had fifteen chapels. In addition to St Francis in Francis Street there were five regular chapels, that is, attached to monastic orders: the Augustinians, Capuchins, the Carmelites, of whom there were two orders, and the second Franciscan chapel in Cook Street. Three other chapels were attached to the convents. The six parochial chapels were St James's Watling Street, St Catherine's Dirty Lane, St Andrew's Townsend Street, St Paul's off Arran Quay, St Mary's Liffey Street and St Michan's Bull Lane.

Chesterfield is also remembered for his embellishments of Phoenix Park – the groves of trees he planted there, and the graceful Phoenix Column erected at his own expense. He was patron of the Dublin Society. His efforts after he left Ireland obtained it a Royal Charter in 1750. The Society, the first of its kind in Europe, had been founded in 1731 by fourteen Dublin gentlemen for the improvement of husbandry, manufacture and the useful arts. Educated men were very much conscious of the precarious state of the economy – a number of banks had failed, and it was realized that the economy was basically lopsided, with too much emphasis on commerce and not enough on manufacture. Among other projects, the Society founded the Botanic Gardens at Glasnevin in 1759 in order to assist Irish agriculture and horticulture by experiments with plants most suitable to the climate. The man who did most to establish the Society was Thomas Prior, author of the *List of the Absentees of Ireland* which calculated the amount lost out of the country by those who chose to live elsewhere. Other early members included the killjoy, Samuel Madden, author of *Reflections and Resolutions Proper to the Gentlemen of Ireland*, Dr Delany, Thomas Sheridan and Sir Thomas Molyneux, who as Dr Molyneux, had belonged to the old Dublin Philosophical Society over forty years before.

Chesterfield's short eight month stay in Ireland was nothing but beneficial, and when he left he was universally regretted. 'Lord Chesterfield's influence, like the departing sun, has left a warm and serene sky behind it' wrote Lord Orrery fulsomely. Lord Orrery, a translator of Pliny's letters, kept up a wide, rather peevish correspondence full of complaints about 'the malignant air of Dublin...' 'the fog of Stillorgan...' 'the wicked air of this wide town...' In a letter to the Bishop of Cork he wrote how 'Dublin stands just where it did...I hear nothing but the creaking of unoiled cars...I smell nothing but the mud of the Liffey...I taste nothing but tough meat...' As a footnote he added, 'there are great riots in the city'. For many years he had been one of the small group of friends who dined with Dr Delany on Thursday nights and with Swift at the Deanery on Sundays. His 'shabby' *Life* of his old friend was regarded as a particular betrayal by the circle that used to meet so happily and regularly. One of his most eloquent critics was Dr Delany; his wife shared his views. 'I am indeed so vexed with him about his manner of treating Swift that I can hardly allow him any merit.'

After a ten year interval Mrs Pendarves had returned and married Dr Delany on 9 June 1743. Now her life rotated round their exquisite eleven-acre estate of Delville. Delville was situated at Glasnevin, a fashionable neighbourhood with villas inhabited by members of an intellectual society which included Addison and his executor, the poet, Thomas Tickell. The house survived until 1951, 'a fine example of an old interior' a visitor wrote in 1907 'with its spacious rooms lit by great windows, the little panes of which are set in wooden frames of tremendous thickness'. Here Mrs Delany painted, played the harpsichord and made flower decorations. She loved gardening and birds, letting chaffinches and robins feed out of her hands. Landscape gardening, including a ninepin bowling alley and a deer park with eighteen head of deer, together with lavish entertainment, reduced the Delanys to near-penury.

Daily routine was punctuated by meticulously served meals. Breakfast was at 9 a.m.; in summer they ate it in the garden under the nut trees, while a harper played nearby. Dinner was at 3 or 4 p.m., tea or coffee in the 'afternoon' and supper between 8 and 11 p.m. – not unlike the hours Spaniards keep today. Early in married life, when they invited Lord Chesterfield to breakfast, Delville had to look its best. 'To work went all my maids...stripping covers off chairs, sweeping, dusting etc and by eleven o'clock the house was as spruce as a cabinet of curiosities.' Enormous dinners were prepared as lumbering coaches and even sedan chairs made their way to

Glasnevin. Starters for a first course might include turkey, endive, plum pudding, venison pasty and roast loin of veal, to be followed by a second course consisting of partridge, collared pig, crabs, creamed apple-tarts and pigeons. A meal for Primate Stone and his sister and the Bishop of Derry and his wife had among other items, pickled salmon, quails, 'rabbits and onions', strawberries and cream, orange butter, cherries, 'blammage' and Dutch cheese. Sending this letter to her sister, Mrs Delany wrote: 'I give as *little hot meat* as possible, but I think there could not be less considering the grandees that are to be here; the invitation was for the *beef stakes* which we are famous for.' And sure enough, they, too, are included as an item in the first course.

Outside Delville life was busy. 'I have made fourteen visits last Thursday in the afternoon and propose doing as much nearly this day' she wrote in February 1752. We learn in the same year that 'high living is too much the fashion here...you are not invited to dinner to any private gentleman of £1,000 a year or less that does not give seven dishes at one course and Burgundy and Champagne'. There were visits to the theatre, routs, fashionable masquerades and balls. Acquaintance was resumed with rich Mrs Clayton. In the National Gallery of Ireland there is a portrait of Bishop Clayton and his wife who wears a brown dress fringed with gold. This may be the very dress Mrs Delany refers to when she describes a visit both ladies paid to Dublin Castle in 1751. 'I went to Madam in my coach at twelve o'clock; she was in her sedan with her three footmen in Saxon Green with orange-coloured cockades marched in state – I humbly followed. Can you tell why she desired me to go with her? I can. She was superb in brown and gold and diamonds; I was clad in the purple and white silk I bought last year in England, and my littleness set off her greatness.'

A glimpse of slightly less exalted circles than those in which Mrs Delany moved can be obtained from the account book of Mrs Katherine Bayly, wife of a minor government official who lived in Peter Street in the heart of the city in easy middle class circumstances. Some details of the Baylys' domestic life are luxurious, like the list of the contents of their ample wine cellar which held, among other wines, 'four bottles of my son's champagne'. The accounts indicate hours of leisure to be filled up with visits to the theatre, buying garden tickets for Dr Mosse's lottery in aid of his Lying-in Hospital, and taking a coach to

Phoenix Park to see the soldiers in their camps. In 1745 the family
rented rooms in the countrified atmosphere of Harold's Cross 'to
take the air at Templeogue', where there was a spa. 'Have this day
agreed with Mrs Middleton for two middle rooms. The street
closet, use of the parlour and kitchen, with a bed for my man
servant, the dairy and leave to walk when we please in the garden at
the rate of 15/- a week.'

The Baylys' involvement in art and education was limited. Mr
Haskings received £1.2s.9d. to teach the five girls to write, in
addition 'I am to give a guinea a quarter for the three biggest girls
and what I please for the other two, say a crown more for them.' In
1754 one of the girls was efficient in reading and ciphering, being
perfect 'as far as ye rule of subtraction'. They had dancing lessons,
perhaps from someone like Mr Lalanze who had been to Paris and
advertised in 1731 that 'he will teach ladies and gentlemen, young
Misses and Masters after the newest and best manner practised at
Court Assemblies'. £1.2s.9d. was paid to a Mr Murphy for teaching
two to sing and play on the spinet. In 1751 three books were bought
for the servants and family, *The Pious Parishioner*, *The Great
Importance of Religious Life* and *New Weeks Preparation*. Other
books kept in the house were *The Female Spectator*, *The Works of
Shakespeare* and a romance called *Cornelia*.

Mrs Bayly liked gaming and cards. 'Lost at cards at Mrs Lodges,
paid for the cards 6d.' 'Won at Mrs Bensons after paying for the
cards 3s 9d.' Cards and dice, which were taxed, could only be made
in Dublin and Cork, and were wrapped in their own stamps and
cipher. Quadrille parties were a fashionable afternoon
entertainment for women as well as men. Mrs Pendarves played
whist, quadrille which was a four handed game requiring forty
cards, and commerce. Swift admonished Stella for her card
playing; he wrote that ladies played into the small hours of the
morning, gambling until they had lost their housekeeping money
and the plate had to be pawned. Perhaps on these occasions players
used the odd language commented on by the English traveller, John
Loveday. 'Even ye gentry when talking to you will call you honey.
Even ladies make use of expressions bordering too near
swearing...''the devil if any'' is a common phrase among ye
vulgars.' Lady Morgan's mother told her that conversation among
ladies in mid-century was notably coarse. There are hints of this in
Swift's *Genteel and Ingenious Conversation*, the collection of

conversational clichés he made over the years in 'a large table-book' which include many expressions still in use. (Lady Smart: 'Madam, do you love Bohea tea?' Lady Answerall: 'Why, Madam, I must confess I do love it, but it does not love me.') The party where these are spoken in the form of dialogues is fairly boisterous; a cup is broken, and Miss Notable, filling a dish of tea for Lady Smart, sweetens it and tastes it before handing it across. When Colonel Atwitt kisses her she struggles a little and says: 'Well I'd rather give a knave a kiss for once than be troubled with him; but upon my word, you are more bold than welcome.' A lady of Lady Morgan's generation would have been less likely to reply to Mr Neverout's 'Pray, Miss, why do you sigh?' with the abrupt 'To make a Fool ask, and you are the first.'

The dialogues, published in Dublin in 1738, give pleasant social details – the quantities of bread and butter consumed, the kettle singing on the fire, the maid bringing in boiled cream. Taking cream in tea was a fashion that started around 1725; Americans still sometimes drink it this way, although not warmed. Silver teapots of simple round design, copying Chinese pots, first made their appearance at the beginning of the century. But, for about forty years the price of tea, imported from China, and coffee which came from Arabia, was relatively high so that many families favoured chocolate. Silver chocolate pots had a removable finial so that a rod could be inserted inside them to stir the chocolate which had to be piping hot. It was a messy, difficult drink to make, and around the mid-century coffee and sweetened tea became more widely drunk. However the widespread popularity of tea was a slow development. Sugar was bought in cones – hence the name of the Sugarloaf mountains – which were ground up before being served.

The death of Mrs Bayly's servant meant extra expenses. This was an age when society marriages and funerals were usually held in the evening or at night. Swift's wish to be buried 'as privately as possible and at twelve o'clock at night' was arranged without difficulty. The rich were buried solemnly, the mourners wearing linen scarves, a fashion introduced around 1729 with the aim of encouraging linen manufacture. In that year at the funeral of a Miss Fitzpatrick, 'a young lady of great beauty and fortune' her hearse, according to the *Dublin Intelligencer,* was 'adorned with white or virgin plumes...the bearers having fine linen scarves...This young lady is the fourth who was buried in the same manner, the others being Colonel Groves, the late Rt Hon William Conolly and Mrs Masson, wife of Mr Masson, an eminent clothier in Essex Street.' At William Conolly's pretentious funeral on 8 November 1729, the long procession from his house in Capel Street to Celbridge included not only the Lord Mayor and 'Poor Men in black Cloath Serge Gowns in number 67 according to his age', but 'Nobility and Gentry two and two, and all with linen scarves of Irish manufacture'.

Coffins came into general use towards the end of the seventeenth century; previously ordinary people were buried in shrouds. Undertakers advertised their wares, like Ann Sherrard at the Sign of the Plough in Francis Street and William Wheeling at the Sign of the Bear and Scales in the Coombe. Thomas Raper, operating from the Sign of the Coffin, supplied 'Plain Oak Coffins neatly furnished' for 16 shillings, or a more elaborate 'fully mounted Coffin, silvered, lined and covered' for £3.19s.7½d. Phil Conolly, Mrs Bayly's servant, probably had to make do with something like 'deal coffins of all sizes, ready made'. He died without fuss. 'Mr O'Byrne the surgeon, for bleeding him on both arms when he found him dead, 2s.2d. Cash to his wife to provide things for his wake, besides sending candles, sheets and other necessaries, 5s.5d. Paid Ben, Mr Lodge's man, when he paid for a room to wake poor Phil in, and for drinks he gave the men that carried the corpse 3s.4d.'

Household expenses in Ireland were much less than in England. When Swift resigned himself to living in Dublin, he found one of the compensations was the difference in the price of food and wages paid to servants. Among the numerous small city shops, each carrying its own sign, many advertising the latest fashions and goods from England, were the Royal Leg in Castle Street which sold stockings, the Golden Peruke in Essex Street for gentlemen's shirts and the Spread Eagle in the Coombe for corsets. Mrs Bayly bought poplin from the Half-Moon and Seven Stars in Francis Street. The Hen and Chickens in Werburgh Street specialized in Drumcondra printed linens which did not fade. The Blue Tea Tub and Lace Lappet in Capel Street sold Mechlin and Brussels lace. Stock at the Bee Hive in Bridge Street, a linen drapers, included bordered ruffles for ladies, striped and plain Scotch kentings, sprigged Silesia lawns, coloured pillow fustians, thick-set barragons, nankeens and grandurells for gentleman's wear, cherry-derries and Indianoes for ladies' gowns and gentlemen's waistcoats. Mr Doran, the silk dyer at the Blue Hand and Rainbow in Watling Street prepared 'rolls for printing and watering, Paragons, Chinas, Arrateens and Kidderminsters... Tabbies, Armazeens, Ducapes and Paduasoys'. Of tobacco shops the best known was Mr Lundy Foot's at the sign of the Virginia Planter, whose popularity lasted for well over a century. Early stock of tobacco included Bristol Roll, Common Roll, High and Low Scotch Snuff, Irish Rapee, Pig Tail and Superfine Pigtail for Ladies.

A frequent entry in the Bayly accounts concerned visits to the theatre, a popular pastime among all classes of society. When Thomas Elrington, an early manager of Smock Alley returned to Dublin after a year in England, he was greeted with public bonfires and ringing bells. For a time alternative theatrical entertainment had been provided by Madame Violante, pantomimist and tightrope walker, whose company played first at Fownes Court – her house there was taken over by Dr Mosse for his Lying-In Hospital – and then in George's Street. It offered a repertoire of comic routines performed by French dancers, in addition to the thrills on the wire perpetuated by Madame and her daughters. In 1728 she turned to theatre, producing *The Beggar's Opera* with a company of children called the Lilliputians. They included a charming little girl named Peg Woffington, who ceased to help her mother sell fruit and vegetables, and took up an acting career at the age of eight, playing Macheath.

In 1747 Thomas Sheridan, son of Swift's schoolmaster friend, became a leading theatrical manager in Dublin by taking over Smock Alley. His purpose of producing 'good and chaste plays' and making theatre respectable was hard to achieve. Theatre-going was exhausting entertainment. Outside the actual premises, the narrow streets invited riots among waiting chairmen. At Smock Alley a special crush bar had to be built so that playgoers could wait in safety for their chair or coach. The opening of Crow Street Theatre in October 1758, resulted in a riot where gentlemen's servants and chairmen fought each other, causing several fatal casualties. Inside the audience was usually dominated by the mob element in the pit and upper storey which often threw oranges and bottles at the orchestra and stage. The stage might be thronged with figures who were not actors at all, since fashionable young men vied with each other to become unwanted extras, by paying their way, scraping acquaintance with actors, or merely by threats. Sometimes a member of the audience managed to clamber on stage and cut up the scenery or fondle an actress's bosom or strip off her clothes. Peg Woffington had indecent advances made to her on stage while she was playing Cordelia to David Garrick's Lear. In 1747, during a performance of Vanbrugh's *Aesop* at Smock Alley, a young Galway rake named Kelly climbed over the railings that formed an ineffective barrier between audience and stage and frightened away all the actresses with his drunken abuse. After Sheridan had given him a thrashing, the subsequent 'Kelly riots' which destroyed much of the theatre lasted for two days; Edmund Burke remarked that they 'divided the town into parties as opposed as Whigs and Tories'. A subsequent riot in 1754 arising from Sheridan's attempt to censor *Mahomet the Imposter* which contained lines about political corruption that might allude to the unpopular Lord Lieutenant, the Duke of Dorset, finally put an end to Sheridan's theatrical career. Not even Peg Woffington's presence on stage could prevent the audience from running amok. 'Sheridan is undone' wrote George Faulkner. 'His theatre in Smock Alley has been torn to pieces on the inside, and he will appear no more, he says, on the stage.' After this riot a committee met and suggested rules of conduct for theatre-goers. It was quite ineffectual.

George Faulkner, bon viveur, Swift's 'prince of Dublin printers', a fat little man with a wooden leg 'his wooden understanding', who once sold Mrs Bayly *A Short History of Man* for 7½d., was one of the great literary characters of the time. He operated in Essex Street 'next door to the Merchant's Coffee-house' according to his publicity handout, 'opposite the bridge, and continues to do all manner of printing work at reasonable rates and sells all sorts of new pamphlets, poems and plays as they are published in London or Dublin.' Since there was no copyright, pirated editions of English books were common. With the increase of population there was a corresponding increase in printers whose numbers rose from three in 1691 to thirty-three in 1760. Of the newspapers that sprung up Faulkner's *Dublin Journal* was the most consistently successful, in spite of vigorous opposition from long-lived periodicals like the *Dublin Intelligencer* and *Pue's Occurrences*. As newspapers strived for circulation there were complaints of 'innumerable phamphlets and flying papers constantly thrust into the hand of every man who wears a good coat by those Pests, the Newsboys'.

One reason for their difficulties in attracting circulation was their reluctance to encourage Catholic readership, even though there was now some acknowledgement of the existence of a large Catholic population. As the force of the Penal Laws declined, polemics against Popery lessened. The *Dublin Gazette* could report in 1737 the theft of a priest's vestments 'just as he was going to celebrate Mass' and approve the apprehension of the 'sacrilegious Villain'. Another report in the same paper praised a priest who rescued a small girl from abductors 'tho' he was a Priest he was by much a Heroe than the Chrispian [sic] knight'. The *Dublin Daily Post,* published by Ebenezer Rider, showed a particular interest in Catholic bishops and priests and made a speciality of printing obituary notices of Catholics. Although there was no organized pro-Catholic press before the nineteenth century, a number of Catholic printers flourished. Since the late seventeenth century provision had been made for enrolling them as 'quarter brothers' in the Stationers Guild; upon payment of quarterly dues they were permitted to become printers, while remaining exempt from any oaths and responsibilities concerning the guild. These Catholic stationers and printers worked closely with each other, although they do not seem to have formed any official guild or clandestine organization. They specialized in devotional books and chap-books for the country trade, their stocks being aimed at the Catholic population. They concentrated in High Street and Cook Street, probably because of the existence of so many chapels in the area.

The only Catholic concerned in the printing of newspapers before 1760 was Faulkner's partner, James Hoey, whose ability as a 'Compiler, Writer, Corrector and Author' contributed to the *Dublin Journal*'s long success. Faulkner was one of the few publishers to show sustained sympathy for the trials of Catholics. His friend, Lord Chesterfield, claimed that as Lord Lieutenant he had been guided by the liberal bookseller's advice. 'From my time down to the present' he wrote to him after he left Ireland 'you have been in the position of governing the governors of Ireland, whenever you have thought fit to meddle with business.'

Much of the *Dublin Journal,* like the contents of other contemporary newspapers, is ordinary stuff, giving details of shipping, marriages, deaths and plays. James Carson, 'the facetious Jemmy Carson' who published the *Dublin Intelligencer* on Saturdays, described how he got his news items. 'I must go to balls, masquerades, operas and plays; I must frequent the Exchange, Lucas', Templeogue, the Green to pick up news for the ladies.' In addition there were reports of everyday goings on. 'Last night a gentleman was attacked by two fellows in St Mary's Lane, one of whom knocked him down and gave several blows, while another robbed him of half a guinea and some silver.' Newspapers constantly reflected the violence of the time, a duel at Lucas' ('both contestants were wounded, one of them dangerously, but 'tis hoped, not mortally') a gentleman stopped and stripped of his velvet cloak, the forcible abduction by two villains of a child diverting himself on the low ground at Ringsend. Traffic chaos is recorded in such items as this attempt to introduce two-way lanes: 'All coaches, carts, cars, drays, carriages and chairs passing over...Ormond Bridge to Oxmantown area to pass on the side of the bridge next to Essex Bridge.' (The idea of ordering traffic to keep to the left did not come in for more than a century.) In 1764 'constant reader' complained to the *Freeman's Journal* about the dangers to life caused by a man breaking horses in Dame Street. On another occasion he had to take refuge in a shop from a carriage and four 'driven about in the same inhuman manner...What gentleman will walk about our city to be put in dread and fear of his life, having his pockets picked by beggars that are innumerable or his leg broke by bad pavements?' In 1770 the *Dublin Journal* recorded how 'a decent-looking antient woman was run over by a hackney carriage and lost both legs.'

Advertising progressively increased. 'To be Sett* for one year...two very good houses in St Martin's Lane...N.B. the said Martin's Lane is remarkable for as good air as any about Dublin.' 'Charles Murphy Britches maker in Buck, Doe, Goat, Ram and Lamb.' 'Edmund Nolan offers the latest fashions direct from London; a wide range of clothes including greatcoats, storm bags and duffer coats for ladies...' 'Dominicans that cover the head and shoulders and save the wig from wind and rain when riding...' (Umbrellas came in during the last quarter of the century.) There were countless offers of rich assortments of imported foodstuffs and tempting home-produced articles of food and drink. A grocer in Fishamble Street at the sign of the Golden Key advertised 'ten thousand gallons of rum shrub, brandy shrub, whiskey shrub,

* The Irish equivalent of 'To be let'.

angelica shrub made out of the finest Seville oranges'. Among newspaper readers there seem to have been few who took notice of Samuel Madden's resolution 'that as masters of families we will banish from our tables the luxurious way of living which is too common and pernicious to the gentlemen of Ireland'.

The expansion of the middle decades produced great houses like Kildare House and Tyrone House. In 1756 the first accurate map of the city was made by John Rocque a Londoner of Huguenot extraction. He reckoned he had delineated 338 streets, lanes, rows and other buildings. Dubliners considered that the map was 'the best of that kind ever published'. It showed that the city had taken on a familiar shape, although the great squares, Merrion, Fitzwilliam and Mountjoy were not yet in existence. 'Populous, overgrown and slothful' one contemporary observer considered it.

In 1759 the massive west front of Trinity was completed and at much the same time Provost Andrew rebuilt the Provost's house in sandstone imported from Liverpool. A year before an era had come to an end when another of Swift's enemies, Provost Baldwin, died at the age of ninety-two. The forty-one years of Baldwin's provostship not only marked the beginning of the period when Trinity became the appointed nursery for the rising professional classes, but encouraged an atmosphere which produced the most famous names associated with the College. Berkeley was a Fellow for seventeen years in Baldwin's time. The medley of the old Provost's students, varying from the sons of peers and baronets in gowns trimmed with gold or silver lace according to rank, to the sons of shopkeepers and innkeepers in plain black, included Thomas Southerne, William Congreve and George Farquhar. And Goldsmith and Burke entered in 1744 when Baldwin was, according to Burke 'an old, sickly looking man'.

Burke, the child of a mixed marriage, was the model student, the founder of the debating club which was the forerunner of the College Historical Society. Perhaps Goldsmith fitted better into the shabby atmosphere of Trinity which is conveyed by John Winstanley's *Inventory of the Furniture of a Collegian's Chamber* written in 1742:

> Imprimis, there's a table blotted;
> A tattered hanging all bespotted;
> A bed of Flocks as one may rank it
> Reduc'd to rag and half a blanket;

A tinder-box as people tell us;
A broken-winded pair of bellows...

Goldsmith, the son of an impoverished clergyman, gained his Trinity education with a sizarship, which meant servitude. He had to carry dishes up from the kitchen to the Fellows' dining-room, wait upon his betters, and clean up Front Square. When he went walking in town he had to wear a conspicuous red cap. He relieved his poverty by writing street ballads and selling them in the Reindeer Repository in Mountrath Court for five shillings each, stealing out of college at night to hear them sung. He neglected his Greek lectures, earned buttery fines and was involved in the Black Dog riot of 1747 when students rescued one of their number from gaol, killing several people in the process.

Trinity was a violent place where an unpopular Junior Dean, Edward Ford, had been murdered by students in 1734. Others followed Dr Theckler Wilder's hint as to how to deal with a bailiff they were ducking: 'Gentlemen, for the love of God, don't nail his ears to the pump.' Antagonism between town and gown took sectarian forms; students used massive keys tied to pieces of cloth to support the Liberty Boys, the weavers in the Liberties, in their running feuds with the butchers of Ormond Market, who were mainly Catholic. Fights between the factions could leave whole areas of the city desolate, and usually there were fatalities; John Wesley observed how 'the Ormonde mob and the Liberty mob seldom part till one or more are killed'. Once the formidable butchers strung up several students on hooks like legs of mutton, tying them with their breech bands and gowns.

The proportion of Catholics in the population increased, in spite of newcomers to the town like those Huguenots who landed in August 1752 '...from Rotterdam 96 foreign Protestants, men, women and children; they all seemed in good health and spirits and went in the afternoon to the French Church in Peter Street where there was a large collection for them...' Their sailing experiences are not recorded, although the majority of visitors had horrible voyages. The actor, Tate Wilkinson, took three weeks to recover from a passage made in 1756. Handel's journey to Dublin was interrupted for almost a fortnight at Chester by bad weather. And yet, by now tremendous improvements had been made to Dublin Bay, which, noted Mrs Delany, viewing it from Delville, was 'always full of shipping'. The number of passenger vessels increased until there would be twenty-one by 1791. The approaches to Dublin from the sea had been cleared of their age-old barriers of sand by the building of the North and South Walls extending into the harbour. The Ballast Board, created in 1707, formulated plans for dredging a proper channel, and four years later work began on the Strand Wall which became known as the North Wall. The South Wall, begun in 1715, incidentally destroyed the oyster beds at Poolbeg. By 1728 both walls were complete as far as Ringsend. They were constructed with oak staves driven into the seabed; numerous small flat-bottomed boats known as gabbards – in the ordinary way they ferried goods about in the harbour – were then used for sinking baskets of 'kishes' of stones to make the bases of the walls. The first lightship, a sloop provided with an anchor, was placed at a point known as Pole's Head at the site of the present Pigeon House, which derived its name from a house erected by the Ballast Office for the overseer of their employees, whose name was Pigeon. By 1761 the South Bull had been extended a further two miles to Poolbeg where a lighthouse was erected. In September 1767, Sir John Rogerson's Quay was filled with crowds assembled to see the first light of the George Dublin Lighthouse, as it was officially called, the first lighthouse in the world to use candles rather than a simple beacon of coals. (The playwright, John O'Keefe, has left a description of how in 1788 he and his friends picnicked above the Howth lighthouse looking down on its great iron pan 'from which the coal fire blazed all night'.) The harbour was finally completed in 1820 by the Bull Wall from Clontarf to within 100 feet of the Poolbeg light. Apart from the city walls, this long project was the most important civic undertaking in Dublin's history.

But harbour walls could not prevent storms. When Mrs Pilkington returned to Dublin divorced and destitute, accompanied by her son, her miseries were compounded by the weather. At Parkgate – the alternative embarkation port to Holyhead, twelve miles from Chester – she met Lady Kildare, who lent her the passage money and allowed her to spend much of the night huddled in her coach. Wealthy passengers often travelled with their coaches, and sitting up in them was the most comfortable way of enduring these voyages. For the rest of the time Mrs Pilkington and her son stayed on deck. 'I am always deadly sick at sea...' The ship docked at Dunleary but to avoid the expense of having to hire a coach, she decided to wait on board until it reached Ringsend. That night a storm blew up and the ship was thrown onto the North Bull, a notorious place for shipwrecks, where the local inhabitants made good pickings salvaging goods from wrecked vessels. Mrs Pilkington's boat was washed up on the sand, and she and her son were able to step off 'so that without expense or difficulties' she concluded gamely 'we walked to Ringsend'.

Her later picaresque adventures as society's outcast make sad reading. Her debts were paid by kind Dr Delany, but nothing went well for her. She died in 1750 and was buried in St Anne's, Dawson Street. When she was ill she was visited by the tireless John Wesley. Wesley came over to Ireland on twenty-one occasions between 1747 and 1768. From the pulpit in St Mary's church he preached his first sermon in the city to 'as gay and senseless a congregation as I ever saw'. He thought the churches in Dublin were 'small and mean, both within and without' while Stephen's Green was 'rough and uneven as a common and surrounded by poor houses'. A poem published in 1762 supports his poor opinion of the Green:

> Mid trees of stunted growth, unequal roes
> On the coarse gravel trip the belles and beaus.
> Here on one side extends a length of street
> Where dirt-bespattering cars and coaches meet.
> On t'other in the ditches' lazy flood
> Dead dogs and cats lie bloated, drench'd in mud.

Wesley's diary for 1749, written during his second visit, when Methodism was making its initial impact, indicates the nature of his barn storming missions. At the new Methodist House in Dolphin's ·Barn, converted from a weaver's shed, he was received triumphantly. 'It was some time before my voice could be heard from the noise of the people shouting and praising God.' On Monday, 14 March 'I began preaching at five in the morning, a thing unheard of in Ireland.' On Sunday 20th he preached at Oxmantown Green and on Wednesday 23rd to the prisoners in Newgate 'but found no stirring among the old bones'. On Friday 25th he returned but with no better results. 'I am afraid the Lord refuses his blessing to this place.' Much the same could be said for the pensioners in Kilmainham. 'Oh what is wanting to keep these men happy? Only the knowledge and love of God.' Perhaps they were discontented. John Loveday had noted that they were lodged in rooms that contained three beds each, and the regulation number of persons to a bed was two.

In general accommodation for visitors in Dublin was inadequate. A traveller might stay at a quayside tavern, but the quays were not a respectable part of the city. Elsewhere service was poor; John Loveday, staying at the White Hart in 1732, thought it 'like ye hotels in France, dresses no meat for ye guests – we had our dinners brought up from a cook's shop'. Commenting on inns, John Bushe author of *Hibernia Curiosa,* published in 1764, considered that 'there is not one absolutely good in the town...in which an Englishman of any sense or decency would be satisfied with his quarters'. He advised travellers to go to any of the coffee-houses round Essex Street and the Custom House and enquire the names of lodgings instead.

Bushe noted that 'the whole extent of the city may be one third of London, one fourth of which has been built within these forty years.' He wrote about the heavy drinking and laughed at the decrepit types of transport available like the Chaise Marine 'the drollest and most diverting kind of car with one horse' which, when not used for carrying something like manure, took up to a dozen passengers pushed inside with their feet scraping the ground. He described the familiar noddy as 'an old castoff one-horse chaise or chair'. The noddy, deriving its name from its motion, was a shaky little carriage accommodating two people, the driver sitting in front on the shafts. A less exclusive Dublin vehicle for hire was the jingle, the noisy high-springed one-horse car which could hold six people sitting sideways and face to face. There was a jingle stand behind King William's Statue. Bushe neglected to mention the form of public transport which now worked fairly efficiently. Dublin had become the coaching centre for the country. The stage coach which from 1737 set off every morning at eight o'clock sharp from the London Tavern on Usher's Quay to Athlone, had been joined by others. By 1740 there were regular services from Dublin to Cork, Drogheda and Kilkenny. In 1752 a coach service linked Dublin and Belfast.

According to Bushe the general topic of coffee-houses was the proposition that the English spoken in Dublin was better than that spoken in London and that Dublin was on the whole more genteel. 'But how the devil the inhabitants of this metropolis' exploded the English author, 'whose dress, fashions, language and diversions are all imported from London, should come as a superiority in either, unless from a natural genius or capacity to improve upon their originals, is beyond my comprehension.' Things went the other way when Dubliners travelled to England, where, just as in Elizabethan times, they were mocked because of their accents. Betsy Sheridan mentions in her diary that Irish people visiting a fashionable resort like Bath 'speak French to hide their brogues'.

10

The Triumph of Elegance 1760–1800

By 1776 the population of Dublin, one of the larger European cities, had reached 150,000 and may have been larger. 1762, the year when Merrion Square was laid out, has been considered a good date to mark the beginning of modern Dublin. Other developments that affected a fundamental transformation included the completion of the South Wall of the harbour, the enclosure of the city in the great oval of the North and South Circular Roads, and its siting as the terminus of the Royal and Grand Canals. But the most important step in the creation of a leading European capital had taken place in 1757 with the formation of the Wide Streets Commission, which was responsible for Dublin's present street structure, including the modern layout of the quays. Its most spectacular achievement was the concept of the north-south axis which shifted the whole emphasis of the city. Before 1794 Capel Street and Henrietta Street on the north side, linked to the south of the river by its most important bridge, Essex Bridge, had been Dublin's commercial and fashionable centres. Some way to the east, parallel to Capel Street, stretched Gardiner's Mall, or Sackville Street Mall, with the Rotunda at its northern end. It was 890 yards long and 150 yards broad and lined with elms; there was a coachway at each side with walls adorned with globes and obelisks. Rutland Square to the north of the Rotunda had already superseded Henrietta Street as the most desirable residential quarter, where Lord Charlemont, the Duke of Ormonde and numerous peers and bishops had their town houses. In the 1790s when Carlisle Bridge was built, replacing a ferry, to remain for a long time the lowest bridge on the river, Sackville Street was extended to meet it and to become part of an important new thoroughfare which stretched right across the city from Stephen's Green to the Rotunda. The importance of the Capel Street–Essex Bridge link immediately declined, while Grafton Street on the south side, just below Stephen's Green, which had been a quiet residential area, after becoming part of this new cross-city route, changed to a commercial centre.

The Commissioners, whose work was supplemented in 1773 by the 'Corporation for Paving, Cleansing and Lighting the Streets of

Dublin' were a body of men whose ideas were years ahead of their time. Their ruthlessness was embodied in the spirit of their most prominent member, John Beresford, a throwback to the old Elizabethan adventurers with his particular combination of energy and cruelty. Their very first job was to open a new and wider road from Essex Street Bridge to Dublin Castle – what is now Parliament Street. The owners of various houses due to be demolished agreed to sell, but later changed their minds. The Commissioners, whose powers included compulsory purchase, started to strip off the roofs without warning; 'the terrified inhabitants bolted from their beds into the streets under the impression the city was attacked'. Where the Commission hesitated, Dublin has paid the price. For example, they failed to drive a wide street through Merrion Row, which has remained a traffic bottleneck to this day.

By the end of the century Dublin had a matchless display of public and private buildings. The great public buildings of the later decades included the Royal Exchange and an enlarged Linen Hall, both with their own coffee-houses, Thomas Ivory's new Blue Coat School on the opposite side of Blackhall Place from its predecessor, and James Gandon's masterpieces: the Law Courts, adapted from a design of Ivory's, King's Inns and the Custom House. He also enlarged Pearce's Parliament House. In 1792 the seat of Grattan's Parliament was actually provided with central heating from flues under the floor and around the ceiling. They were not wholly successful. On one occasion one caught fire and nearly burnt the place down, while another, which opened through vaults at the head of the table where the mace lay, caused many a member coming to be sworn to be 'kept dancing on the hot grating at the mouth of the flue in the utmost agony among sulphurous vapour and smells'.

The proposal to build a new Custom House and Bridge further down river met with a storm of criticism when merchants realized that it would change the established pattern of importing. At the Parliamentary Enquiry of 1774 only two merchants supported the plan, while others argued about the probable increase in the price of food. Imported corn had traditionally landed at George's Quay, salt at Aston Quay or Crampton Quay, rock salt at George's Quay, potatoes at Crampton Quay and coal at Aston Quay or Batchelor's Quay from where it was carried to the Coal Quay in lighters. These landing places would no longer be available if the Custom House shifted its position below river of them. The poor would suffer. The newly proposed bridge would prevent ships which could not lower their masts from moving up stream and encourage the loss of timber exports... and so on. But in spite of passionate opposition the work went ahead; the upper part of the old building was unsound, and it would have to be replaced in any case. James Gandon arrived in Dublin in April 1781, and backed by his patron, Beresford, overcame the immense obstacles to his work and stayed in Dublin until his death in 1823. The site of the Custom House on reclaimed slobland compounded his difficulties; so did the hostility of dissatisfied citizens. The work took ten years to complete at the enormous cost of £400,000.

Wealthy peers continued to build magnificent private mansions like Belvedere House, Moira House, Clonmell House, Powerscourt House and Aldborough House, the last to be erected before the Union. At Charlemont House in Rutland Square visitors regularly inspected Lord Charlemont's cabinet of minerals or his paintings brought back from the Grand Tour which included a Titian and a doubtful Rembrandt. In addition to trophies from abroad the great houses, and also the less ostentatious, contained much local craftsmanship. A proportion of house furniture came from England where Wyatt and Adam set the fashion. A nobleman could fill his house with items ordered by catalogue from England: china, furniture, centre panels for chimney pieces and moulds of stucco medallions of familiar subjects like the *Aldobrandini Marriage* by Poussin made popular by Angelica Kauffman. But many chose to buy in Ireland, and much of the elegance had a specifically Irish idiom. Luxury industries flourished. Dublin was noted for its fine coaches, and before the Union there were forty coach building factories giving employment to around 2,000 people. At the height of the building boom more than a hundred firms in the city specialized in decorative plasterwork. The earlier Rococo style of Robert West producing the big white free-standing birds at room corners which sometimes provided bucks with targets for their pistols, gave way to a rigid classical vogue inspired by Adam, whose most famous Irish practitioner was Michael Stapleton.

Domestic silver was of a high standard, its smiths including a number of Huguenot craftsmen. By 1770 the earlier flamboyant style with its elaborate repoussé work was being succeeded by the more severe lines of neo-classical design influenced by Adam, which encouraged the work of the engraver. Heavy gauge metal was being replaced by silver of lighter weight to satisfy increasing demand. Handles and legs with little horses' hoofs were often imported from Birmingham and stuck to local sauceboats and sugar basins by Dublin silversmiths.

Irish craftsmen of the period never took to making fine china, which had to be imported. Wedgwood opened showrooms in College Green in 1772. However, like Waterford and Cork, Dublin had its glass-works belching clouds of yellow smoke. The bottle-shaped Glass House in St Mary's Lane turned out drinking glasses, water bottles, jelly glasses, cupping glasses, weather glasses and other domestic objects, advertised as following the latest London fashions. But large boat-shaped bowls came to be an Irish speciality, and so did piggin glasses whose shape was derived from wooden pails in humble cottages. There was local emphasis on engraving to 'any pattern required', whether a Jacobite or Williamite toast or a Volunteer motto. Other Dublin glass factories were Mulvaney's on the North Strand, the William's Glass House on Marlborough Green which made coloured glass and plate glass for coach windows, and the Venice factory near Ballybough Bridge whose products included 'a set of magnificent lustres' for Dublin Castle.

Irish-made furniture, known as Irish Chippendale, had reached a peak of excellence before 1750. The style, favouring very dark imported Cuban mahogany, was characterized by grotesque masks and carefully carved lion's paw feet emphasizing claws and toe knuckles. (In England chairs and tables preferred scroll or claw and ball feet.) Around the late sixties Adam once again changed fashion; pale satinwood and fruitwoods were substituted for mahogany, carving gave place to Adam's ubiquitous and monotonous decoration, and furniture-making ceased to retain its striking Irish characteristics.

The orderly proportions of the terraces of houses resulting from the strict control of the Wide Street Commissioners, meant that the new Dublin was built in an international uniform style, so that similar terraces abound as far away as St Petersburg. And yet they have a quality of their own, partly due to their rose red brick and partly because of minor local architectural differences. The uniformity of the exteriors contrasts with the immense variety of interiors. The building boom, after all, had to cater for a good many different sections of society. Not only did the richest lords erect their big houses, but lesser peers, who were constantly being created, had to have stylish accommodation. Country gentlemen, even if they were living uncomfortably in draughty converted tower houses, now felt obliged to have town houses in Dublin instead of in their country town as hitherto. But there were those who were prudent enough to limit expenditure by taking lodgings. Maurice Craig considers that much of the speculative housing, particularly round Mountjoy Square, was erected as lodgings to be let out for the season, or as boarding-houses; he derives his conclusion from the plainness of their interior ornamentation. Some had provision for caretaker's flats. We do not know much about life in lodgings and boarding-houses. Mrs Pilkington had a good deal of experience in them. 'Took lodgings in Abbey Street up two pairs of stairs...' Philip Skelton, retired from his remote Donegal parish in 1780, lodged first with a clergyman, then with a snuff merchant and finally a grocer. Jonah Barrington gives a good description of a house in Frederick Street where 'eight or ten select persons' of varying eccentricity (including Lieutenant Johnson who 'without being absolutely disgusting...was certainly the ugliest man in Christendom') were 'most plentifully served in company by plain Mrs Kyle, wife of an ex-trooper, a gentlewoman by birth'.

Society in the 'cheerful little capital' was small and intimate. 'All persons of a certain condition were acquainted with each other' Lord Cloncurry remembered. Its pivot was Parliament; Grattan's Free Parliament, containing 247 peers, 22 spiritual members and 300 ordinary members, without a Catholic among them, provided a focal point for the season which took place in winter. 'Nothing can be so gay as Dublin is' wrote Mary Herbert in 1782, 'the Castle twice a week, the opera twice a week, with plays, assemblies and suppers to fill up the time.' As they had been in Mrs Delany's time, parties were notable for their crush. The most popular form of assembly was the masked ball, which became a regular feature of the season around 1776. Before one began, the masked guests, stared at by the plebeian crowds who pressed round them as they moved, would visit various noblemen's houses from seven to twelve at night, when their costumes would be admired and they would be served wine and cakes. The climax of the season was a grand Ridotto ball or masquerade, held in the Music Hall in Fishamble Street. Rooms were specially decorated – the supper room had murals of waterfalls, hills and painted villages. Five hundred guests dined on 'every style of cooking, from that of the plain viands of our ancestors to the appetite-provoking culinary arts of France'.

At the Rotunda half a dozen yearly assemblies were held in the round room which could hold up to 2,000 people. At other times, mainly on Sunday evenings, when often a third of the House of Commons was to be seen, society promenaded in the Rotunda Gardens. Although there was no music, tea and coffee was served at tea tables to the sound of a bell. Around 1771 tightly corseted ladies favoured scarlet silk stockings, cloaks of gold and silver and feathered hats, while gentlemen wore white silk and carried shoulder-high canes with heavy gold heads. Clothes in general were brilliantly coloured; John O'Keefe once called on his brother 'in sea green tabinet coat, green waistcoat edged with gold and hair full dressed'. His memoirs are full of recollections of odd bright figures like portly Lord Trimleston in scarlet and black hunting cap, Lord Gormanstown in a suit of light blue and Lord Taaffe in dove-coloured silk. Lady Morgan describes concerts at the Rotunda under the direction of Dr Fisher 'dressed in a brown silk camlet coat, lined with scarlet silk, illustrated with brilliant stones'. The most notable dresser of all was Francis Higgins, government toady and attorney, known as the Sham Squire after he had posed as a man of property to marry an heiress. He was to be seen on the Beaux Walk on Stephen's Green near his house dressed in a canary coloured vest and breeches, a three-cornered hat fringed with swansdown, violet gloves with rings on his chubby fingers, and gold tassels on his Hessian boots. Later, Volunteer and Yeomanry uniforms largely replaced extravagant male fashion, while ladies, following the French mode, took to wearing hight waisted muslin.

For a decade or two the Ranelagh Gardens, opened in 1776, rivalled the Rotunda as a fashionable place of entertainment. An advertisement of the period offers: 'Attractions of the Ranelagh: On Tuesday evening there will be a grand concert in the gardens of vocal and instrumental music . . . to conclude with a grand fireworks on the water and a ball in the Long Room.' From the Ranelagh Gardens in 1785 Richard Crosbie ascended into the Dublin sky in a balloon emblazoned with the arms of Ireland. This and subsequent balloon flights were not very successful, but for a time the idea of ballooning was fashionable. Scores of toy lamp balloons were released to light up the sky every evening, while ladies wore 'balloon puffed petticoats'.

When they were satiated with the attractions of the gardens, people could take their leisure farther afield. The lonely cliff road through Booterstown towards Bray made of rock and sea-sand known as the Rock Road to Dublin followed a stretch of wild coast where many ships were cast on the rocks; it was also a haunt of highwaymen. But it led to Blackrock, which, according to Walker's *Hibernian Magazine* in 1783, was 'on fine evenings as crowded with carriages as the most populous streets in the city'. It was a venue for seabathing, and the *Dublin Journal* advertised in 1770 a new bathing house there with dressing-rooms and a protection against the east wind. Many rich people built second residences out at Blackrock. John Wesley thought Lady Arabella Denny's garden surrounded by green fields overlooking the sea one of the pleasantest he had ever seen. At Frescati Lord Edward Fitzgerald laboured with his coat off at 'clearing the little corner to the right of the house, digging around roots of trees, raking ground and planting thirteen two-year-old laurels and Portugal laurels'. Lord Clonmell's garden at Neptune House was ruined during his feud with John Magee when Magee organized the grand Olympic Pig Hunt to run over his grounds.

There was another bathing lodge at Irishtown and one at the mouth of the Tolka where Lord Charlemont took sea baths. Swimming was fashionable, the more so since 1759 when a Dubliner made an epic swim from Dunleary to Howth. Ringsend was, according to different accounts 'very clean, healthy and beautiful with vines trained against the houses' or 'a wretched village, full of smoke and swamps'. The view across the crowded harbour was unprepossessing at close quarters, since such a large proportion of vessels approaching the city were colliers. Suburbs were really villages, many with 'charming villas' like Dolphin's Barn, Finglas and Drumcondra which was also well known for its tea-houses and public gardens. Dorothea Herbert's mother owned a 'tenement' at Phibsborough; 'it consisted of a large Garden, a field and the House – the Garden open'd on the Canal by a Wicket and the packet boats sailed by the windows'. Lewis' *Dublin Guide* of 1787 describes Donnybrook as 'a large and pleasant village... good accommodation to be had there, particularly at two principal tea houses. One at the sign of the Rose, the other kept by Mrs Derby'.

According to Lord Cloncurry an excursion favoured by 'all the great folk' was a carriage outing on the newly built North Circular

Road which he compared to Hyde Park in London. 'I have frequently seen three or four coaches-and-six and eight or ten coaches-and-four passing slowly to and fro in a long procession of other carriages and between a double column of well-mounted horsemen.' Among well-to-do Catholics a favourite Sunday outing was to the two famous St Catherine's Wells at Leixlip, both of which were known for their cures. An observer in 1794 counted 1,200 people passing one day under his window on their way to Leixlip. Four hundred and fifty travelled on horseback, while others passed in 55 coaches, 29 post chaises, 25 noddies, 82 jaunting cars, 20 gigs, 6 open landaus and 221 common cars. Together with Lord Cloncurry's coaches this seems a pretty good summary of the different kinds of Dublin traffic, although it necessarily excludes sedan chairs. These were to be seen parked in the hallways of all great houses. No rich woman walked, but took her gaudily decorated private sedan – the actress Ann Bellamy's sedan had opulent silver livery. In the seventies and eighties it might have a specially made canopy to protect towering hairstyles. In addition there were shabby public sedans for hire – 400 in 1771 – which did not go completely out of business until the second half of the nineteenth century. It seems surprising that a more convenient form of this servile mode of transport – something like the rickshaw – was never developed.

By now the quality of the theatre may have declined. The Chevalier De La Tocnaye who visited the city in 1796 found 'the public playhouse ugly enough, the theatre poorly attended, and the acting nothing better than what is to be found in a little provincial town'. But interest in theatricals remained constant, and large houses like Marlay and Aldborough House had their private theatres. At Lady Borrowes' private theatre in Kildare Street the young Thomas Moore made his debut at eleven years of age, reciting an Epilogue entitled 'A Squeeze to St Paul's'.

Public theatres were relatively small. Since audiences were just as rowdy as they had been in Thomas Sheridan's day, two soldiers with fixed bayonets constantly guarded the stage. The galleries were particularly noisy. Women were now allowed to sit in the pit, while in the boxes both sexes dressed as ornately as if they were at court. A Dublin guide of 1787 gives a list of admission prices – five shillings for a seat in the boxes, three shillings for the pit, two for the gallery and one shilling for the upper gallery. There were no half prices for late-comers as in London. The rivalry between

Smock Alley and Crow Street continued until Smock Alley closed down in 1790.

John O'Keefe wrote how 'it was the invariable custom...when the hero died to bring down the curtain by applause and hear no more...the end of the play was lost... Not a line was heard of the fate of Lady Randolph and Horatio's Farewell Sweet Prince.' When the principal character was about to die, two stage hands would enter with a carpet for him to expire on. After about 1760 scenery grew more elaborate and both scenery and costume more appropriate to the roles actors played. Thomas Sheridan, according to Barrington, played Cato wearing 'a huge white bushy well-powdered wig (like Dr Johnson's) over which was stuck his helmet'. Lighting was generally by tallow candles stuck into tin rings over the stage, sometimes supplemented by rows of candles in front of the galleries. Later, glass chandeliers were introduced over the boxes, once at Smock Alley setting fire to a lady's high headdress. Wax candles were used when managers felt affluent, often on gala occasions when Shakespeare was performed. Wax continued to be a luxury from medieval times right up until the introduction of gas; it smelt less and gave a more brilliant light. When the Rotunda was having a special entertainment the sense of occasion was usually highlighted in advertisements which stated that the entire building would be illuminated *with wax*, for which higher admission prices were charged.

Dublin audiences had a partiality for plays by Sheridan and Goldsmith and also for Charles Macklin's ever-popular patriotic farce *The True Born Irishman*. They saw a good deal of Shakespeare, and towards the end of the century opera and pantomime. Lord Camden, the Lord Lieutenant, was watching *Robin Hood* at the Theatre Royal when he heard the news of the arrest of Lord Edward Fitzgerald. They liked English actors; Mrs Siddons remembered with pleasure the reception she got from 'the warm hearted Irish', and well she might, since she cleared £1,000 when she came over in 1783. The disgraceful financial position of local actors was not eased by the differences of actor-managers like Thomas Mossop (nicknamed 'Teapot' from his favourite way of arranging his arms on stage) Spranger Barry and the duellist, Richard Daly. O'Keefe described how actors stood around the theatre door before performances, taking money as it came into the box office, so that they could get the clothes needed for the evening's entertainment out of pawn and buy candles to light up their dressing-rooms.

Among amateur devotees of the theatre, one of the most indefatigable was Samuel Whyte who ran a school at 75 Grafton Street where Bewley's Café is now. He made a point of teaching drama to his pupils who included Richard Brinsley Sheridan, Thomas Moore, Robert Emmet, the antiquarian George Petrie and the Duke of Wellington. Other schools included Dr Burrow's Academy, attended by Lord Cloncurry, who naturally had for fellow pupils 'eighty to a hundred, all of rank and of the first families of the kingdom'. Mr Ball had a school in Ship Street beside the old round tower; Henry Grattan suffered under him, and so did Jonah Barrington who was flogged, not only for 'not minding my emphasis in recitation' but every Monday as a matter of course. Barrington claimed that he learned more classics in one year from his tutor, the Rev. Patrick Crawly (whose son, he could not refrain from mentioning, was hanged for murdering two old women with an ice-pick) than he had done in six at Dr Ball's.

The education of the majority of young ladies was in the hands of governesses. Elementary schooling at home was summarized by Barrington as 'Horn-book, Primer, Spelling-Book, Reading-made Easy, Aesop's Fables etc.' Dorothea Herbert, a rustic nine-year-old staying with her aunt in Gloucester Street, makes no mention of formal education – her family was more interested in the 'stay maker, the Mantua maker, and the hairdresser to attend to the toilette of Miss'. However, she did have lessons from 'my Dancing Master, my Drawing Master and my Music Master'. Convents catered for wealthy Catholic girls, while those of the established faith could attend certain schools for young ladies like that run by Mrs and Miss Knowles, relatives of Thomas Sheridan, at No. 48 York Street. Mr Whyte himself took classes for young ladies and also visited them in their homes for three guineas for eight weeks. Lady Morgan wrote in detail about her school at Clontarf which was run by a Huguenot named Madame Terson. The regime was strict with hours of rising at six in summer and seven in winter, to be followed by bread and milk for breakfast. No girl was taught writing until she had made a shirt. During meals all conversation was in French. One of her classmates was Mary Ann Grattan, who was tiresome about her father. 'My Papa is the greatest man in Ireland. What is your Papa?' One compensation was escaping

through a door in the garden to the seashore on Dublin Bay where
the school had a bathing machine.

Besides boasting Mr Whyte's Academy, Grafton Street was the
location of the art and drawing school founded in 1767 by the
Royal Dublin Society. It not only trained Irish sculptors and
painters, but the craftsmen whose skills contributed to the gracious
new building schemes of the city. John O'Keefe spent some time in
the school's drawing department, a room heated by a metal stove
and backed with tall wooden presses containing antique busts
which were in use by the present College of Art until quite recently.
Fortified with apples, oranges, peanuts and crayons supplied by the
school porter, each student used a mahogany drawing-board five
feet high for his copy, which was either a figure 'with the skin off'
to show its muscles, or a live model hired at four shillings an hour.

Trinity, embellished by new buildings, encouraged by a series of
able Provosts, among them the thrusting political jobber, John
Hely Hutchinson, was, according to Cloncurry, 'a nursery of
genius and patriotism'. From John O'Keefe, who was a fellow
commoner with Henry Grattan, we learn of the medieval kitchen
with five or six spits of roasting mutton and the college ale, known
as Lemon October. Barrington wrote accounts of gambling,
throwing crackers out of a coach window into glassware shops and
plunging streets into darkness by placing gunpowder squibs in
lamps. A pamphlet published in 1791 tells of 'drinking parties in
rooms, breaking furniture, baiting the badgemen [college
servants]...slipping into brothels, reeling to the theatre, carving
names on tables...' Together with such antics went a vigorous
strain of student politics, particularly after the French Revolution
when radical opinions flourished. Chancellor Fitzgibbon with his
'oblique glance and hatchet sharpness of countenance' felt obliged
to make his celebrated 'visitation' to purge revolutionary students
and members of staff and affect young Thomas Moore with its
'awfulness'.

A more tranquil seat of learning was the Royal Irish Academy to
promote the study of Irish history and antiquities, established in
1785 with the versatile Lord Charlemont as its first President.
There was a revived reverence for learning and culture. Lord
Charlemont, Lord Clonmell and Lord Mountjoy were among those
who put down libraries like port. Lord Clonmell's 6,000 books
were housed in a room in his Harcourt Street house which was

lavishly decorated with Gobelin tapestry. Lord Charlemont, whose Rockingham Library, filled with busts and statues, was one of the sights of the city, has described how when libraries went up for sale, customers went book mad. Books were still being pirated by Dublin publishers, a practice which only ceased with the Copyright Acts of 1801.

Visitors found that society people behaved better and that coarse conversation and heavy drinking were less obvious. The Englishman, Philip Luckombe, who came to Dublin in 1779, described how 'the bottle freely circulated, but not to that excess we heard of and, of course, dreaded to find'. By 1796 De La Tocnaye could write that 'they drink infinitely less in Dublin than I could have believed. Generally in the principal houses, an hour, perhaps only half an hour after the ladies have quitted the dining-room the master of the house pushes his glass to the middle of the table'. However these opinions directly contradict the reminiscences of Jonah Barrington and John Walshe, who were recalling, perhaps in exaggerated fashion, the days before the Union. 'The great end and aim of life in the upper classes' wrote Walshe 'seemed to be convivial indulgence to excess.' Barrington quotes the adage that the first question asked of a newcomer was whether he was good company over claret.

According to the same source, another important question was 'does he blaze?' By the 1770s the epidemic of duelling was said to be on the decline, although Walshe gives figures of 300 duels taking place between 1780 and 1800. An English traveller in 1790 still considered that duels were 'much more prevalent than in any other city I ever visited'. Students at Trinity frequently fought each other. The most prominent group of 'blazers' were the fashionably dressed bucks, and Dublin was a centre of their activities. A shop in Dame Street specialized in selling walking-sticks for bucks engraved with mottos like 'Who's Afraid?' or 'Who dare sneeze?' Men like Buck English, Buck Jones, and George Robert Fitzgerald who used to push passers-by into the street and then demand satisfaction were people to avoid.

In many bucks the spirit of violence was sublimated in the form of gambling. Gambling for high stakes was carried on at well-known haunts like Madden's at the Globe, Reilly's Tavern and Ben Jonson's Head, and there was a well-known hazard table in Smock Alley by the theatre. But the most popular haunt of fashionable rake-hell bucks came to be Daly's Club in College Green which had started as a simple chocolate house, but in 1791 was completely rebuilt to become 'the most supurb gambling house in the world'. Bucks and members of the nearby House of Commons could gamble day and night in sumptuous surroundings; during the afternoons blinds were drawn and chandeliers kept lit to simulate darkness. The Kildare Street Club – from its beginnings a conservative institution catering for the landowning aristocracy – which was founded in 1782, began to flourish as a result of a reaction to the excesses of Daly's.

Bucks like the engaging Buck Whaley, political job-seekers, cultured aristocrats like Lord Charlemont and impoverished eccentrics such as Richard Pockrich and the drunken poet, Thomas Dermody, are the people most frequently recalled in memoirs and reminiscences. We hear less about the middle classes. But one autobiography gives an account of the life of a middling well-off Catholic Dubliner who lived in the city at a time when penal laws had lost much of the power to make life miserable: the *Recollections* of John O'Keefe, the playwright. O'Keefe was born in Abbey Street in 1747. The Dublin that he knew as a child was still relatively modest without its spacious late Georgian proportions. He could remember the Earl of Meath's Liberty as having 'the...largest and richest streets in Dublin'. He was educated in Father Austin's school in Saul's Court, played marbles in the back yard of Dr Sheridan's school and watched from a window in his aunt's house in Dorset Street the trains of artillery passing on their way to oppose Thorot's landing at Carrickfergus. The pageant of Riding the Fringes passed his eye at a time when the Guild of Upholsterers was preceded by a man dressed entirely in feathers.

He had a short spell at Trinity where he watched an anatomy lecture. 'The professor of Anatomy had his subject on a board before him, part of the human body, and as he dissected, frequently put the knife in his mouth.' In spite of efforts by Provost Hely Hutchinson, who also advocated Catholic emancipation, Catholics were still unable to take degrees. Another permanent annoyance was their lack of burial grounds and the fees they had to pay to Protestant clergymen for interments. There were certain cemeteries which had come by custom to be used by Catholics, like St Kevin's, the burial place of the martyred Archbishop Dermot O'Hurley. Another was St James's churchyard; on St James's Day the Pope offered a Pontifical Mass in Rome for the Catholic dead of St James's. On that day, also, according to O'Keefe, the friends of those buried there decorated the graves with flowers, chaplets, cut paper ornaments and pious texts. And then there was Bully's Acre, actually three and three quarter acres near Kilmainham, which were not subject to the irritations of other cemeteries because they consisted of common land.

O'Keefe was closely associated with the theatre, and some of the most entertaining passages of his *Recollections* are concerned with the difficulties of aspiring and impoverished actors in Dublin. Other pages are full of leisure and pleasure. Excursions included trips down to Wicklow where there were sites for picnics and opportunities of viewing the estates of rich men like Lord Powerscourt, Lord Monck, Peter La Touche, and at the end of the century, Henry Grattan, who was given £50,000 by a grateful nation. People travelled out to see them in low cars fitted with a bed or mattress, carrying provisions and wines for the day. O'Keefe described other outings to Ringsend to eat cockles, an adventurous sea trip to a picnic at Howth, or trips to Dunleary by noddy or jingle with his friends to a coffee-house which supplied a sea-food breakfast consisting of 'a wash hand basin full of seagull and other birds' eggs and fried flounders'. This was unusual, because Dublin coffee-houses, unlike those in London which supplied meals, normally served only tea, coffee and chocolate.

One of O'Keefe's favourite coffee-houses was the Globe in Essex Street, frequented by merchants, physicians and lawyers. At the Globe's entrance, the shoeblack, Blind Peter, had his stand, equipped with a three legged stool, blunt knife, painter's brush or old wig for obtaining a shine and polish made from eggs and lampblack. Blind Peter was famous for his reply to Lord Townshend who had asked change for half a guinea: 'Half a guinea, your honour! By G-, Sir, you may as well ask a Highlander for a knee buckle!' With other characters like legless Billy the Bowl and Prince Hackball from an earlier era, he headed the great tribe of Dublin's beggars. Their numbers continued to astonish visitors; Arthur Young commenting on 'the wretchedness of the canaille', found walking through filthy slippery streets crowded with supplicating poor 'a most uneasy and disgusting experience'. De La Tocnaye was also revolted. 'The splendid carriages and the apparent wealth of the principal houses render the more displeasing the sight of the beggars...they may be seen hanging on for hours to the railings of basements, forcing charity by depriving those who live in these places of light and air.' Beggars clustered round shops, crowding customers going in and out. They were filthy, unmannerly, unshaven and strikingly blasphemous.

The contrast between the splendour and squalor of Dublin is attempted in Malton's *Picturesque and Descriptive View of the City of Dublin*, a series of handsome, if bland, prints published between 1792 and 1799. The convention of placing a beggar in a formal Dublin scene was already well established – an early eighteenth-century print of Dublin Bay shows a group of beggars at Beggar's Bush, where country vagrants traditionally assembled before making their descent on the city. Francis Wheatley sketched a beggar under the portico of the House of Commons in his drawing of 1782. Malton's views contain many glimpses of everyday life – gossiping farmers, merchants on horseback, women at open windows, a couple of chairmen at the specially-built sedan stop outside Lord Charlemont's house. Social detail includes a minute study of a tallow chandler's shop in Thomas Street beside the Tholsel and the ramshackle butchers' stalls at the west door of St Patrick's. The early version of the Parliament House on College Green shows two pigs, which were later changed to a solitary dog. The story that the House of Commons, mindful of its dignity, insisted on the change, may be apocryphal.

The very poor inevitably form part of the scene. Opposite the Rotunda a beggar holds out his cap, another supplicates near St Patrick's. Outside St Catherine's Church a notice indicates the consolation of the poor: 'Rum, Brandy, Meed, Whiskey, Arrack, Wholesale and Retail. Publican Denis Plunket.' A contemporary estimate gives 2,000 ale-houses, 300 taverns and 1,200 brandy shops in Dublin. In his print of Essex Bridge Malton, by a carefully assembled crowd, emphasizes that this point is still the centre of the city, although the old Custom House, visible on the south bank, is no longer in use. Ships still come up to the bridge, and one is seen leaning in the Liffey mud. But Carlisle Bridge was almost complete by the time the print was published in October 1797; it was finished by 1798 when the scaffolding that still enshrouded it was used as an impromptu gallows. In the early version poverty is indicated by a beggar and a blind man; less destitute hucksters are also in evidence, one drawing attention to his wares with a bell. On the east side of Capel Street are two lottery offices. These offices, encouraged by government support, were numerous; Gilbert mentions six in Dame Street alone. In his *Letters to the Irish Nation* George Cooper described how they 'are generally papered with green and gold and lighted up with a profusion of most expensive cut glass chandeliers... In these shops are crowds of the most miserable ragged objects...staking their daily bread on the chance of gain.' The draw took place in a hall in Capel Street, the tickets being selected from drums by two boys from the Blue Coat School.

Although there were some industries, mostly run by water power in the suburbs – Palmerstown, for example contained six calico mills, two oil mills and lead and iron works clustered beside the river – most of the city's industrial activity was concentrated in the Liberties. Here in addition to weaving were located trades like coach-building, glass works and breweries. Limekilns, slaughter houses and carrion houses created their stench. By the end of the century the Liberties had become hopelessly squalid slums. The streets were filled with filth flung from the windows of overcrowded tenements; sometimes it came up to the level of the first floor. Covered-in cesspits, dug before the doors of houses, tended to overflow; when they were emptied their odours filled the streets. Pollution from coal fires and from glass-works clouded the air, affecting the brickwork. The Quaker, Dr Rutty, wrote in 1772 of the brackish drinking water: 'The inhabitants of the city are chiefly supplied by water conveyed in wooden pipes to their houses for washing and drawing tea – yet the kettles that have been used to boiling it exhibit a brown crusty matter.' Elsewhere people depended on public fountains for their water. Some were extremely elegant like the one near the Rotunda and the Memorial Fountain erected to the memory of Lord Rutland the Lord Lieutenant who died of one of Dublin's fevers in 1797. Cheerful contemporary prints show women filling and carrying away tubs and buckets from these fountains, while small boys use large black kettles. Their good humour is illusory; many who lived near the Rutland fountain lived in miserable circumstances. 'The inhabitants of Merrion Square' wrote Dr Whitley Stokes in 1799 'may be surprised to hear that in the angle between Mount Street and Holles Street there is now a family of ten in a very small room of whom eight have had fever in the last month...' The city's inadequate plumbing would continue to ensure the importance of fountains. The *Dublin Journal of Medical Science* reporting on the condition of the poor in 1845, commented that 'nothing marks their poverty more than when congregating round their public fountains, struggling to have their little supply... There are many lanes and courts in which a tumbler of water could not be had for drinking...'

In 1798, the summer of the rebellion, the Reverend James Whitelaw, vicar of St Catherine's in Thomas Street, took it upon himself to do a census. 'The most dense population is found within the walls of the ancient city, comprehending the parishes of St Werburgh, St John, St Michael, St Nicholas Without, the eastern parts of St Audoen and the Deanery of Christ Church.' Many houses contained thirty or forty people, and one was quoted to him as having 108. 'I have frequently surprised from ten to sixteen persons of all ages and sexes in a room not fifteen feet square stretched on a wad of filthy straw, swarming with vermin, and without any covering save the wretched rags that constituted their wearing apparel.' A most unpleasant experience was visiting a sick and undernourished family in a leaking stinking house in Joseph's Lane, where an inundation of 'putrid blood, alive with maggots' from a nearby slaughter yard had burst the back door and flooded in to a depth of several inches. The tenants waded through the stuff quite unconcerned. Whitelaw's census proved remarkably accurate when compared to the official census early in the next century. He calculated the total population of Dublin at 172,091 with a further 10,000 people comprising the garrison, Trinity, the Castle and various institutions. This made it more populated than any city in England apart from London.

The poverty and lack of officially distributed aid for the poor encouraged private philanthropy. Probably most gentlewomen devoted part of their day to some form of poor relief, like Mrs Delany, who in 1745 wrote how 'after supper I make shirts and shifts for the poor naked wretches in the neighbourhood'. In the Liberties Whitelaw worked among the destitute, eventually dying of fever contracted when visiting the sick. Priests like Thomas Betagh, S.J. and Father John Austin devoted their lives to the poor. Father Austin spent his days 'visiting them in cellars and in garrets; never a day passed that he did not give food to numbers, including houseless children'. But although the proportion of

Catholics to Protestants in the city was by now five or six to one, most organized charities were Protestant orientated. One of the recognized means of obtaining funds for them was the 'charity sermon' delivered by a well-known clergyman to a packed and affluent congregation. A typical sermon, advertised in the *Dublin Evening Post* in 1780 announced that 'On Sunday 19th of March a Sermon will be preached at Capel Street Meeting House and a collection made for 21 poor boys who are annually clothed and carefully instructed in the principles of the Christian religion.' The best-known exponent of the popular theatrical style of preaching – which De La Tocnaye despised as 'ridiculous frenzies' – was the Reverend Walter Blake Kirwan whom public opinion considered to rival Garrick as King Lear or Mrs Siddons as Isabella. After listening to him a congregation was usually moved to give away large sums. Barrington, describing his 'unprepossessing appearance', wrote of his 'extraordinary powers' and how he knew of a gentleman who, after listening to him, threw his watch and purse on the plate. Once when he was ill, Kirwan had only to mount the pulpit and point to the picturesque group of orphan children, which as usual was grouped strategically round its base, muttering 'There they are!' to receive one of his largest collections.

Some of the myriad nineteenth-century charities, like that for Sick and Indigent Roomkeepers survive. In St Anne's in Dawson Street Lord Newson's curved wooden shelves contain the loaves of bread that are distributed after evening service on Sundays to the poor of the parish without religious distinction. Lady Arabella Denny, descendant of William Petty, founded the Magdalen Society which still offers facilities 'for the reception of such unfortunate females as abandoned by their seducers, prefer a life of penitence and virtue to guilt, infamy and prostitution'. At their House in Leeson Street each of these 'Magdalenes' was assigned a number, and in the registry of inmates Lady Arabella would write her personal comments. 'Mrs One...brought no effects into the house. She was bred in France to the business of making trimmings for ladies' clothes and to cooking. She was expelled for misbehaviour the next year and supposed to be out of her reason at times.' 'Mrs Fifteen is this day restored to a good father and kind stepmother. She is very young and uncertain in her temper which raises fears for her...she is very handy with her needle and can get her bread by it.'

Lady Arabella was also concerned with the Foundling Hospital. In 1772 the old Dublin workhouse had been divided into two separate institutions – the House of Industry near Oxmantown Green and the new Foundling Hospital rebuilt in James Street. In addition to giving more than £4,000 towards building costs and premiums to the nurses, Lady Arabella donated a special grandfather clock which rang out every twenty minutes. A brass plate recorded its purpose: 'To mark that as children rear'd by the spoon must have but a small quantity of food at a time, it must be offer'd frequently, for which purpose this clock strikes every twenty minutes, at which notice all ye infants that are not asleep must be discretely fed.' But her efforts and those of like-minded ladies were pathetically doomed to failure. Amid vermin, dirt and neglect children continued to die. Between 1784 and 1796 more than three quarters of the infants admitted to the Foundling Hospital perished.

The reorganized House of Industry was supported by the government and by the charitable, receiving such miscellaneous free provisions as a cartload of cabbages from the nursery garden at the Foundling Hospital and 'turneps' and two bunches of 'celeri' from the Paving Corporation. Once the Lord Mayor provided rolls of bread and butter and a sow and seven piglets which had been seized in the streets. De La Tocnaye was impressed by the inmates' diet: 'Their food is better than on the tables of peasants. They have meat once a week, bread, potatoes, and other vegetables every day.' In times of emergency the House of Industry fed thousands; during the winter of 1776 hungry people were given a daily ration of a pound of bread, a herring and a pint of beer if they could produce a certificate to show they were starving. At other times it took in two main categories of inmates: those who entered voluntarily, forced by extremes of necessity, and those who were 'compelled' who included a proportion of fettered lunatics from the Bridewell. The dreaded black cart of the House of Industry toured at night; often battles took place between the beadles and those who wished to avoid their clutches. An incident reported in the *Dublin News* of 1780 described how the beadles seized a woman standing in a doorway in Marlborough Street; when the lady of the house sent a chairman to get her release, there was a riot in which two people were dangerously wounded. Another reported riot resulted, not only in some fatalities, but in the complete destruction of the cart.

Proper policing of the city was still disorganized and the various means of ensuring civil law and order were ineffective. (But when disorder became really dangerous there was always the military presence.) Most policing was done by patrolling watchmen who got their jobs as a result of charitable efforts by different parishes. As a result they were often old and feeble. William Le Fanu described these 'charleys' with their lanterns, long frieze coats and capes with low-crowned hats. Their only weapon was the 'crook' on the end of a pole for catching offenders. One of the traditional sounds of Dublin was their voices calling out the hour and the weather '...past twelve o'clock and a cloudy night'. Le Fanu and other student bloods used to amuse themselves teasing these elderly guardians of the law; 'to overturn his watchbox face downwards on the ground was the grandest feat of all'. A corps of police was formed in 1786, but it was ineffective; 'it began like an armed force and ended like a band of invalids'.

The poor policing system paradoxically helped to keep the prisons full; authority took no chances. Although the people of Dublin were aware of the continued scandal of their condition, they were still characterized by overcrowding, drunkenness and gaol fever, while the underpaid gaolers extorted as much money as they could from prisoners, a large proportion of whom were debtors. Numbers were still reduced by hanging, transportation and the age-old punishment of whipping. A favourite whipping course was from Newgate to College Green or the Toll House in St James Street. William Grace who stole a copper teakettle and a coal scuttle was sentenced 'to be whipt from the Tholsel to St James Street on Wednesday week'. Maurice Fitzgerald, sentenced for housebreaking, was 'publically whipped from Newgate to Essex Bridge three times'. Public whipping continued until 1815, when the last to suffer, William Horish, was whipped from the gates of Green Street Courthouse to the Royal Exchange.

De La Tocnaye attended a hanging as a routine entertainment. Criminals of Dublin County were hanged at Kilmainham; the place of execution for criminals of Dublin city was a point between Upper Fitzwilliam Street and Lad Lane, the site of the old Viking Hang Hoeg. Whenever possible murderers, particularly if their crime had taken place in the suburbs, were marched out by a troop of soldiers and hanged at the scene of the crime on a specially constructed gallows. The hangman wore a grotesque mask and a hump on his back formed by a large wooden bowl to fend off stones from hostile crowds. Remnants of barbaric medieval custom were preserved in the beheading of rebels after death and in the sentence of drawing and quartering that could be passed on criminals like the poisoner, Lanegan. According to Barrington, the hangman commuted this to four cuts on his limbs which helped to revive him, together with applications of hot vinegar on his neck by his mother, who noticed a spark of life in him after he was cut down. Larry, the hero of the famous ballad, who must have been convicted of murder, feared that he would be 'cut up like a pie' after he was stretched on the city gallows, although his friends assured him:

> A chalk on de back of de neck
> Is all dat Jack Ketch dares to give you...

Violent aspects of society were remembered later with censure by J.E. Walshe who wrote of 'fights in the street, gambling upon coffins, bucks, bullies, rapparees, duelling, drunkenness, bullbaiting, idleness, abduction clubs and a thousand other degrading peculiarities which marked the higher as well as the lower classes'. Amid the brash new elegance Dublin was a city of beggars, brawling chairmen, bootblacks, penny boys who drove their cattle to Smithfield with knobbed sticks, scores of street sellers crying out about Dublin Bay herrings or cockles and mussels, and odd characters like chalkers who practised 'houghing' or cutting the tendons of pedestrians' legs, pinkindindies who nipped their victims with concealed swords, pluckers, employed by shops to push prospective customers inside, and couple-beggars, degraded clergymen who earned their living by marrying for a reduced fee any couple who asked without question. Dubliners had a wide range of amusement including cockfighting, throwing oranges from the pit of the theatre, cheap days at the Rotunda, and old festivals to be enjoyed – the crowning of the King of Dalkey – which ceased after 1797 – holy wells like St John's to be visited, the week long orgy at Donnybrook to be enlivened with whiskey.

Meanwhile political pressures were increasing. The eighties were a time of political calm and prosperity that seemed permanent. Within a few years the pyramid of wealth and power collapsed. The fanciful parades of the Volunteers were succeeded by the furtive atrocities of the Yeomanry Corps.

As the century wore on, Catholics became increasingly restless at their treatment as second class citizens. Concessions might be made, and there was a greater understanding of Catholic aims, but most Protestant leaders were equivocal when it came to the question of Emancipation. With their own parliament and institutions they continued to feel morally and socially superior. John Keogh, the leader of Catholic radicals in Dublin, used to say you could tell a Catholic by the way he slunk along the street. Members of the two religions kept apart socially; in the summer of 1791 Wolfe Tone, who was about to write *An Argument on Behalf of the Catholics in Ireland*, declared that he was not at the time acquainted with a single member of the Catholic community.

Excluded from the franchise, the army, the guilds and government service, many enterprising Catholics, like similarly deprived non-conformists, entered trade. Some became rich. John Keogh himself was a successful wholesale mercer. Edward Byrne of Mullinahack, a fellow member of the Back Lane Parliament, became the wealthiest Catholic trader in Ireland after making a fortune out of baking and distilling. The Catholic Committee petition presented to Parliament in 1792 – it was rejected – had been signed by fifty of the 'most respectable commercial characters' among the Dublin Catholics who spoke for their whole community. Sir Boyle Roche, who, in spite of his eccentricities held down a job in the Castle, described these worthies as 'turbulent shopkeepers and shop-lifters;' and rambled on about their meeting in chop-houses and plotting against the government as they drank their porter.

'We rejoice in the late privileges an enlightened legislature has extended to them' stated an Assembly Roll of 1784 concerning Catholics; 'but we can never consent to any measure which may weaken or endanger the Protestant establishment in church or state.' A year before, the Volunteer Convention of November 1783 had decisively suppressed Catholic aspirations.

The Volunteer Movement had been reluctantly allowed to gather momentum after 1778 when it was formed to fight off a possible French invasion at a time when England needed all the spare troops for the American wars. Military ardour seized Ireland, and soon there were 100,000 volunteers. Not only did they parade about in their dashing uniforms, but they actually pressurized the government in England to granting concessions like the repeal of laws forbidding the export of wool and other goods. Could they go further? Since Catholics were forbidden by law to bear arms, they could not join the Movement. But they supported the Volunteers eagerly, hoping for further relaxation of the penal and trade laws. There was a possibility of Emancipation which would allow them to enter Parliament. It was their misfortune that at the great Volunteer Convention their champion was Frederick Hervey, Earl of Bristol and Bishop of Derry. The Bishop, a liberal, and an Englishman, believed in Emancipation. But he did not make a very effective advocate. He may have dazzled the Dublin crowds as he drove through in an open landau drawn by six horses and escorted by a contingent of dragoons; they cheered his rotund form swathed in princely purple, his knee and shoe buckles blazing with diamonds and large gold tassels hanging from his gloves. They were enraptured by the tricorned hat of a Volunteer Colonel which topped his purple. But Hervey was no match for the conservative Lord Charlemont, who opposed any concessions to Catholic demands, and his attempts to bring in liberal legislation by a bill which advocated Catholic franchise was defeated. 'From that time' Lecky considered 'the conviction sank deep into the minds of many that reform in Ireland could only be effected by revolution, and the rebellion of 1798 might be foreseen.' Reforms such as the continued relaxation of the Penal Laws, the founding of Maynooth and the eventual admission of Catholics to Trinity were not sufficient to placate radical opinion. Revolutionary fervour, encouraged by events in France, gave rise to a hardening opposition. 1795 saw the formation of the Orange Society. Barrington had described its extraordinary celebration of King William's birthday when 'every man unbuttoned the knees of his breeches and drank the Orange toast on his knees'.

Soldiers in Dublin in May 1798 amounted to 1,500 troops in the garrison; there were also army camps at Loughlinstown and Bray and an artillery camp at Chapelizod. These soldiers were supported by 4,000 members of the Yeomanry who formed a home guard. Their numbers included a corps of old gentlemen recruited from Merrion Square who on wet evenings would patrol the streets in a long line of sedan chairs, their muskets sticking out through the curtains. Meanwhile the public continued to enjoy its pleasures. Theatres were open; in the unseasonably hot weather there was an abduction, and the first grand piano arrived in Ireland. Citizens were treated to an unusual spectacle when Lord Kingston, accompanied by an executioner with his steel axe draped in black, was tried by his peers for the murder of his half-brother. The United Irishmen considered surrounding the Parliament building on College Green during the trial and seizing public figures like the Lord Chancellor, Fitzgibbon and the Lord Lieutenant, Lord Camden. But this plan was defeated by an informer's vote.

Lord Edward Fitzgerald's requirements for insurrection included 50 hammers, 50 grooving irons and 150 hooks for scaling ladders. On 19 May, the day after Lord Kingston was acquitted, the noble revolutionary, interrupted while reading *Gil Blas*, was captured by Major Sirr during an affray in the house of a feather merchant named Murphy in Thomas Street. They found his uniform of the United Irishmen, a bottle-green braided suit with crimson cape and a cap of liberty two feet long. He was taken mortally wounded to the Castle in a sedan chair.

In spite of this setback, insurrection was to go ahead, signalled by the burning of mail coaches and the extinguishing of street lights on the 24 May. Part of the programme was carried out. 'I well remember the feeling of awe in the city by the street lights being put out one after the other,' Thomas Moore recalled. His observation indicates that at last street lighting had become efficient. No longer was it necessary for servants, like the footman advised by Swift, to accompany their masters when they walked abroad or took carriages, carrying lanterns or flambeaux lit with pitch. For decades there had been complaints that street lamps were insufficient, inadequately supplied with oil (paraffin was used), that the globes were imperfectly cleaned and were 'frequently out at five in the morning'. But in 1785 the Paving and Lighting Board introduced a new improved lighting plant, using oil lamps with double burners. There were plenty of them; in Malton's Essex Street print eighteen are located on Essex Bridge alone.

On the hot night of the 24th drums beat the garrison to arms, while the yeomanry assembled with orders to occupy Smithfield. Jonah Barrington belonged to the Attorney's Corps. 'Nobody knew his station or could ascertain his duty...more confused, indecisive and unintelligible arrangement of a military nature never appeared.' They stood about in the dusk 'all the barristers, attorneys, merchants, bankers, revenue officers, shopkeepers, students of the University, doctors, apothecaries and corporators of an immense metropolis in red coats with a sprinkling of parsons, all doubled up together awaiting...for invisible executioners to despatch them without mercy'. Later in the night the panic subsided with calls for refreshments. In fact there were no more than a few hundred leaderless United Irishmen in Dublin wandering around in search of orders.

Next day showed the first fruits of rebellion – three mutilated bodies outside Lord Castlereagh's office in Lower Castle Yard, which were considered by a shocked Barrington as the 'most frightful spectacle which ever disgraced a royal residence, save a seraglio'. (One of them turned out to be alive, and obtained a pardon.) The practice of exhibiting rebel bodies in Castle Yard continued during the summer. Dublin's experience of the ninety-eight was mainly as witness to reprisals, first evident in the dispatching of some disloyal lamplighters, and scenes like the hanging of Dr John Esmonde from the scaffolding of Carlisle Bridge, his yeomanry coat turned inside out to indicate that he was a traitor. Rebels attended by pikes were hung up here and there; a captured blacksmith was paraded on horseback 'his bellows borne before him and his person hung over with the pikes that had been found on him'. The Royal Exchange became a temporary barracks for the Yeomanry where members could indulge in flogging; so did the old Custom House where the dreaded Dumbarton Fencibles arranged pitchcapping and flogging at triangles. Other temporary barracks were improvised on the site of the Shelbourne, in Baggot Street, Henry Street and Kevin Street. Lord Beresford's mansion, Tyrone House in Marlborough Street, became known as Beresford's Riding House Establishment where his own corps of Yeomanry learned not only riding, but torture; someone wrote on a board outside it: 'Mangling done here by John Beresford and Company'. Croppy's Hole, on waste land between the Royal Barracks and the river, filled up with corpses, some without their heads. The theatres finally closed, a curfew was imposed and further volunteers joined the different corps of yeomanry. It seemed every gentleman wore uniform. In the courts the only people in civilian clothes were the prisoners.

The failure of the insurrection emphasized the sterile political ideals, both of the United Irishmen and the Patriots. When Pitt promised Emancipation and greater prosperity as a result of union with England, there were those who found it a reasonable idea. But Dublin felt its interests as a capital city threatened, and the defeat of the government motion in January 1799, resulted in scenes of wild enthusiasm. Barrington saw the 'vast multitude' that crowded round Parliament House, the galleries inside filled with 'ladies of distinction' assembled to witness 'the fate of Ireland'. After the respite, Speaker Foster's coach was drawn triumphantly home by the mob, while that of the ever-unpopular Earl of Clare, who had secured a pro-Union resolution in the Lords, was bombarded with stones. Lord Castlereagh swiftly adjusted the balance with the promise of fifteen promotions in the peerage, the creation of fifteen new peers and numerous other bribes. In the House of Lords annuities awarded by a grateful British government varied from £3,978.3s.4d. for the Earl of Clare to £4.11s. to Andrew Bowen, a water-carrier. In the Commons Speaker Foster received £5,038.8s.4d. a year, while the pension of a firelighter, Thomas Seavers amounted to £4.11s. A front door-keeper was given £168.4s.9½d. and fourteen messengers were paid off with £36 each.

11

From the Union to the Famine 1800–1847

In the words of the *Gentlemen's and Citizens' Almanack*: '1801. Jan 1st. The Imperial United Standard was first displayed upon Bedford Tower, Dublin Castle, in consequence of the Act of Union becoming an operative law.'

The economic repercussions following the wholesale departure of members of Parliament were immediate. The eighty-two peers were estimated to have spent £624,000 a year in Dublin, much of which percolated to tradesmen and shopkeepers. In 1805 J.W. Croker was already complaining of the apathy of shopkeepers who displayed 'a sullen surliness' and 'seemed to prefer extortion and stagnation to quick returns'. In the same year Sir John Carr noticed that many of the larger houses in Mountjoy Square and Stephen's Green were empty or had been let out as lodgings. As the century advanced, the skills that had created and embellished the great town houses declined. There was less demand for craftsmen to supply luxuries. In 1807 John Murphy, a member of the gang that robbed and murdered Father McCartan near Lucan, declared that he would not have come so close to the gallows if it had not been for the Union; before the Act, his trade, that of a silver plater, had been an exceedingly good one. As late as 1836 when the suburban boom was beginning, 'paper stainers, house-smiths, paper hangers, stucco workers and plasterers' were all said to be in a bad way. The new professional classes had less style and less money to throw around than their predecessors.

Houses of the nobility had to find new uses. In 1815 Leinster House was sold to the Royal Dublin Society. Aldborough House became a school. Moira House, whose sumptuous salon with its mother-of-pearl window had been admired by Wesley, was transformed into the grim Mendicity Institute after its top floor had been sheared off. The empty Archbishop's Palace of St Sepulchre – by now located in a slum area – was converted into barracks, while the Archbishop moved to more fashionable quarters in Stephen's Green. By 1806 the Castle was run down, the state carriage needed regilding and the Halberdiers' uniforms needed replacing. In the same year, the Tholsel, ruinous even when

Malton drew it, was finally pulled down. The gravel paths of Stephen's Green were choked with weeds, while the Green itself had been denuded of trees after a firework display had got out of hand. Profits from the Rotunda declined from £1,450 to less than £300 in fifteen years.

By 1821, when the slump was aggravated by the end of the Napoleonic wars, the value of houses had fallen in twenty years by thirty per cent. In the depressed Liberties, where unemployment was as savage as it had been in Swift's time, it had fallen fifty per cent. The Linen Hall, deprived of its old function since the collapse of the linen trade, was staggering towards its demise. There were more beggars than ever.

And yet post-Union Dublin was not all gloom. Sir Walter Scott, who paid a visit in 1825, admired it without reservation. In a letter to Maria Edgeworth he described it as 'splendid beyond my expectations... They tell me the city is desolate (as a result of the Union) of which I can see no appearance'. His son-in-law, Lockhart, echoed his sentiments, talking of 'a very magnificent city'. They may well have been mellowed by the bowing shopkeepers and their wives who bobbed to them on every street corner, and the theatre audience who greeted their arrival with 'a perfect cataract and thunder of roaring'. But it was true that Dublin did not lose every aspect of elegance at the moment of Union. Georgian development had not yet run its course. Neither Fitzwilliam nor Merrion Square were completed until well into the century. Mountjoy Square, whose development was held up by the death of the 2nd Lord Mountjoy, owner of the Gardiner estates, at the Battle of New Ross in 1798, was finished in 1815, with its interior levelled and enclosed around an immense circular lawn surrounding a weeping ash. Francis Johnston continued the great tradition of architecture with St George's Church, the Post Office and the Chapel Royal. In 1815 Catholics were confident enough to erect St Mary's pro-Cathedral, the only work of an amateur architect named John Sweetman. It should have gone up in the wide spaces of Sackville Street, but Protestant opposition would not allow it so conspicuous a position, and it was pushed back out of sight into the miserable confines of Marlborough Street. Nelson's Pillar was subscribed to by merchants and bankers and inaugurated in 1808 with a procession of dignitaries including the Fellows and Provost of Trinity and the Lord Lieutenant and his wife dressed in deepest mourning, who walked from the Royal Exchange to the Rotunda.

Emblems of progress during the early years of the new century varied from the modernized gallows room at the Newgate 'in which' wrote Sir John Carr 'is a windlass and machinery for raising or depressing the bodies of criminals when they are executed' to the Dublin Oil Gas Station, a handsome building in Brunswick Street founded by Act of Parliament in 1824 'to light the city of Dublin and environs with oil gas'. Initially the venture was not very successful. The Alliance Gas Company, advertising its newly introduced gas meters in 1837, admitted that the use of gas had not made much progress since it was expensive and the supply was defective. (Matches did not replace flint and steel until the 1840s.) New seamarks were the Kish Lightship, first anchored in 1811, and the fifteen useless Martello Towers, all about forty feet high with walls eight feet thick, modelled on a tower at Cape Mortella in Corsica which English troops had found difficult to storm in 1793.

Post-Union society regretted the past. A monument in St Patrick's to the Rt. Hon. George Ogle who died in 1814 noted that 'he exhibited a perfect model of that exalted refinement which in the best days of our country characterized the Irish gentleman'. (It is only fair to add that George Ogle was on Barrington's list of duellists; he 'fought Barney Coyle, a distiller, because he was a Papist'.) People sought to console themselves by becoming bourgeois. The change is indicated in a comparison of Malton's prints with those of the Brocas family published about twenty years later. In Malton the beauty of the buildings is stressed, almost exalted. In the Brocas family's twelve views of Dublin which appeared between 1818 and 1829 the physical background is the same. The Georgian idiom of architecture would remain a basic style for another fifty years, but the Brocas family transforms the architecture into a mere backdrop for something tangibly more bustling and plebeian. Their views of Carlisle Bridge and the Half-penny Bridge are crowded with members of the new middle classes – men in top hats and women in respectable poke bonnets holding parasols.

The old conviviality and high living had given way to a more placid, family-orientated routine. Gone were the occasions when innumerable bottles of claret were consumed at a sitting. Duelling ceased to be a social mannerism. William Le Fanu described one of

the last duels which took place on the North Bull in 1838; a
participant shot himself through the leg and was brought back to
the city with the leg sticking out of a carriage window 'to keep it
cool'. Public morals were deemed to have improved, and there
were less 'unfortunate females' roaming the streets. In 1808 the old
Charleys had been replaced by a new corps of men 'stout, young
and able bodies', and the city was divided into six police districts.
Thirty years later the Dublin Metropolitan Police came into being
with 6 superintendents, 24 inspectors, 100 sergeants, 1,000
constables and 20 supernumeraries.

The theatre was less rowdy. In 1820 the old Crow Street theatre
closed; the Green Room became a workroom for manufacturing
hats and other parts of the building were now 'a place for rubbish
for the neighbourhood'. Audiences at the new theatre in Hawkins
Street with its gilded interior shaped like a lyre, failed to provide
the restless bawdy atmosphere of eighteenth-century theatrical
performances. Smock Alley, long gone, had been replaced by a
Catholic church on its site. Ranelagh Gardens was planted with a
convent, while a new venue, the Coburg Gardens – named for
Leopold, not Albert – attracted menaders. Astley's Amphitheatrre
in Peter Street, which had delighted generations with its equestrian
displays, became a house of worship and an asylum for blind
females. Instead of watching ladies perform on horseback, society
could occupy itself more suitably by passing tranquil hours at the
Royal Dublin Society's new Museum in Leinster House or at the
Panoramas with their collections of wild beasts and waxworks. The
Zoological Gardens in Phoenix Park opened in 1830; in the first
year over 30,000 visitors saw the animals which included a leopard,
a wolf, a hyena and a lioness supposed to be in cub.

Warburton and Whitelaw's *History of the City of Dublin*
published in 1818, considered that with the new emphasis on family
life the citizen 'does not meet a friend at a tavern, but at his own
house... For this convivial gratification he neglects the theatre, the
tavern, the gardens...' The old simple amusements like eating
from picnic hampers carried out to Howth and Dalkey became
family pastimes. All classes now partook of pleasures such as
shooting plover and blackbirds in Bloody Fields or hiring a jingle
from the jingle stand at the end of Baggot Street to Dalkey,
Dunleary or Howth, or taking the daily coach to the spreading
suburb of Blackrock which Scott noticed as 'thick with villas and

all the signs of ease and opulence'. The craze for bathing on beaches like Irishtown, Blackrock and Sandymount intensified. Ladies bathed at seperate localities from men. Their bathing machines, which in seaside places in England would have brought them right down to the water, here in Dublin Bay left them 'marooned' on dry land so that they had to walk into the sea past itinerant women selling cockles and crabs from baskets. Men bathed without clothes. 'The swarm of naked figures thus seen on the shore from Ringsend to Sandymount' commented one bemused visitor 'is as singular as it is surprising.' The Fortyfoot at Sandycove, which still tolerates naked men, is a remnant of the old widespread practice.

In 1811 John Gamble described the resident nobility as 'a sickly delicate plant' while the gentry, behaving like swallows, took an annual flight to London. By 1821 John James McGregor's *New Picture of Dublin* claimed that the gentry of the city consisted of a mere 200 families that included clergymen, physicians and attorneys. Doctors had come up rapidly in the social scale, not solely because they could count among their numbers famous medical names like Stokes and Colles. In 1811 Gamble, himself a doctor, noted 'the truth is a physician here is almost on the pinnacle of greatness; there are few resident nobility and gentry here since the Union, and the·professors of law and medicine may be said to furnish the aristocracy of the place'. In 1832 Jonah Barrington was moaning: 'everything is now changed...that class of society is no more; neither men nor names are the same'. By 1841 700 doctors, 1,900 lawyers, 15,000 attorneys and their dependents were struggling to form an aristocracy. In his 1837 diary William Blacker considered that in pre-Union days someone so socially low as an attorney's wife 'would as soon have thought of dancing the ordeal over red-hot ploughshares as of venturing near the Vice-Regal drawing room... Now the courtly doors were thrown open to almost anyone and there was a scramble for tickets...' Thackeray was scathing about the newly emerged Dublin Society. 'Its magnates are tradesmen; brass plates are their titles of honour. O that old humbug of a Castle! It is the greatest sham in Ireland.'

Thackeray was one of the more distinguished tourists of the period. Visitors arrived in increasing numbers after sea travel became less of an ordeal. The crossing of the Irish Sea was revolutionized by the introduction of the paddle boat. At the beginning of the century packets had generally landed at Howth; then in 1817 the foundation was laid of the new east pier at Dunleary, and five years later mail steamers were calling in at Kingstown, rechristened⁺ after George IV's visit. Before the steamboats started their run, the voyage over the Irish Sea retained its eighteenth-century miseries. In 1807, Sir Richard Colt Hoare took twenty-three hours to cross from Holyhead on the *Union Packet*, one of the last sailing ships on the crossing. The coastline was notoriously dangerous, and between 1797 and 1803 as many as 124 ships were wrecked or seriously damaged round Dublin Bay. Broken hulks and masts sticking up over the sands were normal spectacles for those taking the sea air. A particularly dreadful tragedy took place in November 1807 when two military transports sailing from the Pigeon House were driven on shore in thick snow and a violent easterly gale. Hundreds perished on 'the ensanguined strand of Merrion'. The other terrible nineteenth-century shipwreck also involved a sailing ship, the iron-clad clipper, *John Tayleur*, which struck off Ireland's Eye in 1852 drowning nearly 300 people. Steam made sea voyages far less perilous.

Transport generally was becoming more efficient. Stage and mail coaches carried passengers fairly swiftly; by 1824 it was possible to leave Dublin by coach at 9 a.m. and arrive in Carlow by 2.30 p.m. The canals still prospered. Flyboats with their promenade decks drifted along, drawn by two or three horses, often at a gallop. The hotel at Portobello was the starting point for the Grand Canal and Broadstone Harbour for the Royal. But mail coaches and canal boats suddenly found they had a rival – the railway.

The railway between Dublin and Kingstown was begun in 1832 under the direction of Willian Dargan. The first train was drawn by horses on 31 July 1834; locomotives arrived in October and on 17 December 1834 the first train drawn by steam-power, carrying a party of Directors and their wives, was cheered out of Westland Row. It was followed by the first regular passenger train, the *Hibernia*, filled with a fashionable concourse of people. The little carriages, pulled by a high-stacked engine, were painted different colours, purple-lake, yellow-green and Prussian blue according to class. The journey to Kingstown took nineteen and a half minutes. Ten years after the first service was inaugurated, an 'Atmospheric Railway', catering for holiday traffic, the first of its kind in the world, linked Kingstown and Dalkey. Soon the capital was the

centre of a nationwide network and Thackeray commented that
Dublin was 'railway mad'.

The middle classes began to move out. For half a century the
North and South Circular Roads and the canals with their lines of
elms planted to provide water pipes, had bounded the city. Little by
little the area 'beyond the canals' became suburban. The most
genteel residential areas developed south of the Liffey where
Ranelagh, Rathmines and Harold's Cross were connected to the
city by lines of terraces; soon, however, development near Harold's
Cross would be inhibited by the presence of Mount Jerome
Cemetery. Houses in such suburbs were still Georgian in design
with some variations; the single-story terrace, so characteristic
of Dublin was beginning to appear. The most prosperous
developments were those along the railway route. Charles Lever
has a description of the sort of people who travelled on the fast-
growing suburban line. 'The 8.30 train is filled with attorneys; the
ways of Providence are inscrutable; it arrives safely in Dublin.
With the 9.00 train comes a fresh jovial looking sort of fellows with
bushy whiskers and geraniums in buttonholes. They are traders.
9.30 the housekeeper train. 10 o'clock the barristers... fierce faces
look out at the weather... 11 o'clock the men of wit and pleasure.'
Kingstown, which had at first refused to have a railway station,
became, according to Thackeray 'a town irregularly built with
many handsome terraces, some churches and showy-looking
hotels'. At the time of his visit many terraces were incomplete. The
rents of houses taken by Dublin families during the summer were
considered exorbitant.

Kingstown grew at the expense of Blackrock which had been
wrecked by railway engineering. The railway did nothing for the old
Rock Road either, which was in an increasingly neglected state.
Jaunting cars suffered. An illustration prefixing the thirteen views of
the new railway published by the *Dublin Penny Journal* shows the
driver of a jaunting car calling for fares. 'Goin' out, Sir? Get up, your
honour – here's a seat; I'm just off – only waiting for two like
yourself – Tim Dunn, ye'd betther lend me the two gemmen you've
got on your car...' However, the discriminating preferred such old
fashioned transport. Thackeray took a car through the suburbs,
noting 'rows of neat houses fronted with gardens...pretty market
gardens with trim beds of plants and shining glass houses'.

The Industrial Revolution had brought in some industry, most of which was located along the canals, beside the port or along the Liffey and its tributaries. On the Dodder there were mills and factories from Ringsend at its mouth right up to Ballyboden. Donnybrook had a bleaching green, while Ballsbridge boasted its 'hammersmith works' and a calico printing factory. (However, by 1838 the cotton industry had virtually deserted Dublin for County Antrim.) The quays on the north side supported two vinegar works, a vitriol works and a glass works; those south of the river possessed the gas works, a salammoniac factory, and chemical works and the coachworks for the railway beside the Grand Canal Docks. West and north-west Dublin never became residential. The western approaches to the city were fairly squalid because of the industry located beside the Liffey, while the north-west contained a disproportionate number of institutions like the Royal Barracks, the workhouse, a prison and a lunatic asylum. The slums continued to centre on the Liberties.

Lewis's *Topographical Dictionary of Ireland*, published in 1837, stated that the city could be roughly divided into four by the Liffey crossed with a line drawn from the King's Inns to the north through Capel Street to the Castle and Aungier Street south of the river. The western sections including the Liberties were extremely dilapidated. The south-east area with Stephen's Green, Merrion Square and Fitzwilliam Square fostered 'the nobility, the gentry and members of the liberal professions' while the north-east section, which contained Rutland Square and Mountjoy Square was inhabited by the merchant and official class. That this north-eastern area of the city continued to maintain a prosperous Protestant population is indicated by the continued building of churches: St George's Church in 1815, the grandiose chapel of ease known as the Black Church in 1830 and Findlater's Presbyterian church later still.

By the early nineteenth century Dublin could welcome visitors with numerous comfortable hotels. In 1821 McGregor listed forty hotels for a traveller to choose 'suitable to his ability and inclination'. At that time Morrison's Hotel at the bottom of Dawson Street was the most fashionable; it contained a thirty foot long sitting-room overlooking College Park, the usual assortment of coffee-rooms and a tavern. A traveller in 1825 tells how he and a friend were casually greeted by a waiter at Morrison's: 'Well, gentlemen, I shall be putting on a bottle of sherry and another sauterne while you're thinking of what you'll have besides.' The diners chose salmon 'very crisp and good, but the soles tasted of the

hot weather...griddled potato cakes were delicious'. In the same
street was located the still surviving Hibernian Hotel from where in
due course Bianconi would dispatch his long cars all over Ireland,
and Mackens, or the Royal Mail Hotel. At Mackens General
Humbert and his officers had been accommodated while they were
on parole after the Battle of Ballinamuck in 1797; when they left
for France they gave the proprietor their swords. Before the packet
station was transferred to Kingstown it was from Mackens that
passengers for Holyhead would take the Royal Mail Coach for
their ship anchored at Howth.

An advertisement for a new hotel in Sackville Street in 1842
mentions a coffee room with 'viandes of the choicest description,
wines of the 1st vintage, hot joints. Every evening at five o'clock,
soup, chops, steaks, tea and coffee always ready. The daily and
weekly papers taken in. Wax and tallow chandeliers.' In the same
year Thackeray stayed at the Shelbourne, where for six and
eightpence a day – which he considered very moderate – he was
provided with 'a copious breakfast in the coffee room, a perpetual
luncheon is likewise there spread, a plentiful dinner is ready at six
o'clock; after which there is a drawing room and a rubber of whist
with *tay* and coffee and cakes in plenty'. His room was less
satisfactory: 'a queer little room and dressing-room on the ground
floor looking towards the Green' which he persuaded the 'black-
faced, good humoured chambermaid' to clean, after which she
opened his window to the sun, propping it up with a broomstick.

The eye of a stranger notes details which inhabitants often do not
think worth recording. Sir Richard Colt Hoare, for instance, was
struck how in 1807, four years after Robert Emmet's rebellion,
some of the barricades put up at the time still blocked the streets.
Dr Gamble observed in 1811 how pots of geraniums grew in almost
every window. Thackeray, used to the spreading blight of
industrialization in England, found the city countrified. 'You pass
from some of the stately fine Dublin Streets straight into the
country.' After leaving Eccles Street the potatoes began at once.
'You are in a wide green plain diversified by occasional cabbage
plants.' The macabre inspection by many tourists of prisons and
workhouses gives an impression of these institutions which is
difficult to garner from elsewhere. One of the earliest post-Union
travellers, Sir John Carr, made a particularly diligent tour of the
Foundling Hospital, a fever hospital, the House of Industry and

Newgate to provide material for his pompous book *The Stranger in Ireland,* which earned him some ridicule and Byron's title of 'Green Erin's Knight and Europe's wandering star'.

Shelley came in 1812 with his wife and sister-in-law to rouse people against injustice, showering them with pamphlets from his hotel window. One, entitled *An Address to the Irish People*, had been printed 'at the lowest possible cost – 5d....because it is the intention of the author to awake in the minds of the Irish poor a knowledge of their real state...' But the ninety-eight was too recent a memory; so was Emmet's rebellion. Daniel O'Connell said of that doomed enterprise: 'I ask you whether a madder scheme was ever devised by a Bedlamite? Here was Mr Emmet, having got together about £1,200 in money and seventy-four men; whereupon he makes war upon King George III with 150,000 of the best troops in Europe and with the wealth of three kingdoms at his command. Why, my good sir, poor Emmet's scheme was as wild as anything in romance.' At the time of Emmet's rebellion O'Connell was still a member of the Lawyers' Yeomanry Corps. Once in later years he pointed to the Grand Canal Hotel in James Street. 'I searched every room in that house one July night in 1803...for Croppies.' He may have been right in his opinion; Emmet, equipped like Lord Edward Fitzgerald with a green and white uniform crowned with a cocked hat and feathers, was merely another deluded romantic. At least Shelley departed with only the boos and threats.

In contrast the first appearance of royalty since King James's hasty departure inspired a huge carnival. Nothing can disguise the fact that the visit of George IV in 1821, like that of his niece Victoria thirty years later, was greeted with enormous enthusiasm by all classes. The dazzled monarch, quite unused to such popularity, drove into the city in an open carriage wearing military uniform. Lieutenant-Colonel Blacker, who was watching from a window observed 'His Majesty's bloated person...as he stood up in the barouche dressed in scarlet and holding in his hand his hat decorated with an immense bunch of shamrock, which he took care should not escape the notice of the nobility as he repeatedly pointed to it with his finger.' An ode to this shamrock was later composed by George Petrie.

Sir Walter Scott arrived in 1825 to visit his son Walter. Young Captain Walter Scott of the 15th Hussars and his wife shared a house in Stephen's Green with a brother officer. Lockhart noted that the fate of many grand houses after the Union was to be let out cheaply. No. 9, a magnificent town residence, encrusted with plasterwork by the Francinis, was let with all its fine old furniture at £150 a year as garrison lodgings. (In 1840, with the patronage of Daniel O'Connell, it became the ecumenical Stephen's Green Club.) Scott had little opportunity to make pertinent observations about Dublin, since he was ruthlessly lionized by dignitaries of the city such as the Protestant Archbishop, the Attorney-General, the Commander of the Forces, the Chief Remembrancer of the Exchequer, the Provost and professors of Trinity and the Vice-Treasurer of Ireland. Unlike Scott, Thackeray, who came to Ireland seventeen years later specifically to make money out of writing a travel book, paid his visit when he was virtually unknown. We are more inclined to believe him than the author of *Waverley*, when he wrote that the greatest part of the buildings were in 'gaunt decay'. His walk through the city on a sunny summer's day gives a picture of apathy. 'A stand of lazy carmen, a policeman or two with clinking boot heels, a couple of moaning beggars leaning against the rails, a fellow with a toy and bookstall where the lives of St Patrick, Robert Emmet and Lord Edward Fitzgerald may be bought for double their value, were all the population of the Green.' His observations of Dubliners led him to sum them up as 'the car-drivingest, tay-drinkingest, say-baythingest people in the world'.

Miss Ann Plumptre was another visitor who came over to write a travel book. Jackie Barrett, the eccentric Fellow of Trinity, considered it 'too silly and too ill-mannered for a public library'. Besides retailing a number of anecdotes about Barrett's meanness, Miss Plumptre gives a glimpse of Dublin's most flourishing literary salon. When she arrived at the Pigeon House in 1814, she was delayed by sailors arguing about the price of rowing her ashore. To pass the time she read Lady Morgan's novel, *O'Donnel*. Later, like numerous other fortunate visitors, she achieved the distinction of being invited to one of the author's soirées.

Lady Morgan had taken to writing novels after a shaky career as a governess. In 1812 she married the Marquess of Abercorn's physician, and such was the social prominence she had reached by her literary abilities, that he was specially knighted for the occasion. She now had a secure position in Dublin's new middle-class world. A house was acquired in Kildare Street which was in typical post-Union condition, 'an old dirty dismantled house' she wrote to her friend, Lady Stanley, 'and we have turned our piggery into a decent sort of hut enough'. In the drawing-room, hung with chandeliers and brocaded curtains, she entertained local celebrities like Mrs Felicia Hemans, author of 'The Boy Stood on the Burning Deck', who had retired to Ireland to live with her brother in Dawson Street, and guests from abroad like Paganini and the German Prince von Pückler-Muskau, friend of Goethe. Scholars and people of every religion and shade of political opinion met in her house. In 1835 she wrote: 'my soirée was very fine, learned, scientific and tiresome. Fifty philosophers passed through my rooms last night.' Her enthusiasm for harp playing encouraged her to invite Thomas Moore on a number of occasions. He was familiar with her house, where as a boy he had performed at Lady Borrowes' private theatricals. Now: 'I had a little dinner got up in a hurry for Moore yesterday; it was thus got up. I threw up my windows and asked the inmates of the cabs and carriages of my friends as they passed... Moore sang some of his most beautiful songs in the most delightful manner without stopping, some of them twice over.' All over fashionable Dublin Moore sang songs and made people cry; Lady Morgan was often moved to sadness by them, while 'tears dropped like dew' from her sister.

The new flourish of Dublin's social and intellectual life was largely stimulated by the political inertia imposed by the Union. The emphasis was on home-based decorous entertainment. Even the dancing and quadrille parties held several times a week by the eccentric Reverend Charles Maturin drew no breath of scandal. Maturin, author of an influential horror novel, *Melmoth the Wanderer*, inspired by the soirées he had attended at Lady Morgan's, began entertaining himself in his gaudy York Street drawing-room, which he decorated with rich carpets, ottomans, scenes out of his novels and 'ceilings painted to represent clouds with eagles in the centre from whose claws depended brilliant lustres'. His parties, often held in daytime with the curtains drawn, helped him towards bankruptcy.

The famous Dr William Stokes entertained such notables of the bar as John Philpott Curran and Charles Kendal Bushe. Later in the century Charles Lever had a salon in his chaotic house at Templeogue. Lever, many of whose novels are autobiographical, qualified as a doctor at Trinity. After becoming a successful novelist his favourite amusements were whist and entertaining. Once he played whist all night, missing the Kingstown boat in the morning. His friends were loquacious. 'I have drawn about me a circle of men of great and varied powers. I may be believed when I assert that conversation took a range and was maintained with a brilliancy that left us nothing to regret of the more famous gatherings of Holland or Gore House.' Talkers at Templeogue included the young Isaac Butt and Joseph Sheridan Le Fanu.

In contrast to the chatter of sumptuous or cosy salons, was the existence of the poet, James Clarence Mangan, a life-long Dubliner and a creature of the shadows. Born in Fishamble Street, the son of a grocer like Tom Moore, he spent his adult life in an apartment in a slum house in Chancery Lane: 'one of the smallest domiciles perhaps to be met with in the forlorn recesses of a city in Europe'. It consisted of 'two wretched rooms, or rather holes, at the rear of a tottering old fragment of a house, or, if the reader please, hovel . . .' It lacked windows and doors, and ladders connected the floors. Mangan's hair was bleached, his eyes very blue, his features 'corpselike' and he took opium and dressed eccentrically. He was a familiar figure in the Bleeding Horse in Camden Street or the Phoenix Tavern in D'Olier Street. Beside him as he drank he always kept handy a bottle of Bishop Berkeley's Tar Water which he called 'the Emperor of Specifics'. Even with this he was unable to survive the effects of starvation and cholera in the epidemic of 1849.

The beautiful Georgian capital was horribly unhealthy. Much of the land on which Dublin was built was reclaimed slob, considered impervious to drainage; tidal waters affected the inadequate sewers and there was widespread pollution. In spite of assets like a good water supply, gas lighting and an established police force, the squalor of the eighteenth century had intensified. Of the 'fevers' that killed the Dublin poor the most lethal was typhus. Fever hospitals were opened to receive patients, the earliest in Hardwicke Street in 1802 and in Cork Street in 1804. According to McGregor, a patient would be brought to a fever hospital 'in a covered carriage placed on springs, and when stripped in the reception room his clothes are put in cold water'. The Board of Health was established in 1818; after the epidemic of 1826 each parish had to employ a body of people to disinfect clothes, and clean up premises. Dr Corrigan, writing in the *Lancet* in 1830, considered these useless measures. 'Much money was expended in

this way; in cleaning out depots of filth for those who were too indolent
to do it for themselves and in whitewashing rooms for poor creatures
who then had not the price of fuel to dry their wet walls.'

The annual reports of the Cork Street Fever Hospital give grim
details. In 1814, for example, not an outstanding year for 'fever',
there was a heavy fall of snow that made the streets nearly
impassable for three weeks. 'The mere effluvia arising from a
number of persons crowded together in unwholesome and badly
ventilated situations may acquire a degree of malignity capable of
occasioning a fever.' When a patient's filthy clothes were stripped
off and he was issued with new garments, they were often pawned
immediately after he left hospital.

Many doctors were selflessly dedicated. A Dr George Hagen was
'totally regardless of himself and heedless of risk whilst engaged in
combating the suffering of the wretched or in medicating the means
of their relief, he was alike unconscious of personal inconvenience
and privation'. In addition to treating patients in hospital doctors
went on visits. 'Catherine Corcoran aged 36. No very urgent
symptoms, complaining only of a slight cough and sore throat.
Ninth visit, much worse. Died.' 'John Kelly aged 11. Water on the
brain, effusion having taken place. Died after 3rd visit.' 'Catherine
M'Caul aged 50. Typhus fever. Died after 6th visit. Treatment
included camphor mixture, wine cordials and friction of the
feet...' The sick were often found in atrocious conditions. A
report of 1822 described how 'with some difficulty we ascended an
ill-lighted, tottering and filthy stair to a garret...to a patient who
lay in a remote corner on a wad of straw. On turning back a piece
of the carpeting – the bed covering of the poor woman – her person
was naked, only a tolerable thick tunic of dirt adhering to her skin.
In the room was no other article of furniture than just a broken jug
holding some liquid to drink.' During the virulent epidemic of the
winter of 1826-1827, a doctor from Meath hospital lamented how
'you would be shocked at our distress aggrevated by disease under
which the lower classes are labouring. They are literally lying in the
streets under fever, turned by force out of their wreathed lodgings,
their bed the cold ground and the sky their only roof – God help the
poor.'

A visitor in 1822 considered the Liberties as 'something out of
the infernal regions'. Barrack Street was 'filled with public houses
exhibiting a degree of depravity and consequent wretchedness

scarcely to be met with anywhere else – women in the lowest state of degradation'. He added: 'I have seen some of these wretched outcasts running about furiously intoxicated and in a state very nearly approaching nudity.' In 1807 William Thomson had noticed the amount of drunken women 'many of them mechanics' wives and others of the lower classes will drink without being much intoxicated 3 or 4 noggins of half pints of whiskey per day'. At the beginning of the century there were fifty-five breweries and twenty-five distilleries in the Dublin area. Dan Donnelly, who retired from boxing to become a publican in the Liberties, was perhaps the most famous of the city's victims of alcoholism. Festive occasions like the pattern to St John's Well on St John's Day and Donnybrook Fair were occasions for whiskey, pig's feet and revelry. Donnybrook Fair was notoriously boozy. Of the many disapproving descriptions, Prince von Pückler-Muskau's is vivid, mentioning the ragged tents, the 'heat and dust, crowds and stench'. 'I saw things eaten and drunk with delight which forced me to turn my head quickly away.' Another commentator, observing 'the painted prostitutes, drunken youths and lassies' considered that 'there is more misery and madness, devilment and debauchery than could be found crowded into any equal space of ground in any part of the globe'. The Fair was stopped in 1855, partly because of public disapproval, partly because of its vicinity to respectable suburbs.

For a time during the forties Father Mathew's campaign produced a remarkable reduction in the consumption of liquor. The Apostle of Temperance made his first visit to Dublin in March 1840, to preach against the pernicious evil for which the capital was famous. A huge crowd assembled in pouring rain in a boggy space behind the Custom House where it was estimated that about 4,600 people took the pledge. By the end of the year about 100,000 people in Dublin were said to have sworn to give up drink. Brewers and distillers were frantic. One bankrupt brewer wrote wildly that 100 distilleries and breweries had been closed and thousands put out of work. He continued 'after causing the ruin of the country and its bone and sinew, find if you can, a single individual out of a thousand who took Father Mathew's pledge and did not break it'. His cynicism was justified and people soon started drinking again.

William Carleton's writings give us some idea of the atmosphere in which typhus and other diseases lurked. A countryman, he arrived in Dublin almost penniless so that he was reduced to dossing down in subterranean cellars and to take lodgings in down and out houses in the Coombe. The really destitute, he reported, took to the immediate suburbs where there were about two dozen notorious cellars which accommodated swarms of beggars, ballad singers, strolling fiddlers and flute players. In one 'the inmates were mostly in bed, both men and women indulging in liquors of every description from strong whiskey downwards. The beds were mostly what are called "shakedown", that is, simply straw.' Among the personal effects hanging on the wall were crutches and wooden legs. Admission was 2d.

In his *Miseries and Beauties of Ireland* published in 1837, the Englishman, Jonathan Bins described Dublin as a city of 'lamentable contrasts'. The well planned and ordered areas where the respectable and affluent had their homes were minutes away from the Liberties where 'narrow streets, houses without windows or doors and several families crowded together beneath the same roof, present a picture of ruin, disease, poverty, filth and wretchedness of which they who have not witnessed it are unable to form a competent idea'. The nineteenth-century slums in English towns blighted by the Industrial Revolution were considered less dreadful than the appalling proximity of the prosperous and destitute that shocked visitors to Dublin. Bins saw 'numbers of miserable beings...lying half naked and apparently half dead from cold and hunger on the parapets and steps of the houses'. Beggars, as always, had continued to be a feature of city life. At the end of the Napoleonic wars there was a new influx following the disbandment of soldiers and sailors. An American who came to Dublin in 1824 considered that 'mendicity in my opinion has reached its "ne plus ultra" in this city'. Beggars lay in front of every respectable front door and there were 'females literally strewn along the principal streets'. Prince von Pückler-Muskau kept his pockets full of coppers like Swift and La Touche a century before 'to throw among the beggars like corn among the fowls'. The American missionary, Asenath Nicholson, compared the beggars of Dublin to 'Pharaoh's frogs'. Another visitor complained that he had been stopped eighty-seven times walking from Baggot Street to Dorset Street.

Of the scores of charities most specialized, like the Asylum for Unmarried Ladies, the Widow's Retreat, the Asylum for Aged and Infirm Female Servants, and Simpsons for gouty and blind old men. 'In the spring and summer the gay sound of the flute and violin is often heard from the benches of their little garden, and the whole institution has an air of cheerful content.' Private individuals who eased the lot of the poor included two gifted and dedicated nuns – Mary Aikenhead who started the Irish Sisters of Charity and her contemporary, Catherine Macaulay, foundress of the Sisters of Mercy. But the core of relief came from public institutions. Two notorious eighteenth-century foundations flourished. The lethal Foundling Hospital was still capable of accommodating 1,200 children and killing a good many of them. The House of Industry, on the other hand, seems to have been almost tolerable. In 1816 Miss Plumptre considered it 'a most excellent extensive and well regulated establishment for the reception of the poor'. In 1840, after it had become subject to the Poor Law Act, it was described in detail by Asenath Nicholson. 'The house contained one thousand seven hundred persons of all ages, and all who were able were at work or in school. The rooms were well-ventilated and the floors daily washed. One old lady was pointed out to me who was a hundred and six years old; she could read without glasses and had the use of all her faculties.' In contrast the Mendicity Institute at Moira House where paupers assembled daily to pick oakum in return for two foul meals was a grim and forbidding place. 'Never had I seen so much filth embodied in one mass, with so many ugly, forlorn and loathsome faces.'

An early *Guide to Dublin* has an unwholesome list of prisons and houses of correction. They included the Dublin Female Penitentiary which provided washing and mangling, the corrective punishment invariably imposed on female sinners, and a terrible institution which received female convicts sentenced to transportation. Warburton and Whitelaw's *History of Dublin* gives a rosy picture of Newgate, mentioning its walls whitewashed three times a year, the bread, 'always good and well baked' the herrings and potatoes. Perhaps for Whitelaw, the old vicar of St Catherine's, who had worked in the grimmest conditions among the poor, things could only have improved, for Reid's *Travels in Ireland* published four years later in 1822, found that 'it seldom fall to one's lot to see a worse prison'. Even the women prisoners were distinguished by 'horrible ferocity'.

The system of jailing debtors of sums of ten shillings upwards was not abolished until 1864. As late as 1841 economic depression ensured that five of Dublin's nine prisons were used for this purpose. They included the notorious Sheriff's Marshalsea where 'notwithstanding the prohibition of the sale of spirituous liquors they are constantly introduced through the front windows'. It was here that the eccentric Lord Kingsborough, author of ten volumes of the *Antiquities of Mexico* which attempted to prove the Hebrew colonization of Mexico before the arrival of Columbus in the New World, was imprisoned for debts involved with printing costs in 1837. He contracted typhus and died within a week. But a debtor's prison could be fun, as Thomas Meyler wrote in his biography. He was confined in the Sheriff's Marshalsea for a week in 1841. 'First it was my duty to stand dinner and liquids...I became gay, jolly, ate, drank, joked and sang liveliest.' Another spell in the Four Courts Marshalsea proved equally agreeable. 'Between the novelty of the bagatelle table, the promenade in the square and the attraction of the racket court, I was gradually introduced to most of the upper yards.' A fellow debtor was Joshua Jacob who had founded a sect known as the White Quakers which believed in simplicity of living and plainness of dress, a doctrine its members carried to extremes when Jacob organized a nude procession through the streets of Dublin. Plain living led to debt, so that Jacob 'and his harem' were in the Marshalsea.

The hellish picture of Dublin life presented by visitors often suggests unrelieved misery. But there was an attractive wild energy and wit about ordinary Dubliners, exemplified perhaps by Zozimus. The tall, gaunt, blind ballad singer wandered round the poorer quarters in his long frieze coat with its scalloped cape, his greasy beaver hat, corduroy trousers and 'Francis Street brogues'. The old blackthorn stick in his hand was tipped with an iron ferrule. His home was in the heart of the Liberties.

> I live in Faddle Alley
> Off Blackpits near the Coombe;
> With my poor wife, Sally,
> In a narrow dirty room.

Thomas Meyler has described the market in Meath Street, deep in the Liberties, as a lively scene where the merchandise overflowing the baskets and sieves all over the streets was 'presided over by old and young matrons and young women and girls selling their pieces of vegetables, together with fresh codfish, conger eels, markerel and Dublin Bay herrings'. Fish was sold by public auction in Pill Lane, where the auctioneer was usually a woman 'holding in her hand a plaice or other flat fish by the tail, instead of a hammer'. A rare sturgeon sold at a shilling a pound while Carlingford oysters were six and six a hundred. People ate one main meal a day which included a large serving of potatoes with occasional additions like bacon, butter and monster carrots grown at Rush. A new sight in the streets was the milkcarts with their locked churns so that 'the person who sells it cannot at any time increase the quantity of adulteration'. No description of the city at this time could be complete without mentioning the smoking chimneys and the two great armadas of coaling fleets that poured into Dublin Bay in September and January. Prince von Pückler-Muskau, viewing Dublin from the Three-Rock mountain, thought it 'like a smoking lime-kiln in the green plain'.

Most observers noted the capacity of Dubliners for enjoyment. Even the beggars, wrote William Thompson in 1807, had an 'infectious gaiety' and he proceeded to note down their favourite swear words...'by the living Jesus, by the Holy Paul, by the blood of the Holy Ghost and the like...' Gamble found 'a whimsical and eccentric people who get drunk and make bulls and who cannot open their mouths that something funny and witty does not come tumbling out like pearls...' A hackneyed view. Von Pückler-Muskau, riding about Donnybrook Fair, noted the merriment of the ragged revellers including the young girls with their pipes and sweethearts. 'Not the slightest trace of English brutality is to be perceived; they were more like French people, though their gaiety was mingled with more humour and more genuine good nature; both of which are natural traits of the Irish, and are always doubled by poteen.'

Some time in the early years of the century Catholics formed over seventy per cent of the city's population. 1829, marked by the Catholic Relief Act, has been put forward as the year when Dublin first changed from a predominantly Protestant to a predominantly Catholic city. The transition was perhaps symbolized by an incident in 1836 when King William was blown up with gunpowder. The deafening explosion, which extinguished all the lights on College Green, hurled pieces of him round the neighbourhood. Ratepayers were forced to pay £240 to put him together.

Among Protestants the siege mentality developed, their sense of isolation manifesting itself in minor ways such as a preference for servants of their own faith. As often as not these came from outside. Advertisements in one issue of the conservative *Dublin Evening Post* in January 1845 include: 'As Upper Housemaid in a nobleman's or gentleman's family, an active young Woman – is a native of Scotland...' 'As a footman...a steady young man, a native of the North of Ireland...is of the Established Church'...'As Professed Cook or Housekeeper...a native of England and of the Established Church'. Mrs Meredith and Miss Ellis advertising their school in Monkstown ('Terms...harp not included, 50 guineas a year') emphasize that 'they are Englishwomen and...the Religious instruction of their Pupils is rigorously attended to.' A steady small stream of immigration on the old medieval pattern continuing throughout the century included all sorts – servants, teachers, engineers to build workhouses, soldiers coming and going and others. Zoe, one of the whores of Nighttown, declares: 'No bloody fear, I'm English.'

The final blow to the old municipal establishment was O'Connell's Municipal Corporation Act of 1840 which brought down the whole tottering edifice of the guilds. Henceforth municipal officials were elected by ratepayers. Only a year after the 1840 Act the Liberator became Dublin's Lord Mayor, the first Catholic to hold the position since the time of James II. His burly figure dominated the pageants and crowds. We see him addressing supporters in Conciliation Hall – which he built himself – wearing his green velvet 'Repeal Cap' 'in shape like a Milesian crown ...ornamented with Irish devices'. He was 'a tall man of massive shape with broad shoulders, large chest, a full good humoured face, fresh complexion...he wore a wig and generally appeared in a military cloak...' Thackeray saw the new Lord Mayor 'wearing his crimson velvet robe ornamented with white satin bows and sable collar, in an enormous cocked-hat like the slice of an eclipsed moon'.

In spite of its historical importance he did not enjoy his term of office, and towards its close declared: 'a fortnight more and I shall have the privilege of knocking down any man who calls me My Lord'. In this he was exceptional; for the most part the office of Mayor and Lord Mayor has been a popular one. Between 1390 and 1430 Thomas Cusack held it for a record nineteen times. The Civic Museum in Dublin contains evidence of mayoral pomp and

importance – early scrolls and manuscripts, a card from a late
nineteenth-century Lady Mayoress proclaiming that she is At
Home; in the corner there is a picture of a chef with a ladle and the
words 'Come Early'. For many years the Lord Mayor's procession
wound its way through the Dublin streets every September 30. A
foot company of 'battle-axe guards' in resplendent uniforms
escorted the massive gilded coach which fortunately is still
preserved; the livery of the bewigged coachman was encrusted with
silver shamrocks as he drove the Lord Mayor and 'Madame', his
wife, waving at the cheering throngs. But O'Connell found the old
gold double Mayoral chain 'won from the old rotten Corporation
of Dublin' an embarrassment; the medallion showing King William
prevented him from going to church when he wore it. It still forms
part of the Lord Mayor's insignia.

He made the crowds gather like no one else. They poured out of
Dublin towards Tara for the monster meeting there and jostled at
Clontarf for the great Repeal meeting. In prison O'Connell was
lavishly feted with vast cakes, fish, venison, game, fruit and
flowers. On his dramatic release from the Richmond Bridewell a
procession several miles long escorted him through the streets. He
was borne along on his throne with a harper on the tier below
playing patriotic tunes, and on the lowest level his angelic
grandchildren clustered in green velvet tunics and caps with white
plumes – altogether a sight to make earlier generations of Dubliners
turn in their graves. The last great crowd was at his funeral.
'Notwithstanding the immense assemblage' reported the *Freeman's
Journal*, 'no sound was to be heard – all was silent unutterable
sorrow.'

It was the beginning of the age of funerals – great ones like
O'Connell's or Dan Donnelly's, where 80,000 people followed the
coffin on which reposed his boxing gloves on a silk cushion, and
more modest obsequies. Inglis wrote in 1834 'I have counted
twenty-seven hackney coaches and sixteen cars in the funeral
procession of a person in the humbler walks of life – one might
easily have mistaken the cavalcade for a procession of wedding
guests.' The old eighteenth-century midnight interments lit by
flambeaux and attended by mourners in linen scarves had given
way to an obsession with the panoply of burial among rich and
poor alike.

The irritations suffered by Catholics who had no proper

graveyards reached a climax after an incident in 1823 when Archdeacon Blake, officiating at the funeral of a prominent citizen, was abruptly told that he had to desist in his prayers for the dead by order of the Protestant Archbishop, Dr Magee. The resulting uproar led to O'Connell seeking what was known as Burial Reform through his Catholic Association. But the Easement of Burial Bill of 1826 did not wholly put a stop to the old grievances, and in 1828 a tract of land beside Kilmainham was purchased by the Catholic Association for the Golden Bridge cemetery. The first interment was that of Father Whelan, a priest who had charge of the chapel at Dolphin's Barn during penal days. His body was specially dug up from under the chapel's earthen floor and reinterred at Golden Bridge. Numerous other funerals, many of which had been postponed until the cemetery was opened, followed immediately.

Golden Bridge was located by the Richmond Barracks, and the military authorities objected so long and so vociferously to the nuisance caused by the endless funeral processions, that thirty years later they managed to secure its closure. But meanwhile Glasnevin had been established. There had been so great a demand for admission to Golden Bridge that O'Connell realized that further burial grounds would soon be needed. In September 1831 the Burial Committee of the Catholic Association bought nine statute acres at Glasnevin adjoining the old residence of the poet, Thomas Tickell. A new road was built to this cemetery to avoid the turnpikes and the Finglas and the old Glasnevin roads with their demand for tolls.

In its first year Glasnevin, like other burial grounds, was subject to threats from body-snatchers. The practice of body-snatching only ceased in 1832 with the passing of the second Anatomy Act allowing doctors and students to dissect donated bodies. (In the same year Bully's Acre, the most notorious venue for body-snatchers, swollen with typhus victims, was officially closed.) Hanged criminals were particularly prone to ending up on the surgeon's table. After Larry had 'gone chuck' his friends went to a lot of trouble to save him from this fate. However some condemned men chose to sell their bodies before they died. In some graveyards the traffic in corpses was undertaken by the sexton himself, who was known as the Knave of Spades; at others employees were required to take an oath that they would not involve themselves in the traffic. Often body-snatching involved pitched battles. The *Freeman's Journal* of 1830 records a battle in the old graveyard at Glasnevin whose walls even had watch-towers. A hundred shots were exchanged. At Bully's Acre the unfortunate surgeon, Peter Harkan, died after he had been nearly pulled in two while he tried to make his escape over the cemetery wall. His helpers were holding one of his legs, the cemetery watchers the other. Like Golden Bridge, Glasnevin was patrolled by Cuban bloodhounds; they continued to be used until 1853, when, tired of having no grave robbers to attack, they turned on Dr Kirwan, the city coroner, who had to stand with his back to a tombstone to keep them at bay.

Coffin makers concentrated in Cook Street near Christ Church. They advertised their wares, calling attention to shroud warehouses, mourning coaches and the innovation of 'soft metal coffin furniture'. The brilliantly lit coffin sheds with their clean smells of sawdust and new wood – open to the public, since people did not steal coffins which were unpawnable – contrasted favourably with the dingy surrounding slums.

By the 1860s a visitor commented: 'I must say that in no city in the world do the local horses attend funerals to such a vast extent...the animals could find their way to the different cemeteries – Mount Jerome and Glasnevin – in the dark almost.' An English friend kept a special pair of horses for attending Dublin funerals. George Bernard Shaw described how slow-moving funeral carriages, once they were out of sight of houses and shops, galloped to the cemetery gates before slowing down once more.

'Must be twenty or thirty funerals every day' mused Leopold Bloom waiting for Paddy Dignam's coffin to be unloaded. James Joyce, a tragically frequent visitor to Glasnevin, remembered details for his Hades chapter – the hawker with his barrow of simnel cakes, the horse with its crooked plume, the server with the brass bucket, the plump white-smocked priest, the coffin cart: 'the metal wheels ground the gravel with a sharp grating cry and the pack of blunt boots followed the barrow along a lane of sepulchres'. Sean O'Casey similarly recreated a funeral among the marble avenues at Mount Jerome. Although Glasnevin had interments of all religions – the first important burial there had been of a Protestant, Edward Ruthven, a colleague of O'Connell – the majority of Protestants chose the exclusive Mount Jerome. The proportion of burials reflected the sectarian divide. By 1900 there were something like 1,000 burials a year at Mount Jerome. Around 4,000 paid-up burials took place annually at Glasnevin, while between 2,500 and 3,000 paupers were interred in 'Poor Ground'.

In 1917 'An Englishman' visiting the city a year after the Insurrection, was still amazed by 'the extraordinary number of funerals. All day and particularly on Saturdays and Sundays the long processions wind up Sackville Street on their way to Glasnevin...I have never before in my life been in a town where hearses and coffins and mourning coaches were so much in evidence.' He went on to quote Seumas O'Sullivan:

> As I go down Glasnevin way
> The funerals pass me day by day
> Stately, sombre, stepping slow
> The white-plumed funeral horses go
> With coaches crawling in their wake,
> A long and slow black glittering snake.
> (Inside of every crawling yoke
> Silent cronies sit and smoke...)
> Soon my procession will be on view,
> A hearse, and maybe a coach or two.

12

The Famine and Afterwards

Officials in Dublin were the first to receive news about the blight breaking out in the potato crop in different parts of Ireland during the autumn of 1845. But the effects of the famine in the city were slow. Throughout the summer of 1846 the number of paupers in the Dublin Unions – that is, the workhouses – was well below total capacity. The Balrothery Union in North Dublin was still able to include potatoes in its diet. Suddenly huge numbers of people appeared in the streets. For a time guards were posted at the outskirts of the city to try and stem the flow of 'country paupers'. A proportion of these were solvent and were passing through. Some, described as 'comfortable farmers' from Meath and Westmeath, were said to be arriving in Dublin daily by the hundred 'apparently all of substantial class and well provided for the trans-Atlantic journey'. Others just had the means to buy their passage on coffin ships or to flee to Liverpool and other English ports. But thousands of destitutes who could not escape on outward bound ships also crowded into the city.

The main burden of relief was thrown on the workhouses. The Irish Poor Relief Act of 1838 introduced the system to Ireland where many new workhouses were built to the designs of an English architect named George Wilkinson. However, in Dublin the main workhouses, the North and South Dublin Unions, were old buildings which Wilkinson reconstructed and enlarged. The North Union was the old House of Industry, while the South Union was the enlarged City of Dublin Workhouse. Wilkinson also renovated premises at Cork Street to accommodate the remaining inmates of the Foundling Hospital and 370 'lunatics' from the House of Industry. (But each workhouse would have its quota of 'lunatics'.) For the rest men, women, boys and girls were kept segregrated as part of a regime calculated to make this form of charity undesirable. The walls that separated the Male Yards from the Female Yards had to be very high to keep people apart. Poor Law rules provided for each Union to be run by a Committee of Guardians drawn from magistrates, Justices of the Peace and members of local authorities.

During the winter of 1846-47 the Dublin workhouses filled up. On the whole these institutions did their best to provide a reasonable diet for their inmates. Before the famine they had consumed huge quantities of potatoes. In 1840 Asenath Nicholson, who was allowed to view dinner time at the House of Industry, observed that three and a half pounds of unpeeled potatoes were 'poured from a net' to each individual who ate them with his fingers. Now substitutes had to be found. Adults received one quart of stirabout and half a pint of milk for breakfast and a slightly varied diet for dinner – meal or rice and half a pint of milk or a pound of bread and a pint of soup. But very soon there was nothing like enough accommodation for the starving people clamouring for admission. When the children's quarters in the South Dublin Union could admit no more, whole families were turned away, since the Guardians were bound by the rules – they could not admit parents to their segregated quarters in the company of their children.

Soon tens of thousands had no other sustenance than that provided by outdoor relief. An Act of Parliament, popularly known as the 'Soup Kitchen Act', passed in January 1847, charged local committees with the setting up of kitchens with financial help from the government and from charitable subscriptions, Relieving officers issued one pound of bread per person, reduced to three-quarters or half a pound in the case of families. And then there was soup. The most famous soup was issued by Alexis Soyer, the French chef of the Reform Club, who came over personally to demonstrate his recipe; it contained oxheads without the tongue, maize, carrots, turnips, cabbages, onions, peas, leeks and a good deal of water. He claimed inaccurately that, together with some bread, it was sufficient 'to sustain the strength of a strong and healthy man'. The New Model Soup Kitchen constructed in front of the Royal Barracks to his requirements, had a 300 gallon boiler standing among long tables which contained a hundred bowls to which spoons were attached by chains. People were admitted in clamorous batches of a hundred at a time. The hideous scenes outside the Royal Barracks drew the scorn of John Mitchel who wrote inflammatory articles about the situation, first for *The Nation* and then for *The United Irishman*. At one time 8,750 were served in a day. After the famine the huge soup boiler was used for boiling bath water at the North Union and steaming paupers' clothing.

Typhus was nothing new. Some medical authorities had long

been certain of its source. 'Epidemic fever may be attributed to a mysterious something, an occult quality in the atmosphere' Dr Corrigan had written in 1830, 'but...we find FAMINE invariably preceding or accompanying epidemic fever,...and FAMINE, therefore, we are justified in marking out as its grand cause.' The typhus epidemic in 1847 was unprecedented. It swept into the workhouses which dispatched victims to the fever hospitals, which in turn became hopelessly overcrowded. Extra premises were hired out by the Unions and hurriedly converted to provide male and female wards for hordes of feverish and dying patients. In the five principal fever hospitals 'every corner, including the cellars' and a number of tents were filled up with the sick. The army donated 'hospital marquees' with wooden floors. When the typhus epidemic receded Asiatic cholera appeared and killed James Clarence Mangan and 5,000 others, compounding the miseries of the starving.

Relief had to be paid for. In the Unions men and boys broke stones which were sold to road-making contractors for 1s.4d. a ton. Women and girls did sewing and laundry. At Balrothery they made calico drawers for the male paupers whose trousers went unlined for the time being. Otherwise the cost of relief, including the provisions of the Soup Kitchen Act, went on the rates. Ratepayers protested. The Dublin and Drogheda Railway Company objected to a valuation of £200 per mile. The South Union Guardians sent a collector to distrain on three canal barges belonging to the Grand Canal Company which refused to pay rates on their water-ways. Among citizens who complained about the poor rate was the Chaplain of the Chapel Royal who claimed that since the Queen was exempted from paying rates, so should be occupiers of State Apartments.

Perhaps it is rather too easy to condemn those who ensured that throughout the years of suffering the gay social life of the capital continued without interruption. One can follow the social round in the advertisements and announcements in the *Freeman's Journal*. 'Chamberlain's Office, Dublin Castle, January 25th. There will be a drawing room at the Castle on Thursday 11th of February, 1847 at 9 o'clock.' 'The Drawing Room, Dublin Castle. To those ladies who propose attending the evening Drawing Room Smith begs to inform that he has received several cases of French Boots and Shoes, amongst which are several dozen of white and black satin shoes.' 'February 5th. By command of His Excellency the Lord Lieutenant the Annual Grand Fancy and Full Dress Charity Ball in aid of the Funds of the Sick and Indigent Roomkeepers Society. In the Rotunda, 15th February.' At the Antient Concert Rooms the first Grand Concert of the season took place on 17 February. At the Theatre Royal a play called *Love Spell* was followed by a farce called, rather surprisingly, *Double-bedded Room*. The following year Jenny Lind would sing there in the leading role of *La Somnambula*. The ailing Lord Lieutenant, Lord Bessborough, complained 'that the balls and drawing rooms which knocked him up were not the responsibility of his office'. During his final illness in May 1847, a Mr Warburton complained that 'it was sad to hear the ladies wishing him dead that the gaieties might recommence and the young A.D.C.s fearing not to be "clear" in time for the Derby'.

The other digression from famine and disease was rebellion. In 1848 the streets of the stricken city swarmed with 'red jackets varied by blue uniforms of the artillery and light cavalry' as thousands of extra troops arrived to deal with the young Irelanders who had almost roused Dubliners to open revolt. There were reports of insurgents arming themselves with pikes and penknives bought from cutlery stores. Leading public buildings like Leinster House, the Linen Hall, Trinity, the old Parliament building, the Post Office and Custom House were fortified or turned into barracks. Rebellion was crushed as first John Mitchel was taken in chains to the North Wall and from there by ship to Australia, and later Smith O'Brien was transported.

In August 1849, a month after O'Brien's departure, Queen Victoria paid a state visit. With rebellion and cholera and the aftermath of famine it was an odd time to choose. Dublin was at its most sombre; according to the *Evening Mail* 'the greater number of of good houses in Dame street, Grafton Street and other principal thoroughfares are in a dirty and dilapidated condition, the windows broken, patched with brown paper, or here and there studded with an old hat, the shops closed and the wooden shutters covered over with auction bills, railway timetables, quack advertisements and notices from the Poor Law Commissioners or the Insolvent Court... If we have funds to spare' concluded the paper, 'let them be spent not on illuminations but on Her Majesty's starving subjects.' But contrary to expectations the visit of the royal couple and their young family was a great success. Illuminations went ahead; the most impressive was the electric lighting of Nelson's Pillar by Professor Gluckman. There were cheers, processions, the visit to the veterans of the Royal Hospital – 'I am glad to see you all looking so comfortable' – the tours of Stephen's Green, College Green, the Four Courts and other parts of the city and suburbs, each of which attracted large crowds. At the Queen's departure Kingstown was 'black with people' and the harbour was crammed with bobbing boats.

Although the visit briefly lightened the gloom, the city was in a wretched state. Thomas Carlyle, who saw it in the same year, was shocked to find it 'patched and dilapidated, the harbour at Kingstown empty and the swarms of beggars little short of terrifying'. The famine ensured that certain undesirable aspects of Dublin life were to remain a feature of the city for more than eighty years. The 1851 census showed that while the population of Ireland had as a whole declined by twenty per cent as a result of the famine, that of Dublin had increased by 22,124 or nine per cent. 250,000 people now lived in the city proper, with another 50,000 mainly better-off citizens settled in the suburbs. Housing problems became menacing as overcrowding assumed grotesque proportions leading to woeful health conditions and a high mortality rate. There were further epidemics of typhus and cholera in the next decades. Apart from a few enlightened philanthropic schemes like those of the Dublin Artisans' Dwelling Company and the Iveagh Trust, little significant attempt was made to rebuild the Liberties and the Coombe where houses like the old Dutch Billies grew increasingly decayed. In other parts of the city houses which had been built for the wealthy became tenements, to be designated as such in Thom's *Directory*. A good sized Georgian house might accommodate a hundred people and more. What such overcrowding meant in terms of discomfort may be conveyed in two quotations. One is from a pre-Famine report in the Dublin *Journal of Medical Science* for 1845: 'not an infrequent occurrence is to see above a dozen human beings crowded into a space not fifteen feet square. Within this space the food of these beings, such as it is must be prepared; within this space they must eat and drink; men, women and children must strip, dress and sleep.' The other is Tom Kettle's observation made early this century and quoted by Gogarty: 'I went "home" to one of the ruined drawing-rooms of the eighteenth century with a prostitute. There was a family living in every corner but one of that dilapidated salon. As we approached the prostitute's corner we approached civilization. There was a screen round her bed.'

Among the countless descriptions of the Dublin slums one of the most detailed is that of a French woman, Madame de Bovet, who wrote a travel book on Ireland in 1891. As ever the air of dirt and decay about the streets struck even those tourists who were well used to the general poverty of European cities. Here is her impression of Patrick Street: 'A street consisting of two rows of tumble-down mouldy-looking houses, reeking of dirt and oozing with the disgusting smell of accumulated filth of many generations, with old petticoats hung up instead of curtains and very often instead of glass in the dilapidated windows. On each ground floor shops with overhanging roofs and resembling dirty cellars expose for sale sides of rancid bacon, bundles of candles and jars of treacle...greens, cauliflowers, musty turnips and bad potatoes...at every three doors a tavern... On the pavements strewn with refuse a permanent market is held. There are barrels of red herrings pickled in brine; flat baskets in which are spread out the most disgusting bits of meat...stale cows' feet, overkept sheep's heads, bits of flabby pink veal, ripe intestines, skins and fat of every animal...the smell mixed with that of bad cabbage, tobacco and petroleum which comes out in puffs from the half-opened hovels...'

By the time of Madame de Bovet's visit, Dublin had taken on what might be termed a modern look. The most immediate visible changes had been achieved by revolutionary developments in the transport system. By 1865 all the main railway lines had been laid. In addition to outside cars which still took passengers on fixed routes, an omnibus service had been started in 1840. It covered routes to the south of the city – Clonskeagh, Sandymount and Rathfarnham, further encouraging suburban development in that direction. Two horses pulled an enclosed vehicle which could carry ten passengers on the roof and twelve who climbed through a small door at the back into a stuffy interior lit by small windows whose floor was laid with straw. These omnibuses were not cheap; a journey to Rathfarnham cost 6d. inside at a time when a labourer's wage might be two shillings a day. They were generally used by the middle classes. Victims of the Rathmines omnibus tragedy of 1861, when a bus of a type known as the 'Favourite' plunged, horses and all, into the lock at Portobello Bridge, included Mr Michaél Gunn, father of the lessee of the Gaiety Theatre, and two relatives of the Liberator, Mrs O'Connell and her daughter, Matilda, 'who was at

St Patrick's ball in the Castle a few evenings before and was much admired for her singular beauty'. The more affluent could also hire hackney cars, which, before they were all painted a uniform green, were gay vehicles, their wheels and undercarriages lemon yellow, the lower half of the cab a deep rose, the upper half black.

The era of cheap transport began in February 1872, when a horse tram service was initiated with a route that ran from College Green to Garville Avenue in Rathgar, a journey of twenty minutes in each direction for much cheaper fares than those demanded on the horse omnibuses. The harness of the tram horses was trimmed with red facings to which little bells were attached. 'The inside of the cars' the *Daily Express* noted, 'are richly cushioned in velvet and fitted with sliding shutters of Venetian glass type – the lamps are placed within ornamental coloured plate compartments and the extremities, thus cutting off any unpleasantness from the combustion of oil.' The *Irish Times* was less impressed. 'Only a pair of horses were provided for each tram, and these do not appear to be in breeding or stamina up to the work.'

In 1881 three different companies amalgamated into the Dublin United Tramway Company which ran 186 trams with over 1,000 horses. To assist those who could not read – the 1881 census listed over 99,000 people, twenty-three per cent of the population, as illiterate – each tram had a distinctive colour according to its route. While the drivers were provided with overcoats and top hats, conductors did not have regular uniforms. The trams moved slowly at about five miles an hour so that passengers could mount or dismount while they were moving. 'Scutting' or joy riding by small boys was a permanent nuisance. Conductors were supposed to tout for custom, and a Company Rule Book for 1883 advised: 'keep a sharp look-out for passengers, and by signalling induce persons to travel who would otherwise walk'.

Horse trams persisted until January 1901, when the last of them knocked down a gentleman's gentleman at the corner of Shelbourne Road, breaking both his legs. The first electric tram in May 1896 was welcomed by the Lord Mayor. After that the gaily painted green and yellow trams with their pushmi-pullyu design, garden seats, brass levers, sputtering overhead wires and clanging bells became part of Dublin life. Like the horse trams they carried painted signs for those who could not read bearing such symbols as a Maltese cross, a brown lozenge and two blue diamonds.

Bicycles made their appearance, beginning with the velocipede which only moved when the traveller kicked it along the ground. The penny-farthing was succeeded by the standard bicycle, a development of the late eighties. The medley of horse traffic included jarveys, drays, scores of milk carts, floats, coal cars, refuse and dung carts and the dashing vehicles of the Fire Brigade. In 1862 the Fire Brigade was reorganized and two years later it acquired its first steam-engine to extinguish flames. The animals for all these vehicles had to be accommodated; a huge number of horses, together with cows and pigs were stabled within the area of the city. The traffic did not add up to anything like modern turmoil and side streets were quiet except for the trotting of a passing jingle or the cries of a hawker. The street hawkers of the sixties and seventies included the muffin man, the woman with 'fresh pikelets' – a kind of tea cake – the man peddling oysters at half-a-crown a hundred and the cockle man shouting 'Cockle-Large Cock'. Some street-sellers would linger into the twentieth century like the lavender man, the strawberry man, the honey-man and those who did the rounds on Fridays calling 'Dublin Bay herrings'. Figures of the sixties included Treacle Billy who stood at Carlisle Bridge with a tall hat and white coat tending a coffee stall and selling doughnuts full of treacle. A woman outside the College of Surgeons sold dolls dressed in College robes and mortar boards. Malone, the banjo player, with his song about a poor drunkard's child drove some listeners to take the pledge. The Grand Old Man always sang a song in praise of Gladstone, while another musician played nothing but 'God Save the Queen' on a tin whistle. An itinerant trio known as Hamlet, Dunbar and Uncle had replaced Zozimus and roamed about singing ballads; their best known song was 'Donnybrook is no more'. However, wandering ballad singers were a vanishing group. The child in *Araby* listened to their harsh voices singing about heroes like O'Donovan Rossa, but by the time James Joyce recorded another set of street characters in June 1904, the only ballad singer was indoors giving a rendering of 'The Croppy Boy'.

Beggars and vagrants remained part of the scene. Madame de Bovet saw them 'everywhere on the bridges, on the quays, round the squares...standing against the railings...a greasy hat over one ear...boys in troops dressed in waistcoats without buttons and seatless breeches... Tall fine-looking girls with clogs and a straw hat and feathers offer the passerby little bunches of pale geraniums, withered Indian pinks...' Women's clothes included, 'silk skirts all befrilled, shining embroidery on one side and silk fringes on the other, worn and rusty, stiff with grease and moth eaten; plush hats, once grey-green...' The purchase of clothes discarded by the rich was essential to the economy of the poor. Dealers brought consignments of second-hand garments over from England to sell in Dublin. Madame de Bovet had noted that in Patrick Street 'every other shop is an old clothes shop'. This old clothes market, which had been patronized by William Carleton, continued to find custom well into the twentieth century. In 1907 A. Peters wrote how 'The Madame Worth...or Madame Manning of this West End of Dublin placed her bundle of goods on the pavement of the open street... Everything is here. Dresses, petticoats, underclothing, men's trousers, children's frocks, showy blouses, all bearing evidence of having played a brave part in some show place of the world... Close at hand are the bootstalls with rows of well-polished foot-gear...with great cathedral bells ringing loudly overhead.'

In 1881 the Mansion House supper room and a portion of Dawson Street were lit by electricity. One of the first firms to provide their own plant for electricity was the *Irish Times* in 1884. After 1890 the first mains were laid in Sackville Street, Grafton Street, Henry Street and other thoroughfares in the centre of the city. Photography was providing a new visual record of Dubliners since Fox Talbot had come over in 1842 and photographed the yard at Dublin Castle and a respectable group of citizens outside St George's Church. We can study top hatted gentlemen, barefoot boys, women among their grimy washing in the Liberties, nannies in Merrion Square, soldiers, the diversity of horse-drawn traffic rumbling between the unobstrusive shops with their narrow arched windows and canopies. Small trade empires like Findlater's and Bewley's were providing landmarks. A number of shops still bore signs, two of which have survived; the elephant over Elvery's was once over a tea shop, and the figure in Duke Street over an optician's used to be called Captain Cuttle and hung over an eighteenth-century optician in Capel Street.

Big Victorian buildings were infiltrating among the Georgian terraces – railway stations, the National Gallery on the site of Dargan's exhibition, the National Library and Museum, the brick crenellations of the South City Offices, the façade of the

Shelbourne Hotel with its guard of Nubian princesses. Thomas Deane and Benjamin Woodward, together with the O'Shea brothers, created the splendours of the Engineering School in Trinity and rebuilt the Kildare Street Club, decorating it with floral and animal trimmings after it burned down in 1860, consuming three maidservants. Triumphalism was manifest in huge new Catholic churches like St Audoen's in Cook Street built over a modest post-penal church and the medieval and Romanesque fantasies of J.J. MacCarthy – St Saviour's in Dominick Street, St Paul, Mount Argus and the Star of the Sea at Sandymount. Meanwhile St Patrick's and Christ Church were being overhauled at the expense of a brewer, Sir Benjamin Lee Guinness, and a distiller, Sir Henry Roe, respectively. Butt Bridge wrecked the elegance of the river bank. New statues and monuments sprang up. The Crampton Memorial was erected in 1862 by Sir Thomas Kirk. John Foley adorned Dublin with Surgeon Parkes and three statues on College Green, Burke, Goldsmith and Grattan – Gogarty observed that all three have the same calves. After the erection of O'Connell's angel-girt monument in 1882 for which Foley was also responsible, Sackville Street was called unofficially by its modern name. 'It is useless' commented Madame De Bovet, 'to speak of it to your driver by any other name than that of O'Connell Street; he will pretend not to understand you.' She noted that Christopher Moore's hideous statue of his namesake, Thomas Moore, had 'already taken on a chocolate tint'. Thomas Farrell hewed out Dargan in front of the National Gallery, William Smith O'Brien and Sir Thomas Grey behind O'Connell and Lord Ardilaun at Stephen's Green, the site of his benevolence. Before 1880 the Green had been enclosed, available only to residents, a field of leafy avenues dominated by George II on his horse. Lord Ardilaun, who owned a big house on the south side, conceived the idea of turning the Green into a public park and landscaping it at his own expense with a lake and waterfall whose water was piped from the Grand Canal.

In the sixties Dublin had three theatres; the Royal, destroyed by fire in 1879, the Queen's, formerly the Adelphi, founded in 1829 and Dan Lowry's Music-Hall which started as the Star of Erin and in time became the Olympia. A fourth theatre, the Gaiety, was opened in 1872, while variety shows were still being staged at the Rotunda. Music could be enjoyed at the Antient Concert Rooms in

Great Brunswick Street or the Rotunda or the Royal Academy of Music, founded in 1848. Over the years citizens listened to Liszt, Paganini, Scarlatti and Jenny Lind; they watched Fanny Kemble and Henry Irving perform on the stage. Meanwhile old outdoor amusements were still popular, driving to the suburbs or the sea or the Strawberry Beds with their strawberry-sellers, pipers, fiddlers and pubs. The old popular seaside resorts attracted summer visitors and summer recreations. Respectable Kingstown was considered suitable for cases of 'depressed temperament', who were perhaps cheered up by the ladies George Moore remembered and called 'light o'loves,' who walked on the pier on Sundays all of them beautifully dressed in sea-green dresses and seal-skin jackets.

By the 1860s the crippling taxes on newpapers were discontinued and in 1865 Dublin had 24 newspapers. Five were morning papers – the *Freeman's Journal, Saunder's Newsletter,* the *Daily Express*, the *Morning News* and the *Irish Times*. Daily papers were small, containing four or six pages of minute print. Public libraries started in 1884 when two opened in Capel Street and Thomas Street. Universal education began in 1865 and every parish in Dublin had its national school. The Bluecoat School changed its uniform. Charity uniforms were designed to be practical and avoid changes in fashion – even the paupers eating off their enamel plates in the workhouses were in brown uniform. The Bluecoat boys finally exchanged their long cutaway coats and Geneva bands for something that was like a cross between the uniforms of a soldier and a telegraph boy. The public school era was reflected in Dublin by the founding of St Columba's College at Rathfarnham in 1860 with the intention of producing a civilized blend of the Celt and the English gentleman. Alternative Catholic education was provided by the praiseworthy programmes of the Christian Brothers. In 1860 the more gentlemanly French Holy Ghost Fathers started their college near Blackrock with its military style clothes very similar to those of the Bluecoat boys. In Great Denmark Street in the heart of the city the Jesuits had converted Lord Belvedere's residence to the day-school which educated James Joyce. Irish was not taught at these schools. About the only place where one could briefly learn the language was at the Mechanics Institute in Abbey Street – later the Abbey Theatre – where O'Donovan Rossa gave classes for a time. The Society for the Preservation of the Irish Language, founded in 1879, was followed by the Gaelic League, which,

although it was too late to save a tongue which the peasantry over
most of the country was discarding, would play a fundamental role
in the future of Ireland and its capital.

O'Connell's crowds had been the first visible demonstration of
the strength of united public opinion. James Stephens realized the
potential of such multitudes – alarming to authority – when he
masterminded another great concourse for the funeral of Terence
Bellew MacManus. Stephens had come to Dublin in 1858 where he
printed his newspaper, the *Irish People*, in premises near the Castle
and administered oaths to members of the Irish Republican
Brotherhood who would rename themselves Fenians. Their earliest
indication of public support was MacManus' funeral. After the
Young Irelander died penniless in exile in California, his body was
brought back and buried in Glasnevin, accompanied by a huge
procession of men marching from Kingsbridge Station to the
cemetery with brass bands, black badges and torches. Six years
later another mighty assembly gathered for the funeral of the
Manchester Martyrs who were carried to the new Fenian plot at
Glasnevin to the sound of solemn music and muffled drums.
'Green ribbons etc., mixed with black crepe were universally worn,
and many women and children were in the procession'. Dubliners
expressed their views in other ways; their treatment of Parnell after
his arrest in Morrison's Hotel was affectionate and familiar, since
the piles of smoking caps, green cushions and a green satin quilt
recalled the generosity of an earlier generation to O'Connell on a
similar occasion.

Scenes like the great funeral processions were not quite balanced
by the royal visits which took place at fairly regular intervals after
the Queen's triumph in 1849. The royal family returned in 1853 to
view the five glass domes of Dargan's Exhibition bubbling over
Leinster Lawn. During one drive through Dublin Her Majesty
whipped off the cap of naughty Prince Alfred with one hand and
gave him a resounding smack across the cheek with the other, to the
delight of the crowd. They came again in August 1861 on their way
to Killarney to meet Bertie who was touring the south. The Queen
went again to the Royal Hospital, while the Prince Consort took his
sons on an exhaustive tour of prisons. Bertie came in 1863 to open
the massive Dublin Exhibition on the site of the old Coburg
Gardens between Stephen's Green and Wellington Square. Before
the galleries were opened they were tested by having 7,000 cannon

balls rolled round them for a day, followed by 600 men of the 78th Highlanders, who, together with their band, marched up and down in slow and double quick time. The heir to the throne returned in April 1868, bringing his young Danish wife with him. When she visited Alexandra College which she graciously allowed to be called after her, 'the Princess had a floral shower cast on her by the young ladies'. Although there were a good many more royal visits before they no longer became necessary, between 1862 and 1900 Dubliners had to do without their queen, who wouldn't return, mainly because of the business of Prince Albert's statue which Dublin Corporation refused to erect. But she did come back as an old lady, when she visited Dublin wearing bunches of shamrock, her bonnet and parasol embroidered with silver shamrocks, in April 1900, instead of going on her usual continental jaunt. Europeans were critical of Britain because of the Boer War, and this was a good propaganda exercise. But her visit also came from the heart. She knew how many of her soldiers were Irish; they had served in South Africa and she wished to thank the Irish people in person.

The smiling presence of royalty brought limited assurance to the Protestant minority suffering from declining prestige and power. The last great betrayal was the disestablishment of the Church of Ireland in 1869. The Anglo-Irish of the eighteenth century had felt less self-conscious about their role in Irish life. In the nineteenth century patriots like Thomas Davis, Isaac Butt and Parnell might be Protestant, but they were exceptions in a society that tended to become withdrawn and isolated.

There were a number of prestigious pockets in the city and suburbs where the ultra-respectable clustered. In the town the most fashionable addresses were still among the big squares. On the north side the quality lingered in Mountjoy Square. An old man interviewed in 1957 described his life as a page-boy in Mountjoy Square at the age of thirteen in 1885. 'The butler blew a whistle and shouted for "Tommy!" and I'd be sent to the Post Office to collect letters or to the bank for money. The bank paid in gold and I'd carry back sovereigns in a little bag of leather.'

Successful doctors had their homes and practices in Merrion Square, where some houses still have tunnels connecting house and mews where servants could walk without being untidy or obtrusive objects of vision. It was 'the best part of Dublin' according to young Oscar Wilde. Maurice Craig has pointed out how the changes of address of his father, the ophthalmologist, indicated the stages of his medical career. Sir William Wilde progressed from 199 Great Brunswick Street to 15 and 21 Westland Row – Oscar was born at No. 21 – to No. 1 Merrion Square where Lady Wilde, the formidable Speranza, held her soirées in darkened rooms 'to avoid the butchery of strong lights'. It was not until the beginning of the twentieth century that doctors began to migrate to Fitzwilliam Square. Merrion Square, unlike Stephen's Green, remained closed off from the common mob for another century. William Pryce Maunsell wrote in 1859 how 'a few ladies take within its railings their solitary constitutional walk; an occasional gentleman is seen crossing it, producing his key at the gate and locking it after him as he would a wine cellar'. The medical profession still dominated the plebeian aristocracy; for pretentious practitioners 'knighthoods were despised and laughed at...no physician would have accepted anything short of baronetcy'. However, Sir William Wilde, touched by the breath of scandal, remained a mere Knight Bachelor. A number of doctors were reputed to keep mistresses round Sandymount and Park Avenue, a pleasant gallop away from the Square.

Considering the entrenched social rhythms of this small bourgeois community, it fostered a good many remarkable people. At No. 60 Merrion Square, a few doors down from where the successful young lawyer, Daniel O'Connell, had established his home more than thirty years before, Sheridan Le Fanu retired to drink his green tea and write ghostly fantasies. Some were inspired by the hysterical nightmares endured by his wife when she was alive. Could the celebrated fat moist white hand that haunted the House by the Graveyard be that of Le Fanu's father-in-law? Perhaps there was some effect of gaslight on decayed and shadowy houses in gloomy streets that caused nineteenth-century Dublin writers such as Maturin, Le Fanu and Bram Stoker to concentrate on horror.

The historian, William Lecky, would be wandering through book-shops 'like an inspired giraffe browsing in the topmost boughs of the tree of knowledge'. In Stephen's Green the fidgety English Archbishop, Dr Whately, could be seen playing with his dogs and swinging from the trees outside his palace. The mathematician, Sir William Rowan Hamilton, discovered quaternions while walking on the banks of the Royal Canal ignoring his wife's chatter. Before his bankruptcy Isaac Butt gave

numerous parties in the house he rented in Eccles Street once
owned by Francis Johnston, and containing an organ in the back
parlour reputed to have belonged to Handel. Sir Samuel Ferguson,
President of the Academy and antiquarian successor to George
Petrie, composed poems and pieces of writing that were influenced
by political events. 'In Carey's footsteps' written in 1885 and
described as a Dublin Eclogue, interpreted the thoughts of an
Invincible just before he and his comrades attacked two members
of the Establishment with long surgical knives.

> Yes, here I'm in the Park.
> The People's Garden. No, let dull Carlisle
> Set out his leg among the nursery maids,
> Ay, there General Gough...
> Astride the gingerbread bronze. They set
> Him up to show how masters know to
> Ride over us rebel Irish...

Apart from diversions at the Castle, society amused itself at race
courses like Punchestown or attended reviews in the Park or polo
games or cricket matches at the Viceregal Lodge. Other sports were
becoming popular. The Irish Rugby Union was formed in 1879, the
Fitzwilliam Lawn Tennis Club came into existence in 1883 and by
1891 serious golfing was becoming popular. The main summer
functions were the Trinity Races and the Horse Show. For patriots
who rejected these pastimes the Gaelic Athletic Association,
founded in 1884, created its own forms of exclusiveness when it
encouraged the popularity of Gaelic games.

The vexed question of Catholics entering Trinity – some did –
seemed successfully bypassed when John Henry Newman, later
Cardinal Newman, offered alternative higher education with his
Catholic University, located in the house in Stephen's Green that
had once belonged to the priest baiter, Richard Whaley. Newman
came to Dublin in 1851 and gave a series of lectures entitled 'The
Idea of a University' in the Rotunda Hall, now the Gate Theatre.
Initially he endured the trials suffered by modern actors at the Gate
of having to compete with noise from next door where the band of
the 81st Regiment was playing for a Grand Bazaar. Three years
later Newman was installed as Rector of the new University whose
student body of forty included a grandson of Daniel O'Connell.
University life was pleasant, enlivened by bathing parties on the

Liffey and visits to the Pigeon House Fort from where groups of students would come rattling back in hackney carriages 'with wolfish appetite' to the austere and elegant house on the Green. But Newman was fatally handicapped by lack of proper finance and of support from the hierarchy; his University had no charter and could not confer degrees. He resigned his Rectorship in 1859, and the idea of a Catholic University was shelved for another twenty years until the Royal University was founded on the same premises. Before he departed he was responsible for the splendid University Church, consecrated on Ascension Day 1856. 'My idea was to build a large barn and decorate it in the style of a basilica.' The architect, John Hungerford Pollen, did exactly what he wanted. 'Pollen has made the church gorgeous.'

In 1873 Trinity abolished all religious tests for entrance. For Trinity the second half of the nineteenth century was an age of great Provosts and outstanding dons like Edward Dowden and John Pentland Mahaffy. William Pryce Maunsell's booklet entitled *The College Idler* stressed the College's surprising squalor. 'The first thing that strikes the most careless observer...is that it is the dirtiest place he ever saw in his life'. Across the slippery paving outside Botany Bay the skips carried their buckets of slops. On Sundays the students could be seen leaving Chapel 'in soiled surplices' and flitting across Front Square 'like dirty spectres'. Above Botany Bay Oscar Wilde lived more fastidiously, sharing rooms with his brother, Willie, and avoiding the society of barmaids which fellow students enjoyed. His tutor, Mahaffy, tended to avoid the College altogether and cultivate Lord Lieutenants, Carlisle, Abercorn, Marlborough and Londonderry.

The prosaic nature of society and the seedy atmosphere of Dublin is vividly captured by George Moore in his early novel *A Drama in Muslin* published in 1886, which describes the city before the Celtic revival and the founding of the Abbey Theatre. His picture is melancholy. 'The weary, the woebegone, the threadbare streets – yes, threadbare conveys the moral idea of a Dublin in 1882.' Merrion Square is described as 'exhaling moist and evil-smelling airs' with nothing to be seen but 'crouching cats and the odd policeman'. The recently landscaped Stephen's Green seemed 'like a schoolboy treat set out for the entertainment of charity children'. It was surrounded with 'broken pavements, unpainted hall doors, rusty railings, meagre outside cars hidden almost out of sight in the deep gutters – how infinitely pitiful!' Perhaps he exaggerated the decrepit state of Dublin, perhaps not. His assessment of society during the eighties has the same note of exasperation. It was 'more lamentable and soul wearying than ever before. It presented no new features. The same absence of conviction, the same mousy gossiping and inability to see over the horizon of Merrion Square. The same adoration of officialism, the same meanness committed to secure an invitation to the Castle, the same sing-song waltz tunes, the same miserable, mocking, melancholy muslin hours were endured by the same white martyrs...'

One of the characteristics of their provincial society was the way the army played an important part in the makeup. There were about 20,000 troops in Ireland at any one time, of whom about half were stationed at ten Dublin barracks. Their officers with their villas in Rathmines and their private incomes gave social functions an attractive garrison panache. The modern absence of soldiers is as striking a change as the absence of horses. For centuries military uniforms were an integral part of the city scene. In 1774 Mrs Delany wrote to her sister: 'I am now in Dame Street waiting for the raree show of the city militia who are all in their regimentals and, they say, make a most gallant show.' In the late eighteenth century there was a Teutonic obsession with uniforms among all shades of political opinion. Volunteer variety progressed to the red-coats of the nineteenth century enhanced by the brass of the bands that played all summer long in Phoenix Park or Rutland Square, to Lieutenant Gardner's newly introduced Khaki which made him glamorous in Molly Bloom's eyes. Some uniforms appear oddly out of place like those worn by the underpaid private soldiers of Charles II sneaking through the wilderness of Phoenix Park in 1668 with traps under their red coats to poach partridges; or Thomas Russell's full regimentals of the East India Company worn as he helped cook dinner for Wolfe Tone's family at their seaside retreat at Ringsend; or the cavalry uniform worn by Captain John Hill Foster after he settled in for life at the Sheriff's Marshalsea, unable to pay his debts.

Asenath Nicholson was touched by the soldiers worshipping in Irishtown church one evening during the summer of 1844. They knelt 'cap-à-pie in warlike habiliments, with furbished guns and bayonets in their pews... Never did a hundred of young soldiers in any house of God do more credit to good air, food, and exercise than did these. Each had his prayer-book, and read with as much apparent devotion as though the success of a battle depended on it.'

Private soldiers dressed just as gaudily as officers. 'The leading side drummer in the first battalion of the King's Liverpool Regiment, best shot in the regiment and haircutter to the men' who married Sean O'Casey's sister, wore for his wedding 'his red coat with its white braid and crescent epaulettes, his spiked helmet on his dear dark head and the blue, yellow and green bugler's cord slung around his breast and back with the two gorgeous tassels cascading down his left shoulder...' A good part of the British army was Irish, as Queen Victoria knew. Scarlet uniforms mixed with the green and black of the great funeral processions. After the funeral of the Manchester Martyrs it was reported that 'a number of soldiers, most of whom belonged to the 86th, have been placed under arrest for taking part'.

At times of crisis like 1798 or 1848 the city was filled with temporary barracks. But the number of permanent barracks grew steadily. In the eighteenth century Chapelizod Barracks had followed the original Royal Barracks. In 1810 Portobello Barracks were begun on a site named back in 1770 after the place where Francis Drake died. Beggar's Bush followed in 1827, Marlborough Barracks rose at Grangegorman in 1888, while Wellington Barracks was converted from a penitentiary in 1891.

'The number of troops in the island is proportioned to its disloyalty' observed Madame de Bovet in 1892 as she walked through Phoenix Park noting 'a dragoon galloping away in the distance...in red tunic and helmet of steel...a patrol of Hussars...a company of riflemen in green uniform so dark it is nearly black...Scottish infantry in tartan...' Phoenix Park was a byeword in the British army for its reviews and mock battles. A critic of Lord Cardigan who led the Charge of the Light Brigade noted how in the Crimea 'the Major General amuses us by giving us regulation Phoenix Park Field Days'. In 1849 Queen Victoria viewed 6,000 soldiers led by their regimental bands who charged with a great huzza to within a few yards of the royal carriages. Reviews for visiting royalty were obligatory. In 1868 the Prince of Wales watched a force which, according to the *Illustrated London News*, 'was small, but it was a very complete little division. It consisted of the Carabiniers, 12th Lancers, D field battery, C horse battery Military Train, 3rd Battalion Grenadier Guards, 3rd Buffs, 39th, 63rd, 72nd and 89th regiments.'

Austin Clarke recalled how 'the infantry men in their smart red jackets and dark blue trousers strolled up and down, silver knobbed swagger-cane tucked under arm, chatting with innumerable girls or bantering them in noisy groups'. Joyce places his soldiers in the middle of Nighttown, knowing how:

> The poor and deserving prostitute
> Plays every night at catch-as-catch can
> With her tight-breeched British artillery man.

Privates Carr and Compton stroll 'swagger-sticks in their oxters...their tunics blood bright in a lampglow, black sockets of cap on their blond copper polls.' Their speech is more obscene than that of any other character in *Ulysses*. No doubt it was faithfully reproduced from encounters Joyce had with the soldiery that thronged the Dublin streets.

13

From Parnell's Death to 1916

Parnell's funeral in October 1891, the largest since O'Connell's, was attended by 200,000 people and accompanied by heavenly manifestations. Above the heads of the crowds surrounding the thick matting of funeral wreaths, some inscribed 'Murdered by Priests', among which lay the little bunch of 'immortelles' from the old Fenian, James Stephens, a meteor trailed. Young Maud Gonne saw it, and so did Standish O'Grady who described the sky as 'bright with strange lights and flames'.

A day after the funeral the nine-year-old James Joyce wrote a poem he called '*Et Tu, Healy*' which his proud father printed and distributed sending a copy to the Pope. That Christmas, dinner was ruined by bitter quarrelling over the dead leader. From that time no politician would be worth following. Instead Joyce's obsession would become the trivia of his surroundings. The small boy in *Araby* who accompanied his female relatives when they went shopping on Saturday evening took note as they made their way 'through the flaring streets, jostled by drunken men and bargaining women, amid the curses of labourers, the shrill litanies of shop boys who stood guard by the barrels of pig's cheeks, the nasal chanting of street singers.' The young man walked across the town from Amiens Street station 'because he wished to partake in the morning life of the city. This morning walk was pleasant for him and there was no face that passed him on its way to its commercial prison but he strove to pierce to the motive centre of its ugliness.'

In Paris he recalled to visiting Dubliners the city frozen in time on 16 June 1904. Kenneth Reddin remembered how 'after twenty years absence he challenged us...to name the shops from Amiens Street Station to the Pillar. First one side and then down the other.' The young Austin Clarke, after witnessing similar party tricks – 'Is Mulvaney's shop still there at the corner?' – diagnosed 'a phase of sensitive early experience assuming the continuity of dream-existence sharpened by the files of feverish memory'. Memory, old maps and stop watches, Thom's *Directories*, years of old newspapers contributed to what Yeats described as 'the vulgarity of a single Dublin day prolonged to 700 pages'.

The extraordinary wide-ranging social detail that *Ulysses*

contains gives us copious information about the minutiae of the Dublin of 1904 – pubs, brothels, trams, horse cabs, jaunting cars, shops, newspaper offices, street characters, household groceries such as those collected so dismally in the dresser in the kitchen at No. 8 Eccles Street. Here we can only select and comment on a few of the social themes that are entangled in the orderly confusion; it seems best to concentrate on some of those that preoccupied the city for a thousand years – involving poverty, dirt and pestilence.

By this time instead of pigs, which had ceased to be a municipal problem, it seems better to substitute cattle as a characteristic of Dublin life. Joyce's works, like Irish mythology, rumble with the hoofbeats of cattle. *A Portrait of the Artist* opens with a cow. *Ulysses* opens with the milk woman of Sandycove and progresses to Mr Deasy's preoccupation with bovine misfortune to the complicated symbolism of the Oxen in the Sun. Cattle are a fitting theme of the Bloomsday structure, since they were very much part of Dublin life at the beginning of the twentieth century. So Leopold Bloom is made to be involved with the cattle trade. During the Oxen in the Sun episode we learn that he had once been 'actuary for Mr Joseph Cuffe, a worthy salesmaster that drove his trade for livestock and meadow auctions hard by Mr Gavins Low's yard in Prussia Street.' Thirty cattle dealers were listed in Thom's *Directory* for 1904, although the narrator in *Cyclops* described Cuffe's premises less elaborately as a knacker's yard. While he was reading details about the model farm at Kinnereth, Bloom remembered 'those mornings in the cattlemarket, the beasts lowing in their pens, branded sheep, flop and fall of dung, the breeder in hobnailed boots trudging through the litter, slapping a palm on a ripemeated hindquarter...'

On the way to Glasnevin the funeral cab takes Bloom and his companions near the cattlemarket where it is held up by the weekly flow of beasts. This has been said to represent the stream of life contrasting with the cab and its mission of death, although the two-way contrast was a regular weekly event in north-side Dublin. 'A divided drove of branded cattle passed the windows, lowing, slouching by on padded hoofs, whisking their tails slowly on their clotted bony croups. Outside and through them ran raddled sheep bleating their fear.' An average of 15,000 animals were exported weekly. 'For Liverpool probably. Roast beef for old England.' About 4,000 were cattle; the rest were made up of sheep, pigs, horses, mules and the odd goat. Sean O'Casey, two years older than Joyce, spent part of his childhood viewing this weekly rush of cattle 'in their hundreds, streaming along holding up the traffic...a mist of steam hanging over them as the hot sun dried the falling rain that glistened on their hides...then a herd of pigs...the drovers prodding them viciously behind the ears...'

In addition to beef cattle Dublin was full of cows. Over 600 proprietors of dairies were listed in the 1904 Thom's, a number that did not include the branches of the Lucan Dairy – the branch in Blessington Street employed a man with curly hair admired by Molly Bloom – or the curiously named Educational Dairy. The milkcarts went about as Sean O'Casey saw them 'filled with shining churns having big brass taps sticking out through holes in the tailboard, all polished...the milkman filled a can with a long snout in which rattled the half-pint and pint measures used to dish out milk...to the women waiting...at the doors with jugs and mugs in their hands...' But the term 'dairy' covered a number of categories of selling milk. Only one milkman is designated 'hawker'; twenty are listed as 'purveyors of milk to the city'. Others are the countless small shops which distributed milk from copious different sources, and the many stables located in the heart of the city that contained a cow or two and sold its produce. Four dairies are listed in Tyrone Street in the heart of the brothel area. At one time in the late nineteenth century city dairies were concentrated in Stonybatter. James Larkin approved of this haphazard system of milk supply; he went as far as buying a cow to show Dubliners the advantages of rural economy in urban surroundings.

Thom's does not list dairies in Kingstown and Sandycove; however the street directories mention fourteen dairies in that area whose proprietors were ratepayers. One may well have employed the old woman who supplied the tenants of the Martello Tower with 'Sandycove milk'. 'He watched her pour into the measure and thence into the jug rich white milk, not hers. Old shrunken paps. She poured again a measureful and a tilly.' A tilly was a bit extra like the thirteenth of a baker's dozen or the thirteenth poem of *Pomes Penyeach*.

> The voice tells them home is warm
> They moo and make brute music with their hoofs

The 'patient cow at daybreak in the lush field' that Stephen imagines the old woman milking was probably near by. Suburbs, even seaside suburbs, were still rural. But summer grazing could be some distance away from a milk round. *A Portrait of the Artist* has a detailed account of the routine of a Blackrock milkman, whose cattle were at grass in Carrickmines during the summer. There is an echo of this memory in the Cyclops episode which talks of 'heavy hooved kine from pasturelands of Lusk and Rush and Carrickmines'. Archie, the small boy in *Exiles*, is allowed as a tremendous treat to accompany a milkman on his rounds. 'But when autumn came the cows were driven home from the grass; and the first sight of the filthy cowyard at Stradbrook with its foul green puddles and clots of liquid dung and steaming bran troughs sickened Stephen's heart.'

The filth that so revolted young Stephen was general in milking yards. Unpasteurized milk was a poison, and people were aware of its dangers; Sean O'Casey's mother commented on how the milkmen polished their churns: 'if they were as particular with the insides as they were with the outsides, the milk'd be safer to drink'. Dublin was slow to regulate its milk supply. In most cities in America bottled and pasteurized milk had become compulsory by 1920, while capitals like Toronto had made the change as early as 1914. Although the Craigie brothers in Dublin had changed to pasteurized milk on their own initiative, in 1925, a year later an enquiry into the cleanness and wholesomeness of the milk supply was still commenting on how 'in places like the slums of Dublin...the milk can and the jug that the householder leaves standing in the doorway of the grimy streets must be among the most virulent disseminators of disease.' In the Circe episode, the old milking woman, who earlier represented Mother Ireland, is turned into a figure of doom: 'Old Gummy Granny in sugarloaf hat appears seated on a toadstool, the deathflower of the potato blight on her breast.' Her milk at 2d. a pint may have been dear enough and the connection may have been intentional. Joyce's sister died of typhoid and his brother of what is now assumed to be tubercular peritonitis; both of these diseases could very likely have been conveyed by milk. Of Bloom's six dead friends whom he remembers as a result of 'bellchime and handtouch and footstep and lonechill' two have died of phthisis or T.B. Hospitals were crowded with wards full of patients who not only had pulmonary tuberculosis but so-called surgical T.B. in different forms – T.B. hips, knee-joints, glands, Pott's disease and so forth. There was nearly always at least one child with that most terrible and distressing of conditions – T.B. meningitis.

Adulterated milk was not the only way to contact fatal disease in a city 'paved with dust, horse dung and consumptive spits'. The sad truth was that the majority of people were hungrier and more badly housed than ever. Between 1851 and 1911 the population rose from 321,000 to 398,000, and because of Dublin's lack of industry only a fraction had jobs. In 1910 the Dublin Labour Exchange was the fourth most crowded in the United Kingdom. An inquiry during 1914 found that nearly a quarter of the population lived in one room tenements with an average of six people crammed into one room. A new breed of rentiers had bought up old mansions. The fashionable parts of the north side around Mountjoy Square were finally deserted by the rich and quickly filled up with tenements. 'The bare bones of a fanlight over a hungry door' wrote Louis MacNeice. The inquiry quoted found that fourteen members of the Dublin Corporation owned or had an interest in tenement houses 'some of which were unfit for habitation'. Halls, landings, and yards were invariably filthy; in many houses one squalid lavatory had to accommodate sixty or seventy people. The crowded tenement rooms were sparsely furnished, often with boxes for tables and chairs. D.A. Chart, who wrote a paper on slum conditions in 1914 reported how 'in some tenement rooms the bedstead is not to be seen in its usual place in the corner, but in its stead there is spread on the floor a mysterious and repellent assortment of rags, which few inquirers have had the hardihood to investigate...'

'The population of Dublin' wrote 'An Englishman' in 1917, 'is made up chiefly of doctors and priests with a sprinkling of rentiers, a great horde of officials and finally perhaps the largest proportion of abjectly poor people which is to be found in any city in Europe of the same size.' The streets round Nelson's Pillar reminded him of Hogarth's Gin Alley with its old women 'howling and roaring at each other and dozens of little barefoot children and drunks'. The Reverend John Gwynn, S.J. writing in the *Freeman's Journal*, described children 'crawling in rags along the pavement – whimpering with cold and hunger'. Patrick Pearce calculated that 'half the children attending primary schools are undernourished. I suppose that there are 20,000 families in Dublin in whose domestic economy milk and butter are all but unknown; black tea and bread are their only diet.' D.A. Chart considered that the extreme monotony of a diet of bread, tea, sugar, herrings, dripping or margarine, occasionally varied by a piece of bacon or pig's cheek was a contributing factor to the amount of alcoholism in the city.

One of the most striking effects of these social evils was the high infant mortality rate. About twenty per cent of all deaths in the city occurred among infants under one year; in 1913, the year of the lockout the proportion rose to twenty-five. The death of Bloom's son as the result of a natal complication at the age of eleven days was nothing out of the common at the time which Austin Clarke, whose parents lost eight children out of twelve, called a Herodian era.

For the poor mortality among children was fearful. Winter brought croup which killed off O'Casey's brothers, while in summer there was another horror: during July and August the outpatients' departments of hospitals were inundated with infants suffering from gastro-enteritis known as 'summer diarrhoea'. Teams of medical students would be organized to try and save the lives of scores of dehydrated children with warm saline. Many died with or without hospital treatment. Such annual epidemics were characteristic of overcrowded and insanitary areas of the city; the children of the well-to-do rarely died of summer diarrhoea. In rural Ireland with its absence of dangers inherent in industrial environments the infant mortality statistics were strikingly lower than in the rest of the British Isles. But Dublin, though not primarily industrial, had a higher death rate for children than that of nearly all English cities. Causes which are now forgotten contributed, like the cloud of flies inevitable in a city of horses. Some commentators have attributed the decline in infant mortality in Europe to the introduction of the motor car and the end of horse dung. (The scent of horse manure lingered; it was one of the first things V.S. Pritchett noticed about Dublin when he arrived in the 1920s.)

Other factors included not only the lack of a safe milk supply, but the deficiencies in providing drains and clean water. Few tenements had washrooms or anything but the most primitive sanitation. For centuries the limited sewers were for rain and flood waters only, and although odd ones carried off waste into the Liffey which was even more polluted than it is now, private cesspits were in general use. Between 1892 and 1906 a new system of main and intercepting sewers were laid, two of which were located on either bank of the Liffey. But their adaptation was generally slow. Among the middle classes the water closet was replacing the privy, but for the poor it was different. Disease festered in the privies behind the houses, emptied occasionally by the dung dodgers. O'Casey described the operations of these corporation employees 'who came at stated times to empty out the petties and ashpits in the backyards of the people... Heaps of muck were appearing before the various houses in the street. Each door would have a horrid hill outside of it till a cart came later on to carry them away. In and out, in and out of the houses went the dung dodgers carrying huge baskets on their backs filled with the slime and ashes of the families, their boots and clothes spattered with the mire that kept dropping from the baskets.' In *Tumbling in the Hay* a medical student going down Nassau Street sees 'a heap of ordure... moving into Grafton Street. Why don't they put clay over it and put a lid on it for the sake of public health? thought Weary as he moved through the polluted air.'

'It is an accepted fact' wrote A. Newsholm in 1906 in his *Infant Mortality: A Social Problem* 'that defective scavenging and the retention of excremental matters in privies and pail closets are always accompanied by excessive infantile diarrhoea'.

From Sandymount Strand to Butt Bridge and Eccles Street *Ulysses* resounds with micturition and evacuation. The Calypso episode gives a clear picture of the plumbing arrangements of a seedy middle-class household. There are two lavatories. One is upstairs. 'Heaviness; hot day coming. Too much trouble to fag up the stairs to the landing.' The other at the back of the neglected garden is in poor shape with its crazy door, stale cobwebs and stench of mouldy lime. But it is not a mere privy – 'Did I pull the chain?' – although it would have replaced an old privy dating from the time when dung dodgers served rich and poor alike. In the deeds of many eighteenth-century houses there are provisions for a right of way to the rear for dung carts. Some early bathrooms were tacked onto the backs of houses, often in place of an elegant arched window, and the 'pushout' is still a crazy feature of Dublin architecture. Lavatories were generally installed in houses that were not actually tenements, although there was still plenty of demand for 'bare clean closestools' like those in the window of William Miller, Plumber. The Blooms have a commode which is out of action and covered with cretonne of an apple design; also an orange keyed chamber-pot.

There is no bathroom in Eccles Street and washing arrangements are primitive. Molly Bloom describes how, having set up washing arrangements and found her washing glove, it is difficult to find privacy; Milly keeps bursting in on her. Bathrooms were a luxury and other citizens besides Leopold Bloom took public baths at Usher's Island, Clontarf Road, the Hamman in Sackville Street, and Tara Street and Stephen's Green. The last two advertised 'splendid plunge baths for both gentlemen and ladies' in addition to 'warm, shower, salt, sulphur, pine, iodine, vapour and patent Magneto-Electric baths administered throughout the day'.

In *A Portrait of the Artist* the child Stephen is unfamiliar with sophisticated plumbing. 'Once he had washed his hands in the lavatory of the Wicklow Hotel and his father pulled the stopper up by the chain... There were two cocks that you turned and the water came out: cold and then hot. He felt cold and then a little hot: and he could see the names printed on the cocks. That was a very queer thing.' In the Ithaca episode it is revealed that Stephen's last bath took place eight months before. Critics like Harry Blamires have associated Stephen's reluctance to wash with 'his rejection of his own baptism, his failure to commit himself to womanhood, and to engage fruitfully in artistic creation'. But it was not easy to perform ablutions in the Dedalus household.

> – Fill out the place for me to wash, said Stephen.
> – Katey, fill out the place for Stephen to wash.
> – Booty, fill out the place for Stephen to wash.
> – I can't, I'm going for blue. Fill it out, you, Maggie.

When the enamelled basin had been fitted into the well of the sink and the old washing glove flung on the side of it, he allowed his mother to scrub his neck...

'Well it's a poor case, she said, when a university student is so dirty that his mother has to wash him.'

Adequate sanitary arrangements had long been available to all who could afford them. In 1848 a bath had been installed in Dublin Castle for Queen Victoria to use; it had a thermometer to measure the water, and still functions perfectly. But by the early 1900s advertisements for houses to let or to sell still felt obliged to point out the sanitary facilities: 'All modern improvements'; 'bath': 'hot bath'; 'Rathgar (hot bath) £38'; 'Morehampton Road – sewerage perfect'; 'Monkstown – house in perfect sanitary condition'. Bloom dreamed of 'bathroom, hot and cold supply, reclining and shower: water closet on mezzanine provided with...tipup seat, bracket lamp, brass tiered brace, armrests...' He also stipulated 'separate sanitary and hygienic necessaries' for the servants of Flowerville; Enid Starkie mentions this very up-to-date feature of the house in Blackrock to which her family moved in 1910.

Unlike 8 Eccles Street, the house where Austin Clarke spent his childhood had a bathroom inside the house. The water closet in the backyard could be flushed 'without straining my conscience' during winter months. In summer Clarke's father, a superintendent of the Dublin Waste Water Department, grew anxious about the danger of drought, as the water level at the Roundwood reservoir dropped daily. Ithaca refers to Dublin's chronic water shortage; June 1904 was a time of drought, though not as threatening as the water shortages of 1893 when the Roundwood supply failed altogether. People drank water from the Royal and Grand Canals which the authorities assured them was 'clean and bright, and contains almost no matter in suspension'.

In general plumbing was notoriously inadequate; thirty-three plumbers are listed in the 1904 Thom's, only three more than the thirty listed in a directory for 1847. In hospitals installation of plumbing varied immensely over the years. Sir Patrick Duns had water closets and a proper drainage system installed prior to 1818, while water was available for hot baths. The Rotunda, on the other hand, did not have water closets until 1855. Between 1861 and 1868 three baths were installed; a few years later a very small hot water system was introduced to bathe the patient on admission. Before that patients had been washed with a communal marine sponge. A decade passed before a pressure water supply served the hospital, but not the wards. Such sanitary limitations cannot have helped the Rotunda's long fight against puerperal fever, which early in the nineteenth century had been unsuccessfully combated by fumigation with chlorine gas. Not until 1875 were nurses and students made to wash their hands in carbolic soap, while further antiseptic behaviour, including the use of nail-brushes, was regarded as an intriguing novelty.

The fight against puerperal mortality was not over by 1904; in that year an outbreak of sepsis at the Rotunda cost seven lives. The rugged nature of childbirth was investigated exhaustively by Joyce in the turgid prose of the Oxen of the Sun, although those who seek for social detail may find that Anglo-Saxon does not give a clear picture of the running of a maternity hospital. 'A couch by midwives attended with wholesome food reposeful cleanest swaddles as though forth bringing were now done...'

The National Maternity Hospital where the Oxen of the Sun is located had been opened in 1884 by William Roe, who converted two houses in Holles Street to medical use. The labour ward, according to Gogarty, was situated 'in what used to be a back drawing-room of some forgotten gentle family fifty years ago'. For its first few years it ran at a loss and it actually closed in 1893. Maternity hospitals were always opening and closing. During the nineteenth century they had included: the Western Lying-in Hospital; the Wellesley Female Institution in Mercer Street; the Anglesea Hospital in Peter Street and a sixty-bed lying-in hospital in South Great George's Street. Privately owned and administered, shadowed by fever, these places were vulnerable to financial loss. However, Holles Street reopened after a committee of ladies and gentlemen met on St Patrick's Day 1894 on the hospital premises. They felt an urgent need for a maternity hospital 'managed under Catholic management wholly and solely'. The Lord Mayor, sending a cheque for £5, with a promise of financial assistance, echoed their sentiments. 'I regret the policy pursued by the Rotunda in continuing to practically exclude Catholics.'

'Dublin has more than a dozen hospitals' Gogarty has pointed out; 'Vienna a much larger city, has but one; but then disease in Dublin is a *modus vivendi* and it therefore assumes a religious aspect. There are Protestant, Catholic and Presbyterian diseases in Dublin.' The possible variance of treatment between Catholic and Protestant obstetricians is a theme of the Oxen of the Sun. Young Madden discusses the circumstances of the 'woman of Eblana in Horne's house that now was trespassed out of this world... To whom young Stephen had these words following... Both babe and parent now glorify their Maker, the one in limbo gloom, the other in purge fire.' In addition Gogarty believed that Dublin maternity hospitals were more conservative than those elsewhere when it came to administering anaesthetics to women in childbirth. Pain-killers avoided the punishment of original sin. Bloom thought of them as a novelty ('twilight sleep idea') although he was aware that Queen Victoria used them. Frock-coated obstetricians were slow to apply induction of premature labour or use forceps, while Caesarian section was rarely performed. Mrs Purefoy's three day ordeal in producing young Mortimer Edward was nothing unusual in obstetrical routine. But since she was Methodist, her suffering was enhanced by her presence in the alien and potentially lethal surroundings of Holles Street.

Maternity hospitals with their stream of short staying students have always been notorious for conviviality. In 1904 the Coombe and Holles Street were particularly famous for rowdy parties. In the Coombe they sang:

> Bear down, bear down, good Mrs Brown, bear down,
> I've got my finger on his crown, on his crown...

In *Tumbling in the Hay* Gogarty describes a party in Holles Street attended by Joyce where the author of *Ulysses* is depicted as eager to pick up obstetrical knowledge. During the party seven people consume 140 bottles of stout, a performance which sets Gogarty musing on the origins of the term 'hospitality...' Throughout the night the entertainment is punctuated by sounds from the Labour Ward above. ' "Don't be an idiot...it's only her first pain." The ceiling began to shake...another scream startled the air.' A mass of obstetrical data is exchanged with drunken pomposity and coarseness, Joyce contributing. Perhaps, in spite of its obscurity, the Oxen in the Sun episode was what Shaw found so reasonably true to Dublin life when he couldn't finish *Ulysses*. 'The Dublin "jackeens" of my day' he told Archibald Henderson in 1924 'the medical students, the young bloods about town were very like that. Their conversation was dirty; and it defiled their sexuality which might just as surely have been presented to them as poetic and vital.'

Although Joyce makes the non-medicals, Stephen and Lynch, go on to the brothels, the sequence of settings, maternity hospital, pub and kip was a natural one.

> Tyrone Street of the crowded doors
> And Faithful Place so infidel

were located west of Amiens Street Station in an area known as Monto after one of its main streets named for Elizabeth Montgomery, who married Luke Gardiner, Lord Mountjoy – a title Joyce failed to make use of in *Ulysses*. Once the district was fashionable. In 1780 Dorothea Herbert's relations lodged in houses round about 'a party of nineteen or twenty Cousins Germans in...Three Neighbouring Streets'. Dorothea stayed in Mecklenburgh Street with her aunt Herbert whose garden 'was a large and handsome one...whenever my two Aunts were out we clubbed and had a feast in the Summer House'. James Gandon also lived for a time in Mecklenburgh Street which later became bourgeois. A directory of 1847 lists a good many solicitors' offices there, in addition to several artists, 'Robert Vanston's classical and commercial Academy' and a lady's seminary. Even in Monto's heyday, the upper end of Mecklenburgh Street, the main thoroughfare for the brothels, had a seedy respectability. How the lower end and the surrounding area came to be a red light district is not really known. One theory puts the transformation to the panic of the Emmett rebellion which brought increased numbers of soldiers into Dublin. The barracks available were inadequate and so they were lodged in Mecklenburgh Street. Another widely believed story proposes that the change occurred when two British regiments quartered in Dublin after the Crimean War lodged their camp followers there. By 1887 Mecklenburgh Street had become Tyrone Street in a vain effort to change its atmosphere by changing its name. Dublin Corporation often tried this tactic. In 1862 murky Park Street behind the University became Lincoln Place, while Upper Mercer Street, near Mercer's Hospital had evolved from French Street, the brothel area that preceded Monto. Notorious Temple Street was renamed Chatterton Street by an angry Corporation after the Rt. Hon. Hedges Eyre Chatterton, the Vice-Chancellor, refused to allow the name of Sackville Street to be altered to O'Connell Street. However, it relented and Temple Street became Hill Street.

The combination of soldiery, drink and poverty, and the sanction of the law kept the district flourishing. Sailors flocked there from the port of Dublin in jaunting cars. Over 1,600 prostitutes were estimated to work in the area without any medical supervision. One whole side of Sackville Street was the stamping ground for women seeking custom. They assembled there, not only from nearby tenements, but, according to the Reverend John Gwynn, S.J., 'from the Coombe and other parts of the city...those crowds of young girls who take possession of the city when the darkness comes, and whose demeanour by no means suggests the modesty and decorum we are wont to regard as inseparable from the Irish maiden.'

This gentlemanly reproof is far from the graphic detail of Joyce and Gogarty. Monto consisted of decayed Georgian houses, tenements, shops, and according to Arthur Power, 'a number of thatched cottages'. 'Rows of flimsy houses with gaping doors' noted the directions to Circe, 'rare lamps with faint rainbow fans.' Among the staggered glares of the gas-lamps he evoked a misshapen people wandering in filth: 'a pigmy woman...a form...a gnome...a crone...a bandy navvy...' And Privates Carr and Compton, who like other English tommies patronized the lower numbers of Tyrone Street near Mabbot Lane. Richard Ellman was told that 'these houses were full of religious pictures behind which the ladies kept coshes of lead piping to prevent trouble'. There were better types of houses; in the 'flash' houses further up Tyrone Street coal fires burned instead of turf and girls appeared in full evening dress before a select, usually military clientele which was expected to leave at least £5 after the entertainment. When the Defence of the Realm Acts were passed in the First World War, the attractions of Monto included, not only fornication, but the opportunity to drink after hours when the rest of the city's pubs were closed. Brothel madams made a point of studying the movements of British soldiers, and sent their cards to the officers' mess as soon as a regiment got transferred to Dublin. During good times the girls, in Mrs Mack's phrase, 'had to be floated up to bed in the best of bubbly'.

Circe's palace, belonging to Bella Cohen, was located among the big houses in Upper Tyrone Street. Her girls, as depicted in *Ulysses*, were modelled on well-known prostitutes like Becky Cooper and Fleury Crawford of whom her father said: 'the girl appears to be enjoying herself, and besides, she is a source of income to me'. In *Tumbling in the Hay* Gogarty concentrated on Mrs Mack, owner of 'a brick red face on which avarice was written like a hieroglyphic and a laugh like a guffaw in hell'. She was so well known that the area which Joyce called Nighttown was sometimes known as Macktown. In her parlour there was 'a pianist who sat with his face turned to the wall in front of a cottage piano on which stood a half-empty measure of stout'. Mrs Cohen's too, had music, played on a pianola, "A shade of mauve tissue paper dims the light of the chandelier... The floor is covered with an oilcloth mosaic of jade and azure and azure and cinnabar rhomboids... The walls are tapestried with a paper of yew fronds and clear glades. In the grate is spread a screen of peacock feathers.'

Gogarty's list of the contents of Mrs Mack's bedroom is like an auctioneer's. 'It had opposite to the door a large washstand

containing two jugs in bright yellow basins... A large bed
hammocked with age...open trunks lay on the floor beside a
mirror. A sewing machine, spools of silk, slippers, cigarettes,
empty cigarette tins, greasy curl-papers, a broken alarm clock and
one that was busily ticking, together with half a hundred·odds and
ends of gauzy female gear lay in old chocolate boxes or on the table
in littered heaps. On the mantelpiece, mottled by the marks made
through the years by numerous cigarettes, were several rancid
tumblers and a photograph of a smart trapful of girls'. (It was the
custom for girls to drive out to race meetings; afterwards cabs
crowded with racegoers would gallop back after them to Monto.)
'Magnificent on the dirty coverlet lay the satin nightdress case of
Mrs Mack...'

> There's nothing left but ruin now
> Where once the crazy cabfuls roared...

By 1910 the flash houses were in decline. However, the First World
War brought a surge of business, and Monto continued to offer its
attractions during the period of the civil war, although the
departure of the British army did much to undermine its economic
position. A new Puritan spirit, inspired largely by the newly formed
Legion of Mary determined to close down the demoralized debt-
ridden houses. A Jesuit Mission gave the Legion its backing; in the
pro-Cathedral which stood in the heart of Monto the existence of
certain undesirable features of the neighbourhood was first
mentioned in a sermon during Lent in 1925. In March the Legion
sought the help of the police, and on the night of the 12th police
cars swept in and arrested 120 people, including a Dail Deputy who
protested that he was only there for a drink. Soon afterwards a
procession of a Praesidium of Legion girls made its way through
Monto past the remaining kneeling whores; each former brothel
was blessed and a holy picture was pinned on the door. Today the
area, dominated by the huge church in Gloucester Street where the
reformed drunkard, Matt Talbot, broods in his tomb of Wicklow
granite, has the usual empty spacing resulting from slum clearance,
its bleakness emphasized by Tyrone Street's second change of name
– since 1911 it has been Railway Street.

Although Joyce claimed that Dublin could be rebuilt with the aid
of his masterpiece, his view of the city is not comprehensive. He
had little interest in Georgian architecture. Like Little Chandler he
ignored 'the gaunt spectral mansions in which the old nobility of

Dublin had roystered'. No. 7 Eccles Street is only incidentally a Georgian building; its architectural importance lies in the positioning of its railings and the area below and the relationship between the main bedroom and the kitchen.

Belvedere, where Joyce was at school, had plasterwork by Michael Stapleton. When they took over the mansion in Great George's Street the Jesuits left intact the decorations in the Diana Room and the Apollo Room, although they removed those in the Venus room. The second Leoville of Joyce's life, Newman House, with its stone lion crouching over the doorway also contains magnificent plasterwork. In the chemistry theatre at this 'sombre college' Stephen talked about the nature of the beautiful without making reference to Francini's plump mysterious deities or Robert West's birds and flames that sweep round the cornices of Buck Whalley's town house. Plasterwork, first glimpsed at Newman House, inspired Joyce's fellow student, C.P. Curran, with a life-long passion for this elegant feature of eighteenth-century life. West's musical instruments might have been an appropriate theme for Joyce; shortsighted, he probably never saw them properly.

His view of Dublin contrasts with George Moore's. They complement each other. When Stephen walked past 'Trinity's surly front' he sneered at 'a dull stone set in the city's ignorance'. Moore, tripping down Grafton Street with Yeats on his way to the Abbey, found that 'it was pleasant to allow one's enthusiasm to flow over like a mug of ale at the sight of the front of Trinity, to contrast the curious differences in style that the Bank presented to the College – the College severe and in straight lines, the Bank all curves.'

> 'The Venus facing the Antinous' I cried.
> Yeats laughed a somewhat chilling approval.

Few cities at one period have been subject to such distinguished literary comment. It is from Moore, describing 'a town wandering between mountain and sea' that we get the atmosphere of the south side of the Liffey. In his search for lodgings he looked at Merrion Square where the houses were 'too large for a single man', rushed down Mount Street where the houses were 'ugly, common and expensive' passing Mount Street Crescent 'bending prettily about a church'. In Pembroke Street the houses had flights of steps down which a man could break his leg; Leeson Street had 'fallen into the hands of nuns and lodging house keepers' while in Baggot Street – 'a declining neighbourhood' – he picked up a flea from the caretaker of a shabby house which he only removed by stripping naked in a private room at the Shelbourne Hotel. (Stephen Dedalus calmly removed a louse from the nape of his neck 'tender, yet brittle as a grain of rice'.) The house Moore found was impeccably Georgian, retaining old fashioned squares of glass in its windows and eighteenth-century chimney pieces.

Joyce would have felt none of Moore's horror at the opening of a shop at the corner of Stephen's Green; it would have had far more significance than any architectural detail. For his work, Georgian Dublin merely provided a grubby backcloth, while the formal semi-colonial society that revolved round the Castle was to be parodied. The lists in the Cyclops episode imitate the closely detailed reports in the *Irish Times* which included the daily first class passenger list of the Kingstown mailboat. 'All the toady news. Our gracious and popular vicereine' thought Bloom.

The great bazaars that were an integral part of the social scene played their part in one of the stories in *Dubliners* and in *Ulysses*. There were still many and various charitable societies like the Protestant Shoemakers' Charitable Society, a Home for Aged Governesses and a Reformed Priests' Protection Society 'to extend a helping hand to a priest of good character who conscientiously abandons the Church of Rome for the pure faith of the Gospel'. Many Catholic charities received generous donations from the madams in Monto. Nearly all relied on such money raisers as the 'sale of fancy works and articles of a useful character'. Large institutions and hospitals, which also needed public charity could organize something grander. Hospitals listed in Thom's emphasized their needs. 'Donations are earnestly requested...' 'Subscriptions and Donations will be gratefully received...' For any development scheme a big occasion like a bazaar was needed. The premises at Ballsbridge provided ample room for the Moorish and Venetian settings built by a firm in England which specialized in Bazaars and moved their wooden effects from city to city in the British Isles.

Bazaars made a good deal of money. Mirus – which in *Ulysses* is only mentioned with approval by Kitty the whore – raised over £4,000 and provided Jervis Street with a new operating theatre, an anaesthetic room, an X-ray department and four bedrooms for the Sisters 'all...electronically lighted'. Araby, attended at the last moment by the small boy in *Dubliners,* was also in aid of Jervis Street. It took place a dozen years earlier than Mirus, but its atmosphere was similar. Its attractions included bicycle polo in the jumping enclosure at Ballsbridge and a display by Menotti, the tightrope walker, whose activities were disturbed by rain. The magazine called *The Lady of the House,* a social barometer of the times, gives details of the stalls, of which the most prestigious was presided over by the Vicereine herself 'attended by a bevy of fair ladies picturesquely clad in the homespuns of Donegal'. At the Civic Stall twenty-three young ladies dressed in pink and grey helped the Lady Mayoress sell clocks, Gladstone bags, worktables, work-boxes, umbrellas, books, lamps, vases, gongs, cigars and cigarettes.

There were other social occasions. The Anglo-Irish might feel their authority slipping away, but they remained powerful in one important field – they rigidly controlled social life. (Even this provided insecurities, since they were divided among themselves between those who could afford to send their sons and daughters to England to schools and seasons, and those who had to remain behind and suffer Trinity and the Castle.) They were in charge of institutions like the Royal Dublin Society and the Royal Irish Academy. 'Are Catholics socially inferior to Protestants?' asked Shane Leslie, a convert, in the *Freeman's Journal* in 1914. The answer appeared to be yes. Enid Starkie remembered how it was considered more 'classy' to be Protestant than Catholic. Stephen Gwynn wrote of the 'deplorable separateness' between members of both religions which seemed unchanged since Wolfe Tone's time.

'Do you see anything of these people at home?'
'We just nod when we pass in the streets.'

The sectarian social divide tended to send Catholics to seek entertainment at the Mansion House except for those who aspired to attend occasions which were located in what was once a brooding symbol of alien power, but now functioned largely as a desirable venue for balls. Although Nationalists might boycott its functions, Dublin Castle, 'that bleak fortress situated in the heart of the slums' still gave tone to society. Doctors, barristers, merchants and country gentlemen pressed for invitations and took their daughters to levees. For the afternoon each girl needed 'a Card with her Name and Address, both in Town and Country...and must bring with her on the evening of the Drawing Room two similar Cards, one to be delivered to the proper person in attendance in the Corridor, and the other to be handed to the Chamberlain who will announce the name...'

The season lasted from February to St Patrick's Day when a grand ball was held at which guests wore sprigs of shamrock. *Drama in Muslin* tells how Mrs Barton took her daughters along Ship Street 'plague spotted, pestilential as a corpse, quick with the life of the worm'. At the ball 'behind a curtain of evergreen plants Liddell's orchestra continued to pour an uninterrupted flood of waltz melody upon the sea of satin, silk, poplin and velvet that surged around the buffet angrily demanding cream ices, champagne and claret cup'.

English Lord Lieutenants who came to Ireland were expected to spend liberally to make the Season brilliantly successful. There was a long tradition of these Viceroys bringing over their pictures, furnishings and gold and silver plate. Lord Cadogan, who was Lord Lieutenant from 1895 to 1902, during the period which Conor Cruise O'Brien has called the Indian Summer of Anglo-Irish society, was particularly hospitable. Raymond Brooke believed that his term of office coincided with the height of Dublin's last splurge of social grandeur. 'The dancers were in two long lines facing each other about twenty couples. The Lord Lieutenant opened the dance with the wife of the Chamberlain – and gave you the impression that you might be back in the 18th century.' Lord Cadogan's colours were light blue. 'The footmen of the Castle wore blue and silver liveries, his carriage had a light blue line on the wheels and panels and the horses light blue bands and knots.' The vast Castle staff included ADCs, private secretaries and various gentlemen waiting around in rich plumed hats and ornate uniforms. There was a Master of Horse and a State Steward whom Moore described as 'walking with a wand, like a doge in an opera bouffe'.

Reporting on the ball given by the Lord Lieutenant and Lady Cadogan in honour of the Duke and Duchess of York in April 1899, the *Irish Times* devoted three columns of descriptions to the toilettes – not all of them by any means, a mere selection of seventy-eight. 'The exquisite fuchsia-coloured satin trimmed with *diamanté* lace worn by the Duchess of York was a Dublin creation...Lady Cadogan's gown was of white satin, exquisitely embroidered in fine silver sequins and edged with a narrow band of chinchilla...the famous Cadogan diamonds flashed on her Excellency's hair, neck and arms...Lady Iveagh was in cerise satin and her diamonds were dazzlingly beautiful...Lady Margaret Forbes was in pink satin with shaded red roses forming her shoulder straps...' Men wore court dress, with white breeches and stockings and shoes topped by gold buckles.

Lord Cadogan was succeeded in 1902 by Lord Dudley, another prodigious spender; any suggested economy was 'anathema to him'. A debutante, later the Countess of Fingall wrote her memories of society life during the time of the Dudleys – the balls every night, the sound of waltz music filtering through the tall windows of Fitzwilliam and Merrion Squares, complaints from older residents about noise, and the occasional clip clop of a mounted trooper delivering a coveted Castle invitation to one's Dublin home. The long procession of carriages to a Castle ball or levee was one of the sights of the city. According to Lady Fingall the carriages were mainly for 'staider people'; among the usual army and nobility were country gentlemen 'bringing with them into the street something of the smell of the country'. The younger people 'many of my future partners...soldiers and sailors gay in their uniforms' favoured outside cars. Around the gates to the Castle yard a great pile-up would be created; here the poor gathered to watch. 'They shivered on the pavement in their thin ragged clothes, waiting for hours sometimes so that they might see the ladies in their silks and satins and furs step from their carriages.'

Amid the contrast of diamonds and rags Thackeray's old brass plate society thrived. As a child Elizabeth Bowen 'took this brass plate announcing the owner's name to be the sine qua non of any gentleman's house'. O'Casey, observing from a different viewpoint, noted how plates and knockers were kept polished by legions of maids in black or blue dresses, white aprons and caps with streamers.

Maurice Headlam, an English official taking the train from Kingstown in 1912, found that 'it all seemed Pooter country, I was all neat, ugly, snug and middle class'. A dissection of the various layers of Castle society by Norah Robertson divided it into four groups. The first three consisted of peers, and members of the gentry, mainly from the country. The fourth in which Dublin people dominated, was made up of 'loyal' professional people and a few others. 'Such...formed useful cannonfodder at Protestant bazaars, and could, if they were really liked, achieve Kildare Street.' From this category would come Conor Cruise O'Brien's archetype West Briton, the dentist's wife who collected crests, ate kedgeree for breakfast and displayed a portrait of the Queen on the mantelpiece. She would, no doubt, attend 'carpet dances'. A booklet published in 1902, which called Dublin 'a city of pretty girls' described these informal variations of the functions at Dublin Castle, where the numerous young officers stationed in Dublin were hot in demand, particularly by scheming mothers looking for desirable catches for their daughters.

This staider section of society had a brief prominence during the time of Lord Aberdeen. The Aberdeens were more interesting viceregents than their predecessors. For one thing, they came to be acutely aware of the poverty around them. Lady Aberdeen visited hospitals, founded the Women's National Health Association and was instrumental in providing playgrounds for slum children. In her excruciatingly titled autobiography *We Twa,* she described her attempts to get English cabinet ministers to come over to see the housing conditions for themselves, but 'the cities and towns of Ireland remained a blot and a menace, culminating in Dublin'. She was bossy, and her husband enraged public opinion by choosing 'Tara' for his title – it was hastily changed to 'Temair' – but when they left in 1915 they got a good send-off. However, their political position alienated them from the Unionists. The Liberal party had made an alliance with the Nationalists and Lord Aberdeen's term of office was intended to usher in Home Rule.

The Unionists employed just about the only weapon they had; they withdrew from society, boycotting the Viceregal court. The Castle balls and social activities went on, but lost their glitter. Since only a scattering of peers and gentlemen could be induced to attend, numbers were made up by Dublin professional people whose political scruples were more easily pushed aside when they received a Castle invitation. It was like the days after 1800. 'The people all seem pleasant but not much more' Maurice Headlam considered, 'and all about the same social standing...' As 'Treasury Remembrancer' Headlam was entitled to a third class uniform. 'I had to have extra gold lace to the amount of £25.'

It is difficult to realize that he lived in the same city that Mary Colum found 'reeked with intelligence and nimble wits of all kinds'. More than any social posturings the excitements of the literary renaissance and the Gaelic revival were signposts of the approaching changes. The Irish Literary Theatre began in 1899. *Countless Cathleen* was performed in the Antient Concert Rooms to a storm of clerical abuse. The new Abbey opened in December 1904. Mary Colum arriving in Dublin as a young girl to find it 'drama mad' crossed O'Connell Street passing 'a trampish looking man' carrying a theatrical billboard which advertised Synge's *Riders to the Sea* and Yeats' *Kathleen ni Houlihan*. 'The old part of the city' she wrote 'bristled with movements of various kinds – dramatic, artistic, educational; there were movements for the restoration of the Irish language, for reviving native arts and crafts; for preserving ancient ruins, for resurrecting native costume, an array of political movements; there, too, were the theatres and the tearooms and pubs which corresponded to the café life of the Continental city. In the centre, too, were the headquarters of the Clubs and societies...focused towards one end, – a renaissance. Between Abbey Street and College Green, a five minutes' walk, one could meet every person of importance in the life of the city at a certain time in the afternoon.'

Professors of all kinds from different parts of the world arrived to write books on 'Yeats and the Irish Revival, on co-operation and Horace Plunkett, on J.M. Synge and the folk-drama, on ancient Celtic crosses, and there was one delightful American dreamer who...wrote a book called *The Fairy Faith in Celtic Countries'*. Celtic enthusiasts took to wearing kilts, enlivened by the occasional plaid worn by a visiting Scottish Gael. At his Sunday dinner parties George Sigerson, famous for his *Bards of the Gael and Gall* and for his obsession about his Dublin-Norse ancestry, liked to divide up his guests – those with Celtic names to one side, those with Saxon or Norse names to the other.

George Moore had come back to what was 'no longer a city of barristers and officials pursuing a round of mean interests and trivial amusements, but the capital of the Celtic Renaissance'. He revelled in Dublin life, the pleasures of Stephen's Green with its lake 'curving like a piece of calligraphy' or Grafton Street with its pretty girls. 'That one, Yeats. How delightful she is in her lavender dress.' He noted the characteristics of his friends, AE in his grey tweeds 'his wild beard and shaggy mane of hair', Yeats 'lank as a rook', like an old umbrella forgotten on a picnic party', Edward Martyn 'neckless as an owl'.

Domestic entertainments flourished. Families like the Sheehys had their musical evenings, the Colums their soirées on Tuesdays. Sarah Purser presided at Mespil House entertaining all her friends in her huge sumptuous drawing-room which smelt of damp. Literary figures had their special evenings. On Sundays AE's guests sat on uncomfortable chairs eating cherry cake. AE liked every sort of person and had 'no awareness of class' observed Mary Colum. 'Seated like a sage and Buddha he would boom away with equal interest to any of us.' Yeats was more selective. Guests like Mahaffy or Maud Gonne with her wolfhound could be equally formidable.

The city had an air of informality, indolence and leisure quite removed from the industry and belching chimneys of Belfast. 'One of the most delightful aspects of Dublin is its frugality and lack of ostentation' commented a visitor. 'There is no "money standard" in Dublin, for no one luckily appears to have any money.' Maurice Headlam, entertained at the Green Room in the Abbey, was given tea 'from a brown teapot' and 'thick brown bread and butter' by Sarah Allgood.

The city had seven theatres – the Gaiety, the Theatre Royal, the Tivoli, the Empire, the Queen's, the Rotunda and the Abbey. Bowler-hatted citizens could attend a few good restaurants like the Bailey or the one opened by the Lord Lieutenant's chef, Monsieur Jammet, in Andrew Street which moved to Nassau Street in 1926. Of the eight clubs that served society the Kildare Street Club was the oldest. Edward Martyn called this staunchly Unionist stronghold the Cod Bank after its pop-eyed members. He was one of the few Catholics to belong; his Republican pronouncements, including his objections to King Edward's visit in 1907 led to his expulsion, followed, after a legal battle, by his reinstatement. He continued to tease fellow members by entertaining priests and members of Sinn Fein on the club's premises. 'His idea of a good dinner was certainly not mine' wrote Maurice Headlam. 'Generally it began with oysters, followed by a kipper and then a large porterhouse steak with onions and washed down with strong tea.'

The royal visit of July 1907 was the second last made by a reigning monarch to Dublin (King George V came briefly on a coronation tour in 1911). Although the occasion was marred by the theft of the Irish Crown Jewels from Dublin Castle just before the King's arrival, all was forgotten as Dubliners exhibited their lamentable weakness for royalty. The royal yacht *Victoria and Albert* steamed into Kingstown to a welcome which newspapers considered surpassed that of any other part of the Empire. The King opened the Dublin Exhibition which included attractions like a Canadian watershute and an authentic Somali village filled with round straw huts and Somalis. There was an uproar when a Somali child was kidnapped by the eccentric, Bird Flanagan; however it was safely returned. The site of the exhibition provided a new amenity for the city, Herbert Park. Elsewhere there were bands, rockets and illuminations of the escort of warships in Kingstown Harbour. Down by the Custom House a real convict ship 117 years old was moored where for 6d. Visitors could see the 'world's most remarkable vessel' furnished with wax effigies of convicts. The King went to Leopardstown races where he dined well; as he returned through suburbs thronged with his subjects waving Union Jacks, he was observed to be fast asleep in his open landau.

Dublin was still in a rural setting, and the train and tram meant easy access to suburbs and countryside. Kingstown became almost garish. All summer long the harbour was crowded with yachts; on the east pier strollers listened to the military band, while others crowded the grounds of the new Kingstown Pavilion. The craze for bicycling had begun in the 1890s; a little over a decade later the era of motor cars had a festive welcome with the Gordon Bennett race. Gogarty with his new 40/50 horsepower Rolls-Royce, a reward of his fashionable practice, was an early motoring enthusiast. The neighbourhood of Dublin shrank. Smoking a cigarette, one hand on the wheel, he drove out to Merrion. 'Howth's amethyst hills in the morning light rival Italy.' Off again into Wicklow. 'In no other city in the world that I have seen could you have pleasure like this in the middle of the day's toil.'

When Hugh Lane, Lady Gregory's nephew, came to Dublin there were no modern paintings to be seen. In 1908 he set about to make good the omission by opening a small gallery in the house in Harcourt Street where Bram Stoker and the old hanging judge, Lord Clonmell, had lived. Then Lane rushed about seeking help where he could find it. Would Moore give a lecture? 'Lane, you tempt me. I am the only one in Dublin who knew Manet, Monet, Sisley, Rénoir, Pissarro.' People had to contribute. 'His idea' wrote Lady Fingall 'was that we should pay £50 to be painted by Laszlo and we should give the picture to the gallery.' The place was considered to have a 'pleasant atmosphere, it is cosy and welcoming like a friend's house'. Servant girls on their evenings out spent an hour there between 8 and 9 viewing Monet's *Madame Gonzalez* and Renoir's *Les Parapluies*.

'The improvement in Dublin goes steadily on' observed the social magazine *Irish Life*, in November 1912, 'but it is mostly about the principal shopping centres that it strikes one. Grafton Street is nearly finished in the building way... The adjoining streets are gradually becoming possessed of fine shops, notably Wicklow Street. The handsome front of Messrs Weirs... aroused the envy of their big neighbours, Messrs Switzers, and now we find a magnificent frontage to the latter's huge premises... These large outlays of money tell of business confidence in Dublin...'

But change was imminent. For a while it seemed that the revolution might be a social one. The Dublin masses provided plenty of recruits for James Connolly's Citizen Army. Since to be in employment at all was a matter of good fortune, working conditions were ferocious; a seventy hour week was not uncommon for a manual worker on the docks. O'Casey, who became a secretary in the Citizen Army, considered the tramway workers 'the worst slaves Ireland ever knew'. When they refused to sign a pledge that they would never join James Larkin's Union, Dublin's only significant contribution to the history of international socialism, the strike of 1913, was timed for the most important date in the social calendar. 'On a bright and sunny day, while all Dublin was harnessing itself into its best for the Horse Show' wrote O'Casey, 'the trams suddenly stopped.' Between the end of the horse era and the beginning of the motor era the city had come to depend on trams for communication, and without them its social and industrial life was paralysed. William Martin Murphy, the employers' leader, found himself described as the 'Tramway Tyrant' and a 'blood sucking vampire'; in his turn Larkin was called 'the most foul and vicious blackguard that ever polluted any country'. But sticks and stones were weapons as well as words. The first Bloody Sunday took place.

Throughout Europe police forces generally acted without restraints imposed by authority or public opinion. In Dublin police brutality had been accepted as part of life. Sometimes it was reported; the weekly *Irish Times* wrote how after Parnell's arrest a public meeting was broken up in Sackville Street by police whose 'conduct was such as to appear almost incredible to all who had been witness to it... after every charge they made, men, amongst them respectable citizens... were left lying in the streets, blood pouring from the wounds they received on their heads from the batons of the police'. This report could slip in among the accounts of the events that took place in the same location on 31 August

1913. In among items devoted to a ball at the Rotunda and the Phoenix Park Races ('rendezvous of fashion and society') were the details of 'appalling scenes in city... fierce baton charges... hundreds injured, two men killed'. The scene was like a battle-field 'with the bodies of the injured people, many of them with their faces covered in blood and with their bodies writhing in agony'. The face of Sackville Street itself was scarred and battered, a prelude to its imminent destruction.

The Tramway Strike captured the imagination and raised the hopes of the working classes, but its momentum fizzled out. The power of the Church contributed; Larkin's scheme of sending strikers' children to Liverpool was regarded as dangerous to their souls, and there was the extraordinary spectacle of Archbishop Walsh himself together with some clergy, managing to seize a number from the Corporation Baths as they were being scrubbed down prior to shipment. The strike and the behaviour of the police did have one positive result. The main purpose of Connolly's Citizen Army was to protect strikers from civic brutality. Its recruits were all Dubliners, and they provided the core of the force that fought in 1916. At the same time the movement of National Volunteers, formed in imitation of Carson's Ulster Volunteers, gathered strength.

At the end of the nineteenth century it was said that 'the whole membership of the Fenian movement could have been comprised into a concert hall'. It was true that a new generation of Gaelic Leaguers had arisen who, according to the Under Secretary, were 'intensely disloyal to the English connection'. However, most people supported John Redmond even after the outbreak of the First World War postponed ideas of Home Rule. In the split among the Volunteers, those who followed John Redmond were in the great majority. Larkin called Redmond 'an Irish Judas' and agonized on the way thousands from Dublin were prepared to go and die in Flanders' mud. 'No English city is displaying more enthusiasm... in sending its bravest and best to murder men with whom they have no quarrel.'

The plans for the Rising were loosely based on Robert Emmet's insurrection and also on Connolly's obsessive idea of fortifying certain buildings and holding them against all comers. 'Such excitement' Miss Lily Stokes wrote in her diary, 'Dublin fell into the hands of the Sinn Feiners.' The events of the sunny spring

morning were totally unexpected; the streets were deserted and
holiday makers were cycling, walking or taking the tram to
Kingstown, while the military presence had gone to the races.

The bungled attack on the Castle resulted in the death of an
unarmed policeman. His death and that of the four unarmed
Lancers outside the GPO and the scores of passing citizens caught
in crossfire in the city centre did not put people on the side of the
rebels. Nor did the food shortages. English troops were cheered as
they landed at Kingstown. When food was distributed Ernie
O'Malley wrote 'I heard that the people were so grateful that they
would do anything for the soldiers.' But it did not take an obstinate
and brutal military authority very long to work out the best
possible way of alienating public opinion. The executions, wrote
Lady Fingall even more vividly than Yeats, were like watching 'a
stream of blood coming from beneath a closed door'.

The climax was slow to build up. A contributor to the souvenir
booklet *The 'Sinn Fein' Revolt Illustrated,* who signed himself
J.W.M. walked down Sackville Street on Easter Tuesday. He
found 'neither policeman nor soldier nor tram nor other vehicle;
only a street full of sightseers with something of a holiday air and
frequent houses with barricaded windows and grim silent
men...waiting with rifles in their hands for the attack... At the
Post Office men lounged at the windows that were stuffed with
mail bags, some smoking, some munching rations from their
shoulder-slung haversacks and others exchanging a few hurried
words with womenfolk on the footway...Two slender strands of
barbed wire streeled slackly across the street...'

The bodies of two horses belonging to the Lancers killed on
Easter Monday lay and decomposed all week. In the Gresham
Hotel Mrs O'Donoghue, caught by the rising, was trapped. When
she could get to her diary she wrote: 'I have lived through an eight
days inferno, and my brain is scorched and my hands and feet are
tired with much work and much walking. I have starved or nearly
that, with 200 others in a big hotel.' Elsewhere in the city others
suffered. 'Some friends of mine, incarcerated in the precincts of
Dublin Castle' wrote Constance Spry in her cook book 'found
themselves restricted to a diet of unrelieved salmon for almost a
week. What a blessing to them would have been Madame Prunier's
book giving around thirty ways of dealing with this delicious but
rich fish.' In Stephen's Green guests at the Shelbourne Hotel were

confined largely through the efforts of Countess Markievicz stationed at the College of Surgeons in her home-made green uniform.

The first looting occurred when a packet of flour was taken from a grocer's shop to be made into adhesive paste for some military purpose. After that 'lollipop shops were the first to go' observed J.W.M. Then came the opportunity for the Dublin poor to fulfill an ever-pressing need. 'Bootshops seem to have been quite irresistible.' Women and children dressed themselves in looted clothes, while drink and gold watches were sold for a fraction of their price. Much looting was frivolous; Noblett's sweetshop was emptied and 'Lawrence's toy and photographic shop with its collection of photographs of Ireland was first looted and then went up in flames. Soon Sackville Street was 'deep in broken glass, cardboard boxes, bits of window frames, papers, crushed hats'. 'In Talbot Street a boy arrayed in a suit many sizes too big for him and with the price label still on the breast of the coat was wielding a fine golf driver against a tennis ball. After each stroke he took from his pocket an expensive pair of binoculars and languidly surveyed the course... A pair of factory girls with work-a-day shawls over their heads sauntered down Great Britain Street arm in arm, each carrying an expensive tennis racquet.'

The city started to burn. The first call came to the Fire Brigade at 3.59 pm on Easter Monday reporting a fire at the Magazine Fort in Phoenix Park. At ten that night the first calls came from the alarm at Nelson's Pillar; the Cable Shoe Company in Sackville Street was burning. Then the True-Form Boot Company caught fire, then No. 4 Earl Street, followed by the huge fire at Lawrence's all on the same night. As the military began shelling the district the fires spread. On Thursday the heart of the city was blazing. From a distance Maurice Headlam saw that 'the skies were red with the fires of Dublin'. O'Casey tells how 'the flames were soaring higher till the heavens looked like a great ruby hanging from God's ear'. Not since the approach of Robert Bruce's army had flames seemed more menacing. Watching them from his window, Augustine Birrell, 'an anti-Nero', the Chief Secretary for Ireland, burst into tears. Watching them from the top of the Fire Brigade Tower Ernie O'Malley rejoiced. 'Looking over unhappy Dublin stretching like a map beneath us, we seemed to be reviewing the whole miserable story. From days of lawlessness to the long pernicious Aberdeen regime...year by year bringing authority into contempt.'

14
Post-1916

After the Easter rising Dublin continued to hold the centre of
Ireland's political stage and citizens suffered the usual wartime
range of experience from inconvenience to horror as one bloody
year followed another. The gun duels that office workers and
students could watch from their places of work, the raids and
searches, the random spatter of shots, the curfew lasting from
midnight until five in the morning, the Black and Tans made
pressures accumulate so that by 1921 an English visitor described
the general state of Dubliners as 'exhausted and on the point of
nervous breakdown'. It seems that almost everyone who was
literate has left their memories of the period. Perhaps Sean
O'Casey with his extravagant vocabulary best recreates the
atmosphere of the times: 'Armoured cars clattered through the
city, lorries caged in with wire and crowded with Tans pointing
guns at everyone's breast cruised through the streets; and patrols
with every rifle cocked to the last hair crept along the kerb. Every
narrow lane seemed to be the dark, dazzling barrel of a rifle...'
The less ornate verbiage of newspapers noted forgotten tragedies
like 'The Portobello Affray' of April 1920. The *Irish Times*
reported how 150 odd soldiers from the Berkshire Regiment came
back to their barracks from the Theatre Royal. They were in a
truculent mood. As they walked along Burgh Quay they shouted
'Down with Sinn Fein!' and 'Down with de Valera!' In Grafton
Street they jostled the crowd on the pavement, in Harcourt Street
they hissed the Sinn Fein bank. When they reached their barracks
at Portobello the real trouble began. By this time a sizeable crowd
had accumulated, and the sequence that followed suddenly became
inevitable: the jeers and flung stones, the charge of troops along
Montague Street and then the shots. Nineteen people were injured
and a van driver and a young domestic were killed. By the standard
of the times the casualties were not high.

The Treaty was signed in December 1921. Nine hundred and fifty
years after the Normans arrived the English were leaving. Tommies
abandoned their numerous barracks to the Free Staters and

marched for the Mail Boat and home as bands played 'Come Back to Erin'. The Black and Tans departed in sealed vans. At the Castle some untidy young men led by Michael Collins tumbled out of two taxis to take over 'the Devil's Half Acre'. O'Casey could not resist describing how the last English Lord Lieutenant, the Catholic Earl Fitzalan 'handed over the place known as Dublin Castle and seemed to be doing it all in a dream... "Here's the key to the throne room, and this one's the key of St Patrick's Hall, my good man..." '

The Civil War broke out in June 1922, a turmoil out of which new political divisions would cause bitterness for generations. Six years of violence had left buildings and people scarred. O'Connell Street was still largely in ruins, while many government offices were surrounded by sandbags. Once again the first shots of a conflict were fired in Dublin; once again the aggressors tried Robert Emmet's unreliable old plan of taking over and defending key buildings. Among them was somewhere quite new, the Kildare Street Club, in which, according to Ernie O'Malley, the Dublin Brigade 'played handball and occasionally puffed leisurely at long cigars'. He himself took part in the defence of the Four Courts where the anti-Treaty forces were surrounded by the menacing guns of the Free Staters, caught 'like rats in a trap'. He found time before the fighting began to view from his position on the dome the river and city in the early morning light. The bombardment was savage, and the pillars of the Four Courts still bear the marks of exploding bullets and shells. O'Casey saw how 'thick dust hides the body of the building and dark smoke encircles the huge dome, making it look like the great globe itself trekking the sky through a way of stormy clouds'. The Record Office burned and history vanished in ashes. Over the dome floated the cloud of paper 'all the records of the country, processes, cases, testimonies, bills of exchange and sales of properties to church and private persons, and all hereditaments chronicled since Strongbow came to Ireland, flying up...to come down scorched and tattered in every Dublin back yard and front garden'.

The Civil War ended on 24 May 1923 and the Irish Free State emerged into existence. With serious economic and political problems ahead the divided nation had no cause for celebration. With confidence and some panache the government set about restoring the great buildings that war had reduced to shells. The

Custom House and the General Post Office presented their familiar profiles once again. Amid the rotting tenements O'Connell Street was painstakingly rebuilt with some sense of artistic unity. The Royal Dublin Society was forced to vacate Leinster House at a price of £68,000 so that its premises could house the Dail. Streets were rechristened with the names of patriots. The unarmed Garda replaced the RIC; post boxes, still bearing the embossed initials of English monarchs, were painted green. Statues began to disappear. King William in College Green was finally blown up in 1929. The equestrian statue of George I by Van Nost the Elder that had once graced Essex Bridge, 'where', wrote an eighteenth-century cleric, 'high mounted, the brass monarch rides, looking down the rough Liffey and marking the tides', was sold to the Barber Institute, Birmingham. Benjamin Rackstraw's little image of George II over the Weavers' Hall in the Coombe was taken down in the 1920s; his head and boots survive in the custody of the Old Dublin Society. Van Nost's fine equestrian statue of George II on Stephen's Green was blown up in May 1937 to coincide with the coronation of his descendant, George VI. Queen Victoria outside the Mansion House, known as 'Ireland's revenge', aggressively ugly and weighing 168 tons, had been unveiled by Lord Aberdeen in February 1908; forty years later it was pushed out of sight to Kilmainham Hospital. The dismasting of the city centre by the destruction of Nelson's Pillar, Dublin's most obtrusive imperial relic, celebrated the fiftieth anniversary of the Easter Rising.

Embassies accredited to the Free State sprang up, something new in Irish life. At the Viceregal Lodge Tim Healy 'uniting the charms of devilled almonds, crème de menthe and pêche Melba perfectly blended' took over from the Lord Lieutenant as Governor General. Gogarty, lamenting 'the spacious days of Lord Wimbourne' called the rechristened Arus an Uachtarain 'Uncle Tim's Cabin'.

The new society became notorious for clericalism and for puritanical behaviour. At the theatre riots were provoked for very different reasons from those which ended Thomas Sheridan's career. In the Abbey which O'Casey considered 'a red flower in the slums' there was a repeat of the Playboy riots in 1926 when theatregoers took exception to *The Plough and the Stars*. 'The whole place became a mass of moving roaring people. The high hysterical distorted voices of women kept screaming that Irish girls were noted over the whole world for their modesty and that

Ireland's name was holy; that the Republican flag had never seen the inside of a public house. Up in the balcony people were singing the "Soldiers' Song", while a tall fellow frantically beat time on the balcony rail with a walking stick.'

Soon after O'Casey found he had had enough of his native city. The reasons he formulated for leaving gave a fair idea of its parochial limitations. 'Sean felt that if he stayed in Dublin life would become embarrassing to meet. Dublin was too close to everyone. All its streets led into one square where everyone met, where hands were shaken, shoulders clapped and drinks taken to everyone's health.' This sense of belonging to an extended village, the casually met friends in a crowded street, the time for idleness and venom of gossips, has got on the nerves of Dublin's greatest sons, causing a number of swift distinguished departures.

Readership of the *Irish Times* could still find interest in its Court and Personal column: 'The Prince of Wales returned to York House yesterday...the Duke and Duchess of Devonshire entertained at Chatsworth...' The levees in Phoenix Park were mocked at by Gogarty just as George Moore had sneered at Castle Balls. (Forty years later another assembly in Phoenix Park to meet President Kennedy provoked similar ridicule; Anthony Cronin has recalled how it 'rushed forward and whooping in the accents of Limerick and points west, practically tore the shirt off the poor man's back'.) But the old dominant society had collapsed, even if this was not immediately obvious. V.S. Pritchett on his arrival in 1923 'was slow to see that I was meeting an upper class in decay and at the point when it was disappearing in boatloads from Dun Laoghaire every day'. Those that remained were mainly professional families, a small minority that posed no threat to the new government. They faced the predicament described by Robert Collis: 'Free Staters and Republicans hating each other and what was left of the old Ascendancy of the Anglo-Irish did not know where they stood.' They kept their businesses and two ancient empty cathedrals and sent their children to their own schools. As late as the fifties some of them advertised for servants of their own persuasion. But they submitted like sheep to the Papal *ne temere* decree controlling mixed marriages, even though they knew it to be ethnic euthanasia. They continued to live in their suburbs in large detached houses with ample gardens. There was Temple Road which had been the last word in respectability when Parnell's mother lived there. Christine Longford considered that 'Rathmines has a name for gentility and for decay since the British army left, Ballsbridge is opulent and Palmerstown socially exclusive.' Jimmy O'Dea's genteel suburbanite said: 'Thank god I live in Rathgar' which became a catch phrase. In the late twenties P.L. Dickenson found the inhabitants of 'the Roads' – Clyde Road, Morehampton Road, Elgin Road and Pembroke Road to be 'professional people and many others of good birth and breeding'. Carrickmines and Foxrock had less quality. 'They no doubt harbour many charming people who contribute to Dublin life collectively if they have not made any contribution to Dublin.' Lawns continued to be laid out with croquet hoops and massive teas served by uniformed maids.

AE and Sarah Purser ('second Tuesday every month') continued to run their literary salons. Yeats, now a senator, had to be guarded against assassination attempts. The Abbey disagreed over *The Silver Tassie* and stagnated. In 1928 theatre got a new stimulus when Michael MacLiammoir and Hilton Edwards founded the Gate with the patronage of Lord Longford. 'Since the Irish theatre was created by the English' Christine Longford has commented, 'it has played a part in Dublin life not second even to politics. Dubliners are interested in it even when it breaks up, and when they discuss it without supporting it.' However, what Dubliners supported to a remarkable degree was the cinema. As late as 1909 Joyce could tell his amazed colleagues in Trieste: 'I know a city of 500,000 inhabitants where there is not a single cinema.' Times changed rapidly since the brief period when he tried to attract audiences to the Volta in Mary Street with showings of *The First Paris Orphanage* and *The Tragic Story of Beatrice Cenci*. By 1913 the Rotunda Picture House, the O'Connell Street Picture House and the Phoenix Picture Palace were regularly showing films; by 1921 in the midst of the Troubles long queues were forming in O'Connell Street to see Douglas Fairbanks in *The Mark of Zorro*. Cinema queues took over from funeral processions, catching the attention of visitors, promoting their own folklore and becoming a dominant feature of city life for forty years.

Motorized traffic increased as Dublin with its easy perimeter of hills and becoming countryside attracted the weekend motorist. The mounting toll of accidents made small steady news items. A column in the *Irish Times* in August 1923 headlined 'Negligent Driver Charges' reported a child run down by a man in a motorcar;

a man named Fitzgerald knocked down and injured by a tram driver; Denis Murphy while riding a motor bicycle in Clontarf injured in a collision with a cart.

For the privileged Dublin was cheap, much cheaper than London. P.L. Dickenson was so struck by its low prices in 1929 that he noted down a typical pub menu:

> 'A steak or chop – 6d.
> Potatoes and bread – no charge.
> A glass of draught stout – 1d.
> Cheese, bread and butter – 2d.
> Glass of port – 2d.'

'No wonder' he concluded 'that people could do themselves well in Dublin...and hunt or yacht or go in for any similar sport in incomes that would scarcely have covered living expenses in London.'

For the majority there was no hunting or yachting. The evil poverty had not eased. V.S. Pritchett found 'the tenements...shocking; the women still wore the long black shawl, the children were often barefooted...the poor looked not simply poor, but savagely poor'. Beggars which had haunted the prosperous since medieval times were still regarded as a public nuisance, particularly round Christmas. 'For the past few weeks the streets of Dublin have been invested with beggars of every description' the *Irish Times* commented in December 1921, ' a pedestrian cannot walk more than fifty yards through any of the main streets without being opportuned by persistent beggars, many of whom are able bodied men.' During the thirties many of the worst tenements were demolished, and medical care with the aid of the Irish Hospital Sweeps began to improve. The prospect of eliminating tuberculosis and other diseases of poverty became a reality. But the slums persisted. Patrick Kavanagh arriving in Dublin just before the Second World War 'more helpless than a bull in a mist' spent his first night in the city in a slum lodging house in Gloucester Street. 'I paid sixpence for my bed. There were six other beds in the room which was at the top of a three storeyed house. The stink of that room and those beds has never left my nostrils. My room-mates were the derelicts of humanity...the communal sanitary convenience was a rusty bucket which hadn't been emptied from the night before and had apparently never been scrubbed; it had a scum of many layers...'

The period engulfed the country in a choking atmosphere of puritanism observed nervously by visitors like Lytton Strachey. He arrived in Dublin in 1931 wearing an aggressive suit of orange tweed. He attended a ball at Arus an Uachtarain, toured the National Gallery and made the statutory visit to the Abbey where one of his companions 'grew so restive over the brogue and boredom that she swept out in the middle of the performance with the whole party at her heels'. He could not quite isolate and identify Dublin's particular brand of repression. 'The state of civilization here is curious, something new to me. An odd betwixt and betweenism. The indecency question for instance...certain jokes are permissible, in fact, frequent...but Oh! there are limitations. And I must say I am always for the absolute. And the young men invariably leap to their feet when a young woman enters a room.'

The Second World War came; the Irish, expert at euphemism, called it 'The Emergency'. Neutral Dublin was in the eye of the storm. It was a time of shortages when all the country's imports had to be ferried over from England in half a dozen small merchant vessels. Since cattle could not be exported there was plenty of meat, but not much else. Great stacks of turf were piled in Phoenix Park, a few freakish cars moved about powered by gas or charcoal and the humorous magazine, *Dublin Opinion* observed the antics of the glimmer men, sent out to search whether citizens had exceeded their meagre gas ration. Sometimes searchlights would beam in on unidentified aircraft to the sound of ack ack guns, while in May 1941 a couple of German aircraft absentmindedly dropped some sticks of bombs. Many years later the Federal German Government paid over £327,000 for the damage done. Less newsworthy than bombing was the collapse at much the same time of some tenements in Old Bridge Street killing two people and injuring eleven. The *Irish Independent* reported that the whole street was enveloped in a dense cloud of dust as a garda in Kevin Street heard the crash of falling masonry; from the window he saw the cloud of dust rising and heard the screams of women and children.

There was a brief interlude in the post war years when the capital became the mecca of a hungry Europe. It contained meat. Restaurants like Jammets and the Dolphin, which no citizen can now recall without intense nostalgia and rage that they no longer exist, catered for the demand in steaks and good living. More important were the pubs. 'Dublin to an alcoholic' wrote Ulick O'Connor in a biography of Brendan Behan, 'is like a girls' gymnasium to a sex maniac. Its atmosphere generates a drinking mood.' When city pubs closed at night drinkers took to the country where pubs placed strategically three miles outside the city limits were allowed to serve them for another two hours. They were called Bona Fides because they could serve bona fide travellers. Dubliners were much travelled. By now the old literary soirées where guests had sipped tea or the occasional glass of sherry had long been superseded by literary bars. Patrick Kavanagh, Brian O'Nolan and Brendan Behan tottered around McDaid's, the Pearl, the Palace, the Baily. 'In Dublin the best Irish is drunk. Or in Dublin the best Irish are drunk' mused John Ryan reminiscing about the period in a book whose title is only just accurate: *Remembering How We Stood*.

Clericalism still flourished and Lent was marked by thundering sermons pointing out the perils for Catholics entering Trinity College delivered by Archbishop MacQuaid, who, his defenders are constantly reminding us, had a heart of gold. A new population crowded into the city, emptying the countryside. By 1951 about one third of the residents of County Dublin had been born outside the county. Conservative, restricted, poor, the city waited for the garish momentum of the sixties. The great 'Merc', the Mercedes car that was to become the symbol of parvenu wealth, was still under wraps; no one thought about new office blocks; censorship still caused picturesque and idiotic rows.

Honor Tracy wrote about the early fifties in a book that provoked much anger as touchy people recognized and resented her accuracy. She was no newcomer to the city, having been involved for years with the literary magazine *The Bell*. The first chapter of *Mind You I've Said Nothing* describes disembarking at Dunn Laoghaire. 'The toy harbour looked as quiet and sleepy as ever...there were priests and nuns, shaggy-haired boys, women bowed under the weight of children and brown paper parcels, members of the Ascendancy, purple of cheek and flowering of whisker all wedged together in a cross and hungry mob.' Later she breakfasted at Westland Row, now Pearse Station, 'A forlorn waiter in baggy trousers and dancing pumps brought a glass of sweet fizzy orangeade, a piece of bacon like a sliver of brick and a cracked teapot from which gushed forth a brew the colour of blood and tasting of soaked leather'. For her the frozen era was symbolized by the dismal ritual of St Patrick's Day. One of the first acts of the new government after the English left had been to ban drink to celebrate the national saint. Bars closed except at Baldoyle races or the Dog Show; 'people walked drearily through the wet streets with dull Sunday faces longing for it to be over'. The depression of Dublin ('an odd, and in many respects unhappy place' Anthony Cronin recalled recently) seized her as she wrote, until her book became a *cri de coeur*: 'a city of ghosts...the truth is you are looking at a lovely shell; the old glory had departed, a new one is not yet in sight...perhaps the only village on earth that contains half a million souls, "one great big unhappy family" as a Dublin writer cried out once, burying his face in his hands...'

Today her descriptions seem as remote as those of Thackeray. During the sixties a measure of prosperity drastically changed atmosphere and appearance. The long-lived policy of slum clearance by dispersing those who lived in the heart of the city to distant suburbs cleared huge areas that had once teemed with life. Dublin was one of the last cities in Europe to suffer the office revolution, and it came with devastating thoroughness. Swathes of inconvenient Georgian terraces were mown down to make room for equally inconvenient glass boxes, unsuited to climate and mood. Developers found easy excuses for pulling down fine houses; they were symbols of colonial ascendancy for which something much more progressive would be substituted. Dazed citizens watched for more than a decade while so much that was good was destroyed. However, architectural vandalism is nothing new; no single action by a modern developer can equal the ugliness of Butt Bridge, built in the nineteenth century to blot out Gandon's masterpiece, the Custom House.

The small intimate city that survived the Second World War – just the right size to induce claustrophobia or friendliness – has gone for ever. The era of change will continue; it has been said that the population of County Dublin may treble by 1991 and the suburbs will stretch all the way from Drogheda in the north to Wicklow and Naas in the south and west. The only constants are the sea, the play of light and the same green curve of hills the Vikings saw when they arrived.

Bibliography

Viking Dublin

Annals of the Kingdom of Ireland by the Four Masters, ed. and trans. by John O'Donovan, Dublin, 1848-1851.
The Annals of Connacht, ed. and trans. A.M. Freeman, Dublin, 1944.
The Annals of Loch Ce, ed. and trans. W.M. Hennessy, London, 1871.
The Annals of Ulster, ed. and trans. W.M. Hennessy and B. MacCarthy, Dublin, 1887-1901.
Bronsted, Johannes, trans. by Kalle Skov, *The Vikings,* London, 1965.
Bugge, Alexander, *History of Norsemen in Ireland,* Oslo, 1900.
Clarke, Howard B., ed., *Focus on Medieval Dublin – Supplement to Catalogue of Dublin Arts Festival,* Dublin, 1978.
——*Dublin, c.840-c.1540: The Medieval town in the Modern City,* Map prepared for the Friends of Medieval Dublin, Dublin, 1978.
——*The Changing Face of Medieval Dublin,* lecture in St Audoen's Church, Dublin, 1978.
Foote, P.G. and Wilson, D.M., *The Viking Achievement,* London, 1970.
Goedheer, A.J., *The Battle of Clontarf,* Haarlem, 1938.
Haliday, Charles, *The Scandinavian Kingdom of Dublin,* Dublin, 1881.
Hughes, Kathleen, *The Church in early Irish Society,* London, 1966.
Little, George A., *Dublin before the Vikings,* Dublin, 1947.
Longford, Christine, *The Story of Dublin,* London,1936.
Mackay Brown, George, *Orkney Tapestry,* London, 1968.
Mitchell, Frank, *The Irish Landscape,* London, 1974.
Moody, T.W. and Martin, F.X. (eds.) *The Course of Irish History,* Cork, 1967.
National Museum of Ireland (Catalogue), *Viking and Medieval Dublin,* Dublin, 1973.
O'Corrain, Donncha, *Ireland before the Normans,* Dublin, 1972.
O'Riordan, Brendan, *Viking Dublin,* Dublin, 1973.

Medieval Dublin

Clyn, John, ed. R. Butler, *Annalium Hiberniace Chronicon,* Irish Archaeological Society, Dublin, 1849.
Cullen, L.M., *Life in Ireland,* London, 1968.
Curtis, Edmund, *History of medieval Ireland,* London, 1923.
F.E.R., *Historical Reminiscences of Dublin Castle,* Dublin, 1899.
Fitzgerald, Brian, *The Geraldines,* London, 1951.
Fitzpatrick, Samuel A. Ossory, *Dublin, a Historical and Topographical Account of the City,* London, 1907.

Gilbert, John T., ed. (later Lady Gilbert), *Calendar of Ancient Records of Dublin,* 19 vols., 1889-1944.
——*A History of the City of Dublin,* 3 vols., Dublin 1854-1859.
Gillespie, Elgy, ed., *The Liberties of Dublin,* Dublin, 1973.
Giraldus Cambrensis, *Topography of Ireland,* Dundalgan Press Edition, Dundalk, 1951.
Gwynn, Aubrey and Hadcock, R.N., *Medieval Religious Houses of Ireland,* London, 1953.
Gwynn, Aubrey, 'The Black Death in Ireland', article in *Studies,* Dublin, 1935.
Hervey, John, *Dublin,* London, 1949.
Lydon, J.F., *The Lordship of Ireland in the Middle Ages,* Dublin, 1972.
Maxwell, Constantia, *Irish History from Contemporary Sources,* London, 1923.
Moylan, Thomas King, 'Dubliners 1200-1500', article in *Dublin Historical Record,* An Tostal Issue, Dublin, 1953.
Nicholls, Kenneth, *Gaelic and Gaelicised Ireland in the Middle Ages,* Dublin, 1972.
Orpen, G.H., *Ireland under the Normans, 1169-1333,* Oxford, 1911-1920.
Otway Ruthven, A.J., *History of Medieval Ireland,* London, 1968.
Pullar, Philippa, *Consuming Passions,* London, 1970.
Royal Society of Antiquaries in Ireland, *Account Roll of the Priory of the Holy Trinity,* Dublin, 1895.
Warburton, John and Whitelaw, Rev. James, *History of the City of Dublin,* Dublin, 1818.
Watt, John, *The Church in Medieval Ireland,* Dublin, 1972.
Webb, John, *The Guilds of Dublin,* Dublin, 1929.
Ziegler, Philip, *The Black Death,* London, 1969.

Reformation to 1603

Bagwell, Richard, *Ireland under the Tudors,* 3 vols., London, 1890.
Breffini, Brian and ffolliott, Rosemary, *The Houses of Ireland,* London, 1975.
Canny, Nicholas P., *The Formation of the Old English Elite in Ireland,* O'Donnell Lecture, Dublin, 1975.
Clark, William Smith, *The Early Irish Stage,* Oxford, 1965.
Derricke, John, *Image of Ireland,* republished London, 1883.
Falls, Cyril, *Elizabeth's Irish Wars,* London, 1958.
MacCurtain, Margaret, *Tudor and Stuart Ireland,* Dublin, 1972.
MacGowan, Kenneth, *Our Lady of Dublin,* Dublin, 1970.
Maxwell, Constantia, *The Stranger in Ireland,* London, 1954.
Moran, Rev P.F., *Persecution of Irish Catholics,* Dublin, 1907.
Stanyhurst, Richard, *Description of Ireland,* from Raphael Holinshed's *Chronicles of Ireland,* London, 1571.
——*History of Ireland,* London, 1577.

Seventeenth-century Dublin

Bagwell, Richard, *Ireland under the Stuarts,* 3 vols., London, 1909.
Beckett, J.C., *The Making of Modern Ireland 1603-1923,* London, 1966.
Carroll, Kenneth, *John Perrott, early Quaker schismatic,* Friends Historical Society, London, 1971.
Clarke, Desmond, *Dublin,* London, 1977.
Craig, Maurice, *Dublin 1660-1860,* 2nd ed., Dublin, 1969.
Kearney, H.F., *Strafford in Ireland,* Manchester, 1959.
King, William, *The State of the Protestants in Ireland under the late King James Government,* London, 1691.
MacLysaght, Edward, *Irish Life in the 17th Century,* 2nd ed., Cork, 1950.
Maxwell, Constantia, *A History of Trinity College Dublin 1591-1892,* Dublin, 1946.
Munter, Robert, *The history of the Irish newspaper 1685-1760,* Cambridge, 1967.
Simms, J.G., *Jacobite Ireland 1685-1691,* London, 1969.
Whitehead, Trevor, *Dublin Firefighters,* Dublin, 1976.

Eighteenth-century Dublin

Barrington, Sir Jonah, *Personal Sketches of his own Times,* London, 1827-32.
——*Rise and Fall of the Irish Nation,* Dublin, 1833.
Beckett, J.C., *The Anglo-Irish Tradition,* London, 1976.
Bennett, Douglas, *Irish Silver,* Dublin, 1976.
Boydell, Mary, *Irish Glass,* Dublin, 1976.
Brimley, Johnson R., *Mrs Delany at Court and Among the Wits,* London, 1925.
Cloncurry, Lord, *Personal Recollections,* Dublin, 1849.
Cullen, Liam, *Merchants, ships and trade 1660-1830,* Dublin, 1971.
Curran, C.P., *Dublin Decorative Plasterwork,* London, 1967.
Delany, Mrs Mary, ed., Lady Llanover, *Autobiography and Correspondence,* 6 vols., London, 1861-1862.
Dunbar, Janet, *Peg Woffington and her Times,* London, 1968.
de Vere White, Terence, *The Anglo-Irish,* London, 1972.
Fitzgerald, Desmond, and Hyams, Edward, *Lost Demesnes,* London, 1977.
Fitzpatrick, William J., *Ireland before the Union,* Dublin, 1867.
——*Lady Morgan,* Dublin, 1860.
Johnston, Edith M., *Ireland in the Eighteenth Century,* Dublin,1974.
Joyce Weston, St John, *The Neighbourhood of Dublin,* Dublin, 1912.
Lecky, William, *History of Ireland in the 18th Century,* London, 1892.
Le Fanu, W.R. *Seventy Years of Irish Life,* London, 1893.
Lewis, R., *The Dublin Guide,* Dublin, 1787.
MacDermot, Frank, *Theobald Wolfe Tone and his Times,* London, 1939.
Malton, James, *A Picturesque and Descriptive View of the City of Dublin,* Dublin, 1792-99.
Maxwell, Constantia, *Dublin under the Georges,* London, 1936.

Middleton Murry, John, *Jonathan Swift,* London, 1954.
Morgan, Lady Sidney, *Memoirs,* London, 1862.
O'Keefe, John, *Recollections,* London, 1826.
Pakenham, Thomas, *The Year of Liberty,* London, 1969.
Peters, A., *Dublin Fragments,* Dublin, 1901.
——*Sketches of Old Dublin,* Dublin, 1907.
Pilkington, Laetitia, *Memoirs,* London, 1748.
Swift, Jonathan, ed. William Eddy, *Satirical and Personal Writings,* London, 1932.
Tocnaye, Le Chevalier de la, trans. J. Stevenson, *A Frenchman's Walk through Ireland 1796-97,* London, 1917.
Walshe, J.E., *Ireland 60 years ago,* Dublin, 1847.
Whitelaw, James, *An Essay on the Population of Dublin 1798,* Dublin, 1818.

Nineteenth-century Dublin

An Englishman, *Dublin, Experiences and Reflections,* Dublin, 1917.
Aykroyd, W.R., *The Conquest of Famine,* London, 1974.
Bovet, Madame de, *Three months tour in Ireland,* London, 1891.
Carr, Sir John, *The Stranger in Ireland, 1803,* London, 1806.
Corrigan, Frank, 'Dublin Workhouses during the Great Famine', Article in the *Dublin Historical Record,* March, 1976.
Carleton, William, *Autobiography,* London, 1896.
de Vere White, Terence, *Story of the Royal Dublin Society,* Tralee, 1955.
Dudley Edwards, R. and Desmond Williams, T., eds., *The Great Famine,* Dublin, 1956.
Fitzpatrick, William J., *History of the Dublin Catholic Cemeteries,* Dublin, 1900.
Freeman, Walter, *Pre-Famine Ireland,* Manchester, 1959.
Gwynn, Stephen, *Dublin Old and New,* Dublin, 1938.
Kohl, J.G., *Travels in Ireland,* London, 1844.
Lewis, Samuel, *Topographical Dictionary of Ireland,* London, 1837.
Lyons, F.S.L., *Ireland since the Famine,* London, 1973.
Mangan, James Clarence, *Autobiography,* republished Dublin, 1968.
McDowell, R.B., *Social Life in Ireland, 1800-1845,* Dublin, 1970.
McGregor, John James, *New Picture of Dublin,* Dublin, 1821.
Moore, George, *A Drama in Muslin,* London, 1886.
Meyler, Thomas, *Autobiography,* republished Dublin, 1968.
Myler, Patrick, *Regency Rogue,* Dublin, 1976.
Nicholson, Asenath, ed. Alfred Tressider Sheppard, *The Bible in Ireland. Excursions through Ireland in 1844 and 1845,* London, 1925.
O'Faolain, Sean, *King of the Beggars,* London, 1938.
Plumptre, Ann, *Narrative of a residence in Ireland during the summer of 1814 and that of 1815,* London, 1817.
Thackeray, William Makepeace, *Irish Sketch-Book,* London, 1843.
Warburton, John and Rev. James Whitelaw, *History of the City of Dublin,* London, 1818.

Wilson, T.G., *Victorian Doctor,* London, 1942.
Woodham-Smith, Cecil, *The Great Hunger,* London, 1962.

From the Death of Parnell to 1916

Aberdeen, Lord and Lady, *We Twa,* London, 1925.
Aykroyd, W.R. and Kevany, J.P.; *Mortality in Infancy and Early Childhood in Ireland, Scotland, England and Wales,* London, 1970.
Blamires, Harry, *The Bloomsday Book,* London, 1966.
Bowen, Elizabeth, *Seven Winters,* London, 1943.
Brooke, Raymond, *The Brimming River,* Dublin, 1961.
Cadogan, Sir Edward, *Before the Deluge,* London, 1962.
Clarke, Austin, *Twice around the Black Church,* London, 1962.
Colum, Mary, *Life and the Dream,* Dublin, 1966.
Curriculum Development Unit, *Divided City: Portrait of Dublin 1913,* Dublin, 1978.
Ellmann, Richard, *James Joyce,* Oxford, 1959.
Finegan, John, *The Story of Monto,* Cork, 1978.
Fingall, Elizabeth Countess of, *Seventy Years Young,* London, 1937.
Gogarty, Oliver St John, *As I was going down Sackville Street,* London, 1937.
——*Tumbling in the Hay,* London, 1939.
——*It isn't that time of year at all,* New York, 1954.
Hely Thom, Publishers, *The Sinn Fein Revolt Illustrated,* Dublin, 1916.
Hone, Joseph, *Life of Yeats,* London, 1943.
——*Life of George Moore,* London, 1936.
Joyce, James, ed. Harry Levin, *The Essential James Joyce,* London, 1958.
——*Ulysses,* Re-set edition, 7th impression, Bodley Head, London, 1967.
Larkin, Emmett, *James Larkin,* London, 1965.
Lyons, J.B., *James Joyce and Medicine,* Dublin, 1973.
Norman, E., *A History of Modern Ireland,* London, 1971.
M'Cready, C.T., *Dublin Street Names Dated and Explained,* Dublin, 1892.
McHugh, Roger, *Dublin 1916,* London, 1966.
Moore, George, *Hail and Farewell,* 3 vols., London 1911.
O'Brien, Conor Cruise, *Writers and Politics,* London, 1965.
——*Concise History of Ireland,* London, 1972.
O'Casey, Sean, *Autobiographies,* 3 vol. edition, London, 1963.
O'Connor, Ulick, *The Gresham Hotel,* Dublin, 1966.
O'Donel, T.D. Browne, *The Rotunda Hospital, 1745-1945,* Edinburgh, 1947.
O'Malley, Ernie, *On Another Man's Wound,* London, 1936.
——*The Singing Flame,* Dublin, 1978.
Power, Arthur, *Conversations with James Joyce,* London, 1974.
Pritchett, V.S., *Dublin A Portrait,* London, 1967.
Starkie, Enid, *A Lady's Child,* London, 1941.
Sutherland, Halliday, *Irish Journey,* London, 1956.

Post 1916

Collis, Robert, *To be a Pilgrim*, London, 1975.
Cronin, Anthony, *Dead as Doornails*, Dublin, 1976.
Dickenson, P.L., *Dublin of Yesterday*, London, 1929.
Holroyd, Michael, *Lytton Strachey*, London, 1967-68.
Kavanagh, Patrick, *The Green Fool*, London, 1938.
O'Brien, Conor Cruise, *States of Ireland*, London, 1972.
O'Connor, Ulick, *Brendan Behan*, London, 1973.
Pritchett, V.S., *Midnight Oil*, London, 1951.
Ryan, John, *Remembering How we Stood*, Dublin, 1975.
Tracy, Honor, *Mind You I've said nothing*, London, 1953.

Newspapers, periodicals, etc.

Dublin Evening Post.
Dublin Historical Record.
Faulkner's Journal.
Freeman's Journal.
Illustrated London News.
Irish Times.
Irish Independent.
Irish Ancestor, ed. Rosemary Ffolliott.
Pue's Occurrences.

Directories

Wilson's *Dublin Directory*, later amalgamated with
  Watson's *Almanack*, 1752-1837.
Post Office *Directory*, 1832-1851.
Thom's *Directory*, 1844 onwards.

Index

The Coast of West Cork
Peter Somerville-Large

In 1970 Peter Somerville-Large set off on a bicycle to explore the beautiful, ragged coastline of West Cork. The impressions he gathered then remain as fresh and vivid today, reflecting the impact this most striking section of the Irish coastline — with its mountains, scattered islands and crumbling castles — made on him then. This new edition of his account of the trip, which took him from Clonakilty to Ardgroom, will enthrall readers everywhere, whether they are already familiar with the region or content to be vicarious travellers.

Despite an inevitable increase in tourism over the years, this section of the Irish coastline has remained remarkably unspoilt, thanks largely to the fact that beaches in the area are comparatively few, and the holidaymaker who might otherwise have been tempted to settle there has had second thoughts. Although much of the native industry is in decline, with fish stocks diminishing all the time and fewer fishing boats and trawlers to be seen, the author writes of the region with great zest and with no more than a passing regret.

Peter Somerville-Large is no stranger to West Cork, being related to Edith Somerville, of the famous Somerville and Ross literary partnership, and he writes with a warmth and affection that convey his long acquaintance with this landscape and its people. Moreover, his keen eye and ear for the unusual and the fanciful make the book, from beginning to end, a continual delight.

The People of Ireland
Edited by Patrick Loughrey

From prehistory to modern times many groups of people, each quite distinct in origin, speech, religion and culture, have settled or succeeded one another in Ireland. These various groups that came to make up the people of Ireland did not remain distinct for long, however. They intermarried and interacted in a thousand ways, each influencing and modifying the culture and behaviour of others.

In this book, Ireland's leading historians describe the experiences and achievements of these successive waves of settlers — from prehistoric groups, Celts, Vikings and Normans, through to Scots, English, Anglo-Irish and, most recently, nineteenth- and twentieth-century religious and ethnic minorities.

The People of Ireland challenges the popular conception of 'two traditions' — of planter and Gael, or Protestant and Catholic — in Irish society. With lavish colour and black and white illustrations, it amply demonstrates that there exists in Ireland a broad and diverse range of people, a people who will continue to interact with one another and with the outside world as they have in the past, emigrating, receiving immigrants and settlers, quarrelling, forgetting old ways, and learning new ones.

One Hundred and Fifty Years of Irish Railways
Fergus Mulligan

Fergus Mulligan's highly readable and fully illustrated account of the history of Irish railways devotes chapters to each major railway company, plus the independent standard and narrow gauge lines, and includes a section on that marvellous eccentricity, the Listowel and Ballybunion, or the Lartigue, as it was known. He places the emphasis on the men and women involved, rather than on the more technical aspects of rail operations, on the activities and conditions of travellers, workers and the railway visionaries, whose ambitious schemes were often matched only by railway company bankruptcies. The frenetic activity of those earlier years was certainly a far cry from one passenger's description of a halt at Belcoo, Co. Fermanagh, in 1952, as 'one of those long, silent contemplative pauses during which, without the sound of steam escaping from the engine, you felt you ought to be saying your prayers.'

Ireland's Inland Waterways
Ruth Delany

This absorbing and fully illustrated story of Ireland's inland waterways traces their development, from the building of the Newry Canal in the 1730s, right up to the present day. It focuses on the people who planned and built the waterways and the communities they established, as well as their construction, their economic role and the changes they brought about. With its blend of entertainment, authority and meticulous research, *Ireland's Inland Waterways* has already established itself as by far and away the best book on the subject.

'It covers all the canal, river and lake navigations that have existed, north and south, in Ireland with both scholarship and affection, from their largely commercial origins to their newer recreational possibilities. Its copious illustrations are marvellous.'

Irish Times

'This is a book all waterway enthusiasts will want . . . a loving look at the past, present and future of Ireland's waterways.'

Waterway News

'The definitive work. . . After this all readers will want to explore the Irish waterways.'

Waterways World

Dublin's Vanishing Craftsmen
Kevin Corrigan Kearns

Hidden away in workshops and backstreet yards in the heart of Dublin are a number of old men finishing out their days at the crafts to which they were apprenticed in boyhood. Coopers, signwriters, shoemakers, farriers, saddle-harness makers, stone-carvers and tailors — once part of a large and busy fraternity in the city — now find themselves working in isolation and the knowledge that they are the last of a dying breed.

This book is the record of some of these men's lives, a chronicle of their apprenticeship, adulthood and now declining years spent in perfecting crafts which today are little appreciated by society in general. Their stories have been recorded in their work places and in their own words, and reveal not only an astonishing volume of factual information about fast-vanishing crafts but also an attitude to work and life which has almost disappeared.

Kevin Kearns has sought out and interviewed these last few surviving old masters and sets their descriptions of working conditions and social intercourse among craftsmen against a general background of Dublin in the earlier part of this century.

His book will make every reader more aware of the skills and dedication of the master craftsmen, and is a timely account of a way of life and work now almost extinct.